The Norton Scores

TENTH EDITION
VOLUME II

TENTH EDITION
IN TWO VOLUMES

The Norton Scores

A Study Anthology

Volume II: Schubert to the Present

edited by
Kristine Forney
PROFESSOR OF MUSIC, CALIFORNIA STATE UNIVERSITY, LONG BEACH

with textual notes by
Roger Hickman
PROFESSOR OF MUSIC, CALIFORNIA STATE UNIVERSITY, LONG BEACH

W. W. NORTON & COMPANY
NEW YORK LONDON

Printed in the United States of America

Manufacturing by Victor Graphics, Inc.
Project Editor: Allison Courtney Fitch
Book design by: David Budmen
Production manager: Jane Searle

ISBN 13: 978-0-393-92890-7 (pbk.)
ISBN 10: 0-393-92890-X (pbk.)

W. W. Norton & Company, Inc., 500 Fifth Avenue, New York, N.Y. 10110
www.wwnorton.com

W. W. Norton & Company Ltd., Castle House, 75/76 Wells Street, London W1T 3QT

1 2 3 4 5 6 7 8 9 0

Contents

Romantic Program Music

Romantic Symphony, Concerto, and Sonata

Romantic Choral Music

Romantic Opera and Ballet

Preface

The Tenth Edition of *The Norton Scores* provides a comprehensive approach to the study of the masterworks of Western music literature, from the earliest times to the present. Organized in two volumes, the anthology plays a number of teaching and study roles in the field of music, including the following:

- as a core anthology, or an ancillary, for a masterworks-oriented music class, to aid in the development of listening and music-reading skills;
- as a study anthology for a music history class focused on major repertory, genres, or styles of Western music;
- as a core repertory for analysis classes, providing a wide variety of styles, forms, and genres;
- as a central text for a capstone course in musical styles focused on standard repertory, listening, or score study;
- as an ancillary to a beginning conducting course and an aid in reading full orchestral scores;
- as an independent study resource for those wishing to expand their knowledge of repertory and styles;
- as a resource for music teachers in a wide array of courses.

The Norton Scores can be used independently, as described above, or in conjunction with an introductory music text. The repertory coordinates with *The Enjoyment of Music*, Tenth Edition, by Kristine Forney and Joseph Machlis. Recording packages are available for use with this edition: 8 CDs (in two volumes matching the contents and division of the score volumes) and 4 CDs (selected works).

The anthology presents many works in their entirety; others are represented by one or more movements or an excerpt. Most selections are reproduced in full scores; however, opera excerpts are given in piano/vocal scores. (In the case of some contemporary pieces, issues of copyright and practicality prevent the inclusion of a complete score.) Translations are provided for all foreign-texted vocal works, and each score is followed by an informative text that provides historical and stylistic information about the work.

The full scores in this anthology employ a unique system of highlighting that directs students who are just developing music-reading skills to preselected elements in the score, thus enhancing the music-listening experience. Students with good music-reading skills will, of course, perceive many additional details. Each system (or group of staves) is covered with a light gray screen, within which the most prominent musical lines are highlighted with white bands. Where two or more simultaneous musical lines are equally prominent, they are both highlighted. Multiple musical systems on a page are separated by a thin white band. For more information, see "How to Follow the Highlighted Scores" on p. xv. This highlighting system has been applied to most instrumental works in full scores; in vocal works, the text generally serves as a guide throughout the work.

The highlighting is not intended as an analysis of the melodic structure, contrapuntal texture, or any other musical aspect of the work. Since it emphasizes the most prominent line (or lines), however, it often represents the principal thematic material in a work. In some cases, the highlighting may shift mid-phrase to another instrument that becomes more audible.

Here are some considerations regarding the repertory included in this anthology:

- The repertory is divided into two volumes:
  - Volume 1: Gregorian Chant to Beethoven
  - Volume 2: Schubert to the Present
  - The 8-CD set matches this division
- All major Classical genres are represented:
  - New works in this edition include, in Volume 1, a troubadour dance song, ensemble dance music from the Renaissance, a Handel opera aria, a Scarlatti keyboard sonata, a French Baroque dance piece, a Classical-era trumpet concerto, and a Requiem mass; in Volume 2, a Chopin polonaise, a Gottschalk dance for piano, a Fanny Mendelssohn choral part song, a Ravel song cycle, a symphonic movement by William Grant Still, a mariachi standard *son*, a Boulez orchestral work (derived from his own piano work), a hyperinstrument work by Tod Machover, a song cycle by Libby Larsen, and an orchestral work by Bright Sheng.
  - Complete multi-movement works for study (Baroque concerto and Classical symphony, concerto, chamber music, and sonata)
- Seven works by women composers:
  - Middle Ages to contemporary (Hildegard von Bingen, Barbara Strozzi, Clara Schumann, Fanny Mendelssohn Hensel, Amy Cheney Beach, Billie Holliday, Libby Larsen)

- Wide-ranging genres, including chant, mass, motet, chanson, madrigal (Italian and English), Italian and Luteran cantata, opera, oratorio, Lied, song cycle, choral part song, piano music, sonata, dance music, chamber music, concerto, symphony, ballet suite, ragtime, blues, jazz, musical theater, other orchestral genres, traditional and world musics, and computer music.
- Numerous works influenced by traditional and world musics:
  - Traditional music of the Americas (Gottschalk piano work, Ives song, Copland ballet, Revueltas symphonic work, Bernstein musical theater work, Cajun dance tune, mariachi *son*)
  - European traditional music (Gay ballad opera, Haydn string quartet, Bizet opera, Ravel song cycle, Bartók orchestral work)
  - Middle and Far Eastern influence (Mozart sonata, Puccini opera, Mahler song cycle, Cage prepared piano work, Sheng orchestral work)
  - African influence (Still symphony, Ligeti piano etude, jazz selections)

The appendices to *The Norton Scores* provide some useful pedagogical resources for students and faculty. These include the following:

- a table of clefs and instrument transpositions;
- a table of instrument names and abbreviations in four languages (English, Italian, German, and French);
- a table of voice designations in English, Italian, and Latin;
- a table of scale degree names (in four languages);
- a glossary of all musical terms in the scores;
- a concordance among the scores, recordings, and listening guides in *The Enjoyment of Music*; and
- an index by genre and form of all selections in the anthology.

Volume 1 also has a helpful explanation of some performance practice issues in early music, and, where needed, editor's notes explain particular markings in a score that might not be widely understood.

There are many people to be thanked for their help in the preparation of this Tenth Edition of *The Norton Scores*: my California State University, Long Beach colleagues Roger Hickman, for his informative texts on each musical selection and assistance with the selection of recorded performances, and Gregory Maldonado, for his expert work on the highlighting of new scores; my research assistants Denise Odello (University of California, Santa Barbara) and Sarah Gerk (California State University, Long Beach) for their invaluable help on this project; James Forney (St. Lawrence University) for his work organizing the sound package; Tom Laskey of Sony Music, for his assistance in the licensing and production of the recordings and their coordination with the scores; Courtney Fitch and Graham Norwood, both of W. W. Norton, who ably collected and edited the scores and handled the permissions; Kathy Talalay of W. W. Norton, for her very skillful and painstaking work on the entire *Enjoyment of Music* package; and Maribeth Payne, music editor at W. W. Norton, for her support and guidance of this new edition. I am deeply indebted to them all.

How to Follow the Highlighted Scores

By following the highlighted bands throughout a work, the listener will be able to read the score and recognize the most important or most audible musical lines. The following principles are illustrated on the facing page in an excerpt from Beethoven's Symphony No. 5 in C minor (first movement).

1. The musical line that is most prominent at any time is highlighted by a white band shown against light gray screening.
2. When a highlighted line continues from one system (group of staves) or page to the next, the white band ends with an arrow head (>) that indicates the continuation of the highlighted line, which begins on the next system with an indented arrow shape.
3. Multiple systems (more than one on a page) are separated by narrow white bands across the full width of the page. Watch carefully for these bands so that you do not overlook a portion of the score.
4. At times, two musical lines are highlighted simultaneously, indicating that they are equally audible. On first listening, it may be best to follow only one of these.
5. When more than one instrument plays the same musical line, in unison or octaves (this is called doubling), the instrument whose line is most audible is highlighted.
6. CD track numbers are given throughout the scores at the beginning of each movement and at important structural points within movements. They appear in a □ for the 8-CD set and in a ◇ for the 4-CD set, where appropriate.

6
36
63
1
2
310
320
1.
Fl.
Ob.
Fg.
Cor. (Es)
Timp
Vl.
Vla.
Vc. Cb.
4
3
330
Cl.
cresc.
Vc.
Cb.
5

A Note on the Recordings

Recordings of the works in *The Norton Scores* are available from the publisher. There is an 8-CD set that includes all the works in the two volumes of the anthology and a 4-CD set that includes selected works from both volumes. The recording track numbers are noted at the top of each score, to the right of the title.

Example (for Schubert's *Erlkönig*)

8CD: 5/ [1]–[8]

4CD: 2/ ◇57◇–◇64◇

The first number gives the CD on which the work is included. The numbers in squares or diamonds are the inclusive track numbers of the work. For an overview of which works appear on the various recording sets, see Appendix D, *Concordance Table for Recordings*.

For the 8-CD package, the first set accompanies *The Norton Scores*, Volume 1, and the second set accompanies *The Norton Scores*, Volume 2.

Note: Occasionally, there are differences between the notated scores and the recordings; an editor's note is generally included in the score to explain these performance choices.

Electronic Listening Guides

There are interactive Listening Guides for each work in the Norton scores; these guides interact with the 8-CD and 4-CD sets, and the software is found on the Student Resource CD (packaged with *The Enjoyment of Music*). These guides are a study tool to help students understand the form and style of each work.

The Norton Scores

TENTH EDITION
VOLUME II

I

Franz Schubert

Erlkönig (Erlking), D. 328 (1815)

8CD: 5/ 1 – 8

4CD: 2/ 57 – 64

Editor's note: In performance, this Lied is often transposed to F minor, and occasionally to E minor.

24
Kind; er hat den Kna - ben wohl in dem Arm, er fasst ihn
30
sicher, er hält ihn warm. Mein
f
pp
37
Sohn, was birgst du so bang dein Ge-sicht? Siehst, Va - ter,
f
(pp)
43
du den Erl - kö - nig nicht? den Er - len -
mf
p
48
kö - nig mit Kron' und Schweif? Mein Sohn, es ist ein
mf

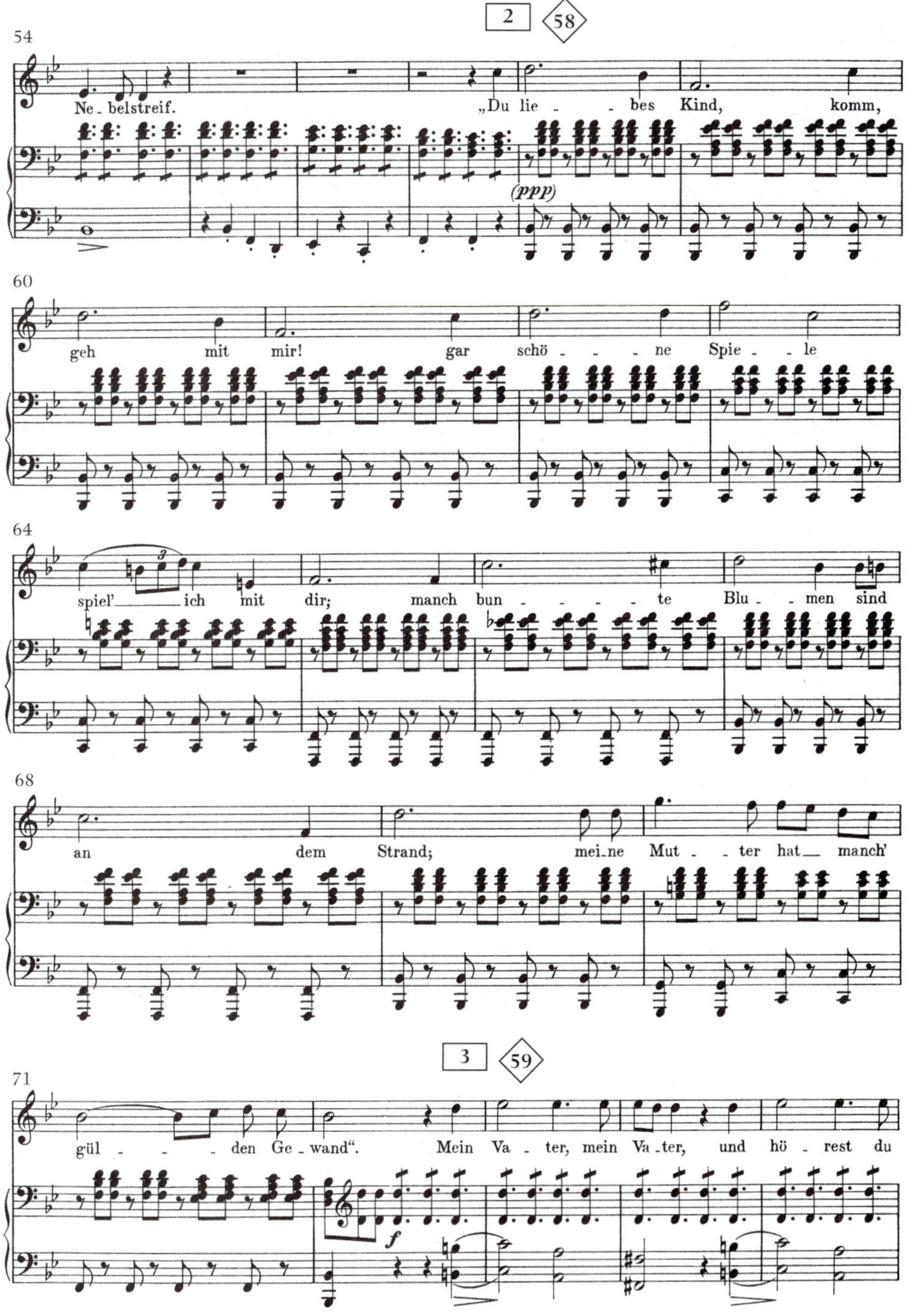
2
58
54
Ne - belstreif.
„Du lie - - bes Kind, komm,
(ppp)
60
geh mit mir! gar schö - - - ne Spie - - le
64
spiel' ich mit dir; manch bun - - - - te Blu - - men sind
68
an dem Strand; mei - ne Mut - - ter hat manch'
3
59
71
gül - - den Ge - wand".
Mein Va - ter, mein Va - ter, und hö - rest du
f

76
nicht, was Er-len-könig mir lei - se verspricht? Sei ru-hig, bleibe
p
decresc.
4
60
82
ru-hig, mein Kind; in dür-ren Blättern säu-selt der Wind. „Willst,
87
fei - ner Kna - be, du mit mir gehn? mei-ne Töch - ter sol - len dich
ppp
90
war - ten schön; mei-ne Töch - ter füh - ren den nächt - li-chen Reihn, und
93
wie - gen und tan - zen und sin - gen dich ein, sie wie - gen und tan - zen und sin - gen dich ein".
f

5
61
97
Mein Va - ter, mein Va - ter, und siehst du nicht dort Erl -
102
kö-nigs Töchter am dü - stern Ort?
decresc.
Mein Sohn, mein Sohn, ich
108
seh' es ge - nau; es scheinen die al - ten Wei - den so grau.
cresc.
ff
6
62
113
„Ich lie - be dich, mich
p
pp
118
reizt dei-ne schö-ne Ge - stalt; und bist du nicht wil - lig, so brauch' ich Ge-

7
63
123
walt". Mein Va - ter, mein Va - ter, jetzt fasst er mich an! Erl - kö - nig
fff
fz
129
hat mir ein Leids ge - than!
8
64
Dem Va - ter
f
134
accelerando
grau - set's, er rei - tet geschwind, er hält in Ar - men das
cresc.
139
äch - zen - de Kind, er - reicht den
ff
144
Recit.
Hof mit Müh und Noth; in seinen Armen das Kind war todt.
Andante.
fp
pp
p

TEXT AND TRANSLATION

Wer reitet so spät durch Nacht und Wind?
Es ist der Vater mit seinem Kind;
er hat den Knaben wohl in dem Arm,
er fasst ihn sicher, er hält ihn warm.

Who rides so late through night and wind?
It is a father with his child:
he has the boy close in his arm,
he holds him tight, he keeps him warm.

"Mein Sohn, was birgst du so bang dein Gesicht?"
"Siehst, Vater, du den Erlkönig nicht?
den Erlenkönig mit Kron' und Schweif?"
"Mein Sohn, es ist ein Nebelstreif."

"My son, why do you hide your face in fear?"
"Father, don't you see the Erlking?
The Erlking with his crown and train?"
"My son, it is a streak of mist."

"Du liebes Kind, komm, geh mit mir!
gar schöne Spiele spiel' ich mit dir;
manch' bunte Blumen sind an dem Strand;
meine Mutter hat manch' gülden Gewand."

"You dear child, come with me!
I'll play very lovely games with you.
There are lots of colorful flowers by the shore;
my mother has some golden robes."

"Mein Vater, mein Vater, und hörest du nicht,
was Erlenkönig mir leise verspricht?"
"Sei ruhig, bleibe ruhig, mein Kind;
in dürren Blättern säuselt der Wind."

"My father, my father, and don't you hear
the Erlking whispering promises to me?"
"Be still, stay calm, my child;
it's the wind rustling in the dry leaves."

"Willst, feiner Knabe, du mit mir geh'n?
meine Töchter sollen dich warten schön;
meine Töchter führen den nächtlichen Reih'n
und wiegen und tanzen und singen dich ein."

"My fine lad, do you want to come with me?
My daughters will take care of you;
my daughters lead off the nightly dance,
and they'll rock and dance and sing you to sleep."

"Mein Vater, mein Vater, und siehst du nicht dort,
Erlkönigs Töchter am düstern Ort?"
"Mein Sohn, mein Sohn, ich seh' es genau,
es scheinen die alten Weiden so grau."

"My father, my father, and don't you see
the Erlking's daughters over there in the shadows?"
"My son, my son, I see it clearly,
it's the gray sheen of the old willows."

"Ich liebe dich, mich reizt deine schöne Gestalt,
und bist du nicht willig, so brauch' ich Gewalt."
"Mein Vater, mein Vater, jetzt fasst er mich an!
Erlkönig hat mir ein Leids gethan!"

"I love you, your beautiful form delights me!
And if you are not willing, then I'll use force."
"My father, my father, now he's grasping me!
The Erlking has hurt me!"

Dem Vater grauset's, er reitet geschwind,
er hält in Armen das ächzende Kind,
erreicht den Hof mit Müh und Noth:
in seinem Armen das Kind war todt.

The father shudders, he rides swiftly,
he holds the moaning child in his arms;
with effort and urgency he reaches the courtyard:
in his arms the child was dead.

JOHANN WOLFGANG VON GOETHE

The Romantic spirit is largely indebted to a generation of poets whose works deal with images of love, heroes, nature, and the supernatural. In the late eighteenth century, musical settings of such poems were homophonic and strophic; thus the music remained subordinate to the text. But Franz Schubert (1797–1828), who composed over six hundred Lieder, elevated the genre to a new artistic level with beautiful melodies and imaginative piano accompaniments. Written in 1815, *Erlkönig (Erlking)* is one of Schubert's earliest masterworks in the genre. The song is a narrative ballad, a subgenre of the Lied that tells a story, usually tragic. Passages of dialogue are not uncommon. This poem, by the great German literary figure Johann Wolfgang von Goethe, relates a story based on the legend of the king of elves, whose touch is deadly to humans. The image of an elf king is well known to those who have seen *The Lord of the Rings.*

Schubert avoids the more typical strophic setting for telling such a story and creates a dramatic through-composed structure. Following an opening statement by a narrator, a dialogue among the father, the boy, and the seductive elf king ensues. Each character in the story has its own voice register and projects its own mood. The climax is created by the rising sequential repetition of the son's terrified, dissonant cries. Unifying the diverse vocal styles is an unrelenting triplet accompaniment in the piano that creates a visual image of the racing horse. The energetic motion only ceases when the narrator returns and tells of the tragic ending.

2

Franz Schubert

Die Forelle (*The Trout*), D. 550 (1817)

8CD: 5/ 9 – 11

17
sah in sü - ßer Ruh des mun - tern Fischleins Ba - - de im
21
kla - ren Bächlein zu, des mun - tern Fischleins Ba - - de im
25
kla - - ren Bächlein zu.
p
10
29
pp
p
Ein Fi - scher mit der Ru - - te wohl

33
an dem U - fer stand, und sah's mit kal-tem Blu - - te, wie
37
sich das Fischlein wand. So lang' dem Was-ser Hel - - le, so
41
dacht ich, nicht ge - bricht, so fängt er die Fo - rel - - le mit
45
sei - ner An-gel nicht, so fängt er die Fo - rel - - le mit

49
sei - - ner An-gel nicht.
p
53
11
Doch end-lich ward dem Die - be
pp
57
die Zeit zu lang.
Er macht das Bäch-lein tük-kisch
cresc.
p
cresc.
61
trü - - be, und eh ich es ge-dacht, so zuck - te sei - ne
p

65
Ru - te, das Fisch - lein, das Fisch-lein zap-pelt dran, und
p
69
ich mit re-gem Blu - - te sah die Be-trog-ne an, und
73
ich mit re - gem Blu - - te sah die Be-trogne an.
77
dim.
pp

TEXT AND TRANSLATION

In einem Bächlein helle,
Da schoss in froher Eil'
Die launische Forelle
Vorüber wie ein Pfeil.
Ich stand an dem Gestade
Und sah in süsser Ruh'
Des muntern Fischleins Bade
Im klaren Bächlein zu.

Ein Fischer mit der Rute
Wohl an dem Ufer stand,
Und sah's mit kaltem Blute,
Wie sich das Fischlein wand.
So lang' dem Wasser Helle,
So dacht ich, nicht gebricht,
So fängt er die Forelle
Mit seiner Angel nicht.

Doch endlich ward dem Diebe
Die zeit zu lang. Er macht
Das Bächlein tückisch trübe,
Und eh' ich es gedacht,
So zuckte seine Rute,
Das Fischlein zappelt dran,
Und ich mit regem Blute
Sah die Betrog'ne an.

C. F. Schubart

In a bright little stream
the good-natured trout
darted about in joyous haste
like an arrow.
I stood on the bank
and watched in sweet repose
the bath of the lively little fish
in the clear water.

A fisherman with his rod
also stood on the bank
and cold-bloodedly watched
the little fish swimming to and fro.
As long as the water stays clear,
I thought, he won't
catch the trout
with his rod.

But finally the wait grew too long
for the thief. He made
the brook all muddy,
and before I knew it,
his rod quivered,
the little fish wriggled at its end,
and I, my blood boiling,
gazed at the betrayed one.

3

Franz Schubert

8CD: 5/ 12 – 18

Piano Quintet in A major (*Trout*), D. 677, Fourth movement (1819)

13

32
tr
8

36
tr
8

14
Var. II
41
p
[p]
arco
mf

44
47
1
2
6
50
p

15

63

65

67
1

68
2

70

72
8

74

76

78

16

89
tr
pp
pp
[pp]
pp
tr
tr
tr
pp tr
tr
tr

91
tr
tr
tr
tr
tr
tr
tr

94
tr
[p]
decresc.
pp
cresc.
p
decresc.
pp
cresc.

97
tr
pp
[pp]
p
decresc.

17

Var. V 101
pp
p
p[p]

105
cresc.
[cresc.]
[p]
1
[pp cresc.]
p

108
pp
pp
[pp]
pp
cresc.

113
pp
pp

117
[>]

121
pp
decresc.

125
[dim.]
[dim.]
dim.
[dim.]
dim.

18
128 Allegretto
p
p

132
p

138
[p]
p
p

140

144
p

149

154
6
p
[p]
[p]
[p]

159

164
decresc.
decresc.
[p]
6
6

168
pp
dim.
pp
[dim.]
6
pp
[dim.]
pp
dim.
decresc.
pp
dim.

Franz Schubert's brief life span coincides with a fascinating period in Viennese history. On the one hand, Vienna was the home of one of the greats of the Classical era, Ludwig van Beethoven. He died just one year before Schubert. On the other hand, Schubert's Vienna embraced fully the Romantic operatic sensations of Rossini. This Classical-Romantic dichotomy is evident in Schubert's instrumental music, in which he fashioned a distinctive combination of Romantic style and Classical structure in his symphonies, piano sonatas, and chamber music. This fusion is critical to nineteenth-century chamber music in general. Of all of the Romantic instrumental genres, chamber music retains the strongest and most consistent ties to Classical structures. But within this Classical framework, composers like Schubert placed an emphasis on melody, color, and theatricality, prominent features of the pervading Romantic spirit.

The expanding color palette of nineteenth-century chamber music is evident in Schubert's *Trout* Quintet, which is scored for the unusual combination of piano, violin, viola, cello, and string bass, rather than the standard ensemble of a piano and string quartet. Typical of Romantic chamber music, the virtuosic weight of the composition lies in the piano part. Composed in 1817, the *Trout* Quintet is set in five movements, reflecting the early freedom of Schubert's chamber works, which range from one to six movements in length. The fourth movement, inserted between a scherzo and the finale, functions as a second slow movement in the cycle. Schubert casts this movement in a standard Classical form of a theme and variations and borrows its theme from his own Lied, *Die Forelle* (*The Trout*).

The song itself is typical of Schubert's Lieder. The poem, by the critic and composer Christian Schubart, has three stanzas and relates a delightful tale of the demise of a trout at the hands of a clever fisherman. The subject matter reflects Schubert's interest in nature, although some symbolism might be read into the tale. The vocal line mirrors the innocence and simplicity of the story with its repeated diatonic phrases, and the piano accompaniment suggests the image of splashing water. The modified strophic form also reflects the simplicity of the narrative; the only variation in the form occurs during the climactic action of the third stanza.

In the Quintet, the theme is reshaped into a binary structure. Each variation features different combinations of instruments, and the theme is increasingly treated more freely. The final section, which can be viewed as a sixth variation, brings back a clear statement of the original theme and incorporates the piano accompaniment material from the song as well.

4

Robert Schumann

Dichterliebe (*A Poet's Love*), No. 1: "Im wunderschönen Monat Mai" ("In the lovely month of May") (1840)

8CD: 5/19 – 20
4CD: 2/65 – 66

TEXT AND TRANSLATION

Im wunderschönen Monat Mai, als alle Knospen sprangen, da ist in meinem Herzen die Liebe aufgegangen.	In the lovely month of May, as all the buds were blossoming, then in my heart did love rise up.
Im wunderschönen Monat Mai, als alle Vögel sangen, da hab ich ihr gestanden mein Sehnen und Verlangen.	In the lovely month of May, as all the birds were singing, then did I confess to her my longing and desire.

Robert Schumann (1810–1856) follows Franz Schubert as the second great composer of Lieder in the nineteenth century. Distinctive qualities of Schumann's songs include the composer's choice of high-quality poetry and his treatment of the piano as an equal partner to the voice. Coming to Lieder composition relatively late in his career, Schumann launched into the genre with a prodigious output in 1840, composing over one hundred Lieder, including the masterful song cycle *Dichterliebe* (*A Poet's Love*). It was during this "year of the song" that he married the young piano prodigy Clara Wieck.

Based on poems of Heinrich Heine, *Dichterliebe* examines the joys and pains of love without relating any specific story. The opening song, "Im wunderschönen Monat Mai," takes a strophic form with a piano prelude, interlude, and postlude. The two poetic stanzas compare the arrival of May to the blossoming of a poet's love. For the final line of the poem, Schumann sustains a mood of "longing" and "desire" with dissonances and harmonic ambiguity. Suspensions and appoggiaturas are frequent, and the harmony seems to hover between A major and F-sharp minor. Moving through several other keys as well, Schumann eventually closes the song on the dominant seventh of F-sharp minor. Although this harmony resolves at the beginning of the next song, the overall sense of unrequited and unfulfilled love is established, preparing the listener for the cynical and disillusioned moods that follow in the cycle.

5

Frédéric François Chopin

Prelude in E minor, Op. 28, No. 4
(published 1839)

8CD: 5/21–22

The preludes of Frédéric Chopin (1810–1849) stand as a Romantic counterpart to *The Well-Tempered Clavier* by J. S. Bach. Like its Baroque model, Chopin's set contains twenty-four works in all of the major and minor keys. But in keeping with the Romantic spirit, Chopin omits the learned fugues, allowing the preludes to stand by themselves. The twenty-four works, which provide a wide variety of moods, styles, and lengths, can either be performed as a unit or individually.

The fourth prelude, in E minor, is justifiably one of Chopin's most renowned compositions, primarily because of its brevity, chromaticism, and emotional potency. The melody, which can be heard as an antecedent-consequent pair of phrases, moves in a restricted range with simple ornamentation, suggesting the lyricism of a vocal line. The expressiveness of the prelude would be enhanced by a rubato performance. In the age of Chopin, rubato would occur in the right hand only; the melody could speed up or slow down depending on the inspiration of the performer, but the left hand would maintain a steady tempo. The accompaniment gradually descends with chromatic alterations, generally with one note changing in each successive harmony. The climax occurs in measures 16–18, where the range of the melody suddenly expands, the rhythmic activity increases, and the rate of harmonic change accelerates.

6

Frédéric François Chopin

Polonaise in A major, Op. 40, No. 1 (*Military*) (1838)

8CD: 5/23 – 27

4CD: 2/67 – 71

12
14
17
20
22

25
69
ff
Ped.
29
3
32
8
ff
35
cresc.
38
8

41
f
Ped.
45
3
48
8
ff
51
cresc.
54
8

26
70
57
31
4
61
64
ritenuto.
cresc
fff
67
3
70
3
8

73
ff
77
80
27
71
f
83
86

89
93
96
99
102

During the nineteenth century, the piano underwent many technological advances to become the most popular musical instrument in the home and the preferred instrument for professional soloists. As a result, an impressive body of new literature was created in which piano miniatures replaced the more formal sonatas of the Classical era. Many of these newer works demanded virtuosic technique, as composers made full use of the instrument's new capabilities.

One of the major figures in Romantic piano music is the Polish-French virtuoso Frédéric François Chopin (1810–1849). Active primarily in Paris, Chopin devoted his compositional output almost exclusively to piano music. His output includes piano exercises (études), dances (waltzes, mazurkas, polonaises), and many other short, lyrical works. Typical qualities of these works include an emphasis on melody, often with elaborate embellishments, expressive chromatic harmony, and rubato.

Chopin never forgot his Polish background. By evoking nationalistic rhythms and melodies, he paid homage to his native country, most notably with his mazurkas and polonaises. In his Polonaise in A major, Op. 40, No. 1 (called the *Military*), Chopin expanded the traditional dance structure to a ternary form in which both the **A** and **B** are rounded binary: **A** (a-a b-a b-a)–**B** (trio: c-c′ c-c′ d-c-c′ d-c-c′)–**A**′ (a-b-a). The **A** section is characterized by a chordal texture and vigorous rhythms. Its pomp and energy evoke a military procession. The trio, in the subdominant key of D major, has a more lyrical quality; a brief descending tune is accompanied by repetitions of the fundamental polonaise rhythm in the left hand. With its unrelenting rhythmic drive, strong crescendos, and fortissimo climaxes, the work has become a showcase for bravura technique.

7

Franz Liszt

La campanella (*The Little Bell*), from *Transcendental Etudes after Paganini,* No. 3 (1838–39; rev. 1851)

8CD: 5/ 28 – 37

31
21
p
24
27
8
31
35
cresc.

32
poco rit.
sempre p

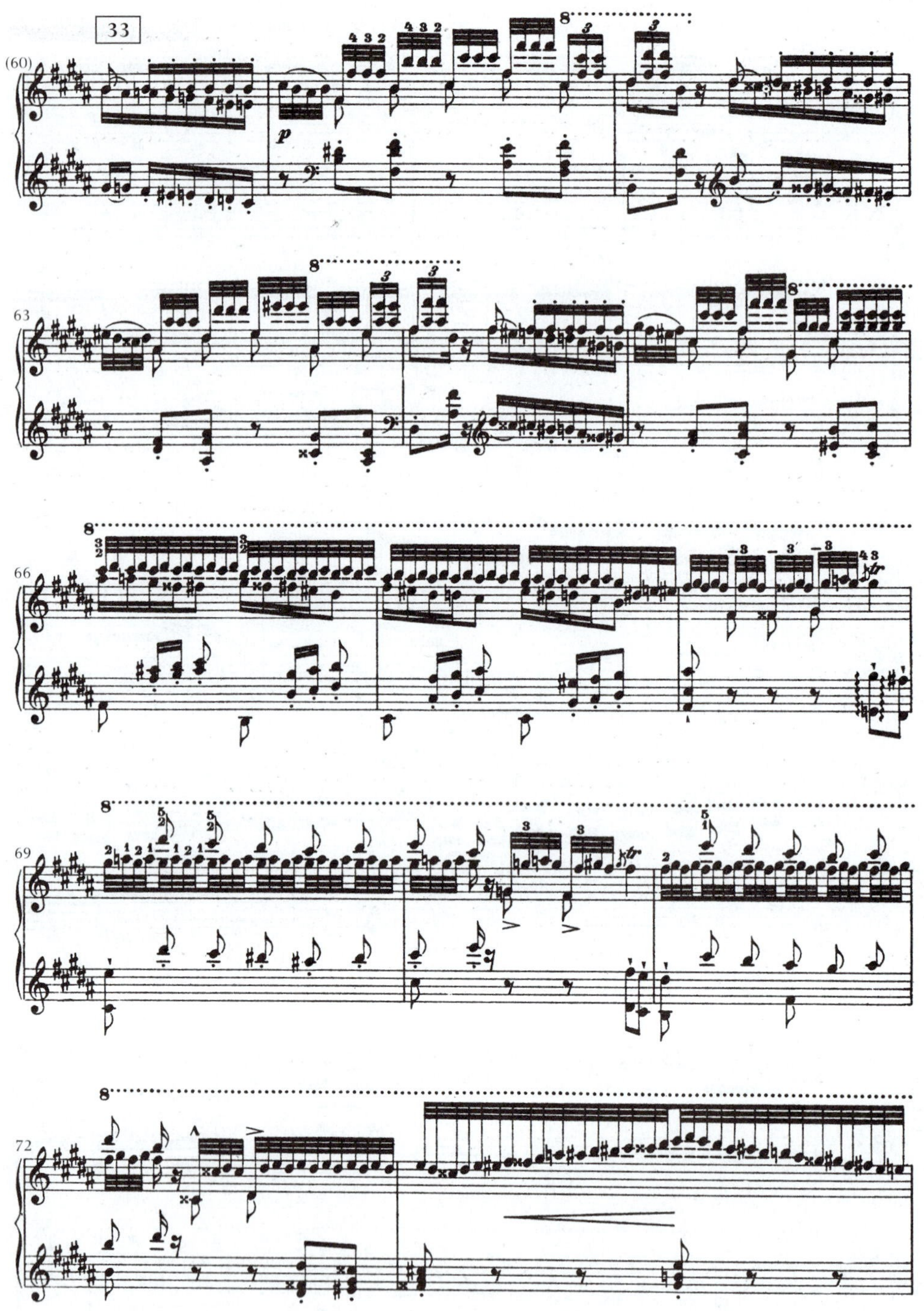
33
(60)
p
63
66
69
72

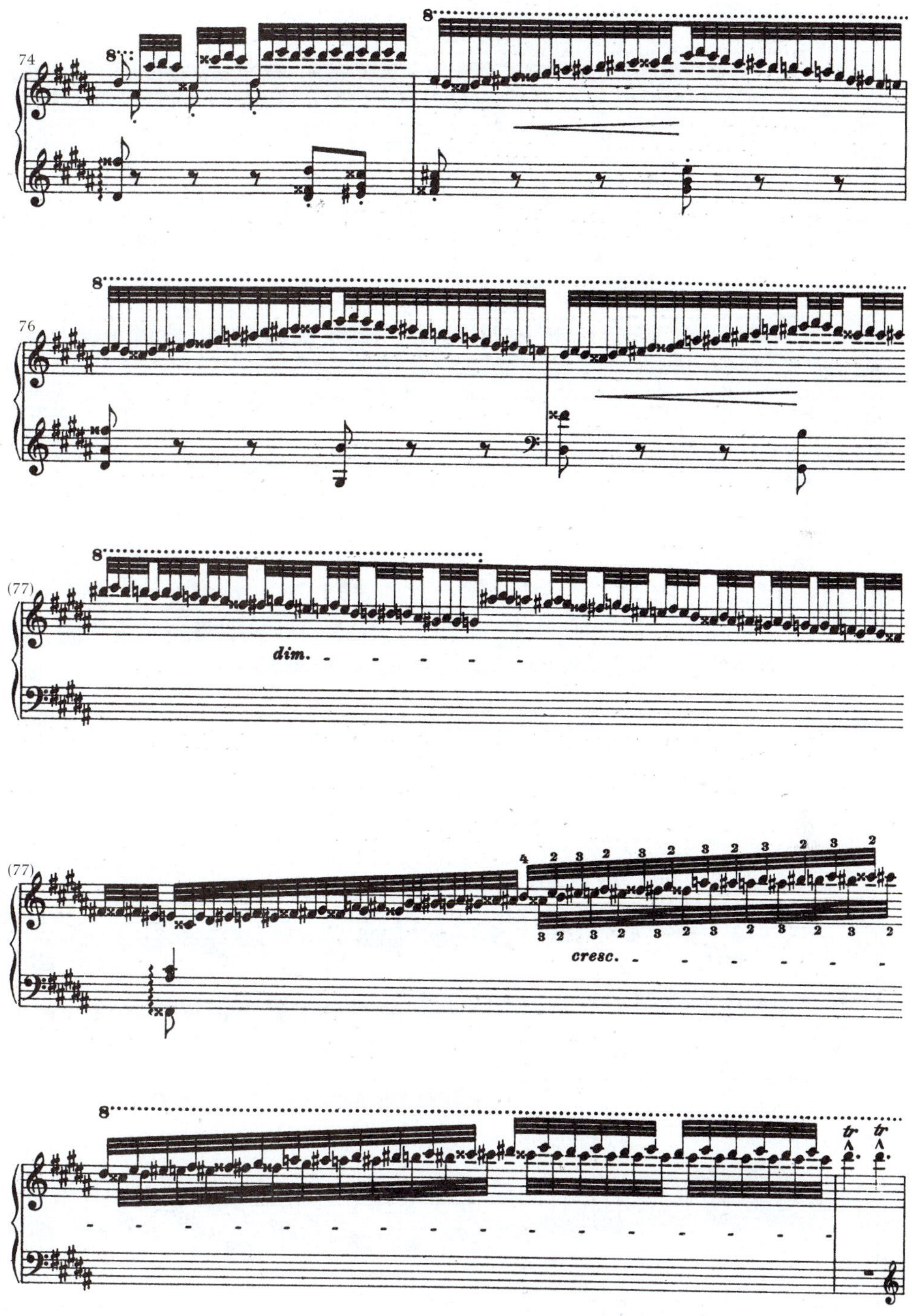
74
76
(77)
dim.
(77)
cresc.
tr
tr

34
79
p
82
84
sempre piano
smorz.
13
87
p
(89)

92
espressivo
94
p
pp
35
Più mosso.
(95)
staccato
98
102
p

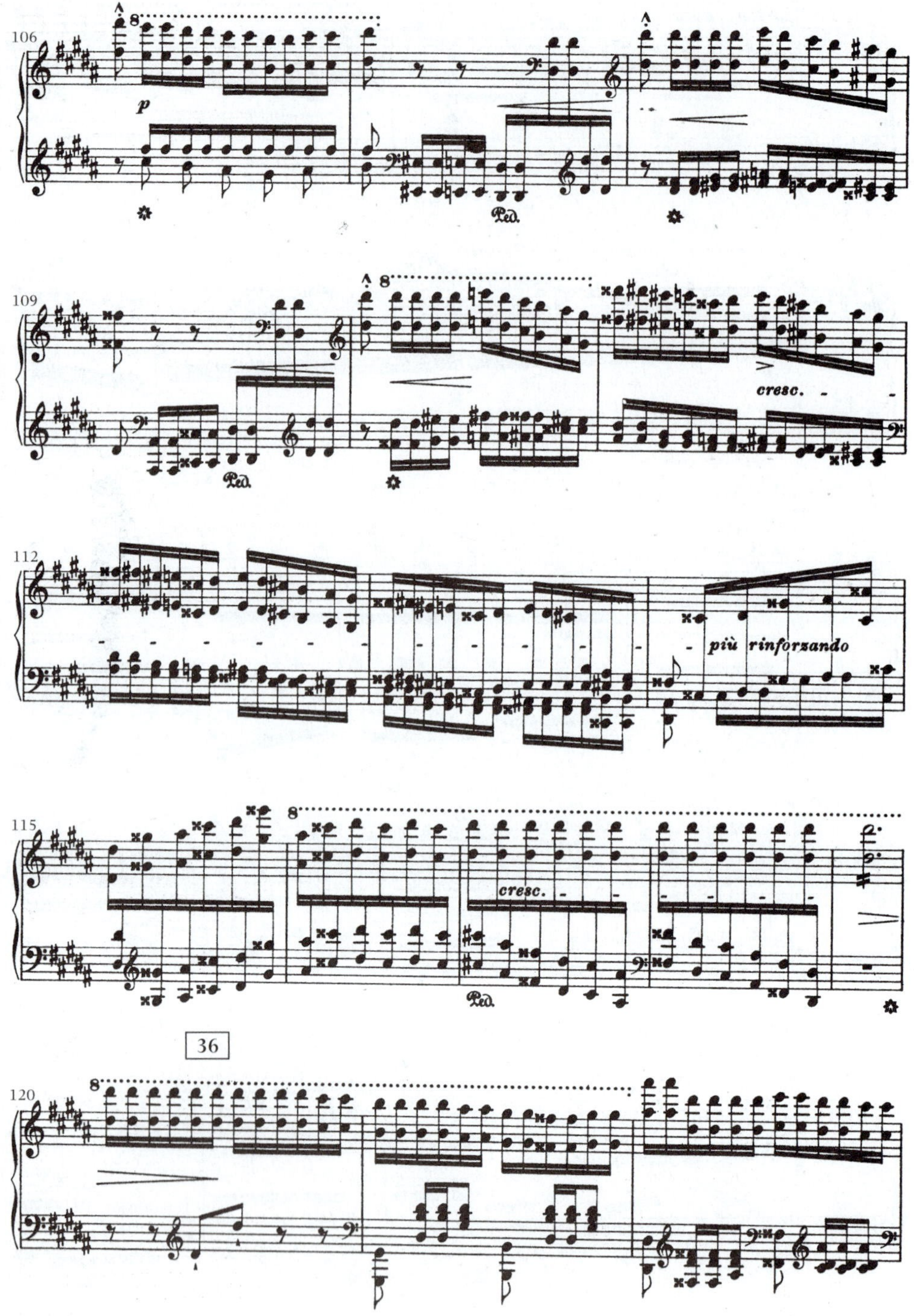
106
p
Ped.
109
8
cresc.
112
più rinforzando
115
cresc.
36
120

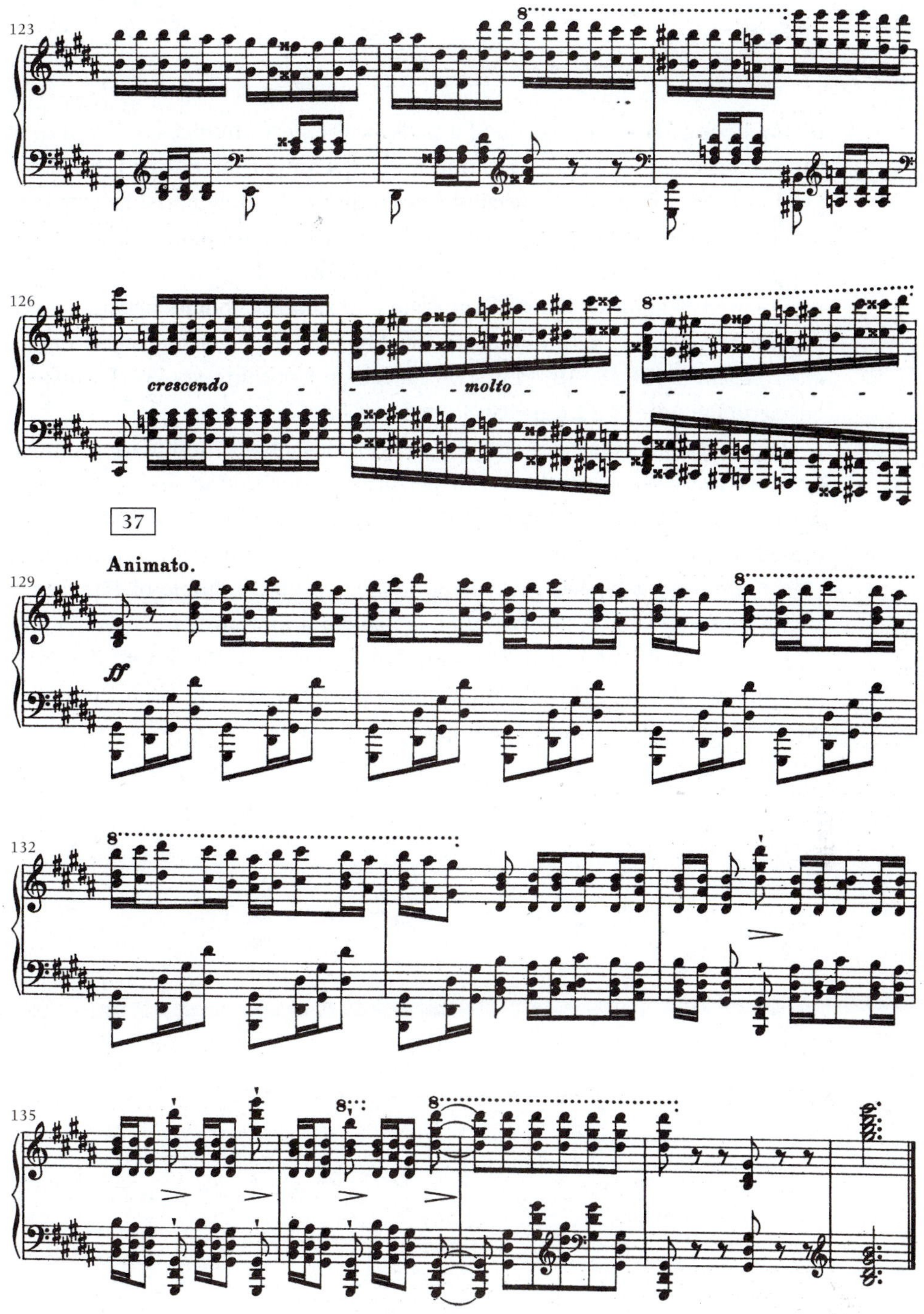
123
126
crescendo
molto
37
Animato.
129
ff
132
135

Instrumental virtuosity reached a peak in the performances and works of the Italian violinist Nicolò Paganini and the Hungarian pianist Franz Liszt (1811–1886). Paganini's dazzling technique and showmanship provided an inspiration for both violinists and pianists, an influence that can be seen in the numerous tributes to his works by other composers. Liszt assimilated Paganini's flamboyant style and raised it to new artistic levels. Paying homage to the violin virtuoso, Liszt created *Transcendental Etudes after Paganini* (1838–39, rev. 1851), which contains six works largely based on Paganini's 24 Caprices for solo violin.

Like Paganini's caprices and Chopin's études, Liszt's études are intended both as exercises to develop the performer's technique and as concert pieces. For Liszt, these études were literally intended to transcend the perceived limitations of the piano. The third étude, subtitled *La campanella (The Little Bell)*, borrows two thematic ideas from the finale of Paganini's Violin Concerto No. 2. The two themes, one in minor and one in major, are freely alternated and varied. The sound of a triangle in Paganini's concerto is imitated by repeated high pitches during the **A** sections, and the whole effect is light, colorful, and dazzling.

8

Clara Schumann

Notturno (Nocturne), from *Soirées musicales* (*Music for an Evening Entertainment*), Op. 6 (1836)

8CD: 5/38 – 41
4CD: 3/1 – 4

* The editor applies this accent to the E in the alto.

** This 8 applies to the octuplet in the R.H.

* This 8 applies to the octuplet in the R.H.

63
sf
67
dim.
[rit. . . . . a tempo]
p
71
mf
[✻]
✻
75
(✻)
✻
animato rinf.
rit.
f
79
espress.
p
(a tempo)

* The editor suggests Tempo I in the second half of this measure.

stretto
cres - cen - do
f
riten.
f
p
sf
(p) ri - tar - dan - do
pp
ri - tar - dan - do
41
4
a tempo ma più lento
con espress.
(pp)
pp
(U.C.)
calando e morendo
(rit.)
ppp

Clara Schumann (1810–1896) was one of the most remarkable musicians of the nineteenth century. Married to Robert Schumann and close friend to Johannes Brahms, Clara was connected to many of the leading performers and composers of the time. Called "the priestess" by her colleagues, she maintained a musical presence while supporting her husband's career and raising seven children. Prior to her marriage, she enjoyed great success in Paris, where she performed six character pieces that were later published as *Soirées musicales* (*Music for an Evening Entertainment*), Op. 6. Among those in attendance at her Parisian concerts were Frédérick Chopin and Robert Schumann.

Perhaps inspired by Chopin's preferred genres, Op. 6 consists of a toccatina, ballade, nocturne, polonaise, and two mazurkas. The Irish pianist John Field was the first to use Nocturne as a generic title in 1812, and Chopin began publishing nocturnes around 1830. The title suggests nighttime music.

Schumann's *Notturno* (Nocturne) has a clear **A**-**B**-**A**′ form. The **A** section is written in an intimate and sensitive style similar to that of Chopin. The left hand establishes a rolling accompaniment, and the right hand enters in the third measure with an unpredictable melody; the harmonies are unstable, and the repetition of the theme, beginning in measure 28, contains rhythmically complex embellishments. When the main melody returns in the final section of the Nocturne, it is again subjected to new ornamentation. The D-minor middle section is characterized by a faster tempo and a firm rhythmic accompaniment. The coda is particularly notable for its lingering chromatic harmonies.

Robert Schumann, enamored of both the music and its composer, gave Op. 6 a glowing review. He was particularly fond of the Nocturne and made reference to it in one of his own pieces. He later described this exquisite miniature as Clara's "most precious" work. After Robert's death, Clara performed widely and championed Robert's compositions. Her own output includes numerous Lieder, a piano concerto, a piano trio, and other short piano works.

9

Louis Moreau Gottschalk

Le banjo (*The Banjo*), Fantasie grotesque (1854–55)

8CD: 5/ 42 – 48

4CD: 3/ 5 – 11

17
pp
21
ten.
ten.
25
cresc.
29
f
pp

33
37
p ben ritmato
42
ben misurato
L.H.
44
7
47
Ossia
8va
f brillante
ff
martellato

51
8va
ff tutta la forza
mf
martellato
55
8va
ff
martellato
59

64

ben misurato

68

45 8

p subito

ff

strepitoso

cresc.

martellato
tutta la forza

fff

ff *p subito*

76
ten.
p
80
6
rfz
84
6
rfz
88
ten.
rfz
ten.
pp

92
96
100
martellato
104
108
46
9
Con spirito
8va
L.H.

ossia
8va
113
ben martellato
f
117
ff tutta la forza
mf
martellato
122
ff
martellato

127
132
martellato
47
10
136
cresc.
cresc.
fff staccato
p subito
martellato
tutta la forza
ff
p subito

140
ten.
p
145
150
dim.
pp
ossia
155
pp
cresc.

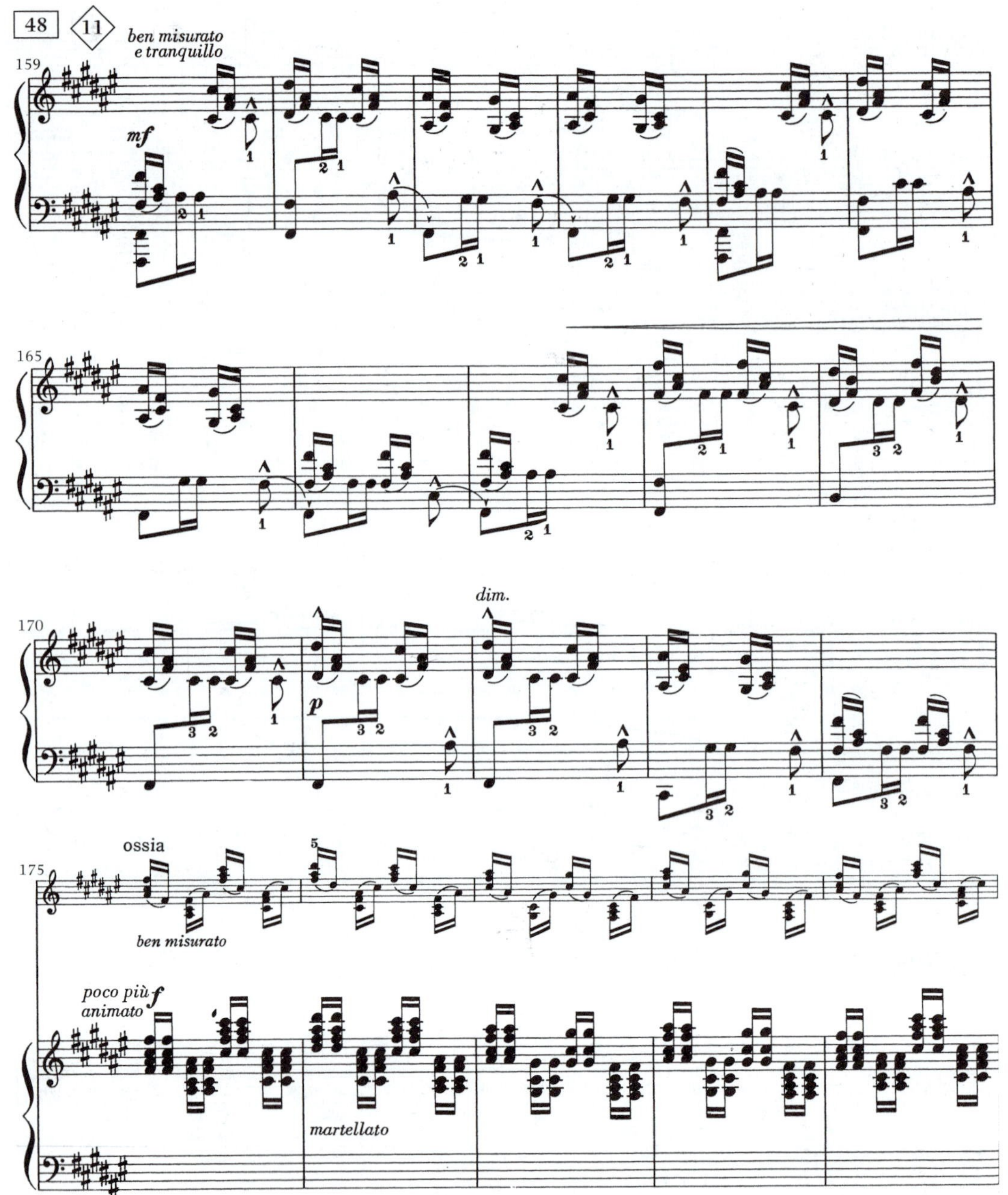
48
11
ben misurato
e tranquillo
159
mf
165
170
dim.
p
ossia
175
ben misurato
poco più
animato
f
martellato

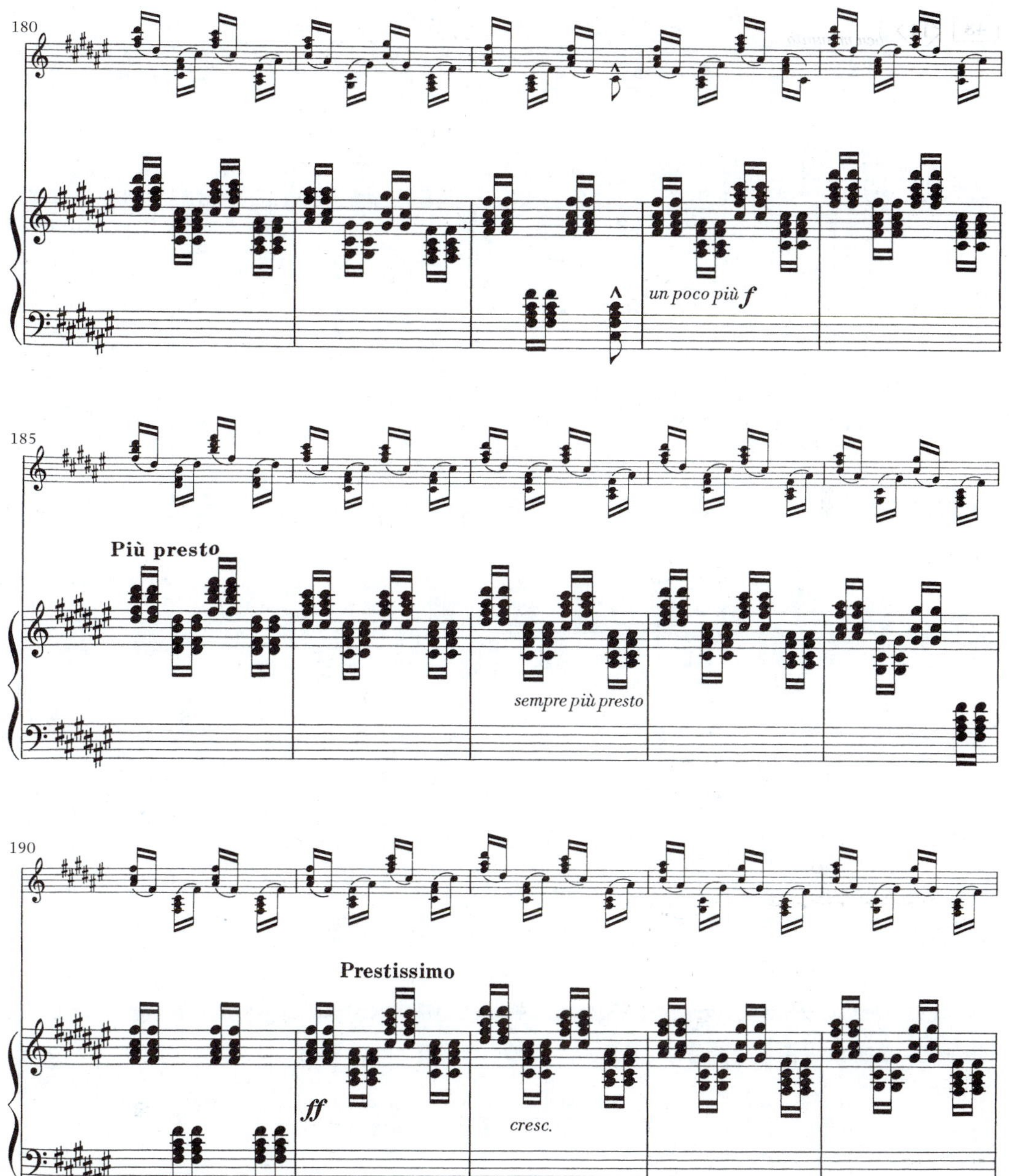
180
un poco più f
185
Più presto
sempre più presto
190
Prestissimo
ff
cresc.

195
velocissimo
tutta la forza
201
fff
Prestissimo
ben martellato
207
8va
fff

Louis Moreau Gottschalk (1829–1869) was the first American musician to receive international recognition. Born in New Orleans, he was a child prodigy and eventually studied piano and composition in Paris. Hearing him play in 1845, Chopin predicted that Gottschalk would become "king of pianists." Gottschalk's music took on a distinctive character, as he blended European styles and genres with vernacular music of the Americas, much of which he learned from his French-Creole mother. He would spend most of his career touring the United States, the Caribbean islands, and South America. Following a scandal involving a young seminary female, he fled to South America. Four years later, he contracted malaria and died from an overdose of quinine.

Le banjo (*The Banjo*) typifies Gottschalk's individual sound. It is labeled a fantasy, linking it to Liszt's fantasies, which are based on well-known melodies. The melodic material of *Le banjo* is derived from Stephen Foster's *Camptown Races* and the spiritual *Roll, Jordan, Roll*. The refrains of Foster's tune and the spiritual begin with the same motive, and this shared melodic idea appears in the introduction of Gottschalk's work. The coda of the fantasy presents the Foster refrain three times with an accelerating tempo. In between the introduction and coda, the melodic ideas are fragmented. Two principal sections alternate to make up a five-part sectional form: **A**-**B**-**A**-**B**-**A**. The **A** sections, set in the low register, consist of four-measure phrases marked by playful rhythmic gestures. The **B** sections are in the upper register and imitate the sounds and gestures of a banjo, the preferred instrument of African-Americans at the time.

10

Hector Berlioz

Symphonie fantastique,
Fourth and Fifth movements (1830)

8CD: 5/ 49 – 61
4CD: 3/ 12 – 17

7
II.
I.
p
p
cresc. poco a poco

15
50
13
Clar.
Corni
Fag.
unis.
Soli
Ctti
Tr.
Tromb.
Oph. I.
cresc.
Timp.
cresc. molto
cresc.
pizz.
Viol.
arco
dim.
unis.
26
Cor. III. IV.
Fag.
cresc
Timp.
Soli
Viol.
Vello. e C.B.
unis.
dim.

34
Timp.
Viol.
dim.
p
39
Fl.
Ob.
Clar.
Corni.
Fag.
C^{tti}
Tr.
Tromb.
Oph. I.
Timp.
ff
mf
p
f
dim.
(dim.

44
Fl.
Ob.
Clar.
Corni.
Fag.
Timp.
Viol.
Soli unis.
pizz.
50
Fag.
Viol.
55
Fag.
unis.
Viol.
dim.
pp

51
14
60
Fl.
Ob.
Clar
Corni.
avec les cylindres tous les sons ouverts.
with the valves, all tones open
Fag.
Ctti
Tr.
Tromb.
Oph. I.
Timp.
Cinelli.
Gr. Tamb.
Viol.
Vello.
C.B.
arco
a 2.
II.
cresc.
53

68
mf
mf
mf
p
pizz.
ff

52
15
75
poco f
p
cresc.
f
pizz.
arco

83
I.
Soli
Soli
II.
Oph. I.
Soli
Soli
poco f
f cresc.
cresc.
Cinelli
Solo
Gr. Tamb.
Solo
arco
pizz.
cresc.

91
a 2.
a 2.
f
f
mf
mf
f
f
ff
ff
ff
ff
ff

96
(>)
(> >)
mf
cresc.
f
ff

101
diminuendo
poco f
Soli
Soli
cresc.
cresc.
cresc.
cresc.

106

a 2.

I.

Soli

Soli

unis.

Soli

Soli

pizz. arco pizz. arco

pizz. arco pizz. arco pizz.

pizz. arco pizz. arco pizz.

pizz. arco pizz. arco pizz.

pizz.

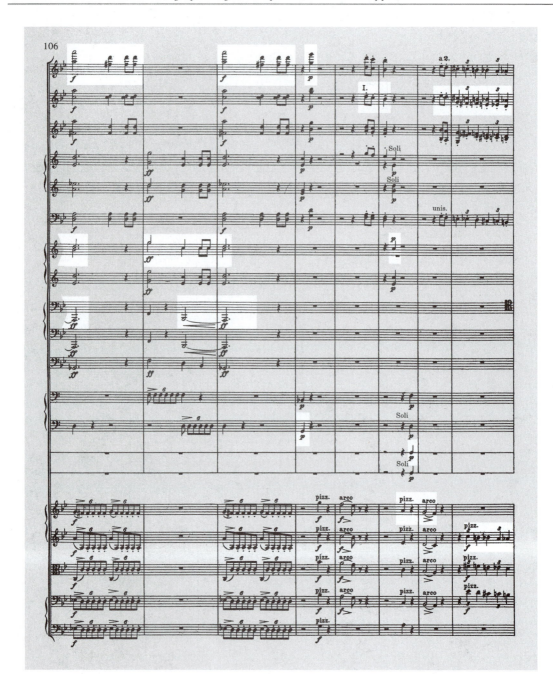

114
mf
a 2.
cresc.
sempre più forte
arco
ff

53
16
119
a2.
Baguettes de bois
Wooden drum-sticks
cresc.

125
a 2.
dim.
p
pp
ff
mf
I.
a 2.

136
a 2.
unis.
sul G

144
a 2.
unis.

151

2 Oph.

a 2.

a 4.

(a 2)

muta in B♮

f dim. mf ff

158
54
17
a 2.
p
pp
ff
I. Solo
pp dolce assai ed appassionato
Trois Timbaliers
Three drummers

167
rall. poco a tempo
a 2.
I. II.
Fag.
III. IV.
a 2.
1. Timpanista.
2. Timpanista.
Soli
3. Timpanista.
Tamburo.
Cinelli.
étouffez le son
damp the tone
Gr. Tamb.
étouffez le son avec la main
damp the tone with the hand
pizz.
arco
rall. poco a tempo

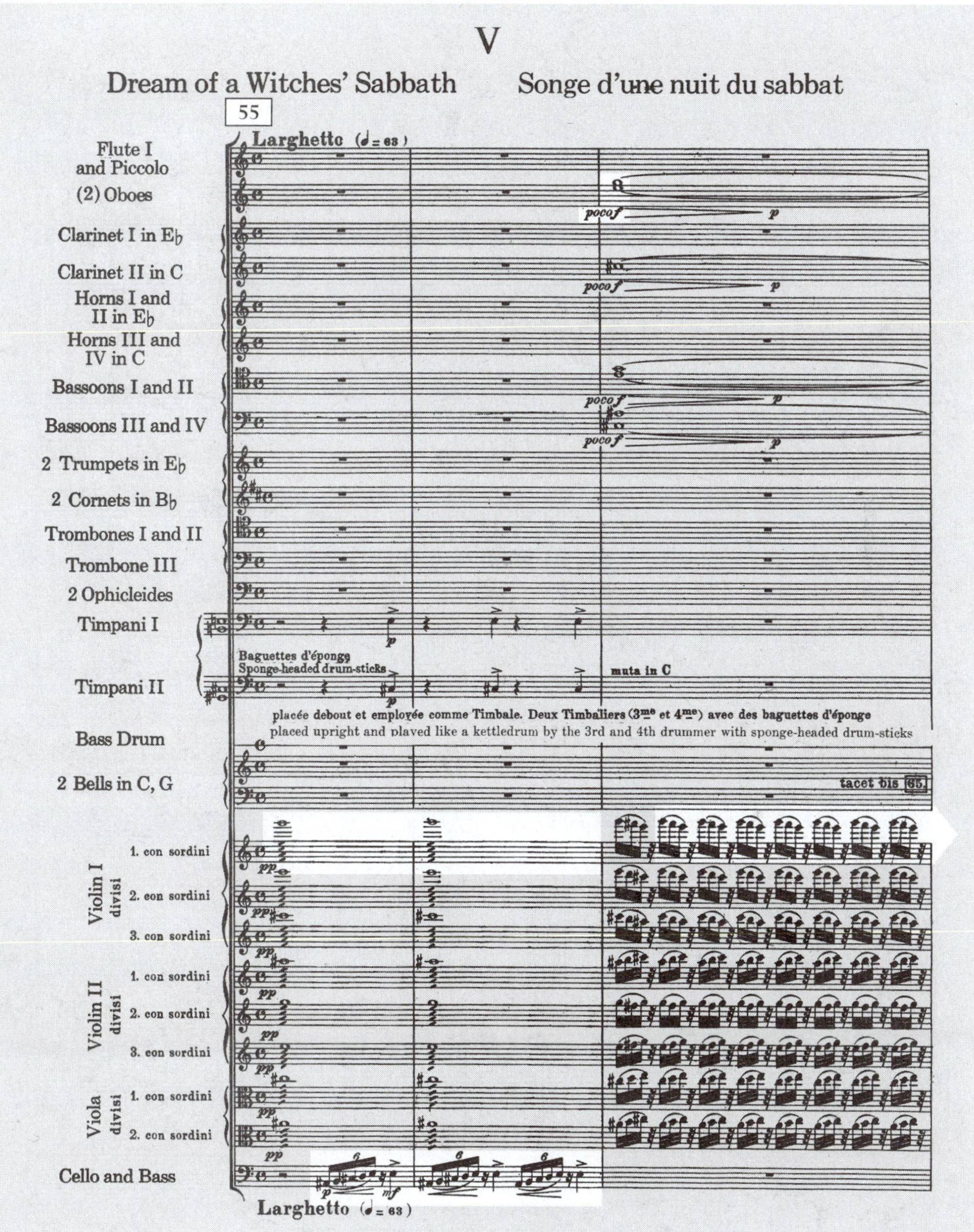
V
Dream of a Witches' Sabbath
Songe d'une nuit du sabbat
55
Larghetto (♩= 63)
Flute I and Piccolo
(2) Oboes
Clarinet I in E♭
Clarinet II in C
Horns I and II in E♭
Horns III and IV in C
Bassoons I and II
Bassoons III and IV
2 Trumpets in E♭
2 Cornets in B♭
Trombones I and II
Trombone III
2 Ophicleides
Timpani I
Baguettes d'éponge
Sponge-headed drum-sticks
Timpani II
muta in C
placée debout et employée comme Timbale. Deux Timbaliers (3me et 4me) avec des baguettes d'éponge
placed upright and played like a kettledrum by the 3rd and 4th drummer with sponge-headed drum-sticks
Bass Drum
2 Bells in C, G
tacet bis 65
Violin I divisi
1. con sordini
2. con sordini
3. con sordini
Violin II divisi
1. con sordini
2. con sordini
3. con sordini
Viola divisi
1. con sordini
2. con sordini
Cello and Bass
Larghetto (♩= 63)

4
dim.
p
f
I.
pizz.
ppp
Vcllo.
div.
mf
C.B.

7
Fl. Solo
mf
dim.
Fl. picc. Solo
a 2.
Soli
I. Solo
Solo III. bouché avec les cylindres
ppp stopped, with valves
dim.
II.
sf > p
Deux timbaliers, roulement avec des baguettes à tête d'éponge sur la Grande Caisse placée debout
Two timpanists, rolling with sponge-headed sticks on the upright Bass Drum.
ppp
arco
sf
pp
mf
unis.
6

13
poco f
p
muta in G
sf
mf

16
Solo I.
dim.
Solo. III. bouché avec les cylindres
dim.
éponges
ôtez les sourdines
ôtez les sourdines
ôtez les sourdines
ôtez les sourdines
ôtez les sourdines
ôtez les sourdines
div.
div.

56

21

Allegro (♩. = 112)

Allegro assai (𝅝 = 76)

Solo lointain distant

ppp

cresc.

ouvert avec les cylindres

open, with valves

a 2.

I.

p cresc. poco a poco

Sur les deux timbales

p

cresc. poco a poco

sans sourdine

sans sourdine

Allegro (♩. = 112)

Allegro assai (𝅝 = 76)

32

a2.

a2.

a2.

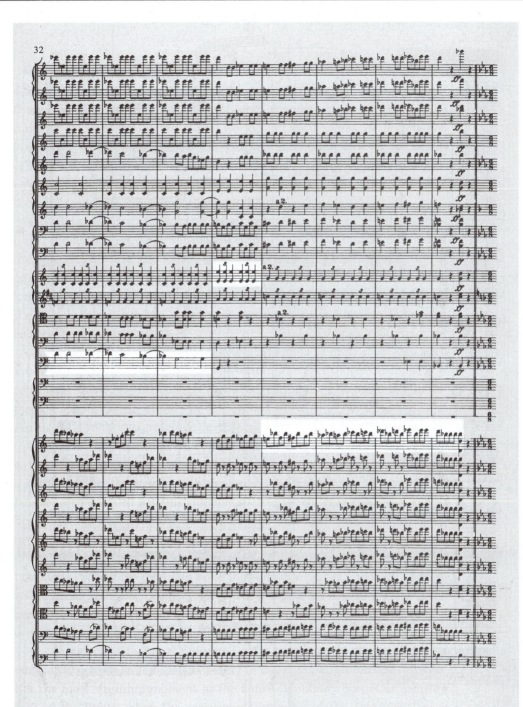

40
Allegro (♩.= 104)
Fl. picc.
Ob.
poco f
Clar. I in E♭
Solo
poco f
cresc.
Clar. II in C
poco f
Fag.
unis.
mf
mf
Viol. I unis.
Viol. II unis.
Viola unis.
Vcllo.
C.B.
Allegro (♩.= 104)
49
Fl. picc.
Ob.
Clar.
Fag.
Viol.
pp
pp

55
Fl.
Fl. picc.
Ob.
a 2
Clar.
Cor.
Fag.
Viol.
61
Fl.
Fl. pic.
Ob.
Clar.
Cor.
Fag.
(cresc.)
Viol. cresc.

67

Fl.

Fl. picc.

Ob.

Clar.

Cor.

Fag.

unis.

a 2.

Tr.

Ctti

Tromb.

Oph.

Timp.

Viol.

ff

74

𝅗𝅥 = 𝅘𝅥.

a 2.

unis.

a 2.

a 2.

a 2.

𝅗𝅥 = 𝅘𝅥.

83
Fag.
unis.
(dim.)
ppp
Viol.
102
57
Tromb.
Timp.
derrière la Scène
behind the Scene
Due campane (2 Glocken) in C (Ut) G (Sol)
con Ped.
A défaut de Cloches derrière le Théâtre, plusieurs Pianos sur l'avant-scène.
In the absence of Bells behind the scene, several pianos on the apron.
Viol.
Soli
poco f

115
Ob. I. Solo
mf
a 2.
f
Cor.
Tr.
Tromb.
ff
Timp.
f
Camp.
p
pp
Viol.
ff
mf
p
58
127 Dies iræ sans presser
Fag. unis.
Oph. a 2.
Soli
f
Camp.
f
Viol.
sans presser

146
59
Fl.
Fl. picc.
Ob.
Clar.
Cor.
Fag.
Tr.
Ctti
Tromb
Oph.
Gr. Tamb.
Camp.
Viol.
pizz.
pizz.
pizz.

159
arco
arco
arco
pizz.
pizz.
H.B.1.

171
pizz.
pizz.
pizz.

184
arco
arco
arco
arco
tenu
arco
tenu

196

209
f
pizz.
pizz.
pizz.

221
a 2.
a 2.
G-Caisse roulante, deux Timbaliers
Bass-Drum roll, two timpanists
arco
arco
arco

231
Fl.
Fl. picc.
Ob.
Clar.
Cor.
Fag.
Tr.
Ctti
Tromb.
Oph.
Baguettes d'éponge
Sponge-headed sticks
Timp.
Baguettes d'éponge
Sponge-headed sticks
Viol.
cresc.
a 2
a 4
a 2.

60

Ronde du Sabbat

Witches' round dance

241 **Un peu retenu**

I.

Un peu retenu

250
I.

257
I.
a 2.
a 2.
unis.

265
unis.
a 2.
a 2.
a 2.
cresc.

272

a 2.

cresc.

cresc.

cresc.

cresc.

cresc.

280

f

f

a 2.

f

f

f

a 2.

sf

f

III.

a 2.

sf

f

p cresc. - - ff

f

f

p f p f p cresc. - - ff

p f p f p cresc. - - ff

p f p f (p cresc. - - ff)

p f p f p cresc. - - ff

p f p f p cresc. - - ff

289
I.
(cresc.)
(cresc.)

297
a 2.
III.
unis.
a 2.

306
Soli
éponges
pizz.
arco

313
f dimin.
f (dimin.
a 2.
ff
p
pp
pizz.
arco
f

320
a 2.
unis.
a 2.
a 2.
a 2.
pizz.
pizz.

327
Soli
I.
III.
dim.
pp
unis. Soli
arco
pizz.
poco f
en dim. toujours
(en dim. toujours)

335
sf > pp
sf > pp
sf > pp
sf > pp
p
dim.
ppp
dimin. sempre
ppp
ppp
p
pp
pp
p
pp

345
II.
Solo
poco f
IV. Solo
poco f
II.
pp
IV.
pp
ppp
II. Solo
presque rien
mf
ppp
presque rien
mf
ppp
pizz.
pp
div. arco
mf
div.
Soli.
ppp
arco
Soli
mf
dim.
presque rien
arco
pppp
mf
dim.

361
cresc. poco a poco
II.
bouché avec les cylindres
IV.
poco sf > p
crescendo
Un Timbalier
One drummer
Solo
pp
cresc. poco a poco
pp
cresc.
Soli
pp
crescendo

371

bouché avec les cylindres
II.
poco sf > *p*

Les deux Timbaliers réunis
Both drummers together
p cresc. poco a poco

p
p
cresc. poco a poco
poco a poco
poco a poco

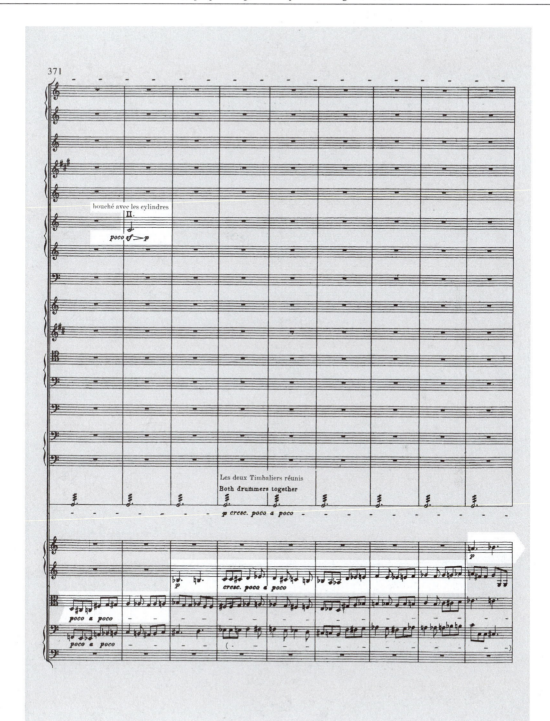

380
mf
cresc.
I.
cresc. sempre
cresc. poco a poco
cresc sempre
f cresc. sempre
cresc. sempre

389

ff

mf

mf

f

unis.

a 2.

cresc. molto

ff

div.

unis.

398

407

sf

sf

sf

sf

sf

61
Dies irae et Ronde du Sabbat ensemble
414 Dies irae and witches' round dance together
a 2.
unis.
a 2.
a 2.
a 2.

423

429

mf

435
p
f
f
f
f
f
f
f
p
f
ff
p
ff
p
ff
p
(ff)

441

a 2.

mf

unis.

frappez avec les bois de l'archet

frappez avec les bois de l'archet

frappez avec les bois de l'archet

(col legno battuta)

div.

448

pizz.
pp
pizz.
pp

456

Soli

p légèrement

I.

p légèrement

p légèrement

I.

p légèrement

arco

464

p

a 2.

p

f

ff

a 2.

I.

arco

pp cresc.

474
Soli
mf
cresc.
I.
a 2.
unis.

483

Solo II.

a 2.

unis.

a 2.

cresc. molto

a 2

a 2.

493

animez un peu

a 2.

a 2.

I.

animez un peu

504

unis.

a 2.

a 2.

I.

div.

unis.

515

tenu

unis.

Coup frappé sur une Cymbale avec une baguette couverte d'éponge ou un tampon
Struck on a cymbal with a sponge-headed drum-stick or a padded stick

Cinelli.

The early Romantic tendency toward the colossal is best seen in the imaginative works of Hector Berlioz (1803–1869). Expanding both the size and the range of colors of his operas, choral works, and symphonies, Berlioz created innovative works that dazzled the Parisian public. *Symphonie fantastique* (1830), a program symphony with five movements, stands as one of the masterpieces of the early Romantic era because of its fanciful story, effective use of thematic transformation, and brilliant orchestration.

For the most part, Berlioz pays only passing homage to Classical structures. While the first three movements primarily present musical tableaus of the poet and his love, the fourth and fifth abound in specific imagery. In his opium state, the poet dreams that he has killed his lover, and, in the marchlike fourth movement, he is led to a scaffold and beheaded. In the last movement, the poet is transported to a Faustian scene, where witches, including his beloved, revel in his demise.

A recurring theme, labeled the *idée fixe* (fixed idea) by Berlioz, appears in all five movements of the symphony. Representing the poet's lover, the melody is continuously transformed to meet the moods of the story. In the fourth movement, it appears briefly at the end. In the finale, the theme, played by the E-flat clarinet, is a rollicking, grotesque jig, reflecting the true image of his love.

Masterful orchestration is evident throughout both movements. The string instruments explore contrasting colors with passages of pizzicato and *col legno* (hitting the strings with the wood side of the bow). The woodwind families are expanded with instruments such as the E-flat clarinet, the English horn, and the contrabassoon, and the flutes are asked to make an unusual sound effect by rolling the mouthpiece away from their lips at the beginning of the fifth movement. The low brass section is also expanded with the addition of two *ophicleides* (obsolete brass instruments, replaced today by tubas). As is evident at the beginning of the fourth movement, the role and size of the percussion section are also increased. One of the most striking passages of orchestration occurs in the fourth movement: following measures 82 and 109, the principal theme is presented with continuously changing colors, often on a note-by-note basis, including a "note" by the unpitched cymbals. But the most stunning moment in the entire symphony occurs at measure 127 of the finale, when the sacrilegious intoning of the *Dies irae* (*Day of Wrath*) chant by the low brass is heard against church bells ringing in the background.

II

Bedřich Smetana

Vltava (The Moldau),
from *Má vlast (My Country)* (1874–79)

8CD: 5/ 62 – 69
4CD: 3/ 18 – 25

62 18

Editor's note: Smaller notes indicate an alternate version for reduced orchestra.

Fl.
Harfe
1.Viol.
2.Viol.
Br.
Klar. (C)
p

25
Fl.
Klar. (C)
1.Viol.
2.Viol.
Br.
p
30
Fl.
Klar. (C)
1.Viol.
2.Viol.
Br.
35
63
19
Fl.
Ob.
Klar. (C)
*2. Ob.
Hr. (C)
I.II.
a 2
Trgl.
p elegante
1.Viol.
arco
p dolce
2.Viol.
lusingando
arco
ondeggiante
Br.
lusingando
*2.Vcll.
p lusingando
Vcll.
p lusingando
pizz.
K.-B.

40
Fl.
Ob.
Klar. (C)
Fag.
Hr. (C)
Trpt. (C)
Pos. Tuba
Pk.
Trgl.
1.Viol.
2.Viol.
Br.
Vcll.
K.-B.
dolce
p dolce
a 2
*1. Ob.
*2. Ob.
*3. Hr.
*2. Fag.
ppp
sf
dim.
sempre ondeggiante

45
Fl.
Ob.
dolce
dolce
Klar. (C)
*2. Ob.
Fag.
dolce
Hr. (C)
Trpt. (C)
Pos. Tuba
Pk.
Trgl.
glockenartig
1.Viol.
2.Viol.
sempre ondeggiante
Br.
sempre ondeggiante
Vcll
sempre ondeggiante
K.-B.

50
Fl.
Ob.
Klar. (C)
Fag.
Hr. (C)
Trpt. (C)
Pos. Tuba
Pk.
Viol.
Viol.
Br.
Vcll.
K.-B.
sf
p
dim.

55
Fl.
a 2
mf
cresc.
sf
Ob.
mf cresc.
Klar. (C)
Fag.
Hr. (C)
p
cresc.
*4. Hr.
Trpt. (C)
Pos. Tuba
p cresc.
Pk.
Trgl.
Harfe
1. Viol.
2. Viol.
Br.
Vcll.
K.-B.

60
a 2
Fl.
Ob.
*2.Ob.
Klar. (C)
*2.Fl.
*2.Ob.
Fag.
Hr. (C)
*4.Hr.
Trpt. (C)
Pos. Tuba
Pk.
Trgl.
Harfe
Viol.
Viol.
Br.
Vcll.
K.-B.
sf
p
cresc.

65
Fl.
Ob.
Klar. (C)
Fag.
Hr. (C)
Trpt. (C)
Pos. Tuba
Pk.
Trgl.
1.Viol.
2.Viol.
Br.
Vcll.
K.-B.
*2.Fl.2.Ob.
cresc.
arco
pizz.

70
Fl.
Ob.
Klar. (C)
Fag.
Hr. (C)
Trpt. (C)
Pos. Tuba
Pk.
Trgl.
Harfe
1.Viol.
2.Viol.
Br.
Vcll.
K.-B.
*2. Vcll.
*2. Ob.
*4. Hr.
*3. Hr.
*2. Fag.
dopo la repetizione muta in C. G.
pizz.

75
Fl.
Ob.
Klar. (C)
Fag.
Hr. (C)
Trpt. (C)
Pos. Tuba
Pk.
Trgl.
Harfe
1.Viol.
2.Viol.
Br.
Vcll.
K.-B.
sf
dim.
p

64
20
80
Forest Hunt
Fl.
Ob.
Klar. (C)
Fag.
Hr. (C)
Trpt. (C)
*2 Ob.
Pos. Tuba
*4. Hr.
Pk.
Trgl.
Harfe
1.Viol.
2.Viol.
Br.
Vcll.
arco
K.-B.

86
Fl.
Ob.
Klar. (C)
Fag.
Hr. (C)
Trpt. (C)
Pos. Tuba
Pk.
Trgl.
1.Viol.
2.Viol.
Br.
Vcll.
K.-B.
*2.Ob.
*3.Hr.
*4.Hr.

92
Fl.
Ob.
Klar. (C)
Fag.
Hr. (C)
Trpt. (C)
Pos. Tuba
*4. Hr.
Pk.
muta in A. D.
Trgl.
1.Viol.
2.Viol.
Br.
Vcll.
K.-B.

97
Fl.
Ob.
*2. Ob.
Klar. (C)
Fag.
Hr. (C)
Trpt. (C)
*3. Hr.
Pos. Tuba
Pk.
1.Viol.
2.Viol.
Br.
Vcll.
K.-B.

102
Fl.
Ob.
Klar. (C)
*2 Ob.
Fag.
Hr. (C)
Trpt. (C)
muta in E
*3. Hr.
Pos. Tuba
*3. Hr.
*4. Hr.
Pk.
Trgl.
1.Viol.
2.Viol.
Br.
Vcll.
K.-B.
f dim.
f dim.
f dim.

107
Fl.
Ob.
Klar. (C)
dim.
sempre dim.
Fag.
dim.
sempre dim.
Hr. (C)
dim.
p dim.
sempre dim.
sempre dim.
Trpt. (E)
sempre dim.
Pos. Tuba
dim.
sempre dim.
Pk.
1.Viol
dim.
sempre dim.
2.Viol.
dim.
sempre dim.
Br.
dim.
sempre dim.
Vcll.
dim.
sempre dim.
dim.
sempre dim.
K.-B.
dim.
sempre dim.

112
Fl.
Ob.
Klar. (C)
a 2
Fag.
Hr. (C)
Trpt. (E)
Pos. Tuba
Pk.
1.Viol.
2.Viol.
Br.
Vcll.
K.-B.
pp
ppp

65
21
Peasant Wedding
118
L'istesso tempo, ma moderato
Klar. (C)
Fag.
Hr. (C)
Trpt. (E)
3. Pos.
1. Viol.
2. Viol.
Br.
Vcll.
K.-B.
a 2
mf
p
cresc.
128

136
Fl.
Ob.
Klar. (C)
Fag.
Hr. (C)
Trpt. (A)
*3.u.4.Hr.
Pos. Tuba
*2.Fag.
*2.Vcll.
Pk.
Trgl.
1.Viol.
2.Viol.
Br.
Vcll.
K.-B.

144
Fl.
Ob.
Klar. (C)
Fag.
Hr. (C)
Trpt. (A)
Pos. Tuba
Pk.
Trgl.
1.Viol.
2.Viol.
Br.
Vcll.
K.-B.
dim.
p

152
Fl.
a 2
Ob.
Klar. (C)
Fag.
*3.u.4. Hr.
Hr. (C)
Trpt. (A)
Pos. Tuba
Pk.
più p
Trgl.
1.Viol.
2.Viol.
Br.
Vcll.
K.-B.

160
a 2
Fl.
Ob.
Klar. (C)
Fag.
Hr. (C)
Pk.
1.Viol.
2.Viol.
Br.
Vcll.
K.-B.
dim.
più p
sempre dim.
*4.Hr.
muta in E H
168
E
muta in B
muta in Es
muta in F
*2.Fag.
pp Solo
pp
ppp

66
22
181
Moonlight: Nymphs' Dance
L'istesso tempo
Fl.
Ob.
Klar. (B)
Fag.
Hr. (Es)
Trpt. (B)
1.Viol.
2.Viol.
Br.
Vcll.
K.-B.
plusingando
*2.Ob.
*Die 1.Stimme blasen
in B
*2.Ob.mit Dämpfer
tranquillo
con sordini
dolciss.
pp ondeggiante
188
Harfe
3. Pos.
*3.Hr.ohne Dämpfer
*4.Hr.

192
Fl.
Klar. (B)
(Es) Hr. (F)
Trpt. (B)
3. Pos.
Harfe
1. Viol.
2. Viol.
Br.
Vcll.
ppp
*3. Hr.
*4. Hr.
p
sempre pp
196

200
Fl.
Klar. (B)
(Es) Hr. (F)
Trpt. (B)
3. Pos.
Harfe
1. Viol.
2. Viol.
Br.
Vcll.
sempre pp
*3. Hr.
*4. Hr.
p
pp
*Die 1. Stimme spielen
204

208
Fl.
Ob.
Klar. (B)
Fag.
(Es) Hr. (F)
Trpt. (B)
Pos. Tuba
Pk.
Harfe
1. Viol.
2. Viol.
Br.
Vcll
K B
dim.
più pp
pp
*3.u.4.Hr.
*3.Hr.
*4.Hr.
p

212
Fl.
Ob.
Klar. (B)
Fag.
*4. Hr.
ppp possibile
(Es)
Hr.
(F)
ppp possibile
ppp possibile
*3. Hr.
*4. Pos.
Trpt. (B)
ppp possibile
Pos. Tuba
ppp possibile
*3. Pos. bläst die Tubastimme
ppp possibile
Pk.
Harfe
p
1. Viol.
2. Viol.
Br.
Vcll.
*2. Vcll.
K.-B.
pp

216
Fl.
Ob.
Klar. (B)
Fag.
(Es)
Hr.
(F)
Trpt. (B)
Pos. Tuba
Pk.
Harfe
1. Viol.
2. Viol.
Br.
Vcll.
K.-B.
ppp
pp
p
sempre pp
*1.u.2. Pos.
*3. Pos. bläst die Tubastimme

220
Fl.
Ob.
Klar. (B)
Fag.
*2.Hr.
(Es)
Hr.
(F)
*3.Hr.
sempre pp
sempre pp
Trpt. (B)
sempre pp
Pos. Tuba
sempre pp
sempre pp
Pk.
Harfe
p
p
1. Viol.
sempre pp
2. Viol.
sempre pp
Br.
sempre pp
V. II.
sempre pp
sempre pp
K.-B.
sempre pp

224
Fl.
Ob.
Klar. (B)
Fag.
(Es)
Hr.
(F)
Trpt. (B)
Pos. Tuba
Pk.
Harfe
1. Viol.
2. Viol.
Br.
Vcll.
K.-B.
pp
p

228
Fl.
Ob.
Klar. (B)
Fag.
(Es)
Hr.
(F)
Trpt. (B)
Pos. Tuba
Pk.
Trgl.
Harfe
1.Viol.
2.Viol.
Br.
1.Vcll.
2.Vcll. K.-B.
pp
*Die obere Stimme.
*Die obere Stimme
*3.u.1.Hr.
in E a 2
p cresc.
pp cresc.
cresc.

231
Fl.
cresc.
Ob.
cresc.
Klar. (B)
cresc.
Fag.
pp
cresc.
(Es)
Hr.
(F)
cresc.
cresc.
Trpt. (E)
a 2
3
3
cresc.
Pos.
Tuba
cresc.
cresc.
Pk.
cresc.
Trgl.
Harfe
cresc.
sf
1.Viol.
cresc.
2.Viol.
cresc.
Br.
cresc.
1.Vcll.
cresc.
2.Vcll.
K.-B.
cresc.

234
Fl.
cresc.
Ob.
Klar. (B)
cresc.
Fag.
(Es)
Hr.
(F)
muta in C
muta in C
Trpt. (E)
Pos. Tuba
*2. Fag.
p
Pk.
1.Viol.
2.Viol.
Br.
1.Vcll.
2.Vcll. K.-B.

67
23
Tempo I
237
Fl.
*2. Ob.
dolce
p
*Die obere Stimme
Ob.
dolce
Klar. (B)
muta in C
Fag.
p dolce
Hr. (C)
Trpt. (E)
Pos. Tuba
*2. Fag.
pp dolce
Pk.
Trgl.
senza sordini
1.Viol.
dolce
2.Viol.
sempre ondeggiante
Br.
Vcll.
*2.Vcll.
K.-B.
pizz.

241
Fl.
Ob.
Klar. (C)
Fag.
Hr. (C)
Trpt. (E)
* 3. Hr.
Pos. Tuba
Pk.
1.Viol.
2.Viol.
Br.
Vcll.
K.-B.
dim.
f
sf
p

246
Fl.
a 2
mf cresc.
sf
Ob.
mf cresc.
*2. Ob.
Clar. (C)
Fag.
Hr. (C)
Trpt. (E)
*3. Hr.
Pos. Tuba
Pk.
Trgl.
Harfe
cresc.
Viol.
Viol.
Br.
Vcll.
C.-B.

251
a 2
Fl.
cresc.
* Die obere Stimme
Ob.
*2.Ob.
sf
cresc.
*2.Ob.
Klar. (C)
Fag.
Hr. (C)
Trpt. (E)
Pos. Tuba
Pk.
Trgl.
Harfe
1.Viol.
2.Viol.
Br.
Vcll.
K.-B.

256
Fl.
Ob.
Klar. (C)
Fag.
Hr. (C)
Trpt. (E)
Pos. Tuba
Pk.
Trgl.
1.Viol.
2.Viol.
Br.
Vcll.
K.-B.
cresc.
arco
pizz.
arco

261
Fl.
Ob.
Klar. (C)
Fag.
Hr. (C)
Trpt. (E)
Pos. Tuba
Pk.
Trgl.
Harfe
1.Viol.
2.Viol.
Br.
Vcll.
K.-B.
*2.Vell.
*2.Ob.
*2.Vcll.
*2.Fag.
dim.
pp
mf
p
sf
pizz.
tr

266
Fl.
Ob.
* 2. Ob.
Klar. (C)
Fag.
Hr. (C)
Trpt. (E)
Pos. Tuba
Pk.
Trgl.
Harfe
1.Viol.
2.Viol.
Br.
Vcll.
K.-B.
sf
dim.
f
p

68
24
271
St. John's Rapids
bei kl. Bes. *1.Fl.nimmt Kl.Fl.bis Schluß
Fl.
Ob.
Klar. (C)
Fag.
Hr. (C)
Trpt. (E)
Pos. Tuba
*4.Hr.
Pk.
Trgl.
Gr.Tr.
Solo
mit Paukenschlägel
Harfe
1.Viol.
2.Viol.
Br.
1.Vcll.
2.Vcll. K.-B.
cresc.

276
Kl.Fl.
1.Fl.
*1.Fl.
2.Fl.
Ob.
Klar. (C)
Fag.
Hr. (C)
*1.Pos.
*1.u.2.Pos.
Trpt. (E)
Pos. Tuba
Pk.
mit Paukenschlägel
Gr.Tr.
1.Viol.
2.Viol.
Br.
1.Vcll.
2.Vcll. K.-B.

281
Kl. Fl.
1. Fl.
2. Fl.
*1. Fl.
Ob.
*2. Ob.
Klar. (C)
Fag.
cresc.
Hr. (C)
Trpt. (E)
Pos. Tuba
*4. Hr.
Pk.
1. Viol.
2. Viol.
Br.
1. Vcll.
2. Vcll. K.-B.

286
Kl. Fl.
1. Fl.
2. Fl.
Ob.
*2. Ob.
Klar. (C)
Fag.
Hr. (C)
Trpt. (E)
*1. Pos.
Pos. Tuba
Pk.
1. Viol.
2. Viol.
Br.
1. Vcll.
2. Vcll. K.-B.

291
Kl.Fl.
1.Fl.
2.Fl.
*1.Fl.
Ob.
Klar. (C)
Fag.
*1.u.3.Hr.
Hr. (C)
Trpt. (E)
Pos. Tuba
Pk.
Bck.
1.Viol.
2.Viol.
Br.
1.Vcll.
2.Vcll. K B.

296
Kl.Fl.
1.Fl.
2.Fl.
Ob.
Klar. (C)
Fag.
Hr. (C)
Trpt. (E)
Pos. Tuba
Pk.
1.Viol.
2.Viol.
Br.
1.Vcll.
2.Vcll. K-B.
*Kl. Fl. loco
cresc.
sf
marc.
*3. Hr.
*4. Hr.
*3. Pos. bläst die Tubastimme

303
Kl. Fl.
1. Fl.
2. Fl.
Ob.
Klar. (C)
Fag.
Hr. (C)
Trpt. (E)
Pos. Tuba
Pk.
Bck.
1. Viol.
2. Viol.
Br.
1. Vcll.
2. Vcll. K.-B.
*1. Fl.
Kl. Fl. loco
cresc.
*3. Hr.
*4. Hr.
*3. Pos. bläst die Tubastimme

309
Kl. Fl.
1. Fl.
2. Fl.
Ob.
Klar. (C)
Fag.
marc.
Hr. (C)
Trpt. (E)
*1. u. 2. Pos.
rfz
Pos. Tuba
* 3. Pos. bläst die Tubastimme
Pk.
Gr. Tr.
Bck.
1. Viol.
2. Viol.
Br.
1. Vcll.
2. Vcll. K.-B.
marc.

315
Kl. Fl.
1. Fl.
2. Fl.
Ob.
Klar. (C)
Fag.
Hr. (C)
Trpt. (E)
Pos. Tuba
Pk.
Gr. Tr.
Bck.
Viol.
Viol.
Br.
Vcll.
Vcll. K.-B.
sempre cresc.
cresc.

K
321
Kl. Fl.
1.Fl.
2.Fl.
Ob.
Klar. (C)
Fag.
Hr. (C)
Trpt. (E)
Pos. Tuba
Pk.
Gr.Tr.
Bck.
1.Viol.
2.Viol.
Br.
1.Vcll.
2.Vcll. K.-B.
fff
sf
ff
muta in A
muta in E
*4. Hr.
mit Schlägeln
dim.
sub. pp

328
Kl. Fl.
1. Fl.
2. Fl.
Ob.
Klar. (A)
Fag.
Hr. (E)
Trpt. (E)
Pos. Tuba
Pk.
pp
sub. cresc.
1. Viol.
pp
sub. cresc. molto
2. Viol.
pp
sub. cresc. molto
Br.
cresc. molto
1. Vcll.
2. Vcll. K.-B.

The Moldau in its Greatest Breadth
333
Più moto
Kl.Fl.
1.Fl.
2.Fl.
Ob.
Klar. (A)
Fag.
Hr. (E)
Trpt. (E)
Pos. Tuba
Pk.
Trgl.
Harfe
1.Viol.
2.Viol.
Br.
1.Vcll.
2.Vcll.
K.-B.

341
Kl.Fl.
*Kl.Fl.loco
1.Fl.
*Kl.Fl.Okt.höher
2.Fl.
*1.Fl.
Ob.
Klar. (A)
Fag.
Hr. (E)
Trpt. (E)
Pos. Tuba
Pk.
Trgl.
Harfe
1.Viol.
2.Viol.
Br.
1.Vcll.
2.Vcll.
K.-B.

350
Kl.Fl.
1.Fl.
2.Fl.
Ob.
Klar. (A)
Fag.
Hr. (E)
Trpt. (E)
Pos. Tuba
Pk.
Trgl.
Harfe
Viol.
Viol.
Br.
Vcll.
Vcll.
K.-B.
fz
f
cresc.
marcatiss.

69
25
Vyšehrad Motive (Symphonic Poem No. 1)
359
L
Kl. Fl.
1. Fl.
2. Fl.
Ob.
Klar. (A)
Fag.
Hr. (E)
Trpt. (E)
Pos. Tuba
Pk.
Trgl.
Gr. Tr.
Bck.
Harfe
1. Viol.
2. Viol.
Br.
1. Vcll.
2. Vcll.
K.-B.

364
Kl. Fl.
1. Fl.
2. Fl.
Ob.
Klar. (A)
Fag.
Hr. (E)
Trpt. (E)
Pos. Tuba
Pk.
Trgl.
Gr. Tr.
Bck.
1. Viol.
2. Viol.
Br.
1. Vcll.
2. Vcll.
K.-B.

369
Kl.Fl.
1.Fl.
2.Fl.
Ob.
Klar. (A)
Fag.
Hr. (E)
Trpt. (E)
Pos. Tuba
Pk.
Trgl.
Gr.Tr.
Bck.
1.Viol.
2.Viol.
Br.
1.Vcll.
2.Vcll.
K.-B.
fz
rinf

374
sempre ff
Kl. Fl.
1. Fl.
2. Fl.
Ob.
Klar. (A)
Fag.
Hr. (E)
Trpt. (E)
Pos. Tuba
Pk.
Trgl.
Gr.Tr.
Bck.
1.Viol.
2.Viol.
Br.
Vcll.
K B.
fz
rfz
ff
*Kl.Fl.loco

383
Kl. Fl.
1. Fl.
2. Fl.
Ob.
Klar. (A)
Fag.
Hr. (E)
Trpt. (E)
Pos. Tuba
Pk.
Trgl.
Gr.Tr.
Bck.
Viol.
Viol.
Br.
Vcll.
K.-B.

392
Kl. Fl.
1. Fl.
2. Fl.
Ob.
Klar. (A)
Fag.
Hr. (E)
Trpt. (E)
Pos. Tuba
Pk.
Trgl.
Gr. Tr.
Bck.
1. Viol.
2. Viol.
Br.
Vcll.
K.-B.
*1. Fl.

401
Kl.Fl.
1.Fl.
2.Fl.
Ob.
Klar. (A)
Fag.
Hr. (E)
Trpt. (E)
Pos. Tuba
Pk.
Trgl.
Gr.Tr.
Bck.
1.Viol.
2.Viol.
Br.
1.Vcll.
2.Vcll.
K. B.
sf dim.
sempre dim.
*1.Fl.
*3.Hr.
*2.Fag.
*Die 2.Stimme bis Schluß

410
Kl. Fl.
1. Fl.
2. Fl.
Ob.
Klar. (A)
Fag.
Hr. (E)
Trpt. (E)
Pos. Tuba
Pk.
1. Viol.
2. Viol.
Br.
1. Vcll.
2. Vcll.
K.-B.
pp
p dim.
ppp
ff
dim.
sempre dim. al

419
rall.
Kl.Fl.
1.Fl.
2.Fl.
Ob.
Klar. (A)
Fag.
Hr. (E)
Trpt. (E)
Pos. Tuba
Pk.
1.Viol.
2.Viol.
Br.
1.Vcll.
2.Vcll.
K.-B.
pp
dim. al ppp
smorz.
ff
fz
rall.

Musical nationalism can most readily be seen in works that create an image or tell a story, such as operas, songs, and symphonic poems. One of the foremost nationalist composers in the nineteenth century was Bedřich Smetana (1824–1884), who came from eastern Bohemia (in the modern-day Czech Republic). He composed a set of six symphonic poems entitled *Má vlast (My Country)* that depicts various images of his homeland. These works can be performed as a group, but they are often heard individually, especially the second member of the set, entitled *Vltava (The Moldau)*. Smetana attached the following description to this movement:

> Two springs pour forth in the shade of the Bohemian forest, one warm and gushing, the other cold and peaceful. Coming through Bohemia's valleys, they grow into a mighty stream. Through the thick woods it flows as the merry sounds of a hunt and the notes of the hunter's horn are heard ever closer. It flows through grass-grown pastures and lowlands where a wedding feast is being celebrated with song and dance. At night, wood and water nymphs revel in its sparkling waves. Reflected on its surface are fortresses and castles—witnesses of bygone days of knightly splendor and the vanished glory of martial times. The Moldau swirls through the St. John Rapids, finally flowing on in majestic peace toward Prague to be welcomed by historic Vysehrad. Then it vanishes far beyond the poet's gaze.

Many of the images in this description are mirrored in the music, from the gentle murmur of two springs to the tumultuous St. John Rapids. Unifying the work is a recurring E-minor river theme that has its grandest statement, with a dramatic turn to major, as the river nears the city of Prague. Smetana's nationalism is not limited to patriotic visions of Bohemia. Folk-music traditions are also reflected in the melody and rhythm. The river theme has a distinct folk character with its limited range and repetitive patterns. Also distinctive are the folk-dance rhythms heard as the river passes the wedding feast.

12

Johannes Brahms

Symphony No. 3 in F major, Third movement (1883)

8CD: 5/ 70 – 72
4CD: 3/ 26 – 28

10
Fl.
Kl.
Fg.
Vl.
Br.
Vc.
Kb.
p
m. v.
espress.
6

Kl.
Fg.
Vl.
Br.
Vc.
Kb.

20
Kl.
Fg.
Vl.
Br.
Vc.
Kb
pp
dolce
pp
pp
dolce
pp
pp

Kl.
Fg.
Vl.
Br.
Vc.
Kb

30
Kl.
Fg.
Vl.
Br.
Vc.
Kb.
dim.
pp
dolce

Kl.
Fg.
Vl.
Br.
Vc.
Kb.
2.
p
dim.

40
Fl.
Hb.
Kl.
Fg.
Hrn. (C)
Vl.
Br.
Vc.
Kb.
mp espress.
p
legg.
p legg.

Fl.
Hb.
Kl
Fg.
Hrn. (C)
Vl.
Br.
Vc.
Kb.
pizz.

50
Fl.
Hb.
Kl.
Fg.
Hrn.
(C)
Vl.
Br.
Vc.
Kb.
p
dolce

71
27
Fl.
Hb.
Kl.
1.
Fg.
Hrn.
(C)
arco
Vc.
Vc.
p dolce
p

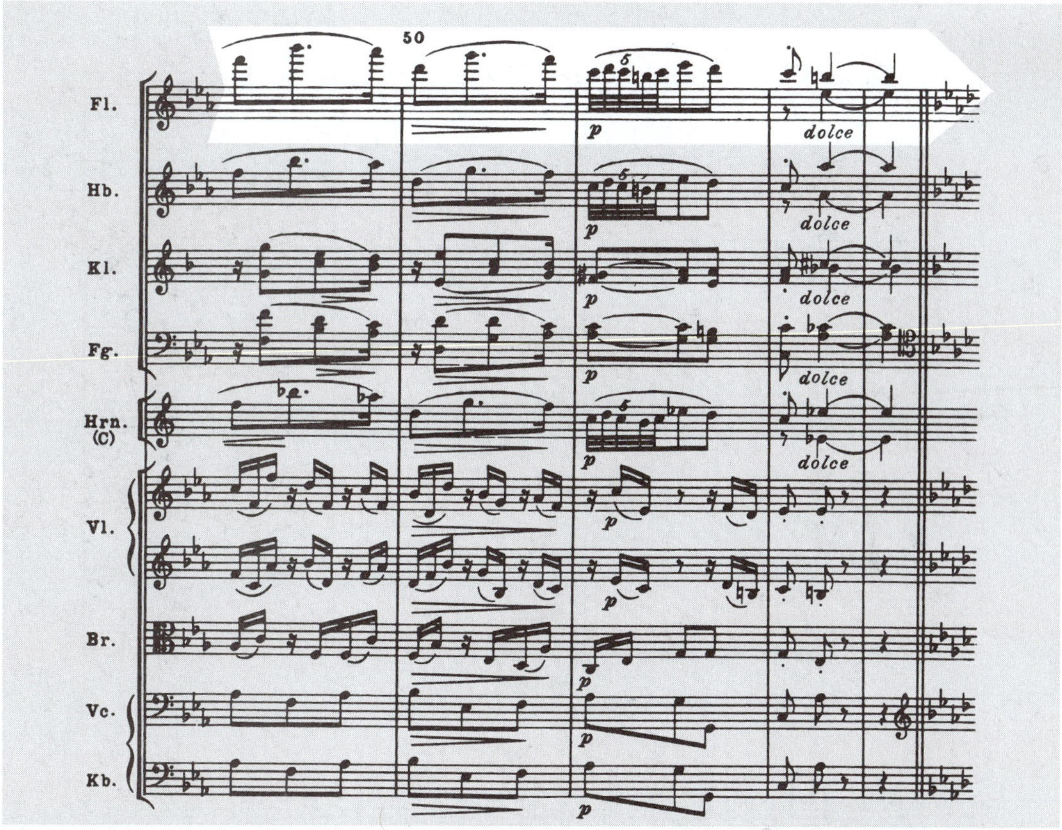

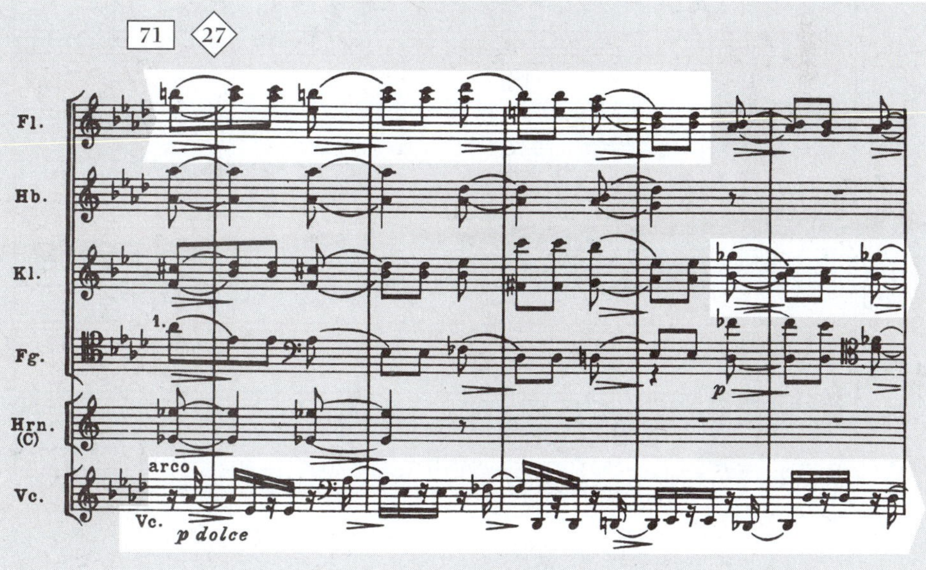

60
Fl.
Hb.
Kl.
Fg.
Hrn. (C)
1.Vl.
Br.
Vc.
dolce
p dolce
p dolce

70
Fl.
Hb.
Kl.
Fg.
Vl.
Br.
Vc.
pp espress.
pp espress.
pp espress.
pp espress.

Vl.
cresc.
f
p dim.
Br.
Vc.
Kb.
arco
p

80
Fl.
Hb.
Kl.
Fg.
Hrn.
(C)
Vl.
dolce
Br.
Vc.

90
Fl.
Hb.
Kl.
Fg.
Hrn. (C)
Vl.
Br.
Vc.
p dim.
p dim.
p dim.
p dim.

Fl.
Hb.
Kl.
Fg.
Hrn. (C)
Vl.
Br.
Vc.
1.
p
lunga
pp dim.
pp dim.
pp dim.
pp dim.

72
28
100
Fl.
p
1.
Hrn. (C)
p espressivo
Vl.
pp legg.
pp legg.
Br.
p
Vc.
p
pizz.
Kb.
p

Fl.
Hrn. (C)
Vl.
Br.
pizz.
Vc.
Kb.

110
Fl.
Hb.
1.
p espress.
Kl.
dolce
Fg.
1.
p
Hrn. (C)
5
Vl.
Br.
arco
Vc.
Kb.

Hb.
Kl.
Fg.
Hrn. (C)
Vl.
Br.
Vc.
Kb.

120
Hb.
Kl.
Fg.
Vl.
Br.
pizz.
Vc.
pizz.
Kb.

Hb.
dolce
Kl.
1.
dolce
Fg.
dolce
Hrn. (C)
pp
Vl.
dolce
dolce
Br.
arco
dolce
Vc. Kb.
Bassi
dolce

130
Fl.
Kl.
Fg.
Hrn. (C)
Vl.
Br.
Vc. Kb
dim.
pp
dolce
p dim.
pp dolce
dim.
dim.
dim.
dim.
più p

Fl.
Kl.
Fg.
Hrn. (C)
Vl.
Br.
Vc. Kb

Fl.
Kl.
Fg.
Hrn. (C)
1. Vl.
Br.
Vc.
1.
p dim.
p
dim.
get.
mp espr.
Vc.
arco
mp espr.

140
Fl.
Hb.
Kl.
Fg.
Hrn. (C)
Vl.
Br.
Vc.
Kb.
1.
p

Fl.
Hb.
Kl.
Fg.
Hrn. (C)
Vl.
Br.
Vc.
Kb.

150
zu 2
Fl.
Hb.
Kl.
Fg.
Hrn. (C)
Vl.
Br.
Vc.
Kb.
p
dolce

160
Fl.
Hb.
Kl.
Fg.
Hrn. (C)
zu 2
Vl.
get.
pizz.
Br.
Vc.
Kb.
arco

Johannes Brahms (1833–1897), a leading figure in the second half of the nineteenth century, embraced the traditions of the Viennese Classical school. He mastered the Classical forms, including sonata and variation, and he composed significant works in all of the major Classical instrumental genres—symphony, concerto, piano sonata, and chamber music. Of these, the symphony was the last to be explored. Feeling the weight of Beethoven's masterworks, Brahms did not begin his first symphony until he was over forty-years old, and he completed only four symphonies during his lifetime.

In his symphonies, Brahms returns to the concept of absolute forms, without programmatic images. Each symphony contains four movements in standard Classical structures; cyclic elements are limited, and even the size of the orchestra is comparable to that of Beethoven. Within this framework, Brahms creates a distinctively Romantic sound by employing effective orchestrations, passionate melodies, complex harmonies, and blurred rhythmic effects.

The third movement of Symphony No. 3 retains the ternary structure of a scherzo, but Brahms replaces the traditionally lively tempo with a melancholy waltz. The cellos open the movement with a passionate, songlike melody accompanied by the murmuring of the upper strings. Each time the theme returns, it is presented in a different setting, most strikingly in the French horn solo at the reprise. The complexities of Brahms's textures, rhythms, and harmonies are particularly evident in the middle section.

13

Antonín Dvořák

Symphony No. 9 in E minor (*From the New World*), First movement (1893)

CD8: 6/1 - 9

7
fz
dim. p
fz
dim. p
ff
ff
ff
p
ff
ff
ff [z]
ffz
ff
ff
ff
ff
ff

12
p
p
p f
pp
a 2
p f dim.
ff
p f
p f
32
pp
fz
fp pp pp
fz
fp pp pp

17
a 2
p
pp
f
a 2
16
16
fz

20
mf
tr
ff
ffz
p
cresc.
fpp
attacca

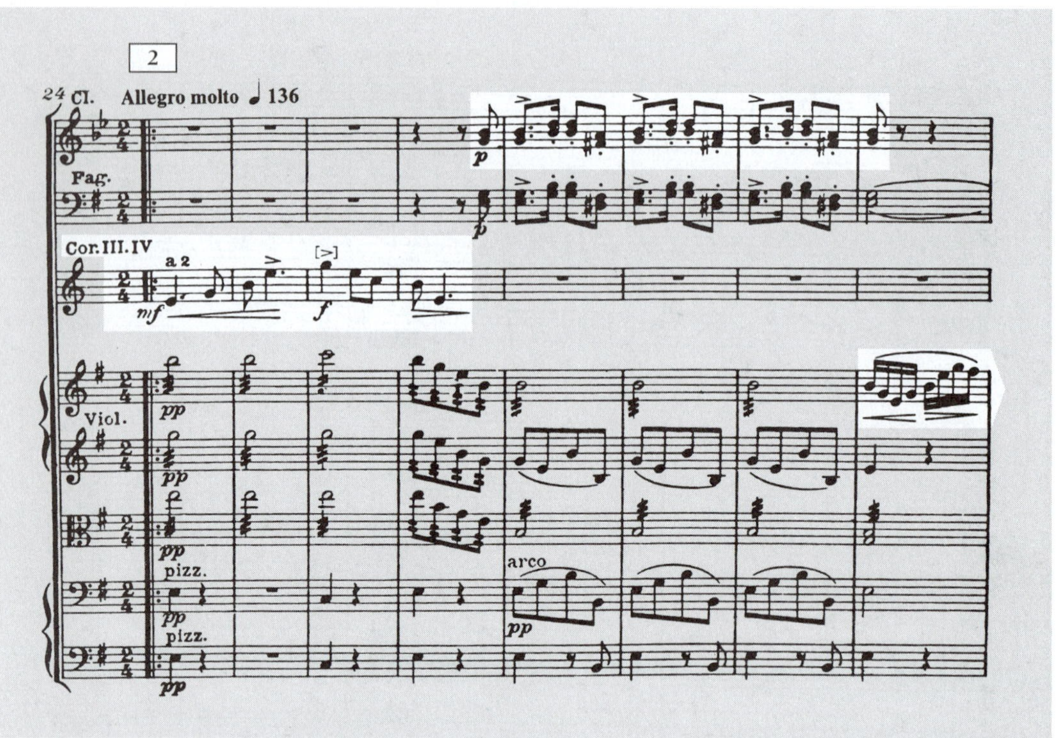
2
24 Cl.
Allegro molto ♩ 136
Fag.
Cor. III. IV
a 2
mf
f
p
Viol.
pp
pizz.
arco

32 Fl.
Ob.
a 2
mf
fz
mp
[mp]
Fag.
p
Viol.
pp
arco

39
a 2
ff
f
a 2

48
ffz
ff
div.
fz
f

61
a 2
a 2
fz
ff
f

67
a 2
ff
ff
ff
[f]
[f]
f
[f]
[f]
[f]
fz
fz
fz
fz
fz
fz
f
f
f

73
fz
f[z]
I.
mp
mp
ff
ff
f
f
f
tr
tr
f
f
fz
fz
mf
dim.
f
f
mp
[f] fz
mf
ffz
mf
mp
ffz
mf
ffz
mf
mp
pizz.
ffz
ffz
mp

79
Cl.
Fag.
Viol.
p
dim.
sempre più dim.
pp

86 Fl.
Ob.
Cl.
Fag.
Viol.
p
pp

3
91 Fl.
Ob.
Cl.
Fag.
Cor. III Solo
Viol.
p
fz
pp
ppp

97 Fl.
Ob.
Cl.
Cor. III.
Viol.
fz
pp
ppp
pizz.

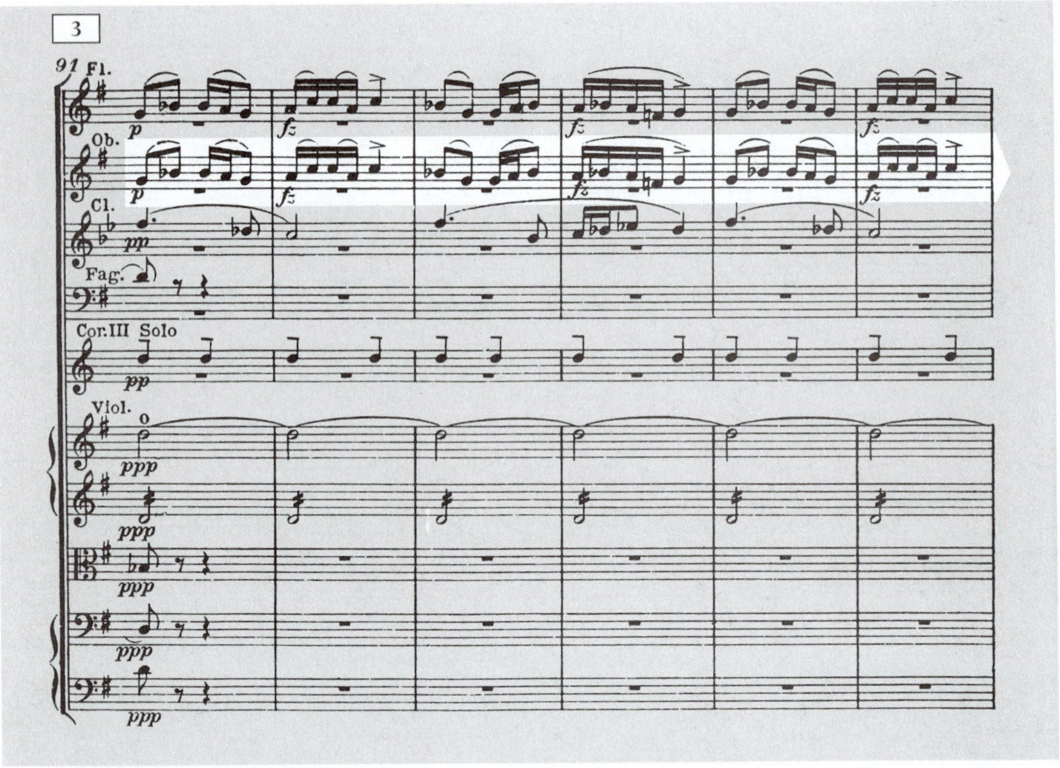

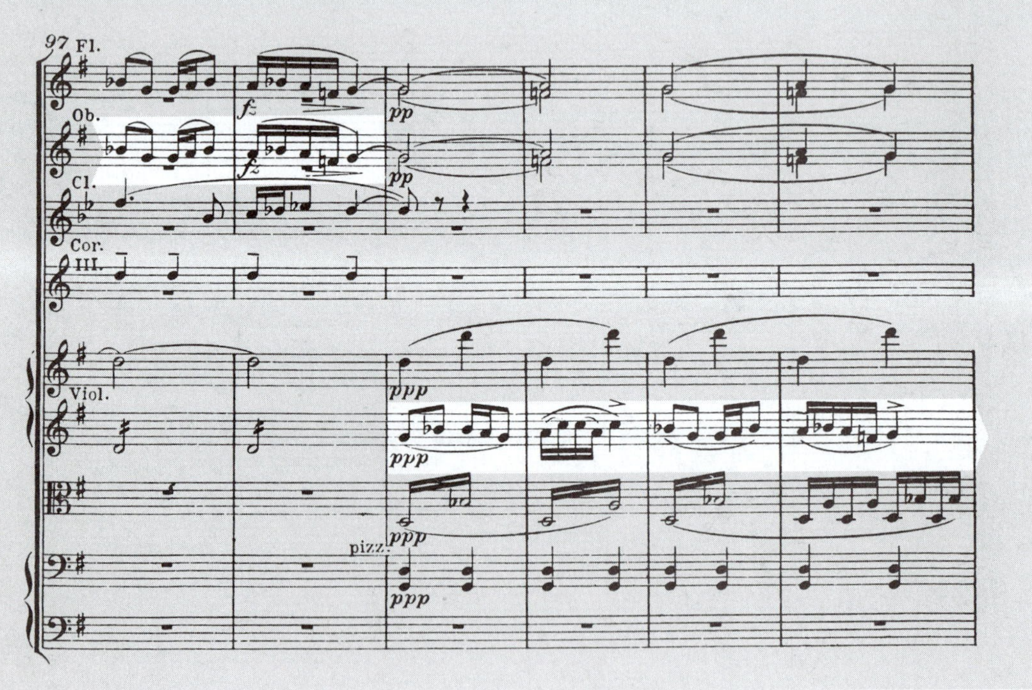

109 Fl.
f p f p
Ob.
f p f p
Cl.
mp [mp]
Fag.
mp [mp]
f f
Viol.
f p f [p]
f p f [p]
f p f [p]
f p f [p]

121
Fl
f
dim.
Ob.
f
dim.
p
Cl.
f
dim.
p
Fag.
f
dim.
Cor.
III.IV.
f
dim.
Timp.
tr
f
dim.
dim.
p
Viol.
f
dim.
p
f
dim.
p
f
arco
dim.
p
dim.
p
f
p

126
Fl.
Ob.
cresc.
f
p
Cl.
cresc.
f
p
Fag.
p
Viol.
cresc.
fz
p
dim.
cresc.
fz
p
dim.
fz
dim.
p
dim.
fz
fz
p
dim.
fz
fz
p
dim.

132
Fl.
Ob.
p
pp
cresc.
f
Cl.
p
pp
cresc.
f
Fag.
[p]
cresc.
f
Viol.
pp
cresc.
f
pp
cresc.
f
pp
cresc.
f
pp
cresc.
f
ffz
pp
f
fz

137 Fl.
Ob.
Cl.
Fag.
Viol.
p
pp
dim.

4
144 Fl.
Solo
Ob.
Cl.
Fag.
Viol.
pp
ppp

153
Fl.
Ob.
Cl.
pp
Fag.
pp
Viol.
[pp]
[pp]
[pp]
[pp]
pizz.
pp

161
Cl.
cresc.
Fag.
cresc.
Viol.
cresc.
cresc.
cresc.
cresc.
arco

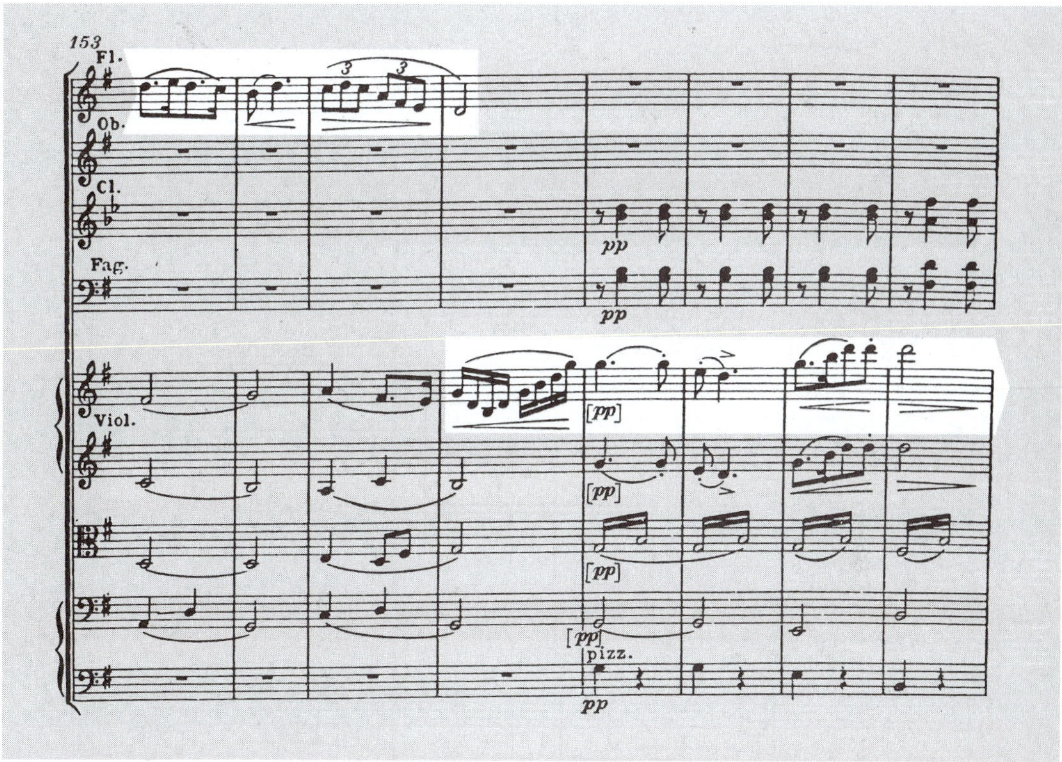

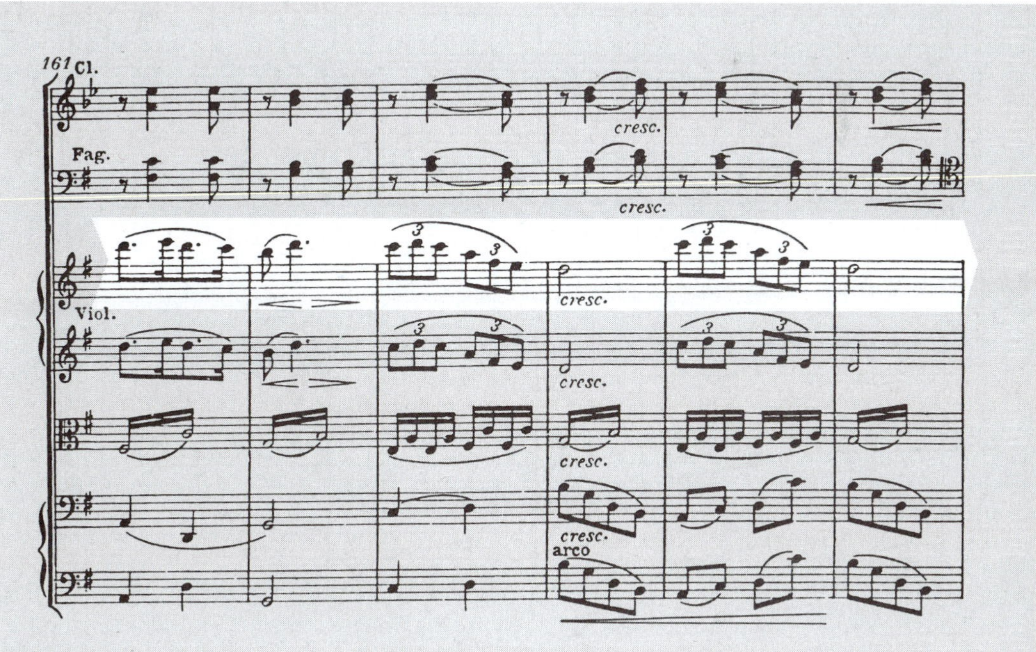

167
ff
tr
f
a 2.
in C
cresc.

174
1.
fpp
fpp

5
177
2.
a 2
ff
f
fz
ffz
3

183
Cl.
Solo
Cor. III. IV.
dim.
Trb.
p
dim.
Viol.
p
leggiero
pp
dim.
dim.
p
dim.
pp
dim.
p
dim.
pp
dim.
p
dim.
pp
dim.

189 Fl.
Fl. Piccolo
p
Cl.
Cor. I
Solo
mp
Trb.
Trombe Solo
a 2
pp
Viol. ppp
ppp
ppp
ppp
ppp
[ppp]
ppp
pizz.
ppp

197
p
pp
p
poco
pizz.
arco
pp
pp
fp
poco

202
Flauto gr. II
mf
mf
f
mf
mf
f
a
poco
cresc.
cresc.
mf
pp
cresc.
cresc.
cresc.
cresc.
cresc.
cresc.
fp
più
fz
f
a
poco
cresc.

208
a 2
a 2
sul G
div.
non div.
arco

215
a 2
ff
fz
a 2
ff
fz
fz
fz
div.
f
f
f

221
ff
a 2.
a 2.
fz
non div.

228
fz
ff

232
ff
a 2
f
[ff]
fz
[>]
[fz]

238
a 2
f
ff
fz

244
a 2
f
[ff]
fz
ff

250
a 2
a 2
fz
fz
fz
fz
fz
fz

256
a 2
fz
p dim.
pp
ff
fz
a 2.
fz
p
pp
fp
p
pp
fp
p
pp
pp
fz

264
Solo
p
I.
p
pp
cresc.
pp
cresc.
pp
cresc.
pp
cresc.
pizz.
pp
cresc.

6
271 Fl.
Cl.
Fag.
Cor. III.IV
a 2
Timp.
Viol.
pizz.
arco
278 Fl.
Ob.
a 2
Cl.
Fag.
Timp.
Viol.

285
a 2
a 2
in E
a 2
arco

293
ffz
fz
f
fz
f

301
Viol. dimin.
dimin.
dimin.
dimin.
dimin.
p
dim.
pp
7
308 Fl.
Solo
[p]
Viol.
legato
dim.
ppp
legato
dim.
ppp
legato
dim.
ppp
pp
dim.
ppp
pizz.
[ppp]
ppp
314 Fl.
Viol.

320 Fl.
p
I.
Cl.
I.
p
Fag.
p
Cor.
II. pp
Viol.
ppp
ppp
pp
pp
326 Fl.
cresc.
fz
Ob.
cresc.
p
fz
Cl.
Fag.
cresc.
fz
Cor. I.II
cresc.
cresc.
f
cresc.
f
cresc.
f
cres.
f
arco
pp
cresc.
f

333
Cl.
mp
[mp]
p
Fag.
mp
[mp]
p
Viol.
f
p
pizz.

338 Fl.
f
Ob.
mf
cresc.
Cl.
cresc.
mf
Fag.
cresc.
molto cresc.

342 Fl.
Ob.
Cl.
Fag.
Cor.
Trb.
Viol.
arco
dim.
347 Fl.
Ob.
Viol. I
II
fz
dim.

352
Fl.
Ob.
Fag.
Viol.
dim.
p
fz
f[z]
cresc.
f
[>]

358
Fl.
Ob.
Fag.
Viol.
[p]
p
pp
dim.
fp

8
365
Fl.
Ob.
p Solo
Viol.
ppp
374
Fag.
p
pp
pizz.

382
Ob.
Cl.
Fag.
p
cresc.
mf
Viol.
arco
389
Fl.
Cor.
in E
a 2
f

9
396
fff
ff
a 2
in C.
fz
tr

405
sfz
sfz
sfz
sfz
ffz
ffz
ffz
ffz
ffz
ff
fz
fz
fz
ff
fz
fz
fz
ff
sfz
sfz
sfz

412
ff
ff
f
f
f
f
f
f
f
f
fz
fz
fz
fz
fz
fz
fz
fz
[fz]
fz
fz
fz
fz
fz
fz
fz
fz
[fz]
fz
div.
fz
fz
fz
fz
fz
fz
fz
fz

420
a 2
a 2
a 2
a 2
a 2
a 2
fz
fz
fz
fz
[fz]

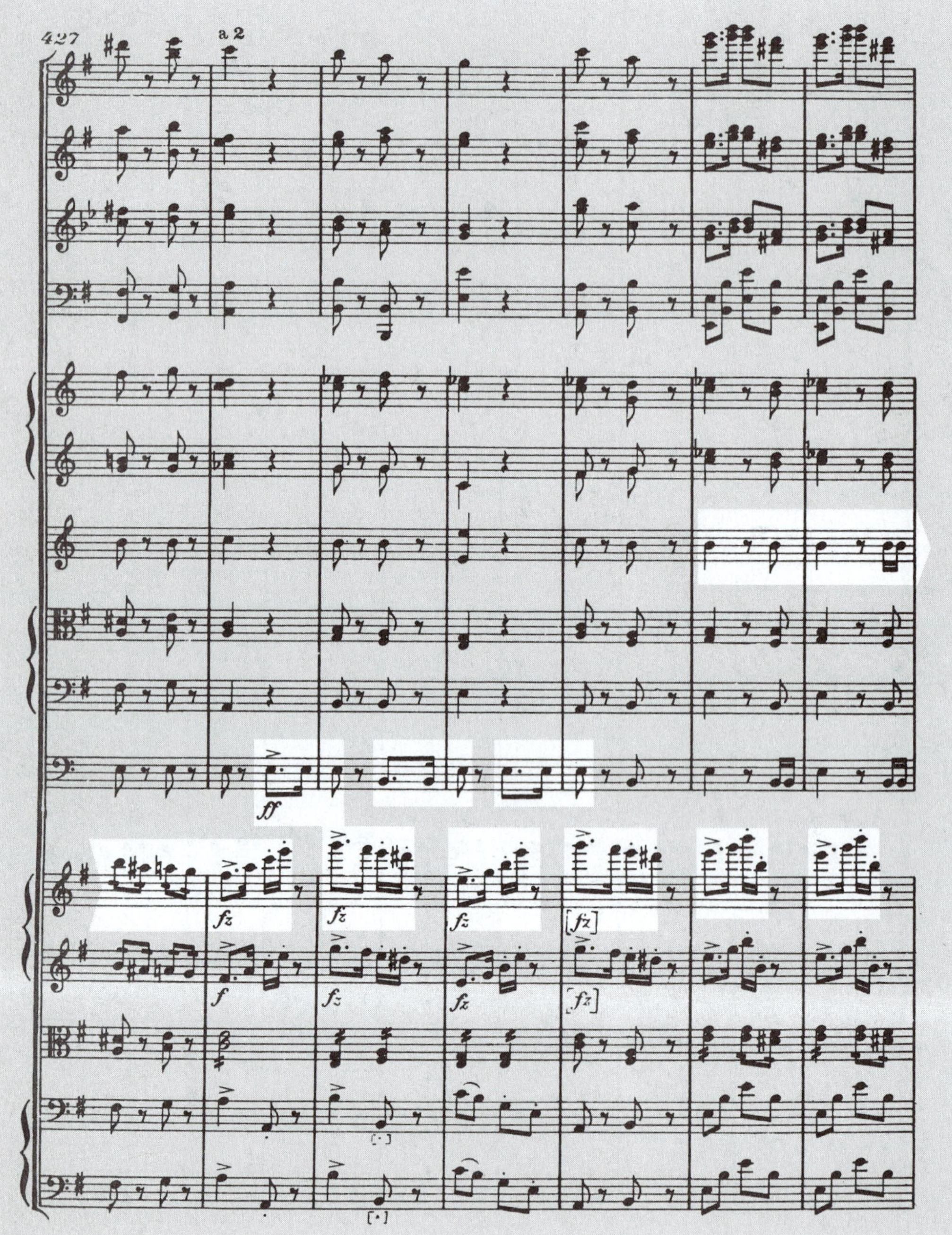
427
a 2
ff
fz
fz
fz
[fz]
f
fz
fz
[fz]

434
tr
fz
a 2
ff

441
a 2
tr
fz
f
[fz]
f[z]

Antonín Dvořák (1841–1904), like his contemporary Brahms, returned to the Classical traditions of the symphony, completing nine works in the genre. Unlike Brahms, however, Dvořák was also a strong nationalist and created a distinctively fresh folk character in his works. Late in his career, Dvořák left his homeland, Bohemia (now part of the Czech Republic), and lived in the United States for several years. He composed and premiered his last symphony in New York in 1893. The work, subtitled *From the New World,* follows the standard four-movement structure of the Classical symphony, but it also reflects some of the Romantic tendencies in the genre. Recurring themes create a strong sense of cyclic unity, and the middle movements, inspired by Longfellow's *The Song of Hiawatha,* suggest a programmatic conception.

This powerful symphony mixes elements of Classical structure, Bohemian folk music, and African-American spirituals. The first movement is a clearly defined sonata-allegro form with a slow introduction. American sounds can be heard in the syncopation of the opening somber melody and in the closing theme, which resembles the spiritual *Swing Low, Sweet Chariot.* Much of the other melodic material seems to be more Bohemian than American, but the overall energetic character has been linked to the untapped power that Dvořák saw in this country over one hundred years ago.

14

Felix Mendelssohn

Violin Concerto in E minor, Op. 64,
First movement (1844)

8CD: 6/10-18

Cl.
Fg.
Vl. pr.
Vl.
Vla.
Vc. e Cb.

10
1.
Fl.
p
Cl.
p
Fg.
p
Cor. (E)
p
Timp.
p
Vl. pr.
Vl.
Vla.
Vc. e Cb.

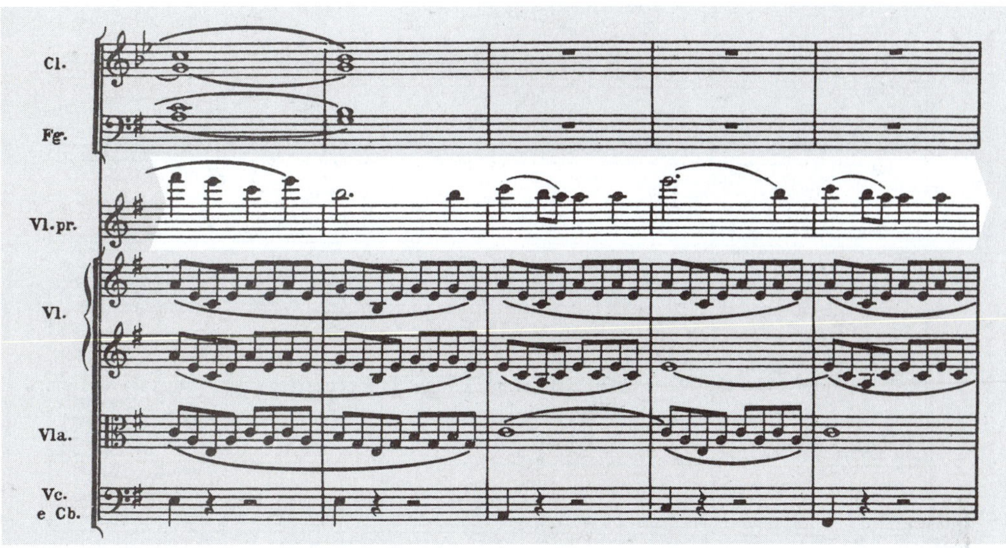

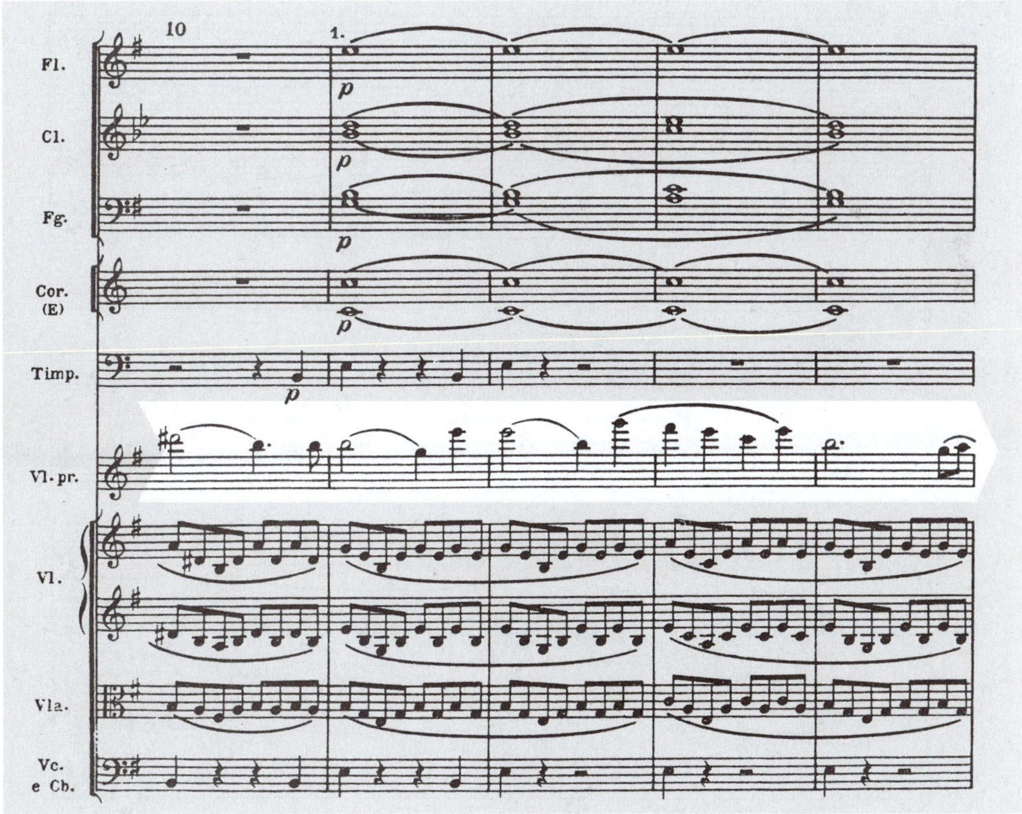

Fl.
Fg.
Vl. pr.
Vl.
Vla.
get.
arco
Vc. e Cb.
20
Fl.
Ob.
zu 2
cresc.
Cl.
Fg.
zu 2
Cor. (E)
Timp.
Vl. pr.
cresc.
Vl.
Vla.
Vc. e Cb.

Fl.
Ob.
Cl.
Fg.
Cor. (E)
Timp.
Vl. pr.
Vl.
Vla.
Vc. e Cb.
30
zu 2

Fl.
Ob.
Cl.
Fg.
Cor. (E)
Timp.
Vl. pr.
Vl.
Vla.
Vc. e Cb.
mf
4ta
cresc.
p
fp
1.
40
cresc.
sf
f
tr

zu 2
Fl.
Ob.
Cl.
Fg.
Cor. (E)
Tbe. (E)
Timp.
tr
Vl. pr.
3
Vl.
Vla.
Vc. e Cb.

Tutti
50
zu 2
Fl.
ff
zu 2
Ob.
ff
Cl.
ff
Fg.
ff
Cor. (E)
ff
sf
sf
sf
zu 2
Tbe. (E)
ff
sf
sf
sf
tr
tr
tr
Timp.
ff
sf
sf
sf
Vl. pr.
Vl.
ff
ff
Vla.
ff
Vc. e Cb.
ff

Fl.
Ob.
Cl.
Fg.
zu 2
zu 2
Cor. (E)
Tbe. (E)
Timp.
tr
tr
f
Vl.
f
f
Vla.
f
Vc. e Cb.
f
60
Fl.
ff
Ob.
ff
Cl.
ff
Fg.
sf
sf
sf
sf
zu 2
Cor. (E)
ff
Tbe. (E)
ff
Timp.
ff
Vl.
sf
sf
sf
sf
Vla.
sf
Vc. e Cb.
sf

zu 2
Fl.
ff
zu 2
Ob.
ff
zu 2
Cl.
ff
Fg.
ff
Cor. (E)
Tbe. (E)
tr
Timp.
Vl.
ff
ff
Vla.
ff
Vc. e Cb.
ff
Fl.
Ob.
Cl.
Fg.
sf
Cor. (E)
zu 2
Tbe. (E)
tr
tr
tr
Timp.
Vl.
Vla.
Vc. e Cb.
sf

11
70
Fl.
Ob.
Cl.
Fg.
Cor. (E)
Tbe. (E)
Timp.
Vl.
Vla.
Vc. e Cb.
zu 2
Solo
80
Vl. pr.

Cl.
Fg.
Cor. (E)
Vl. pr.
Vl.
Vla.
Vc. e Cb.
cresc.
f
p
sf
90

1.
Fl.
p
Vl. pr.
3
cresc.
Vl.
p
p
Vla.
p
Vc.
e Cb.

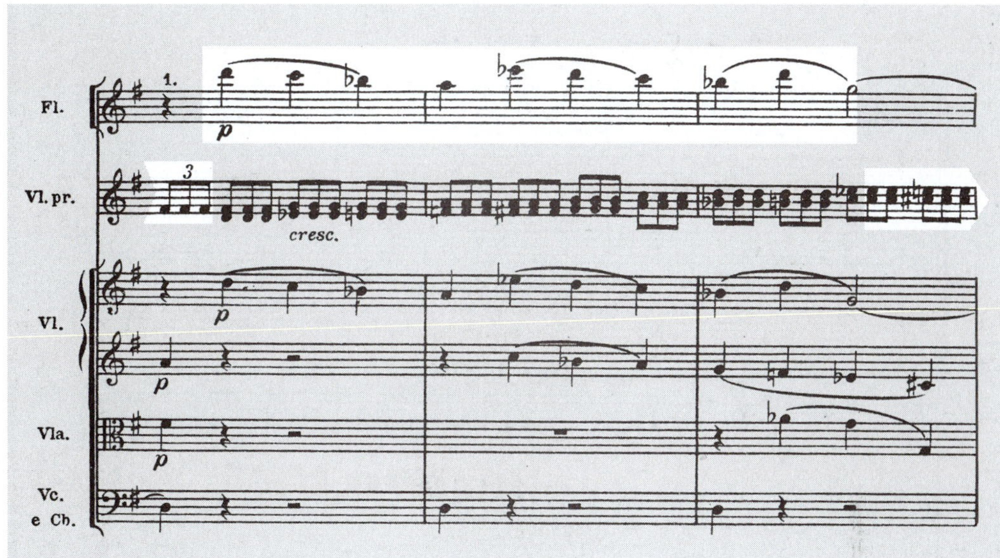

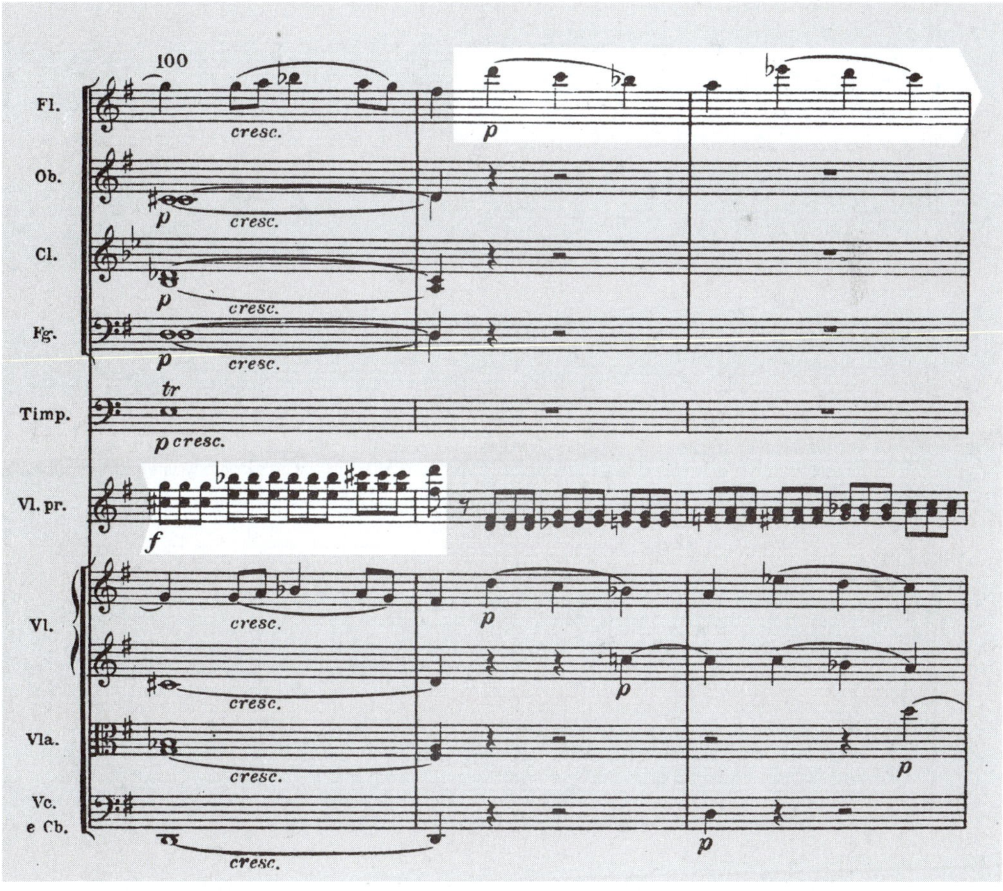

100
Fl.
cresc.
p
Ob.
p
cresc.
Cl.
p
cresc.
Fg.
p
cresc.
tr
Timp.
p cresc.
Vl. pr.
f
Vl.
cresc.
p
cresc.
p
Vla.
cresc.
p
Vc.
e Cb.
cresc.
p

Fl.
cresc.
p
Ob.
cresc.
Cl.
cresc.
Fg.
cresc.
Timp.
tr
cresc.
Vl. pr.
p
Vl.
cresc.
dim.
cresc.
dim.
Vla.
cresc.
dim.
Vc. e Cb.
cresc.
dim.

110
Fl.
Vl. pr.
cresc.
Vl.
cresc.
cresc.
Vla.
cresc.
Vc.
e Cb.
cresc.

Fl.
f
Ob.
fp
Cl.
fp
Fg.
fp
Vl. pr.
sf
sf
Vl.
f
f
f
f
Vla.
f
f
Vc.
e Cb.

120
Ob.
Cl.
Fg.
Vl. pr.
Vl.
Vla.
Vc. e Cb.
dim.
f
Vl. pr.
sempre dim.
Vl.
Vla.
Vc. e Cb.
p
12
130
tranquillo
Fl.
Cl.
pp
pp tranquillo
Vl. pr.
p tranquillo
pp
Vl.
Vla.
Vc. e Cb.

140
Fl.
Cl.
Vl.pr.
pp
pp
pp tranquillo
p cresc.
150
Vl. pr.
sf
Vl.
Vla.
Vc.
160
cresc.

13
Cl.
Fg.
Vl.pr.
Vl.
Vla.
Vc.
e Cb.
pp
cresc.
pizz.
pp Bassi
170
Ob.
p
sf
arco
f
leggiero
cresc.

180
Vl. pr.
cresc.
sf
p
pizz.
Vl.
pizz.
pizz.
Vla.
pizz.
Vc. e Cb.
1.
Fl.
p
1.
Ob.
p
Cl.
p
Fg.
p
Vl. pr.
pp
Vl.
pp
pp
Vla.
pp
Vc. e Cb.
pp
Fl.
Ob.
1.
Cl.
Fg.
Vl. pr.
cresc.
arco
Vl.
arco
arco
Vla.
arco
Vc. e Cb.

190
Cl.
Fg.
Vl. pr.
Vl.
Vla.
Vc.
e Cb.

Cl.
cresc.
Fg.
cresc.
Vl. pr.
cresc.
p leggiero
Vl.
cresc.
Vla.
cresc.
Vc.
e Cb.
cresc.

200
Fl.
Ob.
Cl.
Fg.
Vl. pr.
Vl.
Vla.
Vc.
Cb.
1.
p
pp

Fl.
Ob.
Cl.
Fg.
Vl. pr.
cresc.
Vl.
Vla.
Vc.
Cb.

Fl.
Ob.
Cl.
Fg.
Cor. (E)
Vl. pr.
Vl.
Vla.
Vc. e Cb.
zu 2
210
Tbe. (E)
Timp.
con forza

220
Fl.
Ob.
Cl.
Fg.
Cor. (E)
Tbe. (E)
Timp.
Vl. pr.
Vl.
Vla.
Vc. e Cb.
zu 2
dim.
14
230
agitato
pizz.
cresc.

Tutti
zu 2
Solo
Fl.
Ob.
Cl.
Fg.
zu 2
Cor. (E)
Tbe. (E)
Timp.
Vl. pr.
ptranq.
Vl.
Vla.
arco
Vc. e Cb.
240
1.
Fl.
1.
Cl.
Vl. pr.
Vl.
Vla.
Vc.
Vc. e Cb.
Bassi

Fl.
Ob.
Cl.
Vl.pr.
Vl.
Vla.
Vc. e Cb.
p
p
Vc.

Cl.
Fg.
Vl. pr.
Vl.
Vla.
Vc. e Cb.
250
1.
p
1.
p
cresc.
cresc.
cresc.
cresc.
Bassi
cresc.

zu 2
Fl.
Ob.
Cl.
Fg.
Cor. (E)
Tbe. (E)
Timp.
Vl. pr.
Vl.
Vla.
Vc. e Cb.

260
Fl.
Ob.
Cl.
Fg.
Cor. (E)
Tbe. (E)
Timp.
Vl. pr.
Vl.
Vla.
Vc. e Cb.
f
p
dim.

Cl.
Fg.
Timp.
Vl. pr.
Vl.
Vla.
Vc.
e Cb.
pp
pp
pp
p dim.
p
p
p
p
270
pp
sempre più p
dim.
sempre dim.
dim.
sempre dim.
dim.
sempre dim.
dim.
sempre dim.

Vl. pr.
pp
Vl.
pp
Vla.
pp
Vc.
e Cb.
pp
280
Cor.
(E)
pp
Vl. pr.
pp
sempre pp
Vl.
pp
pp
Vla.
pp
Vc.
Vc.
e Cb.
Bassi
290
Ob.
pp
poco a poco cresc.
Cl.
pp
poco a poco cresc.
Fg.
pp
poco a poco cresc.
Cor.
(E)
poco a poco cresc.
Tbe.
(E)
pp
poco a poco cresc.
Timp.
tr
pp
Vl. pr.
cresc.
Vl.
poco a poco cresc.
poco a poco cresc.
Vla.
poco a poco cresc.
Vc.
e Cb.
poco a poco cresc.

Fl.
Ob.
Cl.
Fg.
Cor. (E)
Tbe. (E)
Timp.
Vl. pr.
Vl.
Vla.
Vc. e Cb.
cresc.
sf ff
15
Cadenza ad lib.
300
Vl. pr.
f

Vl. pr.
8
f

Vl. pr.
8
Tempo I
tr
f

Vl. pr.
310
tr tr tr tr
cresc.
f

Vl. pr.
320
tr
8
a tempo
3 3
f
cresc.

Vl. pr.

Vl. pr.
330
poco a poco dimin.

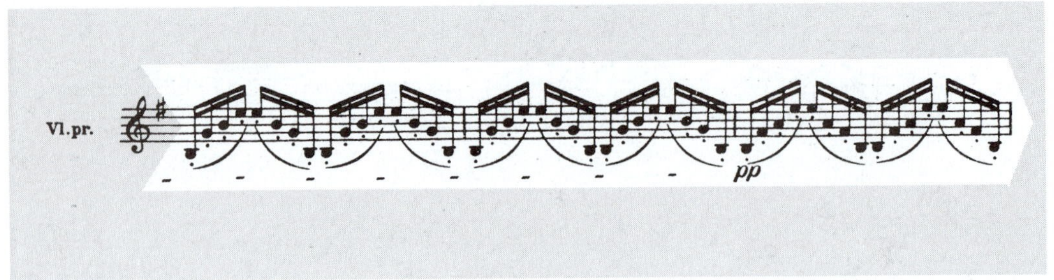

16
1.
Fl.
1.
Ob.
pp
Cl.
pp
Fg.
pp
zu 2
Cor. (E)
pp
Timp.
pp
Vl. pr.
segue
Vl.
pp
pp
Vla.
pp
Vc. e Cb.
pp

Fl.
cresc.
Ob.
cresc.
Cl.
cresc.
Fg.
cresc.
Cor. (E)
p
Timp.
Vl. pr.
cresc.
Vl.
cresc.
cresc.
Vla.
cresc.
Vc. e Cb.
Vc. cresc.
Cb.

Fl.
Ob.
Cl.
Fg.
Cor. (E)
Timp.
Vl. pr.
Vl.
Vla.
Vc. e Cb.

Fl.
Ob.
Cl.
Fg.
Cor. (E)
Vl. pr.
ff
Vl.
cresc.
Vla.
cresc.
Vc. e Cb.
cresc.

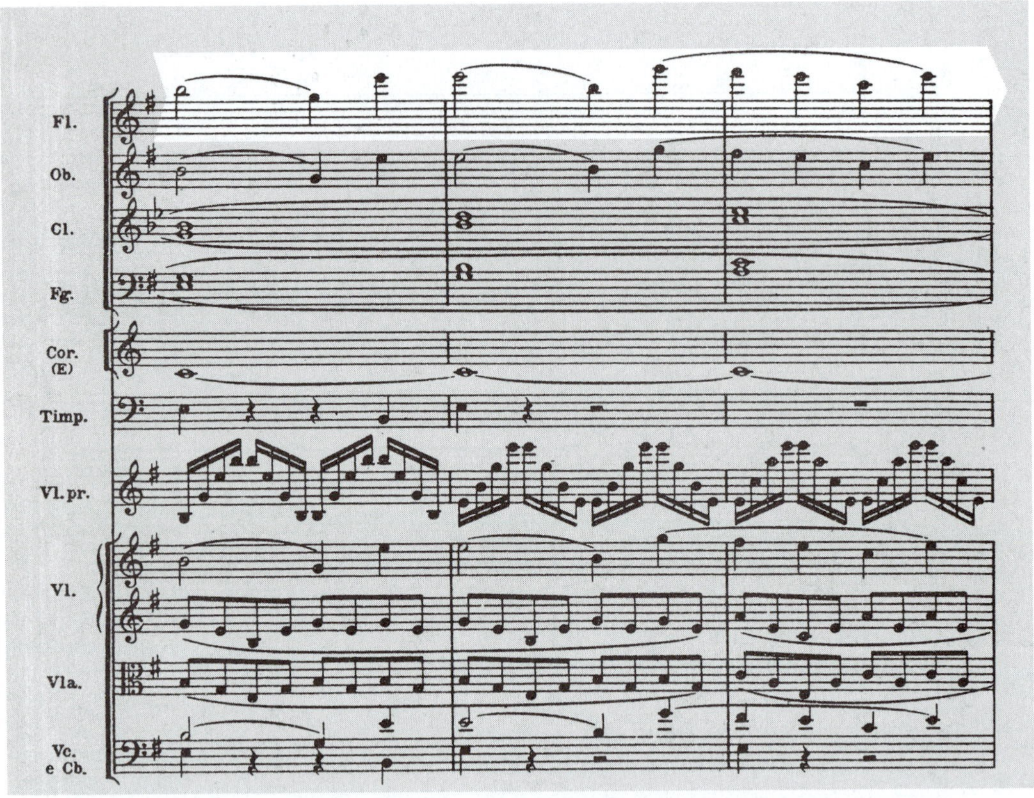

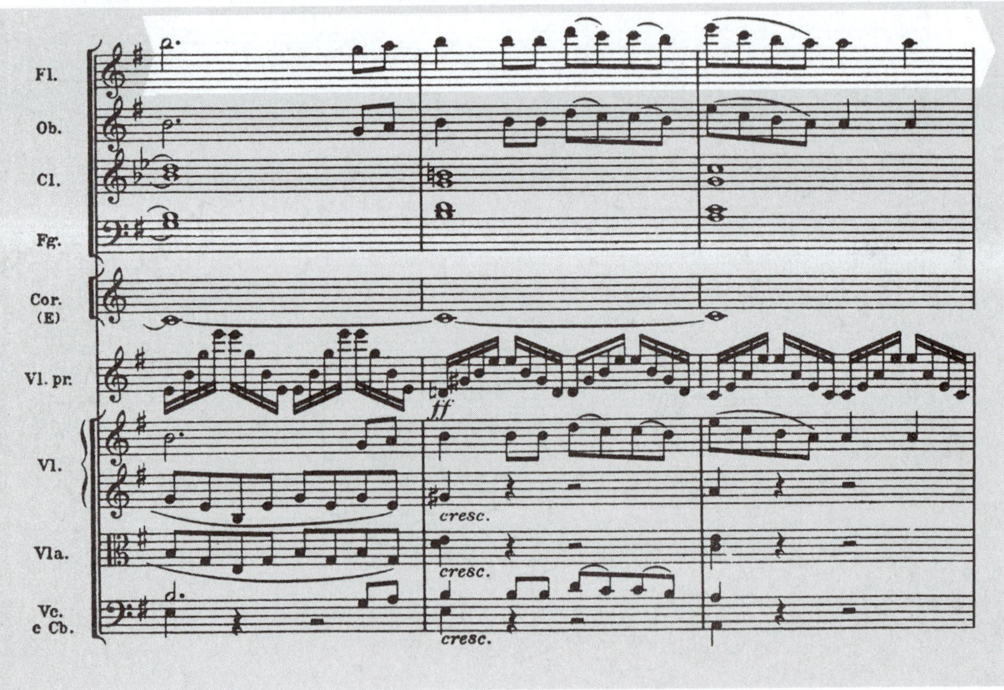

350
Tutti
zu 2
Fl.
ff
zu 2
Ob.
ff
Cl.
ff
Fg.
ff
Cor. (E)
ff
zu 2
Tbe. (E)
ff
zu 2
Timp.
ff
Vl.pr.
Vl.
ff
f
ff
Vla.
f
ff
Vc. e Cb.
Bassi f
ff

360
Fl.
Ob.
ff
Cl.
ff
fp
Fg.
ff
zu 2
Cor. (E)
ff
zu 2
Tbe. (E)
ff
Timp.
ff
Vl. pr.
mf
Vl.
sf
ff
sf
Vla.
ff
sf
Vc. e Cb.
ff
sfp
370
Cl.
dim.
Vl. pr.
dim.
sempre più tranquillo
Vc. e Cb.
Cl.
pp
Cor. (E)
pp
Vl. pr.
Vc. e Cb.

17
380
Fl.
pp
Ob.
zu 2
pp
1.
Cl.
pp
1.
Vl.pr.
390
Fl.
pp
pp
Ob.
pp
Cl.
pp
Cor. (E)
pp
Vl.pr.
pp
Ob.
Cl.
Vl.pr.
cresc.
1
Vl.
p
p
Vla.
p
Vc. e Cb.
p

400

Fl. *pp* 1.

Ob. *pp* 1.

Cl. *pp*

Cor. (E) *pp* zu 2

Vl. pr.

Vl. *pp* *pp*

Vla. *pp*

Vc. e Cb. Vc. *pp*

zu 2
Cor. (E)
pp
1.
Tbe. (E)
pp
Timp.
pp
Vl. pr.
cresc.
Vl.
pp
fsf
pp
fsf
Vla.
pp
fsf
Vc. e Cb.
pp
fsf
p

1.
420
Cl.
p
1.
Fg.
p
Vl.pr.
Vl.
p
p
Vla.
Vc. e Cb.

Cl.
Fg.
Vl.pr.
3
cresc.
Vl.
cresc.
cresc.
Vla.
cresc.
Vc.
e Cb.
cresc.

430
1.
Ob.
p
Cl.
p
Vl.pr.
f p
pizz.
Vl.
pizz.
pizz.
Vla.
pizz.
Vc.
e Cb.

1.
Ob.
Cl.
Cor. (E)
Tbe. (E)
Timp.
Vl.pr.
Vl.
Vla.
Vc. e Cb.
pp
cresc.
sf
arco

440
Cor. (E)
cresc.
Vl. pr.
sf
sf
più cresc.
Vl.
cresc.
cresc.
Vla.
cresc.
Vc. e Cb.
cresc.

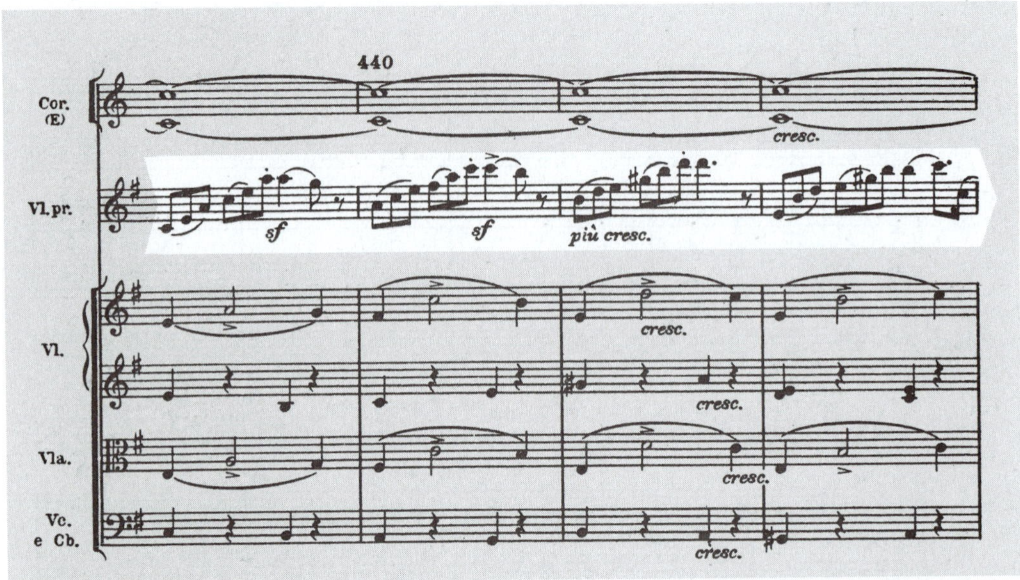

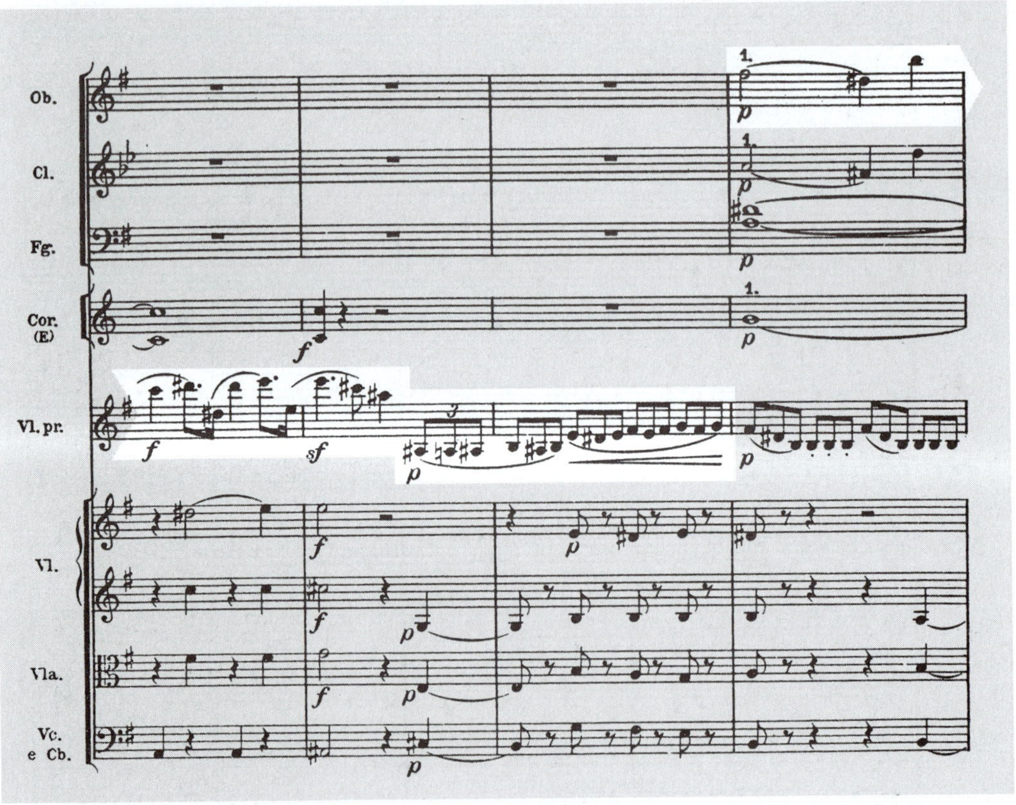

Ob.
1.
p
Cl.
1.
p
Fg.
p
Cor. (E)
f
1.
p
Vl. pr.
f
sf
3
p
p
Vl.
f
p
f
p
Vla.
f
p
Vc. e Cb.
p

Ob.
Cl.
Fg.
Cor. (E)
Vl.pr.
Vl.
Vla.
Vc. e Cb.
450
cresc.
Fl.
Tbe. (E)
Timp.
zu 2
2a e 3a corda

zu 2
Fl.
ff
zu 2
Ob.
ff
zu 2
Cl.
ff
Fg.
Cor. (E)
Tbe. (E)
imp.
l.pr.
Vl.
ff
ff
Vla.

460
Fl.
Ob.
Cl.
Fg.
Cor. (E)
Tbe. (E)
Timp.
Vl. pr.
Vl.
Vla.
Vc. e Cb.
zu 2
470
dim.

18
Più presto
Fl.
Cl.
Fg.
Cor. (E)
Tbe. (E)
Timp.
Vl. pr.
Vl.
Vla.
Vc. e Cb.
zu 2
p
sf
480
Sempre più presto
Ob.
sf cresc.

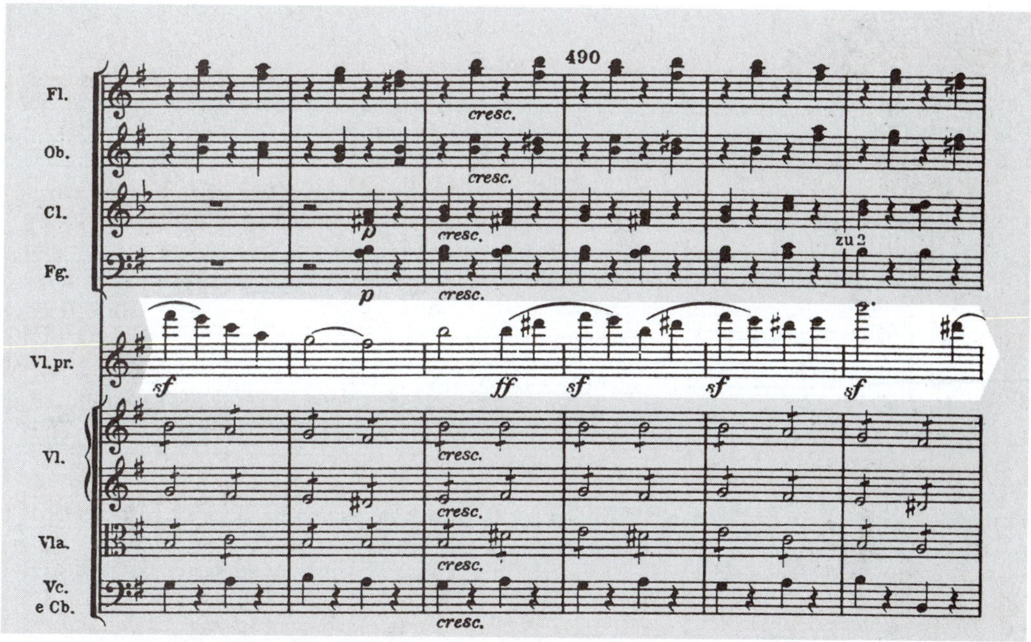

490
Fl.
Ob.
Cl.
Fg.
Vl. pr.
Vl.
Vla.
Vc. e Cb.
cresc.
zu 2
p
sf
ff

Presto
1.
Fl.
Ob.
Cl.
Fg.
Cor. (E)
Tbe. (E)
Timp.
Vl. pr.
Vl.
Vla.
Vc. e Cb.
f
p
sf

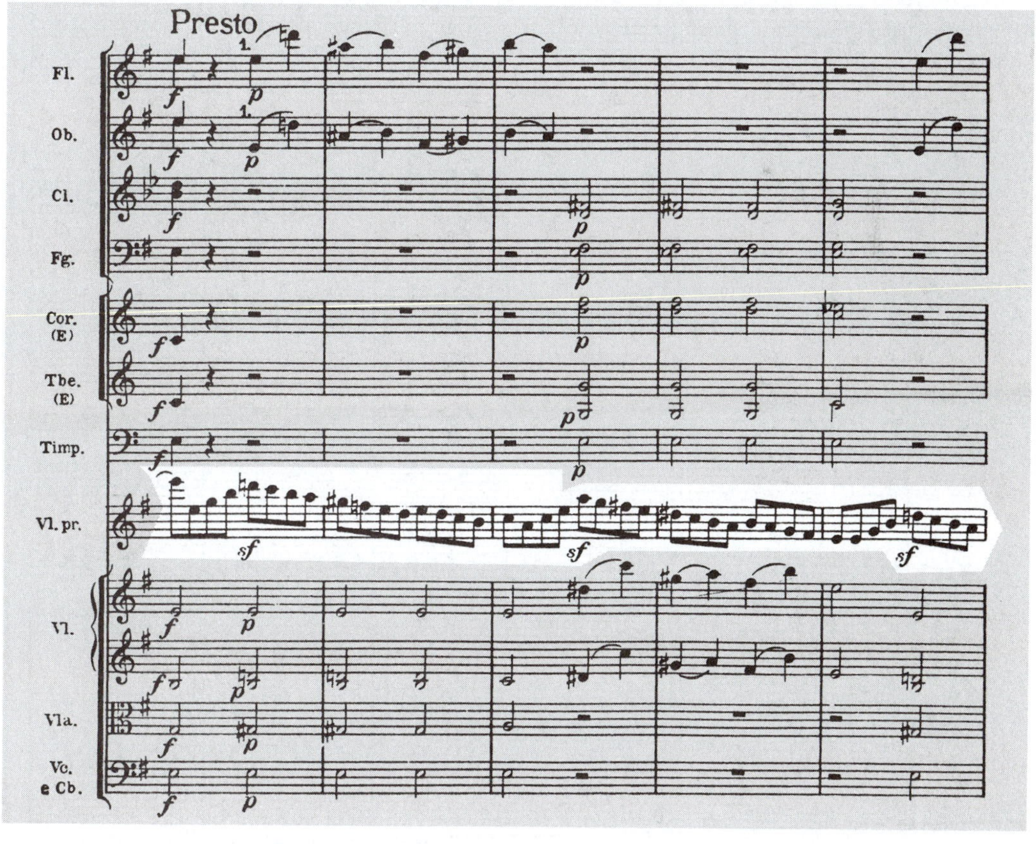

500
Fl.
Ob.
Cl.
Fg.
Cor. (E)
Tbe. (E)
Timp.
Vl. pr.
Vl.
Vla.
Vc. e Cb.
f
cresc.
1.
zu 2
ff
p

510
Ob.
Cl.
zu 2
1.
zu 2
Fg.
cresc.
Vl. pr.
Vl.
Vla.
Vc. e Cb.
Tutti
Fl.
Ob.
Cl.
Fg.
Cor. (E)
Tbe. (E)
Timp.
Vl. pr.
Vl.
Vla.
Vc. e Cb.

520
Fl.
Ob.
Cl.
Fg.
Cor. (E)
Tbe. (E)
Timp.
Vl.
Vla.
Vc. e Cb.
zu 2
sf
p

The Romantic concerto retained many of the traditional features of the Classical genre, including the three-movement structure and the general form of each movement. Distinctive new aspects of these concertos are the abbreviated first-movement structures, the general tendency toward cyclic unity, and the assimilation of the Romantic musical style. The brilliant Violin Concerto by Felix Mendelssohn (1809–1847) illustrates these tendencies well.

Each of the three movements is set in a traditional Classical form, but there are no pauses between the movements, and a musical quotation of the first movement in the second further enhances the cyclic quality. The first movement omits the opening *tutti* section that is standard in the Classical concerto; rather than waiting through an entire orchestral exposition, the soloist enters after one and a half measures. The movement then unfolds in a sonata-allegro form.

While the Classical framework is clearly evident, the movement as a whole projects the passion and virtuosity of Romanticism. Both the opening theme and the second theme are beautiful, lyric melodies. The latter is especially colorful, as the woodwinds initially present the tune over a sustained open G by the soloist. In a masterful stroke, Mendelssohn moves the cadenza from its traditional position at the end of the movement to the close of the development. In the cadenza, Mendelssohn exploits the violinist's technique with multiple-stopped chords and a rapid alternation of notes on all four strings. While the soloist is completing this passage, the orchestra quietly enters with the opening theme, creating an overlap of the development and recapitulation.

15

Amy Cheney Beach

Violin Sonata in A minor, Second movement (1896)

8CD: 5/73–75

25
p
staccato
mf
p
Ped.
mf

p
sf p

35
cresc.
Ped.

41
mf
poco rit.
a tempo
pp leggiero
poco rit.
pp a tempo
Ped.

46
cresc.
cresc.
52
f
f
dim.
dim.
58
p
più dim.
63
più dim.
pp
pp
non legato senza cresc.

74
Più lento. (♩=96.)
69
sf
f
p
p legatissimo
Ped.
76
rit.
pp
a tempo
cresc.
p espressivo
cresc.
83
mf
mf
dim.
p
90
pp
espress.
sempre sul G
pp molto tranquillo
molto tranquillo
legatissimo
pp
cresc.
poco cresc.
mf
dim.
Pedale sostenuto

98
sul D
dim.
pp
pp
105
sempre pp
sempre pp
75
Tempo I.
110
accel.
accel.
p
116
cresc.
poco a poco cresc.

122
mf
rit.
a tempo
pp
mf
rit.
a tempo pp
128
scherzando
cresc.
cresc.
135
f
dim.
f
dim.
141
p
p

147

più dim.
più dim.
pp
pp
Ped.

154

Vivo.
con delicatezza
leggierissimo
sempre pp
Ped.
Ped.
Ped.

161

pp
f
rall.
ff
f
rall.
ff
Ped.

American society looked to Europe for cultural leadership in the nineteenth century. Appearances by composers and performing artists from across the ocean were seen as major events, and serious American-born musicians often traveled to Europe for instruction. By the end of the century, a number of individuals began to lay the foundation for the enormous growth of American music in the twentieth century. New England was a particularly strong center of activity, and one of the most prominent figures to emerge from this region was Amy Cheney Beach (1867–1944).

Beach was a child prodigy and contributed to the New England musical scene both as a concert pianist and as a composer. Encouraged by her husband, she completed a number of large-scale works, including a piano concerto, a Mass, and the *Gaelic* Symphony, all of which were performed by prestigious American ensembles. The concertmaster of the Boston Symphony Orchestra, Franz Kneisel, joined Amy Beach in the premiere of her Violin Sonata in A minor.

The sonata retains the four-movement structure found in some Beethoven sonatas and in the violin sonatas of Brahms, but the order of the inner movements is inverted. The second movement, cast in a traditional scherzo form, is in duple rather than the standard triple meter. Beach draws upon a rich harmonic palette, particularly in the trio, where the tranquil, lyrical mood provides an effective contrast to the lively and energetic scherzo sections that create a *perpetuum mobile* (perpetual motion) character.

16

Johannes Brahms

Ein deutsches Requiem (A German Requiem),
Fourth movement (1868)

8CD: 6/19–23
4CD: 3/29–33

12
Ze - - ba - oth, dei - ne Woh - nun -
Ze - - ba - oth, dei - ne Woh - nun -
Ze - - ba - oth, dei - ne Woh - nun -
Ze - - ba - oth, dei - ne Woh - nun -
Fl.
Hob.
Hr.
Kl.
18
gen, Herr Ze - - ba -
gen, Herr Ze - - ba -
gen, Herr Ze - - ba -
gen, Herr Ze - ba - oth, Herr Ze - - ba -
Viol.
23
oth!
oth!
oth! Wie lieb - - lich sind dei - ne Woh - nun-
oth!
p espress.
espress.
p
con Ped.

30
p espress.
Wie lieb - - - - -
p espress.
Wie lieb - - - - lich
gen, Herr Ze - - - - - ba oth! Wie
p espress.
Wie lieb - - - - - - - - - lich
37
- - lich sind dei - - ne Woh - - nun - gen, Herr Ze - - - -
sind dei - - ne Woh - - nun - gen, Herr Ze - - - -
lieb - - - - - lich sind dei - - ne Woh - - nun - gen, Herr
sind dei - - ne Woh - - nun - gen, Herr Ze - - - -
20
30
42
- - - ba - oth! Mei - ne See - - -
- - - ba - oth! Mei - ne See - - -
Ze - - ba - oth! Mei - ne See - - -
ba - - - oth! Mei - ne See - - -
p
Holzbl.

48
cresc.
le
ver -
cresc.
le
ver - lan - get und
cresc.
le
ver - lan - get und seh - net, ver - lan - - -
cresc.
le ver - lan - get und seh - net, ver - lan - get und seh - net, ver - lan - - -
cresc.
54
f
p
lan - get und seh - net, und seh - net sich nach den
seh - net, ver - lan - get und seh - - - net sich nach den
get und seh - - - - - - net sich nach den
get und seh - net, seh - net sich nach den
Fl. u. Kl.
60
Vor - - hö - fen des Herrn; mein
Vor - - hö - fen des Herrn; mein
Vor - - hö - fen des Herrn; mein
Vor - - hö - fen des Herrn; mein
Hob.

66
Leib und See - le freu - en sich in dem le - ben - - -
Leib und See - le freu - en sich in dem le - ben - di - gen
Leib und See - le freu - en sich in dem le - ben - di - gen
Leib und See - le freu - en sich in dem le - ben - di - gen
Str.
72
- di - gen Gott, freu - en sich
cresc.
Gott, mein Leib und See - le freu - en sich
cresc.
Gott, mein Leib und See - le freu - en sich
cresc.
Gott, mein Leib und See - le freu - en sich
cresc.
78
in dem le - ben - - - - - - - di - gen
in dem le - ben - di - gen, in dem le - ben - - - - - - - di - gen
in dem le - ben - - - - di - gen, in dem le - ben - - di - gen
in dem le - ben - - - - di - gen, in dem le - ben - di - gen

21
31
84
Gott.
Wie
Gott.
Wie
Gott.
Wie
Gott.
Wie
Viol.
Fl.
Kl.
Hr.
90
lieb - lich sind dei - ne Woh - nun - gen, Herr Ze - - ba -
lieb - lich sind dei - ne Woh - nun - gen, Herr Ze - - - - ba -
lieb - lich sind dei - ne Woh - nun - gen, Herr Ze - - - - ba -
lieb - - - lich sind dei - ne Woh - nun - gen, Herr Ze - ba -
Kl.
Viol.
96
oth, Herr Ze - ba - oth, dei - ne
oth, Herr Ze - ba - oth, dei - ne
oth, Herr Ze - ba - oth, dei - ne
oth, Herr Ze - ba - oth, dei - ne
Fl.
Hob.
Hr.

102
Woh - nun - gen, Herr Ze - - - ba -
Woh - nun - gen, Herr Ze - - - ba -
Woh - nun - gen, Herr Ze - - - ba - -
Woh - nun - gen, Herr Ze - ba - oth, Herr Ze - - - ba -
Kl.
Viol.
108
oth!
Wohl de - - -
p
p legato espress.
con Ped.
113
nen,
wohl de - - nen, die

22
32
119
cresc.
in dei - nem Hau - se woh - nen, die
in dei - nem Hau - se woh - nen,
in dei - nem Hau - se woh - nen,
in dei - nem Hau - se woh - nen,
124
lo - ben - dich im - mer - dar,
die lo - ben dich im - mer - dar, im - mer - dar, im - mer,
die lo - ben dich im - mer - dar, lo - ben dich, lo - ben
die lo - ben dich im - mer - dar, die lo - ben, die lo - ben, die
130
die lo - ben dich, die lo - ben dich im - mer -
im - mer-dar, im - mer-dar, die lo - ben dich im - mer - dar,
dich im - mer - dar, die lo - ben dich im - mer - dar,
lo - ben, die lo - ben dich, die lo - ben dich im - mer -

136
dar, im - mer - dar,
die
die lo - ben dich im - mer -
die lo - ben dich im - mer - dar, die lo - ben dich im - mer -
dar, im - mer - dar, die lo - ben dich im - mer - dar,
141
lo - ben, die lo - ben, die lo - ben, die
dar, die lo - ben, die lo - ben, die lo - ben,
dar, die lo - ben, die lo - ben, die lo - ben, die lo - ben,
die lo - ben, die lo - ben, die lo -
147
23
33
p dimin.
lo - ben dich im - mer
lo - ben dich im - mer
die lo - ben dich im - mer
ben, die lo - ben dich im - mer
Fl.
Hob.
pp Str. pizz.
p es-

153
p dolce
dar! Wie lieb - - lich, wie lieb - - lich,
p dolce
dar! Wie
p dolce
dar! Wie lieb - - lich, wie lieb - - lich,
p dolce
dar! Wie
press.
Viol.
espress.
p
159
p
wie
lieb - - lich, wie lieb - - lich, wie lieb - - - lich, wie
p
wie
lieb - - lich, wie lieb - - lich, wie lieb - - - lich, wie
Fl.
Hob.
p
cresc.
Holzbl.
p
165
cresc.
f
lieb - - lich sind dei - ne
lieb - - lich, wie lieb - lich sind dei - - ne
lieb - - lich sind dei - ne
lieb - - lich, wie lieb - lich sind dei - - ne
legato
cresc.
Str.

TEXT AND TRANSLATION

Wie lieblich sind deine Wohnungen, Herr Zebaoth! Meine Seele verlanget und sehnet sich nach den Vorhöfen des Herrn; mein Leib und Seele freuen sich in dem lebendigen Gott.	How lovely is Thy dwelling place, O Lord of Hosts! My soul longs and even faints for the courts of the Lord; my flesh and soul rejoice in the living God.
Wie lieblich . . .	How lovely . . .
Wohl denen, die in deinem Hause wohnen, die loben dich immerdar!	Blessed are they that live in Thy house, that praise Thee evermore!
Wie lieblich . . .	How lovely . . .

The nineteenth century produced a rich and varied repertory of music for chorus. From simple part songs to colossal Requiems, choral music played an important role in European and American society. Johannes Brahms contributed numerous works to the choral repertory of both amateur and professional ensembles. His masterwork, one of the landmarks of the era, is *Ein deutsches Requiem (A German Requiem)* (1868).

A Requiem Mass is generally based on the Latin text of the Catholic Church funeral service. But German Requiems, which have been composed since the time of Schütz and Praetorius, do not use the liturgical text of the Catholic service. Rather, the words are drawn freely from passages in the Lutheran Bible and are in the vernacular, German, instead of Latin. For his Requiem, Brahms chose a variety of texts from both the Old and New Testaments. A prominent theme in these verses is the comfort offered to those who mourn.

The seven movements of Brahms's Requiem can be viewed in an overall arch-like structure. At the heart of the work is the gentle fourth movement, based on a passage from Psalm 84. The opening lines appear three times in the movement, and they are set in a similar fashion each time. Contrasting with these sections are several passages of contrapuntal activity and vigorous rhythms. But the recurring principal theme evokes an ethereal serenity and creates an overall rondo-like form.

17

Fanny Mendelssohn Hensel

Unter des Laubdachs Hut (*Under the Greenwood Tree*) (1846)

8CD: 6/ 24 – 27
4CD: 3/ 34 – 37

10
Keh - len Klang zu lust - ger Vö - gel Sang:
ihn er - nährt, und was er find't ver - zehrt:
stimmt der Keh - len Klang zu lust - ger Vö - gel Sang:
sucht, was ihn er - nährt, und was er find't ver - zehrt:
stimmt der Keh - len Klang zu lust - ger Vö - gel Sang:
sucht, was ihn er - nährt, und was er find't ver - zehrt:
stimmt der Keh - len Klang zu lust - ger Vö - gel Sang:
sucht, was ihn er - nährt, und was er find't ver - zehrt:
25 35 27 37
14
f
1. & 2. Komm ge - schwin-de, ge-schwin-de, ge - schwin - de, komm ge -
1. & 2. Komm ge - schwin-de, ge-schwin-de, ge - schwin - de, komm ge -
1. & 2. Komm ge - schwin-de, ge-schwin-de, ge - schwin - de, komm ge -
1. & 2. Komm ge - schwin-de, ge-schwin-de, ge - schwin - de, komm ge -
18
schwin-de, ge-schwin-de, ge - schwin - de! Hier nagt und sticht
schwin-de, ge-schwin-de, ge - schwin - de! Hier nagt und sticht
schwin-de, ge-schwin-de, ge - schwin - de! Hier nagt und sticht
schwin-de, ge-schwin-de, ge-schwind! Hier nagt und sticht kein Feind ihn

22
kein Feind ihn nicht, hier nagt und sticht kein Feind ihn
kein Feind ihn nicht, hier nagt und sticht kein Feind ihn
kein Feind ihn nicht, hier nagt und sticht kein Feind ihn
nicht, hiernagt und sticht, hier nagt und sticht kein Feind ihn
27
p
nicht als Re - gen, Wet-ter und Win - de, als Re - gen, Wet-ter und
nicht als Re - gen, Wet-ter und Win - de, als Re - gen, Wet-ter und
nicht hier nagt und sticht kein Feind ihn
nicht hier nagt und sticht kein Feind ihn
31
cresc.
f
Win - de, kein Feind, als Re - gen, Wet-ter und Win -
Win - de, kein Feind, als Re - gen und Win -
nicht als Re - ten, Wet-ter und Win - - -
nicht als Re - ten, Wet-ter und Win - - -

35
p
de. Hier nagt und sticht kein Feind ihn nicht, hier nagt und sticht kein
p
de. Hier nagt und sticht kein Feind ihn nicht, hier nagt und sticht kein
p
de. Hier nagt und sticht kein Feind ihn nicht, hier nagt und sticht kein
p
de. Hier nagt und sticht kein Feind ihn nicht, hier nagt und sticht kein

39
f
p
Feind ihn nicht als Re - gen, Wet - ter und Win - de, als
f
p
Feind ihn nicht als Re - gen, Wet - ter und Win - de, als
f
Feind ihn nicht als Re - gen, Wet - ter und Win - de,
f
Feind ihn nicht als Re - gen, Wet - ter und Win - de,

44
p
Re - gen, Wet-ter und Win - - - - de.
p
Re - gen, Wet-ter und Win - - - - de.
p
als Wet - ter und Win - de.
p
als Wet - ter und Win - de.

TEXT AND TRANSLATION

Verse 1	**Shakespeare's original English**
Unter des Laubdachs Hut,	Under the greenwood tree,
wer gerne mit mir ruht,	who loves to lie with me,
und stimmt der Kehlen Klang	and turn his merry note
zu lustger Vögel Sang;	unto the sweet bird's throat.
Chorus	
Komm geschwinde, geschwinde, geschwinde!	Come hither, come hither, come hither!
Hier nagt and sticht	Here shall he see
kein Feind ihn nicht	no enemy
als Regen, Wetter, und Winde;	but winter and rough weather,
(text repeated)	
Verse 2	
Wer sich von Ehrgeiz fornhält,	Who doth ambition shun,
in der Sonne gern,	and loves to live i' the sun,
selbst such, was ihn eruährt	seeking the food he eats,
und was er find't verzehrt;	and pleas'd with what he gets.

Chorus (as above)

Fanny Mendelssohn Hensel (1805–1847) was a talented composer and pianist. Accepting her role as a nineteenth-century European woman, she devoted herself to her husband and child. But she also found time for some performing, and she composed a significant number of works, most notably piano music and Lieder.

The text for *Unter des Laubdachs Hut* (*Under the Greenwood Tree*) is a German translation by Friedrich von Schlegel of a song from Shakespeare's comedy *As You Like It*. In the early years of the nineteenth century, Shakespeare enjoyed immense popularity; all of his plays were translated from English into German. Fanny Mendelssohn's younger brother Felix was active in the Shakespeare movement, writing incidental music for *A Midsummer Night's Dream*, which Fanny must have observed with interest.

Unter des Laubdachs Hut is strophic, featuring two verses and a refrain, "Come hither." The lilting compound meter suggests the idyllic nature of the poem, and the rich harmonic language and the alternation between homorhythmic and imitative textures sustain interest for both performer and listener. The upper and lower voices are paired in the imitative passages.

18

Giuseppe Verdi

Rigoletto, Act III, aria, "La donna è mobile" ("Woman is fickle"), and quartet, "Un dì, se ben rammentomi" ("One day, if I remember right") (1851)

8CD: 6/ 28 – 33
4CD: 3/ 38 – 43

A lonely spot on the shore of the Mincio River, with the towers of Mantua in the background. On the left, a two-story house almost in ruins, the front of which, open to the spectator, shows a rustic inn on the ground floor: a broken staircase leads from this to a loft where stands a rough couch. On the side towards the street is a door, and a low wall extends backward from the house. Gilda and Rigoletto converse in great agitation along the road to the inn; Sparafucile is seated inside the inn. Upon reaching the inn, Rigoletto forces Gilda to watch through a fissure in the wall as the Duke enters, disguised as a cavalry officer.

Canzone (aria). "La donna è mobile" ("Woman is fickle")

pp
D.
in pianto o in ri - so, è menzo - gne - ro. La donna è mo - bil
Frown-ing or smil - ing, Just as she pleas - es. She is ca - pri - cious,
pp
p
f
leggero
qual piuma al ven - to, mu - ta d'ac - cen - to e di pen - sier,
Turns like the weath - er, Sways like a feath - er, Nev - er the same,
Fl.
Ob.
pp
e di pen - sier, e,
Nev - er, the same, nev -
p
pp
con forza
29
39
e di pen - sier.
- er the same.
f
ff
p marcato

D.
p
pp
D.
E sempre mi-se-ro chi a lei s'af - fi - da, chi le con - fi - da
Blind in sim - plic - i - ty Men's hearts are cap-tured, Whol - ly en - rap-tured,
D.
mal cau-to il co - re! Pur mai non sen-te-si fe - li-ce ap - pie - no
Deaf to all warn-ing. Yet full-est hap-pi-ness No man has tast - ed
D.
chi su quel se - no non li-ba a - mo - re! La donna è mo - bil
Whose life is wast - ed Love-less and mourn-ing! Wom-an will wa - ver,
pp
p

D.
f
pp leggero
qual piuma al vento, muta d'accento e di pensier,
Turn like the weather, Sway like a feather, Never the same,
pp

D.
e di pensier, e,
Never the same, nev-
p

D.
con forza
e di pensier!
-er the same.
ff

(Re-enter Sparafucile with a flask of wine and two glasses, which he places on the table; then

with the hilt of his long sword he knocks on the ceiling twice. At this signal, a smiling young
dim.

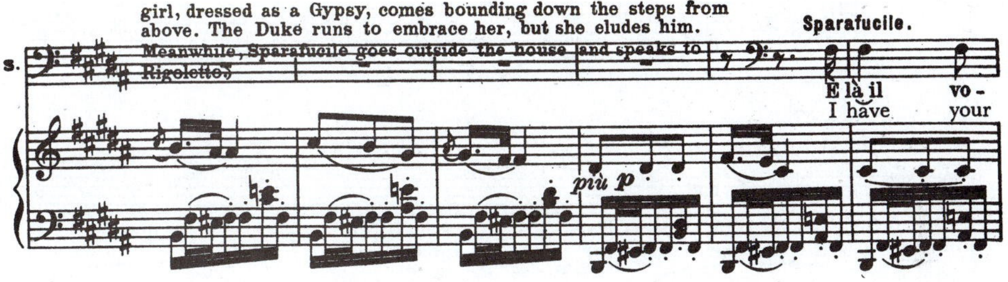
girl, dressed as a Gypsy, comes bounding down the steps from above. The Duke runs to embrace her, but she eludes him.
Meanwhile, Sparafucile goes outside the house and speaks to Rigoletto.)
Sparafucile.
S.
È là il vo-
I have your
più p

Rigoletto.
S.
R.
str'uo - mo... Vi-ver de - e o mo - ri - re? Più
man here. Give your or-ders, I o - bey you. De-
morendo

(Sparafucile goes off behind the house, toward the river.)
R.
tar - di tor-ne-rò l'opra a com-pi - re.
tain him for a while, and then I'll pay you.

Quartet. "Un dì, se ben rammentomi" ("One day, if I remember right")

Gilda.
Maddalena.
In-i-quo! Ah, ah, e ven-t'altre ap-pres - so le
The trai-tor! Ha, ha! No one else be-fore me! You're
do - ra!
dore you.
p

scor - da for - se a-desso? Ha un' aria il si-gno - ri-no da ve-ro li-ber-
tell - ing me a sto-ry. A lib-er - tine, be-lieve me, Could never once de-

Gilda.
Ah pa-dre mi - o!
Ah, dear-est fa - ther!
ti-no...
ceive me.
La-scia-te-mi, stor - di-to.
E-nough of that, it's sil-ly.
Duke (trying to embrace her).
Sì!.. un mostro son,...
Ih che fra-
Yes, I'm ver-y bad . . .
Come, don't be
Fl.
Ob.
cresc.

Maddalena.
Duke.
casso! Stia saggio. E tu sii do-ci-le, non fa-re tan-to
naugh-ty! Be good now! Don't act so prud-ish-ly, Why sud-den-ly be
chias-so. O-gni sag-gez-za chiu-de-si nel gau-dio e nel-l'a-
haugh-ty? Cast all your fool-ish qualms a-way. My dar-ling, you must sur-
Strings
col canto
pp
Maddalena.
(takes her hand)
Scher-
You're
mo-re. La bel-la ma-no can-di-da!
ren-der. Your hand is white as i-vo-ry!
p
pp
Gilda.
za-te voi, si-gno-re. Son brut-ta. I-ni-quo!
mock-ing me, pre-tend-er! I'm ug-ly. Be-tray-er!
No, no. Ab-brac-cia-mi.
No, no! I long for you
f
p

Maddalena.
Ma.
Ebro! Signor l'in-dif - fe - rente, vi pia-ce canzo -
Li-ar! (laughing) It seems to be your fash-ion to jest your way through
D.
D'amor ar - den - te.
with glow - ing pas - sion!
nar? Ne vo-glio la pa - ro-la..
life! Your prom-ise binds for - ev-er! (ironically)
No, no, ti vo'spo - sar. A-ma - bi - le fi -
I want you for my wife! How lov - a - ble and
p
Gilda.
G.
I - ni - quo tra - di - tor!
Maddelena. My heart can bear no more!
Ne voglio la pa - ro-la
Your prom-ise binds for - ev-er!
Duke.
gliuo - la! A ma - bi - le fi
clev-er! How lov - a - ble and
Rigoletto (to Gilda, who has heard all).
R.
E non ti basta an - cor? E non ti basta an -
You want to hear still more? You want to hear still

G.
I - ni - quo tra - di - tor!
My heart can bear no more!
Mn.
Ne vo-glio la pa - ro-la! ne voglio la pa - ro-la, ne voglio la pa -
Your prom-ise binds for - ev-er! Your prom-ise binds for - ev-er! Your prom-ise binds for -
D.
gliuola! a-ma-bi-le fi-gliuo-la! a-ma-bi-le fi -
clev-er! How lov-a-ble and clev-er! How lov-a-ble and
R.
cor? e non ti basta an-cor? e non ti basta an -
more? You want to hear still more? You want to hear still
ff

31
41
G.
Mn.
ro - la!
ev - er!
Andante.
D.
gliuo-la! Bel - la fi-glia del - l'a - mo - re, schia - vo
clev-er! Mad-da - - le - na, I a - dore you, You en -
R.
cor?
more?
Andante. (♩ = 66)
Wood
pp
String pizz.

D.
son de' vez - zi tuo - i; con un detto,un det - to sol tu
slave me and en - chant me; On - ly this one fa - vor you must
D.
pp dolce
puo - i le mie pe - ne, le mie pe - ne con - so - lar. Vieni, e
grant me,Come and love me, be my ra - diant guid-ing star. I im -
Cl. & Bn.
pp
D.
stent.
sen-ti del mio co - re il fre - quente pal - pi - tar, con un
plore you, don't re - fuse me, Be my ra - diant, guid-ing star, grant me
Strings
D.
pp
detto,un det - to sol tu puo - i le mie pe - ne, le mie pe - ne con - so -
this one fa - vor, I im - plore you,Come and love me, be my ra-diant guid-ing

32
42
Gilda.
G.
Ah! co-sì par-lar d'a-
Ah,— I —know— his lips — are
Maddelena.
Ma.
Ah!ah! ri-do ben di co - re, chè tai ba-ie costan po-co;
Talk is cheap, there's no de-ny-ing but your com-pli-ments a - muse me.
Duke.
D.
lar.
star.
Ob. & Vln.
Fl.
Cl.
pp
G
mo - re
ly - ing.
Maddelena.
Ma.
quan - to val-ga il vo - stro gio - co, mel cre - de - te, so apprez -
Pret - ty speech - es don't con - fuse me, I know well how false they
G.
a— me pur l'in-fa-me ho u - di - to!
Ah, — to — think — I once — be-lieved him!
In - fe -
How — sin -
Ma.
R.
zar.
are.
Rigoletto (to Gilda).
Ta-ci, il pian - ge - re non va -
Qui-et, your cry - ing now is use -
Ob. & Vln.

G.
li - - - ce cor tra - di - to, per an -
cere - - - ly did I love him, and he
Ma.
Son av-vez - za, bel si - gno - - re,
Man-y times I heard that sto - - ry,
Duke.
D.
Con un det - to
Don't be heart - less,
R.
le; ta - ci, ta-ci, il pian-ge - re non va -
less! Nev - er mind him, your cry-ing now is use -
G.
go - - - scia non scop - piar, no, no, non scop -
now be - trays me so. Ah, he scorned my
Ma.
ad un si - mi - le scherza - - re, mio bel si -
To be-lieve it would be mad - - ness, It's far too
D.
sol tu puo - i le mi - e
I im - plore you, Come and love,
R.
le, no, non val, no, no, non
less! No, the time for tears has

33
43
G.
piar.
love!
Ms.
gnor!
old!
D.
pe - ne con - so - lar. Bel - la fi - glia del l'a - mo -
ra- diant guid - ing star! Mad - da - le - na, I a - dore
R.
val.
passed.
col canto
pp
G.
In - fe - li - ce
I be - lieved - him,
Ms.
Ah! ah! ri - do ben di co - re, chè tai ba - ie costan po - co,
Talk is cheap, there's no de - ny - ing but your com - pli - ments a - muse me
D.
re, schia - vo son de' vez - zi tuo -
you, You en - slave me and en - chant
R.
Ch'ei men - ti - va,
He was ly - ing,

G.
cor tra -
now he be -
Ms.
quan - to val - ga il vo - stro gio - co, mel cre - de - te, sò ap - prez -
Pret - ty speech - es don't con - fuse me, I know well how false they
D.
i; con un
me; On - ly
R.
ch'ei men - -
He be - -
G.
di - to, ah!
trays me! Ah,
Ms.
zar. Sono avvez - za, bel signo - re, ad un si - mi - le scher-
are. Man-y times I heard that sto-ry, To be - lieve it would be
D.
detto, un det - to sol tu puo - - i le mie
this one fa - vor you must grant me, Come and
R.
ti - va sei si -
trayed you, I have

f
G.
— no, non scoppiar. In - fe-li - ce co - re, cor tra -
— it breaks my heart! All my trust and my de - vo - tion
pp
Ma.
za - - re. Ah! ah! ah!ah! ri - - -
mad - - - ness, Ha,ha, ha,ha! Ri - - -
pp
D.
pe-ne, le mie pe-ne con-so-lar. Ah! con un
love me, be my ra-diant guid-ing star! Ah, Mad - da -
pp
con voce cupa
R.
cu - - ra. Taci, e mia sa-rà la
proved it, But I give you my as -
Fl.
Ob.
G.
pp
di - to, per an-go - scia non scop -
He has scorned, and now I am be -
Ma.
do di cor, ah, ah, ri - - - -
dic - u - lous! Ha, ha! Ri - - - -
D.
det - - - - to sol tu
le - - - - na, I a -
R.
cu - - - ra la ven-det - ta d'af-fret -
sur - - - ance That his crime shall be a -
pp

G.
pia - re, in - fe - li - ce cor tra -
trayed. For all my love and my de -
Ma.
do di cor, ah! ah! ri - - - -
dic - u - lous! Ha, ha! Ri - - -
D.
puo - - i le mi - e
dore you, I read a
R.
tar, ta - ci e mia sa - rà la
venged. my pow - er and en -
G.
di - to, per an - go - scia non scop -
vo - tion, He re - paid me with de -
Ma.
do di cor, ah! ah! ri - - -
dic - u - lous! Ha, ha! Come
D.
pe - - - - ne con - so -
prom - - - - ise in your
R.
cu - - ra la ven - det - ta d'af - fret -
dur - - ance I'll em - ploy on grim re -
pp
pp

G.
pia - re, in - fe - li - ce cor tra -
cep - tion. How I loved him and a -
Ma.
do, ah! ah! ri - do ben di co - re, chè tai ba - ie co - stan
now, Talk is cheap, there's no de - ny - ing, But your com - pli - ments a -
D.
lar; vie - ni e sen - ti del mio
glance. I en - treat you don't re -
R.
tar. Sì, pron - - ta
venge. I am pre -
cresc.

G.
di - to, per an - go - scia non scoppiar, no, no, no, no, no,
dored him, And by him I am be-trayed, ah— And
Ma.
poco, quanto val - ga il vo - stro gioco, mel credete, so apprezzar, sì, sì,
muse me, Pret - ty speech - es don't con - fuse me, I know well how false they are, my friend.
D.
co - re il frequen - te pal - pi - tar, ah, sì,
fuse me, make me hap - py and be - mine, ah, my
R.
fia, sa - ra fa - ta - le,
pared to strike a fa - tal blow.
f

G.
no, no, non scop-
now he broke my
Ms.
so-no avvez-za, bel si-gno-re, ad un si-mi-le scher-
Man-y times I heard that sto-ry, To be-lieve it would be
D
vie-
dar-
R.
io sa-prol-lo ful-mi-nar, io sa-prol-lo ful-mi-
I'll em-ploy all my en-dur-ance to strike a fa-tal
G.
pia-re, in-fe-li-ce cor tra-
heart, My trust and my de-vo-tion
Ms.
zar, ah, ah, ah, ah! ri-
hard, ha, ha, ha, ha! Ri-
D.
ni; ah! con un
ling. Ah, Mad-da-
con voce cupa
R
nar; ta-ci, e mia sa-rà la
blow. Yes, I give you my as-

G.
pp
di - to, per an - go - scia non scop -
he for-got, and now I am be -
Ma.
do di cor, ah! ah! ri - - - -
dic - u - lous ha, ha! Ri - - - -
D.
det - - - to sol tu
le - - - na, I a- -
R.
cu- - - - ra la ven - det - ta d'af - fret -
sur - - - - ance, That his crime shall be a -
pp
G.
pia - re, in fe - li - ce cor tra -
trayed. For all my love and my de -
Ma.
do di cor, ah! ah! ri - - - -
dic - u - lous, ha, ha! Ri - - - -
D.
puo - i le mi - e
dore you, I read a
R.
tar, ta - ci, e mia sa - rà la
venged. All my pow - er and en -
8

pp
G.
di - to, per an - go - scia non scop -
vo - tion, He re - paid me with de -
Ms.
do di cor, ah! ah! ri - - - -
dic - u - lous, ha, ha! Come
D.
pe - - - - ne con - so - -
prom - - - - ise in your
R.
cu - - - ra la ven - det - ta d'af - fret -
dur - - - ance I'll em - ploy on grim re -
pp
G
pia - re, in - fe - li - ce cor tra -
cep - tion. How I loved him and a -
Ms.
do, ah! ah! ri - do ben di co - re, chè tai ba - ie co - stan
now, Talk is cheap, there's no de - ny - ing, But your com - pli - ments a -
D.
lar; vie - ni e sen - ti del mio
glance. I en - treat you, don't re -
R.
tar; sì, pron - ta
venge. I am pre - - -
cresc.

G.
di - to, per an - go - scia non scop -
dored him, And by him I am be -
Ma.
po - co; quanto val - ga il vo - stro gio - co, mel cre - de - te, so ap - prez -
muse me; Pret - ty speech - es don't con - fuse me, I know well how false you
D
co - re il fre - quen - te pal - pi -
fuse me, make me hap - py and be
R.
fia, sa - rà fa -
pared to strike a
G.
piar, no, no, no,no, no, no,no, non scop -
trayed, ah And now he broke my
Ma
zar, sì, sì, sono avvez - za, bel si - gnore, ad un si - mi - le scher-
are, my friend, Man-y times I heard that sto - ry, To be-lieve it would be
D.
tar, ah sì, vie -
mine, ah, my dar -
R.
ta - le, io sa - prol - lo ful - mi - nar, io saprol - lo ful - mi -
fa - tal blow. I'll em - ploy all my en - dur - ance to strike a fa - tal

G.
piar, in - fe - li - ce cor tra - di - to, per ango - scia non scop-
heart. How I loved him and a - dored him, And he so— de-ceived my
Ma.
zar, il vo - stro gio - co— sò ap - prez -
hard. I know these sto - ries,— what they are
D.
ni. sen - ti del co - re il pal - pi -
ling, I read a prom - ise in your
R.
nar, ta - ci, e mia sa - rà la cu - ra la ven-det - ta d'af - fret -
blow. Yes, I give you my as - sur-ance, That his crime shall be a -
G.
piar, in - fe - li - ce cor tra - di - to, per ango - scia non scop-
heart. How I loved him and a - doredhim Andhe so— de-ceived my
Ma.
zar, il vo - stro gio - co— sò ap - prez -
worth. I know these sto - ries,— what they are
D.
tar, sen - ti del co - re il pal - pi -
glance, I read a prom - ise in your
R.
tar, ta - ci, e mia sa - rà la cu - ra la ven-det - ta d'af - fret -
venged. All my pow - er and en - dur-ance I'll em - ploy on grim re -
p

G.
piar, no, non scop-piar, non scop-
heart, he broke my heart, my
Ma.
zar, il vostro gio - co sò apprez-zar, il vo-stro gioco sò apprezza -
worth. How well I know what they are worth. How well I know these pret-ty sto -
D.
tar, vieni, vie-ni, vie -
glance. You shall be mine, be
R.
tar, ta-ci, ta - ci, ta -
venge, I shall em-ploy on
p
pp
G.
piar, ah no!
heart, ah, ah!
Ma.
re, ah sì!
ries, my friend!
D.
ni, vie - ni!
mine, be mine!
R.
ci, ta - ci!
grim re - venge!

In the nineteenth century, Italian opera maintained its traditional emphasis on the voice and the aria. Although changes occurred slowly during the course of the era, a number of new qualities can be observed, including a more direct, cutting vocal line for tenors and more frequent ensemble singing in serious operas (an influence of opera buffa). Giuseppe Verdi (1813–1901) fashioned these musical elements into a dramatic flow and brought about a balance between musical and dramatic needs in opera. One of Verdi's most compelling and popular works is *Rigoletto.* Based on a play by Victor Hugo that was banned in France, *Le roi s'amuse* (The King Is Amused), Verdi's opera is a dark tale of seduction, revenge, and murder set in the Renaissance court of Mantua. Rigoletto, a hunchbacked court jester, seeks revenge against his employer, the Duke, for defiling his only valued possession, his daughter Gilda.

In Act III, the plot for vengeance unfolds in a brilliant musical and dramatic fashion. At the opening of this excerpt, the Duke sings his famous aria of seduction, "La donna è mobile" ("Woman is fickle") to Maddalena, while Rigoletto has Gilda watch through a window. The strophic aria is set to a waltz tempo with a guitarlike accompaniment. At the end of the aria, Rigoletto quietly completes a deal for the Duke's murder with Sparafucile, Maddalena's brother. In the ensuing quartet, four divergent moods are projected simultaneously: the ardor of the Duke, the playfulness of Maddalena, the lament of Gilda, and the resolve for vengeance by Rigoletto. Following this remarkable musical moment, Rigoletto's plans go astray. Ultimately, Rigoletto opens a large sack, expecting to see the Duke's body, only to find that Gilda has allowed herself to be killed for her unworthy lover. She dies in Rigoletto's arms as the curtains close.

19

Richard Wagner

Die Walküre, Act III, Opening (*The Ride of the Valkyries*) and Finale, closing section (1856; first performed 1870)

8CD: 6/ 34 – 44
4CD: 3/ 44 – 49

Editor's note: The Shorter Norton Recordings stop on p. 403. This piano/vocal score includes pedal markings.

f marcato
ff
Der Vorhang geht auf
The Curtain rises
36
46
ff
f

(Auf dem Gipfel eines Felsberges. Rechts begränzt ein Tannenwald die Scene. Links der Eingang einer Felsenhöhle: darüber steigt der Fels zu seiner höchsten Spitze auf. Nach hinten ist die Aussicht gänzlich frei; höhere und niedere Felssteine bilden den Rand vor dem

(On the summit of a rocky mountain. On the right a pinewood encloses the stage. On the left is the entrance to a cave; above this the rock rises to its highest point. At the back the view is entirely open; rocks of various heights form a parapet to the pre-

Abhange.— Einzelne Wolkenzüge jagen, wie vom Sturm getrieben, am Felsensaume vorbei.— Gerhilde, Ortlinde, Waltraute und Schwertleite haben sich auf der Felsenspitze über der Höhle gelagert: sie sind in voller Waffenrüstung.)

cipice.— Occasionally clouds fly past the mountain peak, as if driven by storm.— Gerhilde, Ortlinde, Waltraute and Schwertleite have ensconced themselves on the rocky peak above the cave: they are in full armour.)

GERH.
Helm - wi - ge! Hier! Hie - her mit dem
Helm - wi - ge! Here! Guide hith - er thy
HELMWIGE'S (Stimme im Hintergrunde durch ein Sprachrohr.)
(voice at the back through a speaking trumpet.)
Ho-jo-to-ho! Ho-jo-to-ho! Hojo-to-ho!
Ross!
horse!
cresc.
molto cresc.
Ho-jo-to-ho! Hei - a -
(In dem Gewölk bricht Blitzesglanz aus: eine Walküre zu Ross wird in ihm sichtbar; über ihrem Sattel hängt ein erschlagener Krieger.)
(A flash of lightning breaks through a passing cloud: in the light a Valkyrie on horseback becomes visible: on her saddle hangs
ha!

a slain warrior.)
(Die Erscheinung zieht, immer näher, am Felsensaume von links nach rechts vorbei.)
(The apparition, approaching the rocky cliff, passes from left to right.)
(Alle drei der Ankommenden entgegen rufend.)
(All three calling to her as she approaches.)
GERHILDE.
Hei-a-ha! Hei-a-ha!
Hei-a-ha! Hei-a-ha!
WALTRAUTE.
Hei-a-ha! Hei-a-ha!
Hei-a-ha! Hei-a-ha!
SCHWERTLEITE.
Hei-a-ha! Hei-a-ha!
Hei-a-ha! Hei-a-ha!

(Die Wolke mit der Erscheinung ist rechts hinter dem Tann verschwunden.)
(The cloud with the apparition disappears to the right behind the wood.)
ff
f
P.
P.
38
48
ORTLINDE (in den Tann hinein rufend.)
(calling towards the wood.)
Zu Ort-linde's Stu - te stell' deinen Hengst: mit meiner Grau - en gras't gern dein Brauner!
By Ort-linde's fil - ly fas - ten thy horse: gladly my grey will graze near thy chest-nut!
WALTRAUTE.
(hinein rufend)
(calling towards the wood)
Wer
Who
p
p
HELMWIGE (aus dem Tann auftretend.)
(coming from the wood.)
Sintolt, der Hegeling!
Sintolt, the Hegeling!
hängt dir im Sattel?
hangs at thy saddle?
SCHWERTLEITE.
Führ dei - nen Braunen fort von der Grauen: Ortlinde's Mähre trägt
Far from the grey, then, fasten thy chestnut: Ortlinde's fil - ly bears
p
GERHILDE (ist etwas näher herabgestiegen.)
(coming down lower.)
Als Fein - de nur sah' ich Sin - tolt und Wit - tig!
For foes have been e - ver Sin - tolt and Wit - tig!
Wit - tig, den Ir - ming!
Wit - tig, the Ir - ming!
sf.
cresc.
P.

ORTLINDE (springt auf) (starts up)
(Sie läuft in den Tann) (She runs to the wood)
Hei-a-ha! Heia - ha! Die Stu - te stösst mir der Hengst!
Hei-a-ha! Heia - ha! The horse at-tack - eth my mare!
f
p cresc.
P. marcato
GERH. (lachend) (laughing)
Ha ha ha ha ha ha ha ha ha ha! Der Re - cken Zwist ent - zweit noch die
Ha ha ha ha ha ha ha ha ha ha! The he-roes' strife makes foes of the
HELMW. (lachend) (laughing)
Ha ha ha ha ha ha ha ha ha ha!
Ha ha ha ha ha ha ha ha ha ha!
SCHWERTL. (lachend) (laughing)
Ha ha ha ha ha ha ha ha ha ha!
Ha ha ha ha ha ha ha ha ha ha!
f p f p f
marcato
(auf der Höhe, wo sie für Gerhilde die Wacht übernommen)
(on the topmost point where she has taken Gerhilde's post as watcher.)
WALTR.
Hoio - ho!
Hoio - ho!
GERH.
Ros - se!
hors - es!
(in den Tann zurückrufend) (calling back into the wood)
HELMW.
Ru-hig Brau - ner! brich' nicht den Frie - den.
Quiet, Brown-ie! break not the peace, now.
p cresc. f p
p

WALTR.
(nach rechts in den Hintergrund rufend.)
(calling towards the right hand side of the background.)
Ho-io-ho!
Ho-io-ho!
Sie-gru - ne hier! Wo säum'st du so lang?
Sie-gru - ne here! Where stay'st thou so long?
p
marcato
(Sie lauscht nach rechts.)
(She listens towards the right.)
cresc.
SIEGRUNE'S Stimme (durch ein Sprachrohr) von der rechten Seite des Hintergrundes her.
voice (through a speaking trumpet) from the back on the right.
Ar - beit gab's!
Work to do!
f
dim.
marcato
Sind die
Are the

WALTR.
(nach rechts in den Hintergrund rufend.)
(calling towards the right hand side of the background.)
Ho-jo - to-ho!
Ho-jo - to-ho!
SCHWERTL.
(nach rechts in den Hintergrund rufend.)
(calling towards the right hand side of the background.)
Ho-jo - to-ho!
Ho-jo - to-ho!
SIEGR.
An-d'ren schon da?
o-thers all here?
GERH
(nach rechts in den Hintergrund rufend.)
(calling towards the right hand side of the background.)
Hei-a-ha!
Hei-a-ha!
(Ihre Gebärden, sowie ein heller Glanz hinter dem Tann, zeigen an, dass so eben Siegrune dort angelangt ist.)
WALTR.
Hei-a - ha!
Hei-a - ha!
(Their gestures, as well as a bright light behind the wood, shew that Siegrune has just arrived there.)
SCHWERTL.
Hei-a - ha!
Hei-a - ha!
GRIMGERDE'S Stimme (von links im Hintergrunde.)
voice (from the back on the left)
(durch ein Sprachrohr.)
(through a speaking trumpet)
Ho-jo - to-ho!
Ho-jo - to-ho!
dim.
ROSSWEISSE'S Stimme (von eben daher)
voice (from the same place)
(durch ein Sprachrohr) (through a speaking trumpet)
Ho-jo - to-ho!
Ho-jo - to-ho!
Heia-ha!
Heia-ha!
GRIMG.
Heia-ha!
Heia-ha!
cresc.

39
49
GERH.
(ebenso)
(the same)
Sie rei - ten zu zwei.
To - geth - er they ride.
WALTR. (nach links)
(towards the left)
Grim - gerd' und Ross - weis - se!
Grim - gerd' and Ross - weis - se!
molto cresc.
ff
P.
(In einem blitz-erglänzenden Wolkenzuge, der von links her vorbeizieht, erscheinen Rossweisse und Grimgerde, ebenfalls auf Rossen,
(In a bank of clouds, passing from the left, Rossweisse and Grimgerde appear, illumined by a flash of lightning. Both are on horse-
jede einen Erschlagenen im Sattel führend.)
back and each carries a slain warrior on her saddle.)
8va
sempre ff
HELMW.
Gegrüsst,
We greet
ORTL.
(Sind aus dem Tann getreten, und winken vom Felsen-Saume den Ankommenden zu.)
(Have come out of the wood and wave to the approaching Rossweisse and Grimgerde from the edge of the precipice.)
Gegrüsst,
We greet
SIEGR.
Gegrüsst,
We greet

HELMW.
ihr Reis - si-ge! Ross - weiss' und Grim - ger - de!
you tra - vel-lers! Ross - weiss' and Grim - ger - de!
ORTL.
ihr Reis - si-ge! Ross - weiss' und Grim - ger - de!
you tra - vel-lers! Ross - weiss' and Grim - ger - de!
SIEGR.
ihr Reis - si-ge! Ross - weiss' und Grim - ger - de!
you tra - vel-lers! Ross - weiss' and Grim - ger - de!
p
ROSSWEISSE'S & GRIMGERDE'S Stimmen (durch ein Sprachrohr)
voices (through a speaking trumpet)
Ho-jo - to-ho! Ho-jo - to-ho! Hei-a - ha!
Ho-jo - to-ho! Ho-jo - to-ho! Hei-a - ha!
HELMW. & ORTL.
Ho-jo-to-ho! Ho-jo-to-ho! Hei-a-
Ho-jo-to-ho! Ho-jo-to-ho! Hei-a-
GERH. & WALTR.
Ho-jo-to-ho! Ho-jo-to-ho! Hei-a-
Ho-jo-to-ho! Ho-jo-to-ho! Hei-a-
SIEGR. & SCHWERTL.
(Die Erscheinung verschwindet hinter dem Tann.)
(The apparition disappears behind the wood.)
Ho-jo-to-ho! Ho-jo-to-ho! Hei-a-
Ho-jo-to-ho! Ho-jo-to-ho! Hei-a-
ff
p
p
p

ha! Hei-a - ha! Ho-jo-to-ho!
ha! Hei-a - ha! Ho-jo-to-ho!
ha! Hei-a - ha! Ho-jo-to-ho!
ha! Hei-a - ha! Ho-jo-to-ho!
ha! Hei-a - ha! Ho-jo-to-ho!
ha! Hei-a - ha! Ho-jo-to-ho!
più f
ff
f
P.
Ho-jo-to-ho! Hei-a - ha! Hei-a - ha!
Ho-jo-to-ho! Hei-a - ha! Hei a ha
Ho-jo-to-ho! Hei-a - ha! Hei-a - ha!
Ho-jo-to-ho! Hei-a - ha! Hei a ha
Ho-jo-to-ho! Hei-a - ha! Hei-a - ha!
Ho-jo-to-ho! Hei-a - ha! Hei a ha
più f
ff
P.
Ho-jo-to-ho! Ho-jo-to-ho! Ho-jo-to-ho! Ho-jo-to-ho!
Ho-jo-to-ho! Ho-jo-to-ho! Ho-jo-to-ho! Ho-jo-to-ho!
Hei-a-ha! Heia-ha! Heia-ha! Heia-ha!
Hei-a-ha! Heia-hei! Heia-hei! Heia-hei!
Hei-a-ha! Heia-ha! Heia-ha! Heia-ha!
Hei-a-ha! Heia-hei! Heia-hei! Heia-hei!
f
più f
P.

tr
Hei - - a - - ha!
Hei - - a - - ha!
Hei-a - ha!
Hei-a - ha!
Hei-a - ha!
Hei-a - ha!
Hei-a - ha!
Hei-a - ha!
Hei-a - ha!
Hei-a - ha!
Hei-a - ha!
Hei-a - ha!
f
più f
ff
P.
ff
P.
GERH. (in den Tann rufend)
(calling into the wood)
In Wald mit den Rossen zu Rast und Weid!
Leave there in the for-est your steeds to graze!
p
cresc.
P.

ORTLINDE (ebenfalls in den Tann rufend.)
(likewise calling into the wood.)
Füh - ret die Mäh - - ren
Lead off the mares a -
fern von ein - an - der,
far from each o - ther,
bis uns'rer Hel - den Hass sich ge - legt!
till all our he - roes' an - ger is calmed!
ff
p
cresc.
HELMW.
Der Hel - - den
The grey has
GERH.
(lachend)
(laughing)
Ha ha ha ha ha ha ha ha ha ha!
SIEGR.
WALTR.
SCHWERTL.

HELMW.
Grimm büss-' te schon die Grau- - - e!
paid for the he- roes' an- - - ger!
WALTR.
(lachend)
(laughing)
Ha ha ha ha ha ha ha ha ha
Ha ha ha ha ha ha ha ha ha
SCHWERTL.
(lachend)
(laughing)
Ha ha ha ha ha ha ha ha ha
Ha ha ha ha ha ha ha ha ha
cresc.
f
HELMW.
Ha ha ha ha ha ha ha ha ha ha!
Ha ha ha ha ha ha ha ha ha ha!
Ha ha ha ha ha ha ha ha ha
Ha ha ha ha ha ha ha ha ha
GERH.
Ha ha ha ha ha ha ha ha ha ha!
Ha ha ha ha ha ha ha ha ha ha!
Ha ha ha ha ha ha ha ha ha
Ha ha ha ha ha ha ha ha ha
WALTR.
ha! Ha ha ha ha ha ha ha ha ha ha!
ha! Ha ha ha ha ha ha ha ha ha ha!
SCHWERTL.
ha! Ha ha ha ha ha ha ha ha ha ha!
ha! Ha ha ha ha ha ha ha ha ha ha!
f
più f
ff

Editor's note: The Norton Recordings excerpt fades out at this point, and resumes in the finale of Act III.

Finale, closing section

WOTAN **(Er schreitet mit feierlichem Entschlusse in die Mitte der Bühne, und kehrt die Spitze seines Speeres gegen einen mächtigen Felsstein.)**
(He strides with solemn decision to the middle of the stage and directs the point of his spear towards a large rock.)

Mässig bewegt.

Lo - ge hör'! lau - sche hie-her! Wie zuerst ich dich fand, als feu - ri - ge Gluth, wie dann einst du mir schwandest, als schweifen-de Lo-he; wie ich dich band,

Lo - ge hear! List to my word! As I found thee of old, a glim - mering flame, as from me thou didst va-nish, in wan - dering fire; as once I stayed thee,

WOTAN.
bann' ich dich heut'!
stir I thee now!
Her - auf, wa - bern - de
Ap - pear! come, wav - ing
Lo - he,
fire
um - lod'- re mir feu - rig den
and wind thee in flames round the
Fels!
fell!
(Er stösst mit dem Folgenden dreimal mit dem Speer auf den Stein.)
(During the following he strikes the rock thrice with his spear.)
(Erster Stoss.) (First stroke.)
Lo - ge!
Lo - ge!
(Zweiter.)
(Second.)
Lo - ge! hie - her!
Lo - ge! ap - pear!
(Dritter.)
(Third.)
(Dem Stein entfährt ein Feuerstrahl.
(A flash of flame issues from
p
fp
mf
poco cresc.
dim.
cresc.
più cresc.
f

der zur allmälich immer helleren Flammenglut anschwillt.)
the rock, which swells to an ever-brightening fiery glow.)
f
più f
41
(Hier bricht die lichte Flackerlohe aus.)
(Here flickering flames break forth.)
p
sempre stacc
cresc. poco a poco
sempre cresc.
f
Lichte Brunst umgiebt Wotan mit wildem Flackern. Er weis't mit dem Speere gebie-
Bright shooting flames surround Wotan. With his spear he directs the sea of fire
ff

terisch dem Feuermeere den Umkreis des Felsenrandes zur Strömung an; alsbald zieht es sich nach dem Hintergrunde, wo es nun
to encircle the rocks; it presently spreads toward the background where it encloses the mountain in flames.)
42
sempre stacc.
ff
dim.
fortwährend den Bergsaum umlodert.)
43
p dolce
sempre legato
sempre stacc.
44
WOTAN.
Wer mei - nes Spee - - - - res
He who my spear- - - - point's
cresc. poco -
Spit - - - ze fürch - - - - - - tet durch-
sharp - - - ness fear - - - - - - eth shall
a poco
schrei - te das Feu - - - er nie!
cross not the flam - - - ing fire!

(Er streckt den Speer wie zum Banne aus.)
(He stretches out the spear as a spell.)
f
più cresc.
pesante
marcato
ff
(Er blickt schmerzlich auf Brünnhilde zurück)
(He gazes sorrowfully back on Brünnhilde.)
dim.
p
sehr ausdrucksvoll
dim.
più p

(Er wendet sich langsam zum Gehen.)
(Slowly he turns to depart.)
p dolce
più p
sempre più p
(Er wendet sich nochmals mit dem Haupt und blickt zurück.)
(He turns his head again and locks back.)
mp
pp
(Er verschwindet durch das Feuer.)
He disappears through the fire.
(Vorhang fällt.)
Curtain falls.
più pp
ppp

A cycle of four music dramas, *Der Ring des Nibelungen* by Richard Wagner (1813–1883) stands as one of the most monumental achievements in Western music, both in its size and in its impact on opera, music in general, and all of the arts. One of the work's most innovative features is its continuous dramatic flow. Rather than retaining artificial substructures such as arias, recitatives, and other musical numbers, Wagner developed an ongoing melodic style called "endless melody." In order to unify this free dramatic flow, Wagner created a system of *leitmotifs* (leading motives), in which melodic ideas represent aspects of the drama. Among Wagner's other influential innovations are the sheer length of the work, his use of the low brass, and his exploration of the boundaries of functional harmony.

Die Walküre, the second music drama of the *Ring* cycle, derives its title from the Valkyries, nine female warriors that ride flying horses. The Valkyries are the progeny of Wotan, the king of the Gods, and Erda, the all-knowing earth-goddess. Learning from Erda that the immortality of the Gods will be threatened, Wotan orders the Valkyries to gather bodies of dead heroes and bring them to his fortress, Valhalla. Here, he intends to forge them into a mighty army that will protect the Gods.

At the beginning of Act III, the Valkyries are arriving, each bringing a hero on her steed. The orchestra opens with rapid woodwind trills and a repetitive rhythmic accompaniment. The leitmotif for the Valkyries is intoned by the French horns, and soon the other brass instruments join. The tune itself shifts from minor to major, and the orchestra sparkles with Wagner's brilliant orchestration. The melody is well known to general audiences, primarily because of its extended use in the Bugs Bunny cartoon, *What's Opera, Doc?* (1957) and in movies, most notably *Apocalypse Now* (1979). After the orchestral prelude, the Valkyries begin to sing, expressing joyful exuberance and playfulness.

In the final scene of the drama, Wotan must punish and bid farewell to his only real love, his daughter Brünnhilde, who has disobeyed him. In a tender moment, he kisses her and thereby transforms her into a mortal. Brünnhilde falls into a magical sleep. In order to ensure that a hero will awaken her, Wotan commands Loge (the god of fire) to encircle her body with flames. Only a man without fear—a man truly worthy of Wotan's beloved daughter—will be able to penetrate the fiery circle and discover Brünnhilde. Among the prominent themes in this final section are Magic Sleep (a slow descent), Magic Slumber (a gentle, rocking theme), Magic Fire (crackling sixteenth notes in the woodwinds), Siegfried (a forceful melody sung by Wotan and heard in the low brass), and Fate (a minor/major harmonic twist).

20

Georges Bizet

Carmen, Act I, No. 4, Chorus and No. 5, *Habanera* (1875)

8CD: 6/ 45 – 51

Scene No. 4

46
TENORS.
p leggieramente.
La cloche a son - né; nous, des ouv - ri - è - res, Nous ven-ons i -
Ev-'ry day at noon, you will find us here, Wait-ing for the
p
poco sf
ci guet - ter le re - tour; Et nous vous sui - vrons,
time when the girls ap - pear. Charm-ing to the eye,
poco sf
p
bru - nes ci - ga - riè - 'res, En vous mur - mu - rant des pro - pos d'a -
how we love to court them, Hop - ing that our fond wish-es may come
p
sf
dim.
mour! En vous mur - mu - rant des pro - pos d'a - mour!
true, Hop-ing that our fond wish - es may come true,
sf
dim.
Più lento.
sempre più lento.
lunga.
p
pp
des pro - pos d'a - mour! des pro - pos d'a - mour!
As all lov - ers do, As all lov - ers do.
Più lento.
sempre più lento.
p
pp
lunga.

47
Andantino. (♩. = 60.)
BASSES. (Enter Cigarette-girls, smoking cigarettes, and slowly descending to the stage.)
pp
Voy - ez
Here they
les! re - gards im - pu - dents, Mi - ne co -
are, the bright - eyed co - quettes, Keen and au -
quet - te! Fu - mant tou - tes, du bout des dents
da - cious, I - dly smok - ing their cig - a - rettes,
La ci - ga - ret - - - - te.
And so flir - ta - - - - tious!
sf
p
dim.
pp

(Beat 3/4).
48
SOPRANOS I.
SOPRANOS II.
Dans l'air nous sui - vons des yeux La fu -
Smoke rings make their la - zy way, Soft-ly
Dans l'air nous sui - vons des yeux
Smoke rings make their la - zy way,
mé - e, La fu - mé - e Qui vers les cieux Mon - te,
curl - ing, soft - ly curl - ing. Sky - ward they stray In a
poco cresc.
La fu - mé - e, La fu - mé - e Qui vers les cieux Mon - te,
Soft - ly curl - ing, soft - ly curl - ing. Skyward they stray In a
mon - te par - fu - mé - e; Ce - la mon - te
fra - grant cloud un - furl - ing. Their per - fume per -
mon - te par - fu - mé - e; Ce - la mon -
fra - grant cloud un - furl - ing. Their per - fume
dim.
pp
p

gen - ti - ment A la tête, à la tê - te, Tout dou - ce -
vades the air, Gent-ly steal-ing, gent-ly steal-ing, Sooth-ing our
te gen - ti - ment A la tê - te, à la tê - te,
per - vades the air, Gent-ly steal - ing, gent-ly steal - ing,
poco cresc.
dim.
ment, Ce - la vous met l'â - me en fê - te!
mind To a mel - low pleas - ant feel - ing.
Tout dou - ce - ment, Ce - la vous met l'â - me en fê - te!
Sooth-ing our mind To a mel - low pleas - ant feel - ing.
pp e molto stacc.
Le doux par - ler, le doux par - ler des a - mants,
Those ten - der words you lov - ers say ev - 'ry day
mf
C'est fu - mé - e!
Fade a - way!
pp
Leurs trans - ports, leurs transports et leurs serments,
Your prom-is - es, too, like the smoke in the blue
C'est fu - mé - e!
Fade a - way!

pp
Le doux parler des amants,
Those ten-der words lov-ers say
mf
C'est fu-mé-e!
Fade a-way.
pp
Leurs transports et leurs serments, Oui
Your prom-is-es ev-'ry day They
C'est fu-mé-e!
Fade a-way.
c'est fu-mé-e, c'est fu-mé
fade a-way, they fade a-way.
pp
Oui c'est fu-mé-e, c'est fu-mé-e!
They fade a-way, fade a-way,
sf
dim.
p
e!
Dans l'air nous sui-vons des yeux,
Smoke rings rise and float a-way,
pp
Dans l'air nous sui-
Smoke rings rise and
Dans l'air
Smoke rings
vons des yeux, des yeux, La fu-mé-e!
float a-way, a-way in the blue,
cresc.
nous sui-vons des yeux, La fu-
rise and float a-way, of the
marcato
cresc.

cresc.
La fu - mé - e!
in the blue.
me - e!
sky,
cresc.
La fu - mé - e!
of the sky.
f
Dans l'air
See there,
Ah!
Ah!
f
mosso.
nous sui - vons la fu - mé - e Qui monte en tour -
See them curl - ing and ris - ing and van - ish at
dim.
nant, en tour - nant vers les cieux!
last in the blue of the sky.
p
La fu - mé - e!
See them rise
dim.
pp
dim.

pp
smorzando.
La fu - mé
To the skies.
pp
smorzando.
La fu - mé
To the skies.
ppp
smorzando.
e!
e!
pppp
49
Allegretto molto. (♩.= 108.)
BASSES.
mf
Mais nous ne voyons pas
But where's Carmen to-day?
f
p

Allegro moderato. (♩. = 92.)
(Entrance of Carmen.)
la ___ Carmen - ci - ta!
Why ___ is she mis-sing?
ff
TENORS.
f
La voi - là!
There she is!
BASSES.
f
La voi - là!
Look at her!
p
cresc.
SOPRANOS.
ff
La voi - là!
Where she is
voi - là la Carmen -
there is al-ways ex -
TENORS.
ff
La voi - là!
Where she is
voi - là la Carmen -
there is al-ways ex -
BASSES.
ff
f
ff

ci - ta!
cite - ment!
(to Carmen.)
mf
ci - ta!
cite - ment!
Car - men! sur tes pas nous nous pres - sons
At last! We've been anx - ious - ly wait - ing for
(♩. = 100.)
p
tous!
you!
Car - men! sois gen - til - le au moins réponds-
We men want, at least, an an-swer from
nous,
you.
Et dis-nous quel jour tu nous ai - me - ras!
O Car-men, why must you tease us this way?
sf dim.
p
Car - men, dis - nous quel jour tu nous ai - me - ras!
When will you give your love? Won't you name the day?
p pp

Carmen.
quasi Recit.
mf guily.
(after a swift glance at Don José.)
Quand je vous ai - me - rai? ma foi, je ne sais
When I'll give you my love? Who knows, it's hard to
a tempo Andantino.
colla voce.
p
colla voce.
a tempo.
f
p
pas, Peut - ê - tre ja - mais! peut - ê - tre de -
tell! Per - haps not at all. Per - haps ver - y
a tempo.
p
pp
(resolutely.)
main. Mais pas au - jour -
soon! But one thing I'll
pp
d'hui c'est cer - tain.
say: Not to - day.
pp
mf
attacca.

Scene No. 5

50
Allegretto, quasi Andantino.
Carmen.
Sopranos I & II.
(Cigarette-girls).
Tenors.
(Young men).
Basses.
(Workingmen).
Chorus.
Allegretto, quasi Andantino. (♩= 72.)
Piano.
pp
p
L'amour
Love is
est un oi-seau re - bel-le Que nul ne peut ap-pri-voi - ser, Et c'est
free as the way-ward breeze,_ It can be shy,_ it_ can be bold. Love can
portamento.
bien en vain qu'on l'ap - pel-le, S'il lui con - vient de_ re - fu - ser. Rien n'y
fas-ci-nate, love can tease,_ Its whims and moods are_thou-sand-fold. All at
portamento.
fait, menace ou pri - è-re, L'un par - le bien,_ l'au-tre se tait; Et c'est
once it ar-rives and lin-gers For just how long_ can't be fore-told. Then it

l'au-tre que je pré - fè - re Il n'a rien dit; mais il me
deft-ly slips through your fin-gers, For love's a thing no force can
plait. L'a - mour! l'a -
hold. That's love for
espress.
Sopr. pp legg.
L'a-mour est un oi-seau re - bel-le Que nul ne peut ap-pri-voi -
Love is free as the way-ward breeze, It can be shy, it can be
Ten.
pp legg.
L'a-mour est un oi-seau re - bel-le Que nul ne peut ap-pri-voi -
Love is free as the way-ward breeze, It can be shy, it can be
mour! l'a - mour!
you, That's love
ser, Et c'est bien en vain qu'on l'ap - pel-le S'il lui con -
bold. Love can fas - ci - nate, love can tease, Its whims and
ser, Et c'est bien en vain qu'on l'ap - pel-le S'il lui con -
bold. Love can fas - ci - nate, love can tease, Its whims and

l'a - mour! L'amour est en - fant de Bo - hême, Il n'a ja -
for you! A heart in love is quick-ly burned, It knows no
vient de re - fu - ser!
moods are thou - sand - fold.
vient de re - fu - ser!
moods are thou - sand - fold.
mais, jamais connu de loi, Si tu ne m'ai - mes pas, je t'ai - me; Si
law ex - cept its own de - sire. If I should love you and you spurn me, I'm
je t'aime, prends garde à toi! Si tu ne m'ai - mes pas, si
warning you, you play with fire! If I'm in love with you, don't
Prends garde à toi!
You play with fire!
Prends garde à toi!
You play with fire!

cresc.
tu ne m'aimes pas, je t'ai - me! Mais si je t'ai-me, si je
ev-er, ev-er try to spurn me. My friend, re-mem-ber, if I
Prends garde à toi!
You play with fire.
Prends garde à toi!
You play with fire.
f
pp
cresc.
t'aime, prends gar - de à toi!
love you, you play with fire.
mf
L'amour est en - fant de Bo - hême, Il n'a ja -
A heart in love is quick-ly burned, It knows no
L'a - mour
A heart
mais, jamais con-nu de loi, Si tu ne m'ai-mes pas, je t'ai - me; Si
law ex-cept its own de - sire. If I should love you and you spurn me, I'm
est en - fant de Bo -
in love is quick -

Carmen.
Si tu ne m'ai-mes pas, si
If I'm in love with you, don't
je t'ai-me, prends garde à toi! Prends garde à toi!
warning you, you play with fire, you play with fire!
hê - - - me! Prends garde à toi!
ly burned, you play with fire!
tu ne m'aimes pas, je t'ai - me! Mais si je t'ai-me, si je
ev-er, ev-er try to spurn me. My friend, re-mem-ber, if I
Prends garde à toi!
You play with fire!
Prends garde à toi!
You play with fire!
cresc.

t'ai - me, prends garde à toi!
love you, you play with fire.
cresc.
à toi!
with fire.
à toi!
with fire.
cresc.
51
L'oiseau que tu croy - ais sur - prendre Battit de l'aile et s'en - vo -
Wait for love and you wait for - ev - er, Don't wait at all, it comes to
la; L'amour est loin, tu peux l'at - ten-dre; Tu ne l'at - tends plus, il est
you. Try to grasp it, It's far too clev - er, It flies a - way in - to the

portamento.
là! Tout au - tour de toi vi - te, vi - te, Il vient, s'en va, puis il re -
blue. Love has so man-y forms and shapes, Each day it wears a new dis -
portamento.
vient; Tu crois le te - nir, il t'é - vi - te; Tu crois l'é - vi - ter, il te
guise. Think you've caught it and it es - capes To catch you lat - er by sur -
tient! L'a - mour! l'a -
prise. That's love for
pp legg.
Sopr.
Tout au - tour de toi vi - te, vite Il vient, s'en va, puis il re -
Love has so man-y forms and shapes, Each day it wears a new dis -
Ten.
pp legg.
mour! l'a - mour! l'a -
you, That's love for
vient; Tu crois le te - nir, il t'é - vi - te; Tu crois l'é - vi - ter, il te
guise. Think you've caught it and it es - capes To catch you lat - er by sur -

p
mour! L'amour est en - fant de Bo - hême, Il n'a ja - mais, jamais connu de
you! A heart in love is quick-ly burned, It knows no law ex - cept its own de -
tient!
prise.
loi, Si tu ne m'ai - mes pas, je t'ai - me: Si je t'ai - me prends garde à
sire, If I should love you and you spurn — me, I'm warning you, you play with
toi!
fire!
f
Si tu ne m'ai - mes pas, Si tu ne m'aimes pas, je
If I'm in love with you, don't ev - er, ev - er try to
Prends garde à toi!
You play with fire!
Prends garde à toi!
You play with fire!
f
pp

cresc.
t'ai - me; Mais si je t'ai-me, si je t'ai-me prends gar - de à
spurn me, My friend, re-mem-ber, if I love you, you play — with
Prends garde à toi!
You play with fire!
Prends garde à toi!
You play with fire!
pp
cresc.
mf
toi!
fire!
L'amour est en - fant de Bo - hême, Il n'a ja - mais, jamais con-nu de
A heart in love is quick-ly burned, It knows no law ex - cept its own de -
L'a - - - mour est en -
A heart in
mf
p
f

loi, Si tu ne m'ai - mes pas, je t'ai - me; Si je t'ai - me prends garde à
sire. If I should love you and you spurn — me,. I'm warning you, you play with
fant — de Bo - - - hê - - - - -
love — is quick - - - ly
Carmen.
p
Si tu ne m'ai - mes pas. Si
If I'm in love with you, don't
f
toi! Prends garde à toi!
fire! You play with fire!
me! Prends garde à toi!
burned. You play with fire!
p

p cresc.
tu ne m'aimes pas, je t'ai - me; Mais si je
ev - er, ev - er try to spurn me. My friend, re -
f
Prends garde à toi!
You play with fire,
f
Prends garde à toi!
You play with fire,
f
f
p
f
t'ai - me, si je t'ai - me, prends garde à toi!
mem-ber, if I love you, you play with fire!
p cresc.
f
à toi!
with fire!
p cresc.
f
à toi!
with fire!
p cresc.
f
cresc.
f
f ff

Opéra comique remained France's most unique operatic sound throughout the nineteenth century. Characterized by spoken dialogue and lighter, more popular arias, *opéra comique* can trace many of its characteristics back to the eighteenth century. Despite the genre title, operas in this tradition are not necessarily comedies; romanticism, revolution, and realism all impacted the genre. Georges Bizet (1838–1875) created *Carmen*, the greatest French opera of the nineteenth century, in 1875. Based on a powerful story by Prosper Mérimée, the opera portrays characters drawn from everyday life. Events and passions propel the plot, which culminates in the death of Carmen at the hands of Don José. Exoticism also plays a critical role in the story: the opera is filled with images of Spain and of gypsies, which had captivated the French public's imagination at that time.

At noon a bell rings, signaling a break for the girls working in the cigarette factory. They race out and are greeted by young men who gather daily to flirt and seek love. The men sing a gentle melody, and both the men and woman sing of the enchanted qualities of cigarette smoke. The mood is suddenly broken, as the men ardently seek Carmen. She appears and sings her seductive *Habanera* aria. Literally a dance from Havana, the *habanera* is characterized by a moderate tempo and the alternation of triplets and duplets. Bizet enhances the folk quality of the aria by creating a simple guitarlike accompaniment and limiting the overall range, which features an alluring chromatic descent. The melodic material is exchanged between Carmen and a choir, as she quietly selects her next lover—Don José.

21

Giacomo Puccini

Madama Butterfly, Act II, "Un bel dì"
("One beautiful day") (1904)

8CD: 6/ 52 – 53
4CD: 3/ 50 – 51

But.
dolcemente
rall.
nu - to! Io non gli scen - do in - con - tro. Io no. Mi
told you! But I won't go to meet him. Not yet! I
dolcemente
rall.
pp
Tempo I
con semplicità
met-to là sul ci-glio del col-le e a-spet-to, e a-spet-to gran
wan-der to the rim of the hill-top and wait there. I wait for a
13
pp
rit.
a tempo
tem - po e non mi pe - sa, la lun - ga at - te - sa.
long time but I don't mind it, I'm used to wait - ing.
a tempo
pp rit.
p
animando un poco
E... u - sci - to dal - la fol - la cit - ta - di - na
A man e - mer - ges from the crowd - ed cit - y,
animando un poco

rall. un poco
But.
un uo-mo, un pic-ciol pun - to s'av-via per la col -
a dot on the hor - i - zon: he's set-ting out for our
rall. un poco
p
53
51
Sostenendo molto
Lo stesso movimento
li - na. Chi sa-rà? chi sa-rà? E co-me sa-rà
hill - top. Who on earth can it be? And when at last he
14
Lo stesso movimento
p
rall.
Lento
giun-to che di-rà? che di-rà? Chia-me-rà But-ter-fly dal-la lon -
gets here, what on earth will he say? He will call: "But-ter-fly." I hear him
rall.
ppp
ta - na. Io sen-za dar ri - spo - sta me ne sta-rò na -
faint - ly. But I don't think I'll an - swer, I'll stay a while in

rall. molto
con molto passione
But.
sco - sta un po' per ce - lia, e un po' per non mo-
hid - ing: at first to tease him, but then for fear to
rall. molto
col canto
Andante come prima
con forza
ri - re al pri-mo in-con - tro, ed e-gli al-quan-to in pe - na chia - me-
die in his em-brac - es! Then wor-ried by my si-lence he will
15
con molto passione
ff
p
rit.
rà, chia-me - rà: Pic - ci - na mo-gliet-ti - na o - lez - zo di ver-
call, he will call: "My lit-tle wife, my dar - ling, my fra-grant sweet ver-
rit.
pp
be - na, i no - mi che mi da - va al suo ve - ni - re
be - na..." the names he used to give me when first I met him.
r. h.
cresc.

(to Suzuki)
But.
Tut-to que-sto av-ver-ra, te lo pro-met-to. Tien-ti la tua pa-
That's the way it will be, you may be-lieve me. You have no right to
u-ra, io con si-cu-ra fe-de l'a-spet-to.
doubt it while I with faith un-shak-en a-wait him!
poco rall. e cresc.
Largamente
16
(Butterfly and Suzuki embrace, moved.)
dim.
meno f
rit.
(Butterfly dismisses Suzuki who exits through the door at the left. Butterfly gazes after her sadly.)
pp sostenuto
mf
p

Giacomo Puccini (1858–1924), the leading figure in Italian opera at the turn of the century, composed some of the most popular operas of all time. He is often linked to *verismo* (realism), the Italian operatic movement in which the characters are drawn from everyday life and are subject to real-life passions. These qualities are most readily seen in his operas *La bohème* (1896) and *Tosca* (1900). *Madama Butterfly*, one of Puccini's most beloved works, combines verismo elements with the exoticism of Japanese culture.

The libretto for *Madama Butterfly*, by Giuseppe Giacosa and Luigi Illica, has a complex history. John Luther Long expanded Pierre Loti's original tale *Madame Chrysanthème* into a short story. David Belasco then adapted this story for a stage production, which in turn inspired Puccini to create the opera. Although the premiere for *Madama Butterfly* was a disaster, a revised version became a sensation in subsequent performances.

The plot centers on a young Japanese woman, Cio-Cio-San, who is a *geisha*, the equivalent to the Western courtesan. She renounces her profession and religion to marry an American naval officer, B. F. Pinkerton. After Pinkerton leaves for the United States, Cio-Cio-San gives birth to his son. When Pinkerton finally returns to Japan, Cio-Cio-San learns that he has married an American woman. She gives her child to him, and in a powerful scene, commits suicide rather than go back to the life of a geisha.

Throughout the opera, Puccini brilliantly combines the melody-oriented Italian opera style with Japanese colors, including pentatonic and whole-tone scales, traditional Japanese melodies, and the sound of a *gagaku* orchestra (harp, flute and piccolo, and bells). In the well-known aria "Un bel dì" ("One beautiful day"), Cio-Cio-San envisions the joy of Pinkerton's return to Japan. The aria begins in a dreamlike state, accompanied by a solo violin. As she imagines the arriving ship, the music becomes more intense and speechlike. Finally, the emotional level reaches a powerful climax, with the full orchestra supporting the vocal melody on the text "l'aspetto" (I will wait for him).

22

Peter Ilyich Tchaikovsky

The Nutcracker, Three Dances: *March, Dance of the Sugar Plum Fairy, Russian Dance (Trepak)* (1892)

8CD: 6/54 – 62
4CD: 3/52 – 54

March

54 52

Fl.
Gr. Fl.
Ob.
Cl.
Fg.
pp
mf
Cor. (F)
mp
Trbe. (A)
Tbni. Tuba
Mit Paukenschlägel.
Piat.
Vl.
Vle.
pizz.
Celli
C.-B.

10
Fl.
Ob.
Cl.
Fg.
Cor. (F)
Trbe. (A)
Tbni. Tuba
Piat.
Vl.
Vle.
Celli
C.-B.
pizz.
pizz.

Fl.
Ob.
Cl.
cre - - - - scen - - - - do
f
Fg.
Cor. (F)
Trbe. (A)
Tbni. Tuba
Mit Paukenschlägel.
Piat.
Vl.
Vle.
Celli
C.-B.

20
Fl.
Ob.
Cl.
Fg.
Cor. (F)
Trbe. (A)
Tbni. Tuba
Piat.
Vl.
Vle.
Celli
C.-B.
pizz.
arco
mf
f

Fl.
Ob.
Cl.
Fg.
Cor. (F)
Trbe. (A)
Tbni. Tuba
Piat.
Vl.
Vle.
Celli
C.-B.

30
Fl.
Ob.
Cl.
Fg.
Cor. (F)
Trbe. (A)
Tbni. Tuba
Piat.
Vl.
Vle.
Celli
C.-B.
mf
p
pp
pizz.

Fl.
Ob.
Cl.
Fg.
Cor. (F)
Trbe. (A)
Tbni. Tuba
Mit Paukenschlägel.
Piat.
Vl.
Vle.
Celli
C.-B.

40
Fl.
Ob.
Cl.
pp
cre - scen - do
f
ff
Fg.
Cor. (F)
Trbe. (A)
Tbni. Tuba
Mit Paukenschlägel.
Piat.
Vl.
Vle.
pizz.
Celli
C.-B.
p

55
53
Fl.
Ob.
Cl.
Fg.
Cor. (F)
Trbe. (A)
Tbni. Tuba
Piat.
Vl.
Vle.
Celli
C.-B.
mf
marcato
arco

Fl.
Ob.
Cl.
Fg.
Cor. (F)
Tibe. (A)
Tbni. Tuba
Piat.
Vl.
Vle.
Celli
C.-B.

56
54
Fl.
Ob.
Cl.
Fg.
Cor. (F)
Trbe. (A)
Tbni. Tuba
Piat.
Vl.
Vle.
Celli
C.-B.
marcato
marcato

50
Fl.
Ob.
Cl.
Fg.
Cor. (F)
Trbe. (A)
Tbni. Tuba
Piat.
Vl.
Vle.
Celli
C.-B.

Fl.
Ob.
Cl.
Fg.
Cor. (F)
Trbe. (A)
Tbni. Tuba
Piat.
Vl.
Vle.
Celli
C.-B.
mf
cresc.
pizz.

Fl.
Ob.
Cl.
Fg.
Cor. (F)
Trbe. (A)
Tbni. Tuba
Mit Paukenschlägel.
Piat.
Vl.
Vle.
arco
Celli
arco
C.-B.

60
Fl.
Ob.
Cl.
Fg.
Cor. (F)
Trbe. (A)
Tbni. Tuba
Piat.
Vl.
Vle.
Celli
C.-B.
pizz.
pizz.

Fl.
Ob.
Cl.
Fg.
Cor. (F)
Trbe. (A)
Tbni. Tuba
Piat.
Vl.
Vle.
Celli
C.-B.
mf cresc.
cresc.
ff
Mit Paukenschlägel.

Fl.
Ob.
Cl.
Fg.
Cor. (F)
Trbe. (A)
Tbni. Tuba
Piat.
Vl.
Vle.
Celli
C.-B.
mf
f
pizz.

70
Fl.
Ob.
Cl.
Fg.
Cor. (F)
Trbe. (A)
Tbni. Tuba
Piat.
Vl.
Vle.
Celli
C.-B.
arco
arco
arco

Fl.
Ob.
Cl.
Fg.
Cor. (F)
Trbe. (A)
Tbni. Tuba
Piat.
Vl.
Vle.
Celli
C.-B.

Fl.
Ob.
Cl.
Fg.
Cor. (F)
Trbe. (A)
Tbni. Tuba
Piat.
Vl.
Vle.
Celli
C.-B.
mf
cresc.
pizz.

80
Fl.
Ob.
Cl.
Fg.
Cor. (F)
Trbe. (A)
Tbni. Tuba
Mit Paukenschlögel.
Piat.
Vl.
Vle.
Celli
C.-B.
arco
arco

Fl.
Ob.
Cl.
Fg.
Cor. (F)
Trbe. (A)
Tbni. Tuba
Piat.
Vl.
Vle.
Celli
C.-B.
f
sf
mf
pizz.

Fl.
Ob.
Cl.
Fg.
Cor. (F)
Trbe. (A)
Tbni. Tuba
Piat.
Vl.
Vle.
Celli
C.-B.
mf
cresc.
f
ff
Mit Paukenschlägel.
arco

Dance of the Sugar Plum Fairy

Cl.b.
10
mf
fp
Cel.
f
Vl.
Vle.
Celli
C.-B.
Cl.
I.
p
Cl.b.
p
pp
Cel.
mf
Vl.
p
Vle.
Celli
C.-B.

20
Fl.
Ob.
C.Ingl.
Cl.
Cl.b.
Fg.
Cor. (F)
Cel.
div.
Vl.
Vle.
Celli
C.-B.
arco
arco
arco
arco

58
Fl.
Ob.
C.Ingl.
Cl.
Cl. b.
Fg.
Cor. (F)
Cel.
Vl.
Vle.
Celli
C.-B.
pp
mf
p
sf
arco

Fl.
Ob.
C.Ingl.
Cl.
Cl.b.
Fg.
Cor. (F)
Cel.
Vl.
Vle.
Celli
C.-B.
pp
mf
sf
p

30
Fl.
Ob.
C.Ingl.
Cl.
Cl.b.
Fg.
Cor. (F)
Cel.
Vl.
Vle.
Celli
C.-B.

Cel.
Cel.
59
Fl.
Fg.
Cel.
Vl.
pp a punto d'arco
pp a punto d'arco
Vle.
pp a punto d'arco
Celli
pp a punto d'arco
C.-B.

40
I.
Cl.
Cel.
cresc.
Vl.
Vle.
Celli
C.-B.
p
mf
pp

50.
Fl.
Ob.
C.Ingl.
Cl.
Cl. b.
Fg.
Cor. (F)
Cel.
div..
Vl.
Vle.
Celli
C.-B.
pizz.

Russian Dance (Trepak)

10
Fl.
Ob.
C.Ingl.
Cl.
Cl.b.
Fg.
Cor. (F)
Trbe. (A)
Tbni.
Tuba
Timp.
Tamb.
Vl.
Vle.
Celli
C.-B.

20
Fl.
Ob.
C.Ingl.
Cl.
Cl.b.
Fg.
Còr. (F)
Trbe. (A)
Tbni. Tuba
Timp.
Tamb.
Vl.
Vle.
Celli
C.-B.

Fl.
Ob.
C.Ingl.
Cl.
Cl.b.
Fg.
Cor. (F)
Trbe. (A)
Tbni. Tuba
Timp.
Tamb.
Vl.
Vle.
Celli
C.-B.

61
30
Fl.
Cb.
C.Ingl.
Cl.
Cl.b.
Fg.
Cor. (F)
Trbe. (A)
Tbni. Tuba
Timp.
Tamb.
Vl.
Vle.
Celli
C.-B.

Fl.
sempre staccato
sempre staccato
Ob.
C.Ingl.
Cl.
Cl. b.
Fg.
Cor. (F)
mf
mf
Trbe. (A)
Tbni. Tuba
mf
Timp.
Tamb.
Vl.
Vle.
cresc.
Celli
cresc.
C.-B.
cresc.

40
Fl.
Ob.
a 2.
C.Ingl.
Cl.
Cl. b.
Fg.
Cor. (F)
Trbe. (A)
Tbni. Tuba
Timp.
Tamb.
Vl.
sempre ff
sempre ff
Vle.
Celli
C.-B.

50
a 2.
Fl.
Ob.
C.Ingl.
Cl.
Cl.b.
Fg.
Cor. (F)
Trbe. (A)
Tbni. Tuba
Timp.
Tamb.
Vl.
Vle.
Celli
C.-B.

Fl.
Ob.
Ingl.
Cl.
Cl. b.
Fg.
Cor. (F)
Trbe. (A)
Tbni. Tuba
Timp.
Tamb.
Vl.
Vle.
Celli
C.-B.

62
60
Fl.
Ob.
C.Ingl.
Cl.
Cl.b.
Fg.
a 2.
Cor. (F)
Trbe. (A)
Tbni. Tuba
Timp.
Tamb.
Vl.
Vle.
Celli
C.-B.
ff
sf

Fl.
Ob.
C.Ingl.
Cl.
Cl. b.
Fg.
Cor. (F)
Trbe. (A)
Tbni. Tuba
Timp.
Tamb.
Vl.
Vle.
Celli
C.-B.

stringendo
70
Fl.
Ob.
C.Ingl.
Cl.
Cl.b.
Fg.
Cor. (F)
Trbe. (A)
Tbni. Tuba
Timp.
Tamb.
Vl.
Vle.
Celli
C.-B.
sempre *fff*

Fl.
Ob.
C.Ingl.
Cl.
Cl.b.
Fg.
Cor. (F)
Trbe. (A)
Tbni. Tuba
Timp.
Tamb.
Vl.
Vle.
Celli
C.-B.

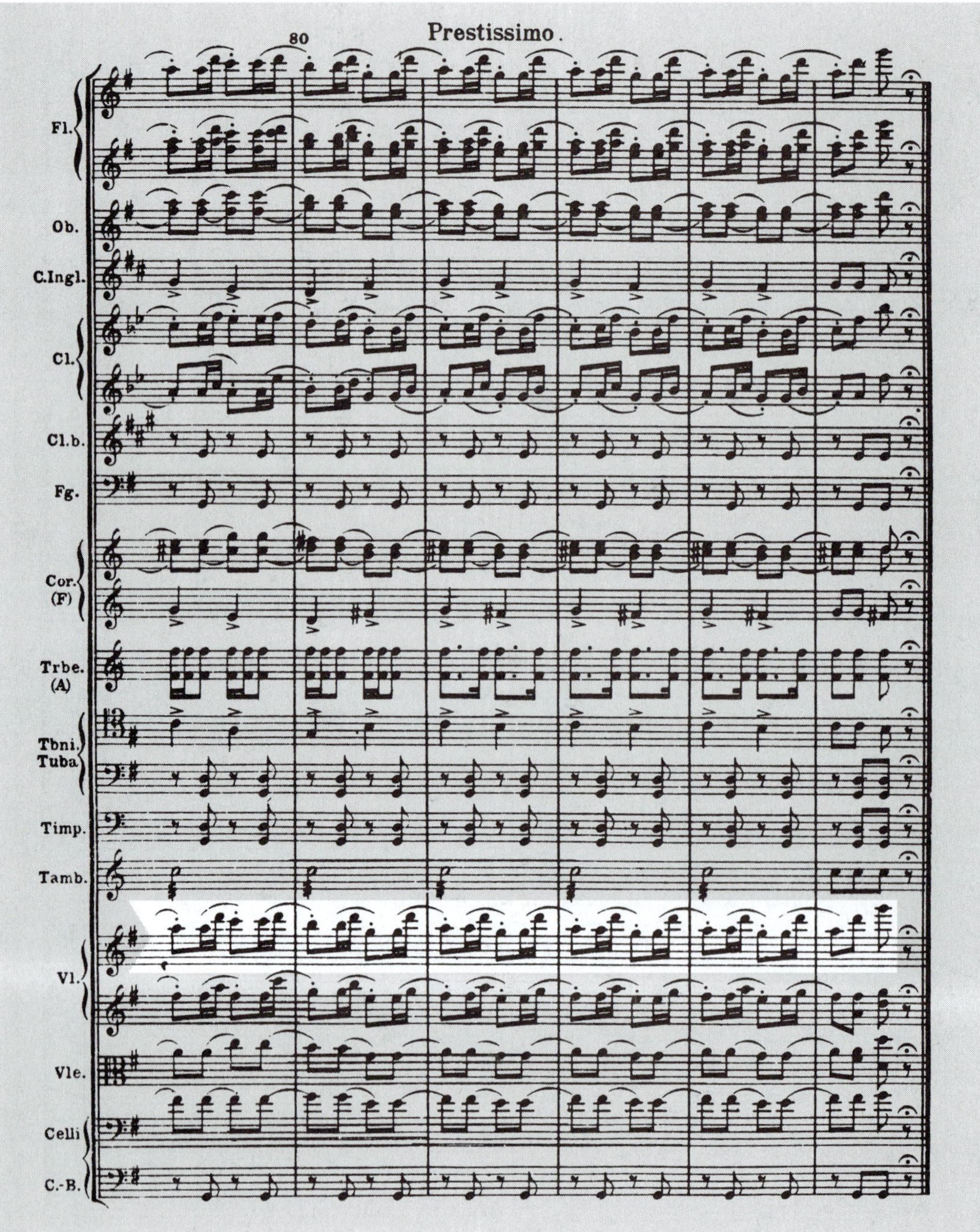
80
Prestissimo.
Fl.
Ob.
C.Ingl.
Cl.
Cl.b.
Fg.
Cor. (F)
Trbe. (A)
Tbni. Tuba
Timp.
Tamb.
Vl.
Vle.
Celli
C.-B.

In the second half of the nineteenth century, Russia became the principal center for ballet, and Peter Ilyich Tchaikovsky (1840–1893) emerged as its first great composer. Of his three masterworks in the genre, *Swan Lake, Sleeping Beauty,* and *The Nutcracker,* the last has become a popular tradition for December performances. The story, set at a Christmas party, is the product of two prominent literary figures: E. T. A. Hoffmann wrote the original story, and Alexandre Dumas *père* created an expanded version that was used as the basis for the ballet's scenario.

The essential elements of the plot occur in the first act. A handsome prince has been cursed, taking the shape of a grotesque nutcracker. The spell can only be broken if someone falls in love with him as he is, and if the evil Mouse King is killed. At midnight, a battle between toy soldiers and giant mice ensues, during which Clara kills the Mouse King. Coupled with her love for the nutcracker, this action breaks the spell, and the handsome prince reappears. The second act, set in the land of the sweets ruled by the Sugar Plum Fairy, is an extended celebration of Clara's heroic deed, in which dancers from all over the world appear in order to entertain and honor Clara.

The success of this ballet is a tribute to Tchaikovsky's ability to create memorable melodies and colorful, rich orchestrations. In keeping with the traditions of French ballet, Tchaikovsky incorporates a number of popular dances into the work. Each of the three excerpts included here is in **A–B–A** dance form. The *March,* which occurs at the beginning of the party scene in Act I, is a nineteenth-century popular dance in duple meter and a moderate tempo. The other two dances are from Act II. The delicate orchestration in the *Dance of the Sugar Plum Fairy* features a solo celesta, a pizzicato string accompaniment, and several brief woodwind solos. A cadenza for the celesta precedes the reprise of the **A** section. A number of the dances from Act II evoke the styles of exotic lands. The *Trepak* is based on a vigorous dance for men that is characterized by the distinctive Cossack *prisiadka* (kicking the legs from a squatting position).

23

Gustav Mahler

Das Lied von der Erde (*The Song of the Earth*),
Third movement, *Von der Jugend* (*Of Youth*) (1908–9)

8CD: 6/ 63 – 66

III. *Von der Jugend* (*Of Youth*)

kl. Fl.
1.2. Fl.
1. Ob.
2. Ob.
1. Kl. in B
2. Kl.
1.2. Fag.
1. Vl.
2. Vl.
Br.
Ten.-St.
Vlc.
cresc.
zu 2
stacc.
lon aus grü-nem und aus wei-ßem Porzel-lan.
Wie der Rücken ei-nes Ti - gers wölbt die

1. Fl.
2. Fl.
1. Ob.
2. Ob.
1. Kl. in B
2. Kl.
1.2. Fag.
Ten.-St.
Vlc.
p subito
zu 2
dim.
pizz.
Brücke sich aus Ja - de zu dem Pa-vil-lon hin - ü - - - ber.

64
32
kl. Fl.
sempre f
1.2. Fl.
zu 2
dim.
1. Ob.
2. Ob.
1.2. Kl. in B
1.2. Fag.
dim. - - - p
1.3. Hr.
in F
2.4. Hr.
1. Trp. in B
in B
mit Dämpfer
Trgl.
sempre pp
gr. Tr. Beck.
1. Vl.
Griffbrett
pp Zart, aber
2. Vl.
Br.
Ten.-St.
In dem
arco
pizz.
Vlc. get.
Kb.

40
kl. Fl.
1.2. Fl.
1.2. Ob.
1.2. Kl. in B
1.2. Fag.
1.3. Hr. in F
2.4. Hr.
1. Trp. in B
Trgl.
gr. Tr. Beck.
1. Vl.
2. Vl.
Br.
Ten.-St.
Vlc. get.
Kb.
zu 2
mit Empfindung.
arco
pizz.
Häus-chen sitzen Freun - de, schön ge-kleidet, trin - ken, plau - dern, man - che schreiben Verse nie - der.

48
kl. Fl.
1.2. Fl.
zu 2
dim.
1.2. Ob.
1.2. Kl. in B
1.2. Fag.
1.3. Hr. in F
2.4. Hr.
1. Trp. in F.
Trgl.
gr. Tr. Beck.
[pp]
1. Vl.
pp espress.
2. Vl.
Br. get.
arco
Ten.-St.
Ih - re seidnen Ärmel glei - ten rückwärts, ih - re seid - nen
Vlc.
pizz.
Kb.
sf

56
kl. Fl.
1.2. Fl.
zu 2
1. Ob.
2. Ob.
1. Kl.
in B
2. Kl.
1.2. Fag.
1.3. Hr.
in F
2.4. Hr.
Trgl.
gr. Tr.
Beck.
Vl. Solo
1. Vl.
2. Vl.
Br.
pizz.
Ten-St.
Müt - zen hok - ken lu-stig tief im Nak - ken.
Vlc.
Kb.
espress.

65
Ruhiger
kl. Fl.
1.2. Fl.
1. Ob.
2. Ob.
1. Kl.
in B
2. Kl.
1.2. Fag.
1.3. Hr.
in F
2.4. Hr.
zu 2
gr. Tr.
Beck.
Ruhiger
Solo-Vl.
cresc.
p espress.
pp espress.
1. Vl.
2. Vl.
Br.
arco
Ten.-St.
Auf des klei - nen,
Vlc.
Kb.
pizz.

72
Langsam
kl. Fl.
1.2. Fl.
1.2. Ob.
1.2. Kl. in B
1.2. Fag.
1.2. Hr. in F
gr. Tr. Beck.
1. Vl.
2. Vl.
Br.
Ten.-St.
klei - nen Tei - ches stil - ler, stil - ler Was - ser - flä - che zeigt sich al - les wun - der -
Vlc.
Kb.

81
Poco rit.
Rit. molto
Tempo (etwas mäßig)
1.2. Fl.
1.2. Ob.
1.2. Kl. in B
1.2. Fag.
1. Hr. in F
2. Vl.
Br.
mit Dämpfer
[mit Dämpfer]
Ten.-St.
lich im Spie - gel - bil - de.
Vlc.
Kb.

66
Rit.
A tempo (mäßig)
Rit.
Molto rit.
Tempo I subito
1.2. Fl.
1.2. Ob.
1.2. Kl. in B
1.2. Fag.
1.2. Hr. in F
4. Hr.
Trgl.
gr. Tr. Beck.
(ohne Dämpfer)
1. Vl.
2. Vl.
Br.
Vlc.
Kb.
espress. molto
p molto espress.
Tutti
arco
pizz.
Dämpfer ab!
zu 2
1. Hr. in F
Ten.-St.
stacc.
Al - les auf dem Kop - fe ste - hend in dem Pa - vil - lon aus grü - nem und aus wei - ßem

105
kl. Fl.
1.2. Ob.
1.2. Kl. in B
1.2. Fag.
Trgl.
1. Vl.
2. Vl.
Br.
Ten.-St.
Vlc.
Por - zel - lan; wie ein Halb-mond scheint die Brük - ke, um - ge - kehrt der Bo - gen.

111
kl. Fl.
1.2. Fl.
1.2. Ob.
1.2. Kl. in B
1.2. Fag.
1. Vl.
2. Vl.
Br.
Ten.-St.
Vlc.
Freun - de, schön ge - klei - det, trin - ken, plau - dern.

TEXT AND TRANSLATION

Mitten in dem kleinen Teiche steht ein Pavillon aus grünem und aus weissem Porzellan.	In the middle of the little pool stands a pavilion of green and of white porcelain.
Wie der Rücken eines Tigers wölbt die Brücke sich aus Jade zu dem Pavillon hinüber.	Like the back of a tiger the bridge of jade arches over to the pavilion.
In dem Häuschen sitzen Freunde, schön gekleidet, trinken, plaudern, manche schreiben Verse nieder.	In the little house, friends are sitting beautifully dressed, drinking, chatting; several are writing verses.
Ihre seidnen Ärmel gleiten rückwärts, ihre seidnen Mützen hocken lustig tief im Nacken.	Their silken sleeves slip backwards, their silken caps perch gaily on the back of their necks.
Auf des kleinen Teiches stiller Wasserfläche zeigt sich alles wunderlich im Spiegelbilde.	On the little pool's still surface everything appears fantastically in a mirror image.
Alles auf dem Kopfe stehend in dem Pavillon aus grünem und aus weissem Porzellan;	Everything is standing on its head in the pavilion of green and of white porcelain;
wie ein Halbmond scheint die Brücke umgekehrt der Bogen. Freunde, schön gekleidet, trinken, plaudern.	like a half-moon stands the bridge, upside-down its arch. Friends, beautifully dressed, are drinking, chatting.

Gustav Mahler (1860–1911) primarily composed in two genres—symphonies and song cycles. Since the symphonies often include voices and the song cycles are generally arranged for orchestral accompaniment, the stylistic differences between the two are minimal. Both genres incorporate large orchestral forces, but, as evident in this work, Mahler skillfully uses the array of instruments as a colorful palette for delicate orchestration. Also typical of both genres are extended lyrical expressions and intricate contrapuntal textures.

Das Lied von der Erde (*The Song of the Earth*), Mahler's foremost song cycle, was composed near the end of his career. It is unique among his works in the genre in that he specifies two solo voices: a tenor and an alto/baritone. The texts of the six songs are based on Hans Bethge's *Chinese Flute.* Reflecting the growing interest and appreciation in nineteenth-century Europe for non-Western arts, this collection contains adaptations of Chinese poetry by a number of writers, most notably the revered eighth-century poet Li-T'ai-Po. In the third song of the cycle, *Von der Jugend* 8(*Of Youth*), Mahler effectively evokes a Chinese character through the use of pentatonic scales and a delicate orchestration; the low brass are omitted, and the woodwinds, solo trumpet, staccato strings, and triangle play prominent roles in support of the tenor voice. The **A–B–A** form of the song, with a contrasting lyrical section in the middle, creates an arch form that can be seen as a musical counterpart to the bridge of jade described in the poem.

24

Claude Debussy

Prélude à "L'après-midi d'un faune" (*Prelude to "The Afternoon of a Faun"*) (1894)

8CD: 7/1–5
4CD: 3/55–59

1 55

5
HAUTB.
CL.
1°
p
più p
CORS
3°
p
p
p
più p
1re HARPE
glissando
2e HARPE
pp
pp
ppp
(sourdine)
Div.
pp
(sourdine)
Div.
pp
(sourdine)
pp
pp
Div. (sourdine)
pp
pp
pp
pp

11
1.re FL.
SOLO
HAUTB.
expressif
CL.
B.ons
CORS
Div. (sur la touche)
(sur la touche)
(sur la touche)
à 2

16
Fl.
1° et 2°
p cre - scen - do f f f
Hautb.
à 2
p cre - scen - do f f
Cor angl.
p cre - scen - do f f f
Cl.
1°
à 2
p cre - scen - do f f
1°
dim. et retenu
Bons
à 2
p cre - scen - do
f
1, 2.
(1)
(2)
Cors
p cre - scen - do f f f
dim.
3, 4.
(3)
p cre - scen - do f f f
dim.
Div.
p cresc. f f f
position nat.
cre - scen - do f f f
position nat.
cre - scen - do f f f
position nat.
cre - scen - do f f f
Unies.
cresc. f

21
1re FL.
SOLO
légèrement et expressif
p
2o
pp
CORS
4o
pp
8
1re HARPE
pp
2e HARPE
pp
pp
pp
Div.
pizz.
pp

23
1re FL.
CL.
Bons
1er COR
1re HARPE
2e HARPE
pp
p
1o
Unis
pizz.

26
p
Fl.
2°
Cl.
Bons
Cors
4°
pp
1re Harpe
2e Harpe p
Div.
arco
Div.
arco
arco

28
Cédez . . .
Fl.
Bons
Cédez . . .
Div.
Unis
dim.
Unis
Div.
dim.
dim.
Div.
arco

2
56
30
1re Fl.
au Mouvt
Cl
sourdines
Cors
sourdines
1re Harpe
au Mouvt
ôtez vite les sourdines
ôtez vite les sourdines
ôtez vite les sourdines
pizz.

32
(Sans trainer)
1re FL.
CL.
Bons
CORS
1re HARPE
(Sans trainer)
pizz.
arco
Div.

35
3
57
En animant (M.M. ♩= 72)
1re FL.
HAUTB.
1° SOLO
doux et expressif
CL.
Bons
1°
CORS
1re HARPE
En animant
pizz.
Div.
arco
pizz
arco
pizz.
Unis

38
HAUTB.
(à 2)
cre - - scen - - do mf
COR ANGL.
cre - - scen - - do mf
CL.
1°
cresc.
(2)
B^ons
cresc.
mf
1. 2.
cresc.
CORS
3. 4.
3°
p
mf
arco
cresc.
mf
cre - - scen - - do mf
cre - - scen - - do mf
arco
cre - - scen - - do mf
Div.
p
arco
mf

42
1°
FL.
2° 3°
Toujours en animant
cresc.
HAUTB.
2°
COR ANGL.
CL.
Changez en Sib
1°
à 2
Bons
CORS
Toujours en animant
Div.
Div.
Unis

45
FL.
HAUTB.
COR ANGL.
CL.
Bons
CORS
mf
f
f très en dehors
1o
f (en dehors)
3o (en dehors)
più f
dim.
Div.

49
retenu
1er mouvt (M.M. ♩ = 60)
FL.
HAUTB.
COR ANGL.
CL.
Solo
p doux et expressif
Bons
CORS
1re HARPE
2e HARPE
(en dehors)
Div.
pizz.
dim.

4
58
54
Cédez un peu . . .
Même mouvt et très soutenu (M.M. ♩ = 56)
p expressif et très soutenu
mf
Fl.
Hautb.
p expressif et très soutenu
Cor angl.
p expressif et très soutenu
Cl.
p expressif et très soutenu
Bons
pp
p
Cors
(3. 4.)
pp
Cédez un peu . . .
Même mouvt et très soutenu
pp
arco

59
Fl.
2° et 3°
Hautb.
à 2
Cor Angl.
Cl.
Bons
1°
Cors
1.2.
3.4.
4°
Unis
Div.
Unis
cre - scen - do
cresc
p cresc
più f

63
En animant
pp subito
FL.
HAUTB.
COR ANGL.
CL.
Bons
pp
à 2
CORS
1re HARPE
2e HARPE
cre
En animant
Unis
très expressif et très soutenu
Div.

66
Toujours animé
scen
do
cre
scen
do molto
Fl.
Hautb.
à 2
Cor Angl.
Cl.
Bons
Cors
3o
4o
1re Harpe
2e Harpe
mp
Toujours animé

69
FL.
HAUTB.
COR ANGL.
CL.
Bons
à 2
CORS
3º
4º
1re HARPE
2e HARPE
mf
f
ff

72
Cédez un peu
(M.M. ♩= 60)
FL.
mf
CL.
1°
p très doux
B^ons
CORS
p espressif et doux
4°
3°
1re HARPE
sfz
V^ons SOLO
Cédez un peu . .
p doux et expressif
sourdines
Div.
pp

76
HAUTB.
1°
pp très doux
ppp
CL.
più p
pp
ppp
CORS
più p
pp
ppp
Von SOLO
p
pp
5
59
79 (M.M. ♩= 84)
Mouvt du Début
1re FL.
doux et expressif
p
HAUTB.
CL.
CORS
pp
1re HARPE
Von SOLO
Mouvt du Début
(1rs Vns)
Div.
pp
Div.
pp
Div.
pp
Div.
pp

82
1re FL.
Un peu plus animé
pp
HAUTB.
1o
p
sf
CL.
pp
Bons
pp
1. 2.
sourdines
pp
CORS
3. 4.
sourdines
3e
pp
1re HARPE
préparez le ton de Mib
Un peu plus animé
pizz.
pizz.
pizz.
pizz.
pp
pp

84
1
FL.
2. 3.
HAUTB.
COR ANGL.
CL.
Bons
CORS
sur la touche
arco
arco
arco
pizz
Div.

86
HAUTB.
1er mouvt
doux et expressif
p
CORS
1re HARPE
pp
2e HARPE accordez sur SI#-DO♮, RÉ#-MI♭, FA#-SOL♭, LA#
1er mouvt
pos. nat.
pos. nat.
Div.
pos. nat.
Unis.
Div.
Div.

89
dans le mouvt plus animé
1.
FL.
2. 3.
1o
HAUTB.
COR ANGL.
sfz
CL.
Changez en La♮
pp
Bons
pp
p
CORS
3o
pp
1re HARPE
2e HARPE
glissando
dans le mouvt plus animé
pizz.
pizz.
pizz.
pizz.
pp
pp

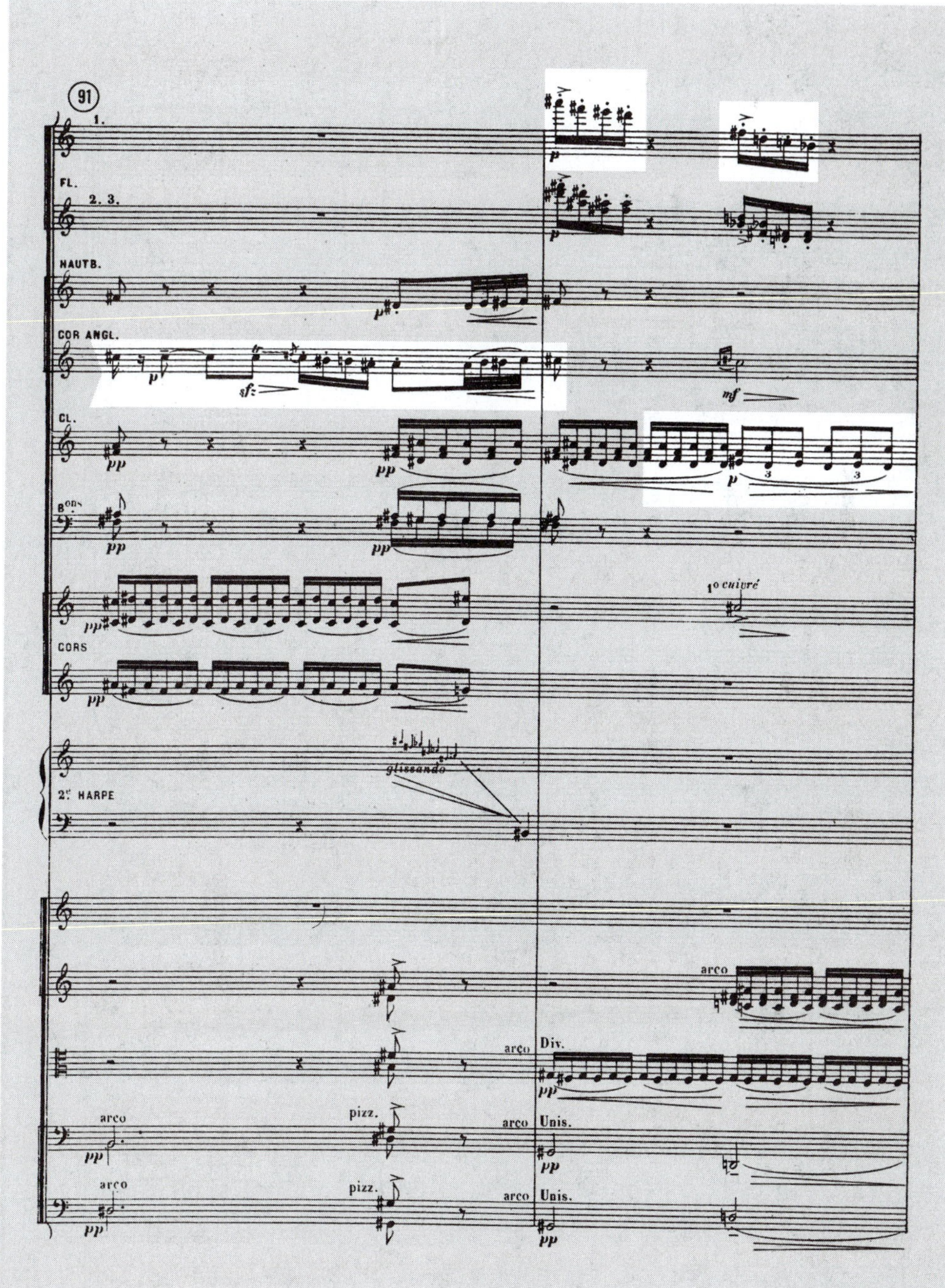
91
1.
FL.
2. 3.
HAUTB.
COR ANGL.
sf
mf
CL.
pp
p
Bons
1o cuivré
CORS
glissando
2e HARPE
arco
Div.
pizz.
Unis.
pp

93
retenu
Dans le 1er mouvt avec plus de langueur
FL.
p expressif et doux
2°
COR ANGL.
CL.
pp
1° bouché
naturel
p
pp
CORS
3° et 4°
CYMB. ANTIQUES
DEUX 1rs Vons
sans sourdines
pp très doux et expressif
retenu
sur la touche
1rs Vons Divisés
2ds Vons Divisés
ALTOS Divisés
Div. sur la touche

96
FL.
HAUTB.
CL.
à 2
B^ons
CORS
1° sourdine
3° et 4°
CYMB. ANT.
1 v^lle SOLO

99
FL.
HAUTB.
CL.
8ons
CORS
sourdine
2°
CYMB. ANT.
1re HARPE
pos. nat.
pos. nat.
pos. nat.
pos. nat.
pos. nat.
pos. nat.
expressif (un peu en dehors)
1 vlle SOLO

102
Retenu
1er Fl.
(a tempo)
Très retenu
HAUTB.
1°
SOLO
COR ANGL.
CL.
B^ons
CORS
2°
(sourdines)
Très retenu
Retenu
(a tempo)

106
Très lent et très retenu jusqu'à la fin
FL.
2. 3.
HAUTB.
1. 2. (sourdines)
CORS
3. 4. (sourdines)
CYMB. ANT.
1re et 2e HARPES
1ère
Très lent et très retenu jusqu'à la fin
Unis
Div.
pizz.
pizz.

In the late nineteenth century, France was the principal center for modern arts. In painting, Monet created a new artistic vision in a movement called Impressionism. Capturing the interplay of light and objects, Impressionism broke with the long-standing Renaissance traditions of perspective. Similarly, French poets embraced a new literary style known as Symbolism, in which images and moods are suggested rather than described. Paralleling these developments, French composers explored innovative approaches to creating a musical work of art.

Claude Debussy (1862–1918) developed a distinctive musical style that is also known as Impressionism. Among the parallels to its artistic counterpart are Debussy's colorful, yet delicate timbres and the frequent vagueness of form, rhythmic pulse, melody, and harmony. The last of these is the most far-reaching innovation of the new style. Rejecting traditional functional harmony, Debussy explores new harmonic techniques, including whole-tone scales, parallel chords, ninth chords, and the establishment of tonal centers without relying on functional tonality.

The *Prélude à "L'après-midi d'un faune" (Prelude to "The Afternoon of a Faun")* is a seminal work in orchestral literature. Set as a single-movement symphonic poem, the composition was initially performed prior to a reading by Stéphane Mallarmé of his Symbolist poem "L'après-midi d'un faune." The poem describes a mythical faun (half man, half goat) who awakens from a dream. He struggles to recall a vague memory of an encounter with three nymphs, and is uncertain whether the event actually occurred or whether it was a dream. Fatigued by the process, the faun finally returns to sleep. The following excerpt is from the opening of the poem:

These nymphs I would perpetuate.
    So light
their gossamer embodiment, floating on the air
inert with heavy slumber.
    Was it a dream I loved?
My doubting harvest of the bygone night ends
in countless tiny branches; together remaining
a whole forest, they prove, alas, that since I am
    alone,
my fancied triumph was but the ideal
    imperfection of roses.

Let us reflect . . . or suppose those women that
you idolize
were but imaginings of your fantastic lust!

Debussy brilliantly captures the moods of the poem in his prelude. The **A–B–A** form mirrors the arch structure that begins with the faun waking and ends with him returning to sleep. The delicate images are reflected in the subtle orchestrations, including an extended flute solo and a prominent harp part; the gentle rhythmic pulse; and the lack of tension that would normally result from functional tonality. The ardor of the faun can be heard in the extended melody from the middle section of the work. The movement comes to a quiet close, highlighted by the gentle sound of antique cymbals.

25

Maurice Ravel

Don Quichotte à Dulcinée (Don Quixote to Dulcinea),
Two Songs (1932–33)

8CD: 7/ 6 - 11

I. *Chanson romanesque (Romanesque Song)*

Editor's note: Because the voice dominates in this work, no highlighting is necessary.

7
Clar.
Fag.
Arpa
Canto
tant tourner vous of-fen-sa, Je lui dé-pê-che-rais Pan-ça: Vous la ver-
hush the winds and seas, my love, I will say to the sun a-bove, "Cease in your
Violini
Viole
Vlli
Contrab.
arco
pizz.
13
7
Fag.
Corni
Tromba
Sord.
Arpa
Canto
-riez fixe et se tai-re. Si
flight, stay in your turn-ing!" If
Violini
Div. pizz.
Viole
Vlli
Contrab.

19
Oboe
Corno I.
Canto
vous me disiez que l'en - nui Vous vient du ciel trop fleuri d'as-tres, Dé - chirant les divins ca - das-tres, Je
ev - er for morning you sigh, The stars I will hide and their wonder, The splendour of heav'n tear a - sun-der, And
Unis
arco
Violini
Viole
Vlli
Contrab.
pizz.
25
Oboe
Fag.
Corni
Tromba
Arpa
Canto
faucherais d'un coup la nuit.
banish the night from the sky.
Violini
Viole
Vlli
Contrab.
pizz.
arco

31
8
Fl.
Oboe
Corno I.
Clar.
Fag.
Corni
Arpa
Canto
Violini
Viole
Vlli
Contrab.
mf
p
senza Sord. 1º
1º
pizz.
arco
Si vous me di-siez que l'es - pa - ce
If space lost in cha-os was o'er— you,
37
Corno I.
Clar.
Fag.
Arpa
Canto
Violini
Viole
Vlli
Contrab.
Ain-si vi-dé—ne vous plait point, Che-va-lier - dieu, la lance au poing,— J'é - toi - le -
Filling your soul with nameless fear, God-like I'd come, shaking my spear,— And sow— the

43
9
Clar.
Fag.
Corni
Arpa
Canto
-rais le vent qui pas - se.
stars, radiant be - fore you!
Mais si vous di-siez que mon sang
But if ev - er I hear you cry,-
1° Solo
Violini
Viole
Vlli
Contrab.
arco
pizz.
mf
49
Est plus à moi qu'à vous, ma Da - me, Je blê - mi - rais dessous le blâ - me
"Give me your life! Prove how you love me!" Darkness will fall, shadows a - bove me,
Col tutti
Div.
Unis
dim.
p

55
Clar.
Fag.
Canto
Violini
Viole
Vlli
Contrab.
Et je mour - rais, vous bé-nis - sant.
Blessing you still, then I shall die!
61
Fl.
Clar.
Fag.
Arpa
Canto
Violini
Viole
Vlli
Contrab.
O Dul - ci - né - e.
O Dul - ci - né - e.

III. *Chanson à boire* (Drinking Song)

7
Canto
Foin du bâ - tard, il - lus - tre Da - me,
Qui pour me perdre à vos doux
La - dy a - dor'd! Where-fore this sor - row?
I live in your glan-ces div -
Violini
Viole
Vlli
Contrab.
pizz.
arco
14
Clar.
Arpa
yeux
Dit que l'a - mour et le vin vieux
Met-tent en deuil mon
-ine,
Say not that love, love and good wine,
Brings to us mor - tals

21
Clar.
Arpa
Canto
cœur, mon â - me! Ah! ah!
grief to - mor - row! Ah! ah!
Violini
Viole
Vlli
Contrab.
27
Clar.
Arpa
Canto
f
mf
mf
ah! Je bois A la
ah! Drink then! drink to
Violini
arco
pizz.
mf
arco
pizz.
Viole
mf
arco
Vlli
mf
Contrab.

34
Fl.
Clar.
Fag.
Tromba
Cast.
Arpa
Canto
Violini
Viole
Vlli
Contrab.
Sord.
pizz.
arco
joie! La joie est le seul but - Où je vais_droit... lors - que_
joy! For good wine makes you laugh like a mer-ry boy! Makes you_
40
Oboi
_ j'ai... lors-que j'ai bu! Ah! ah! ah! la joie! Ah! ah! ah! la
_ laugh laugh, like a boy! Ah! ah! ah! to joy! Ah! ah! ah! to

46
Fl.
Oboi
Clar.
Fag.
Corni
Tromba
Arpa
Canto
Violini
Viole
Vlli
Contrab.
1o
mf cresc.
cresc.
à 2
senza Sord.
joie!
joy!
La...la...la...
La...la...la...
La...la...la...
La...la...la...
Je bois
Drink on,
A la
drink to
arco
pizz.
cresc.
51
11
joie!
joy!
Div.
Unis
pizz.
arco

57
Canto
Foin du ja - loux, bru - ne mai - tres - se, Qui
Who wants a maid, (not I, I'm think - ing,) A
Violini
Viole
Vlli
Contrab.
pizz.
arco
mf
64
Clar.
Arpa
Canto
geind, qui pleure et fait ser - ment D'ê - tre tou - jours ce pâle a - mant
maid - en who mopes all day long, Si - lent and pale, nev - er a song,
Violini
Viole
Vlli
Contrab.

71
Clar.
Arpa
Canto
Violini
Viole
Vlli
Contrab.
mf
mf
pizz.
pizz.
Qui met de l'eau dans son i - vres - se! Ah!
Frowning to see her lov - er a - drink - ing! Ah!

77
Clar.
Arpa
Canto
Violini
Viole
Vlli
Contrab.
f
ah! ah!
ah! ah!

83
Fl.
Clar.
Tromba
Cast.
Canto
Violini
Viole
Vlli
Contrab.
1°
Sord.
arco
pizz.
Je bois A la joie! La joie est le seul
Drink then! drink to joy! For good wine makes you
89
Fag.
Arpa
but Où je vais droit... lors-que j'ai... lors-que j'ai bu! Ah! ah! ah! la
laugh like a merry boy! Makes you laugh, laugh like a boy! Ah! ah! ah! to

96
Oboi
Clar.
Fag.
Canto
joie! Ah! ah! ah! la joie! La...la...la... La...la...la... Je bois
joy! Ah! ah! ah! to joy! La...la...la... La...la...la... Drink on,
Violini
Viole
Vlli
Contrab.
arco
cresc.
pizz.
à 2
102
Fl.
Oboi
Clar.
Fag.
Corni
Tromba
senza Sord.
Arpa
Canto
A la joie!
drink to joy!
Violini
Div.
Viole
Vlli
Contrab.
Unis
gliss.

Maurice Ravel (1875–1937) was asked to write a film score based on the story of Don Quixote in 1932. Produced and directed by the celebrated G. W. Pabst, the movie was to incorporate a number of songs for the legendary Russian opera singer Feodor Chaliapin. Ravel eagerly accepted the offer and began composing songs based on texts from the Paul Morand script, but brain damage, perhaps exacerbated by a car accident in 1932, inhibited Ravel's progress. Subsequently, Jacques Ibert composed the film score, writing his own songs. Ravel's three completed works were published as the song cycle for bass voice and orchestra, *Don Quichotte à Dulcinée* (*Don Quixote to Dulcinea*). This would be Ravel's last composition; he died in 1937 immediately following an unsuccessful brain operation.

Don Quixote (1605–1617), created by the Spanish author Miguel de Cervantes, is one of the first novels in a modern European language. The principal figure is a nobleman who imagines himself a knight errant. Along with his sidekick Sancho Panza and his horse Rocinate, he attempts to right wrongs and protect the oppressed in the name of his imaginary lady Dulcinea. In setting the three songs to Dulcinea, Ravel invoked a Spanish musical character he had mastered in earlier works such as the *Rapsodie espagnol* (*Spanish Rhapsody*).

The cycle opens with *Chanson romanesque* (*Romanesque Song*), in which Don Quixote makes exuberant pledges to Dulcinea. In the last pledge, our wayward knight even promises to kill himself if it would please his lady. Each of the four stanzas is set to different music, creating a through-composed setting. The meter, with a lilting dancelike rhythm, alternates 3/4 and 6/8 measures. The harmony shifts between minor and major, and biting dissonances enliven the orchestral interludes. Typical of Ravel, the orchestration sparkles with delicate colors, including a violin solo.

The cycle concludes with a boisterous ode to drinking. Evoking the spirit of tavern tunes, *Chanson à boire* (*Drinking Song*) is strophic with a refrain. The energetic rhythms suggest a *jota*, a Spanish folk dance from Aragon. Characterized by a triple meter and a quick tempo, the dance features vigorous rhythms and is traditionally accompanied with tambourines and castanets. For the verses, the predominantly string accompaniment mimics the sound of a guitar. The refrain, with its freer vocal style and laughing phrases, recalls flamenco singing. This association is enhanced by orchestration that includes a solo trumpet and castanets.

26

Igor Stravinsky

Le sacre du printemps (The Rite of Spring), Part I, excerpts (1913)

8CD: 7/12–18
4CD: 4/1–7

Introduction (closing)

Danses des adolescentes (Dance of the Youths and Maidens)

15
Fl. picc. 1 2
sf
sf
Ob. 1 2
f
3
C. ing.
come sopra
Cl. picc. in Re
sf
sf
Cl. in Sib 2 3
sf
sf
Cor. in Fa 1.2 3.4 5.6 7.8
come sopra
Solo con sord.
Tr. in Do 1
mf
3
15
pizz.
Vl. I
sf
sf
Vl. II
Vle.
Vc.
Cb.
16
Ob. 1.2 3
1.2 a2
f
C. ing.
Fag. 1 2
mf
tr
Tr. in Do 1
mf
16
Vl. I
(pizz.)
f
Vl. II
Vle.
mf
Vc.
pizz.
poco meno f
Cb.
pizz.
poco meno f

Fl. picc.
Fl. gr.
Fl. alto
Ob.
C. ing.
Cl. picc. in Re
Cl. in La
Cl. in Sib
Fag.
Cor. in Fa
Tr. picc. in Re
Tr. in Do
Vl. I
Vl. II
Vle.
Vc.
Cb.
17
Flttzg.
sempre simile
sim.
con sord.
pizz.
meno f

18
Fl. picc.
Fl. gr.
Fl. alto
Ob.
C. ing.
Cl. picc. in Re
Cl. in La
Cl. in Sib
Fag.
Cor. in Fa
Tr. picc. in Re
Tr. in Do
Vl. I
Vl. II
Vle.
Vc.
Cb.
sim.
muta in Mib
muta in Sib
4 senza sord.
senza sord.
sf sempre
arco
f (non div.)
sempre sim.
come sopra
div.
unis.

14
3
19
1.2 a2
Fag. 1.2 3
C. Fag. 1
Cor. in Fa 1.2 3.4 5.6 7.8
Vl. I
Vle.
Vc.
Cb.
p sub.
Trbn. 1
20
più f
mf

21
Ob. 1 2
1.2 a2
Fag. 1.2 3
C. Fag. 1
Vl. I
Vle.
Vc.
Cb.
p sub.
Fl. gr. 1
piu f
Cor. in Fa 1.5 2.6 3.7 4.8
1.5 a2
2.6 a2
3.7 a2
4.8 a2
Trbn. 1 2
Tbe. 1 2
Timp.
G.C.
Vl. II
pizz.
arco

22
23
Fl. picc.
Fl. gr.
Ob.
C. ing.
Cl. in Sib
Fag.
Tr. picc. in Re
Tr. in Do
Trbn.
Vl. Solo
Vl. I
Vl. II
Vle.
pizz.
arco
Solo
stacc.
marc.
24
2 Vl. Soli
Vc.
sul Sol
col legno sino al segno

15
4
25
C. ing.
p sub.
Fag.
p
tr
Cor. in Fa
mp (mais en dehors)
Solo
2 Vl. Soli
Vl. I
Vl. II
col legno al
mf
Vle.
Vc.
Solo
Fl. gr.

26
Soli
Ob. 1 2
Cl. in Sib 2 3
Fag. 1 2 3 4
Solo
Tr. in Do 1 2
Solo con sord.
senza sord.
2 Vl. Soli
Vl. I
Vl. II div.
Vle.
Vc.
27
Fl. gr. 2
Fl. alto
Solo
Cor. in Fa 5

28
Fl. gr.
Fl. alto
Cl. picc. in Mi♭
Cl. in Si♭
Cl. bas. in Si♭
Fag.
C. Fag.
Cor. in Fa
Trbn.
Timp.
2 Vl. Soli
Vl. I
Vl. II div.
Vle.
Vc.
Cb.
pizz.

16
5
29
Fl. picc.
Fl. gr.
Fl. alto
Ob.
Cl. picc. in Mi♭
Cl. in Si♭
Cl. bas. in Si♭
Fag.
C. Fag.
Tr. in Do
mp cantab.
Trbn.
Timp.
Triang.
bacch. di legno
Cym. ant.
legg. 5.6
legg. 7.8
Tutti div.
Vl. I
Vl. II div.
Vle. div. a 3
3 Soli
Vc.
gli altri
arco
marcatiss. e molto cantabile
Cb.
stacc.

Fl. picc.
Fl. gr.
Fl. alto
Ob.
C. ing.
C. ing. 2 muta in Ob. 4
Cl. picc. in Mib
Cl. in Sib
Cl. bas. in Sib
Fag.
Fag. 4 muta in C. Fag. 2
Cor. in Fa
sim.
Tr. in Do
Trbn.
Timp.
Triang.
Cym. ant.
Vl. I div.
Vl. II div.
Vle. div. a3
3 Soli
Vc.
gli altri
Cb.

30
Cl. picc. in Mi♭
Cl. in Si♭
Cl. bas. in Si♭
sempre sf
Vl. I div.
p sub. e stacc.
Vl. II div.
pizz.
p sub.
meno f
4 Sole
Vle.
le altre
sul Sol
3 Soli
Vc.
gli altri
Cb.
p sub.
sf
31
Fl. picc. 1
Solo
mf grazioso
Ob.
C. ing.
mf
muta in Re
C. Fag.
a2
Cor. in Fa 4
cresc.
(pizz.)
sim.
(sempre sim.)
Tutte
sff
Tutti div.

32
Fl. picc. 1
Fl. gr.
Fl. alto
Ob.
C. ing.
Cl. picc. in Re
Cl. in Si♭
Fag. 3
C. Fag.
a 2
(a 2)
Cor. in Fa
Tr. in Do
Vl. I div.
Vl. II div.
Vle. div.
Vc. div.
Cb.
arco
mf cresc.
unis. arco

Fl. picc. 1 2
Fl. gr. 1 2
Fl. alto
Ob. 1 2 3 4
C. ing.
Cl. picc. in Re
Cl. in Sib 1 2 3
Fag. 1 2 3
C. Fag. 1
Cor. in Fa 1.2 3.4 5.6 7.8
Tr. picc. in Re
Tr. in Do 1 2 3 4
Tbe. 1 2
Vl. I div.
Vl. II div.
Vle. div.
Vc.
Cb.
f sempre
sim.
Flttzg.
mf
mf cresc.
arco
f

33
Fl. picc. 1 2
Fl. gr. 1 2
Fl. alto
Ob. 1 2 3 4
C. ing.
Cl. picc. in Re
Cl. in Sib 1 2 3
Fag. 1 2 3
C. Fag. 1 2
Cor. in Fa 1.2 3.4 5.6 7.8
Tr. picc. in Re
Tr. in Do 1 2 3 4
Tbe. 1 2
Vl. I div.
Vl. II div.
Vle. div.
Vc. div.
Cb.
Flttzg.
sempre sim.
stacc.
a 2
sim. sempre
pizz.

34
Fl. picc. 1 2
a2
ff
Fl. gr. 1 2
Flttzg.
Fl. alto
Ob. 1 2 3 4
stacc.
C. ing.
Cl. picc. in Re
Flttzg.
Cl. in Sib 1 2 3
Flttzg.
Cl. bas. in Sib
Flttzg.
f
ff
Fag. 1 2 3
a2
a3
C. Fag. 1 2
a2
Cor. in Fa 1.2 3.4 5.6 7.8
f
Tr. picc. in Re
f
Tr. in Do 1.2 3.4
f
Trbn. 1 2 3
f
poco più f
Tbe. 1 2
poco più f
34
Vl. I div.
f assai
Vl. II div.
ff
f assai
Vle. div.
ff
ff
Vc. div.
ff
arco
sim.
ff
Cb. div.
ff
ff

Fl. picc. 1 2
a 2
35
Fl. gr. 1 2
Fl. alto
Ob. 1 2 3 4
C. ing.
Cl. picc. in Re
Cl. in Si♭ 1 2 3
Cl. bas. in Si♭
a 3
Fag. 1 2 3
a 2
C. Fag. 1 2
Cor. in Fa 1.2 3.4 5.6 7.8
Tr. picc. in Re
Tr. in Do 1.2 3.4
Trbn. 1 2 3
Tbe. 1 2
secco
Timp.
come sopra
Vl. I div.
Vl. II div.
unis.
div.
Vle.
Vc. div.
Cb. div.

36
a 2
Fl. picc. 1 2
Fl. gr. 1 2
Fl. alto
Ob. 1 2 3 4
C. ing.
Cl. picc. in Re
Cl. in Sib 1 2 3
Cl. bas. in Sib
a 3
tr
Fag. 1 2 3
a 2
C. Fag. 1 2
C. Fag. 2 muta in Fag. 4
sff
gliss.
Cor. in Fa 1 2 3 4 5.6 7.8
Tr. picc. in Re
Tr. in Do 1.2 3.4
Trbn. 1 2 3
Tbe. 1 2
Timp.
36
Vl. I div.
Vl. II div.
div.
unis.
Vle.
Vc. div.
Cb. div.

Jeu du rapt (*Game of Abduction*)

17 ◇6

37 Presto ♩. = 132

38

Fl. picc. 1 2 — a 2 — *f* — Fl. picc. 2 muta in Fl. gr. 3

Fl. gr. 1 2 — a 2 — *ff* — *f*

Fl. alto — *f*

Ob. 1 2 3 4 — *ff* — *f*

C. ing. — *f*

Cl. picc. in Re — *ff marcatissimo* — sim.

Cl. in Si♭ 1 2 3 — *f*

Cl. bas. in Si♭ — *f ben tenuto*

Fag. 1 2 — *f*

Cor. in Fa 1 2 3 4 5 6 7 8 — a 2 — *f*

Tr. picc. in Re — Solo — *f*

Tr. in Do 1.2 3.4 — *f*

Timp. gr. — *f* — secco — *f*

G. C. — poco *sf*

37 Presto ♩. = 132

38

Vl. I — non div. — *f*

Vl. II — non div. — *f*

Vle. — non div. — sempre *f*

Vc. — unis. — *sf* — pizz. — (pizz.) — *f*

Cb. — unis. — *sf* — (arco) — *f*

39
4/8+5/8
Fl.gr.
Fl. alto
Ob.
sim.
f
Ob.4 muta in C. ing. 2
C. ing.
Cl. picc. in Re
muta in Mib
Cl. in Sib
Cl. bas. in Sib
Fag.
Cor. in Fa
secco
Soli a 2
Solo
f assai
Trbn.
Timp. picc.
Timp. gr.
4 Vl. Soli
détaché
div.
Vl. I
Vl. II div.
Vle. div.
Vc.
Cb.
pizz.

40
Fl. picc. 1
Fl. gr. 1 2 3
a 3
Soli
a 2
Cor. in Fa 1 2 5
bouché
Tr. picc. in Re
Tr. in Do 1 2 3 4
Tutti unis.
pizz.
Vl. I
Vl. II div.
Vle. div.
p sub. cresc.
Vc.
Cb.

41
Fl. gr. 1 2
Fl. alto
Ob. 1 2 3
sim.
C. ing. 1 2
Cl. in Sib 1 2 3
ben ten.
Cl. bas. in Sib
Fag. 1 2 3
Cor. in Fa 2 4 6 7 8
a3
a2
f secco
Tbe. 1 2
Timp. picc.
Timp. gr.
f secco
arco
Vl. I div.
Vl. II div.
Vle. div.
Vc.
Cb.
f come sopra

42
crescendo poco a poco
Fl. picc.
Fl. gr.
Fl. alto
Ob.
C. ing.
Cl. picc. in Mib
Cl. in Sib
Cor. in Fa
Tr. in Do
Trbn.
4 Vl. Soli
Vl. I div.
Vl. II div.
Vle. div.
Vc.
Cb.
pizz.

18
7
43
Fl. picc.
Fl. gr.
Fl. alto
Ob.
C. ing.
Cl. picc. in Mi♭
Cl. in Si♭
Fag.
Cor. in Fa
Tr. in Do
4 Vl. Soli
Vl. I div.
Vl. II div.
Vle. div.
Vc.
a2
arco
pizz.

Fl. picc.
Fl. gr.
a2
Fl. alto
Ob.
C. ing.
Cl. picc. in Mib
Cl. in Sib
Fag.
muta in C. Fag. 2
Cor. in Fa
Tr. picc. in Re
Tr. in Do
Trbn.
Timp.
Tutti
unis.
Vl. I
Vl. II
Vle.
Vc.

44
45
Fl. picc.
Fl. gr.
a2
Fl. gr. 3 muta in Fl. picc. 2
Fl. alto
Ob.
C. ing.
Cl. picc. in Mib
Cl. in Sib
Cl. bas. in Sib
Fag.
C. Fag.
1 Solo
marc.
Cor. in Fa
Tr. picc. in Re
Tr. in Do
p sub. cresc.
Trbn.
Tbe.
Timp.
Vl. I div.
p sub. cresc.
gliss.
Vl. II div.
p sub. cresc.
Vle. div.
div.
unis.
Vc.
Cb.
arco

46

Fl. picc. 1 2
Fl. gr. 1 2
Fl. alto
Ob. 1 2 3
C. ing. 1 2
Cl. picc. in Mi♭
Cl. in Si♭ 1 2 3
Cl. bas. in Si♭
Fag. 1 2 3
C. Fag. 1 2
Cor. in Fa 1 3 5 7 2.4 6.8
Tr. picc. in Re
Tr. in Do 1 2 3 4
Trbn. 1 2 3
Tbe. 1 2
Timp.
G. C.
Vl. I div.
Vl. II div.
Vle.
Vc.
Cb.

C. ing. 2 muta in Ob. 4
f stacc.
(pavillons en l'air)
loco

47
Fl picc. 1 2
a2
Fl. picc. 2 muta in Fl. gr. 3
Fl. gr. 1 2
Fl. alto
Ob. 1 2 3 4
C. ing.
Cl. picc. in Mib
Cl. in Sib 1 2 3
Fag. 1 2 3
a3
C. Fag. 1 2
Cor. in Fa 1 2 3
Tr. in Do 3 4
Timp.
Vl. I
unis.
Vl. II
Vle.
Vc.
Cb.

Fl. picc.
Fl. gr.
Fl. alto
Ob.
C. ing.
Cl. picc. in Mi♭
Cl. in Si♭
Fag.
C. Fag.
Cor. in Fa
Tr. in Do
Trbn.
Tbe.
Timp.
G.C.
Vl. I
Vl. II
Vle.
Vc.
Cb.
sim.
secco
molto sf
non div.
div.
Cl. 3 muta in Cl. bas. 2

The earliest creative period of Igor Stravinsky (1882–1971) saw a rapid transition from post-Romanticism through Impressionism to what is generally known as Primitivism. Unifying these varied approaches is a strong sense of nationalism that can be seen in the Russian models for his works, in the Russian stories of his ballets, and, especially with his later works, in a distinctive Russian style. The culminating point of this early phase is the landmark ballet *Le sacre du printemps* (*The Rite of Spring*). Commissioned by the impresario Sergei Diaghilev, the ballet was premiered in 1913 by the Ballet Russes, causing a riot at the first performance. The ballet is based on Russian legends that describe a number of primitive spring rituals. Modernisms dominated the production, with Vaslav Nijinsky's stunning and energetic choreography and Nicholas Roerich's innovative costumes and scenic designs. But it was Stravinsky's modern musical sounds that had the most enduring impact.

The Russian sound can most readily be heard in the melodies, with their limited ranges and repetition. Indeed, Stravinsky is able to interweave a number of authentic folk melodies into the work unobtrusively. Another critical link to Russian traditions is the music's static nature. Contrasting moods are simply juxtaposed, and development, in the traditional Western sense, is absent. The most memorable features of the work are its primitive qualities, huge orchestral force, powerful dissonances, and pounding rhythms. These rhythms, created by Stravinsky's innovative treatment of metric pulse, influenced later twentieth-century art music immeasurably.

At the end of the introduction, a solo bassoon reprises the melody that opened the ballet. Derived from a Lithuanian folk song, the melody floats freely, without a clear metric pulse. The entrance of pizzicato strings serves as a transition from the introduction to the opening scene, entitled *Danses des adolescentes* (*Dance of the Youths and Maidens*). The repetitive eighth-note figure anticipates the harmony and establishes the basic duple pulse that will run throughout the first dance.

The *Danses des adolescentes* begins with thirty-two repetitions of the same chord, played as eighth notes with percussive down-bow articulations in the strings. The chord, a combination of an F-flat minor triad and a first inversion E-flat seventh, contains seven different pitches, all of which can be found in the A-flat harmonic minor scale. Strong accents in the horns contradict the established meter, but the duple pulse is quickly reinstated. The conflict between an established pulse and unpredictable accents provide much of the energy of this dance. The opening section forms a block of sound that returns three times. In the intervening sections, several folk-like melodies appear, the first of which is an authentic folk tune. Unifying these diverse passages are the unchanging harmony and constant eighth-note motion.

The *Jeu du rapt* (*Game of Abduction*) features a new folk melody, brash horn calls, scurrying melodic figures, and strong accented beats. In this dance, there is no established meter, and the accents occur at unpredictable moments. The overall effect is primitive and lusty.

27

Igor Stravinsky

L'histoire du soldat (*The Soldier's Tale*), *Marche royale* (*Royal March*) (1918)

8CD: 7/19–23

*Pist. 26³⁻⁴. These two staccato dots are in the 1924 score and part.

*Pist. 37-38. Phrasing thus in both mss. and 1924 part.

*Fag. 61, 63 etc. Phrasing thus in both mss.

**Pist. 68-70 Phrasing thus in both mss. and 1924 part.

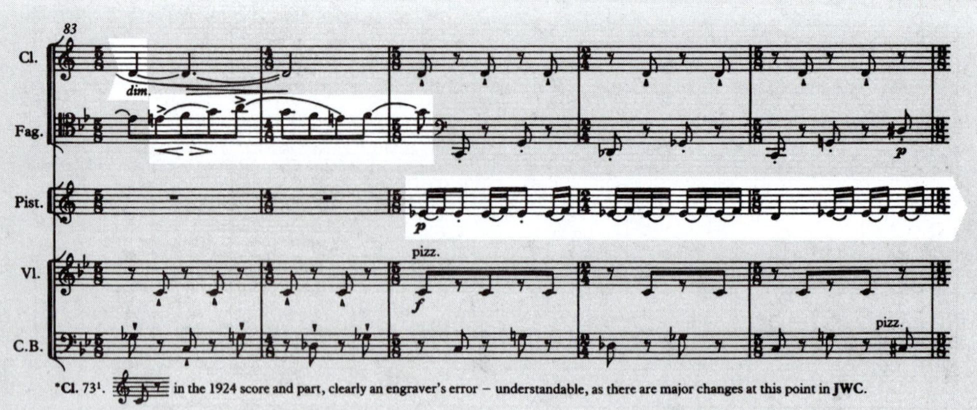

*Cl. 73[1]. in the 1924 score and part, clearly an engraver's error – understandable, as there are major changes at this point in **JWC**.

*Cl. 88-89. Phrasing thus in both mss. and 1924 part.
**Vl. 100. *p* from 1924 part.

22
101
Cl.
Fag.
Pist.
Trb.
Bat.
Vl.
C.B.
ff sub.
sub. meno f
Solo
f (mais moins fort que les bois)
f sub.
S.D.I (unsnared)
B.D. + Cym.
cresc.
sf secco

108
Cl.
Fag.
Pist.
Trb.
Bat.
Vl.
C.B.
Solo
B.D. (edge & centre)
[sim.]
S.D.I
leggiero
(accompagnando)
pizz.
arco

114
Cl.
Fag.
Pist.
Trb.
Bat.
Vl.
C.B.
Solo
B.D. + Cym.
poco
molto
stacc.
(accompagnando)
arco
pizz.
sub. meno f
p sub.

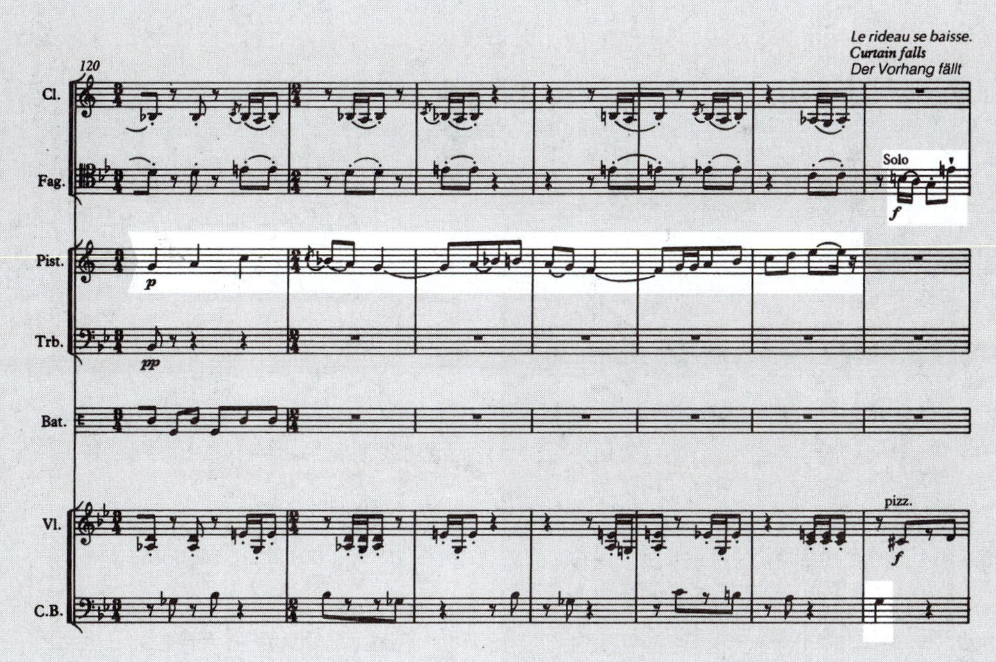
Le rideau se baisse.
Curtain falls
Der Vorhang fällt
120
Cl.
Fag.
Pist.
Trb.
Bat.
Vl.
C.B.
Solo
pizz.

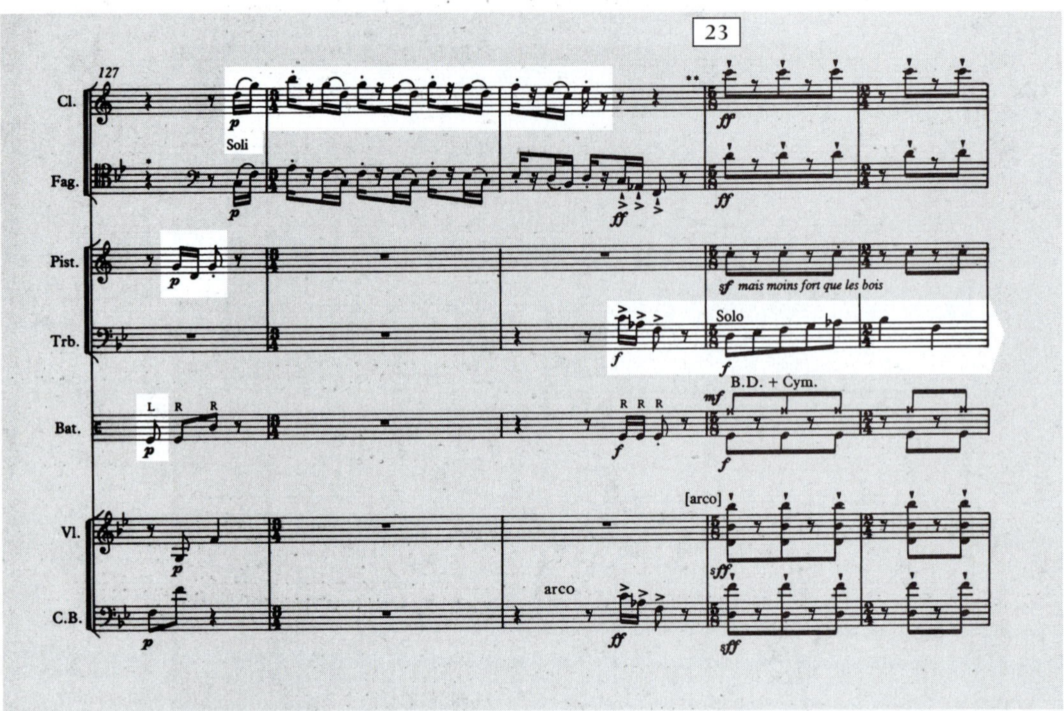

*Fag. 127^{1}. in both mss. and in the 1924 part (but c.f. fig.3). ***139^{1}. in both mss.

**129. Both mss. show that originally there was a break for dialogue at the end of this bar.

L'histoire du soldat (The Soldier's Tale) is a dramatic work for narrator, dancers, and a small chamber ensemble. Created near the end of Stravinsky's Russian period (1918), the story is based on a Russian folk tale in which a soldier exchanges his violin (his soul) for a book that foretells the future. The soldier's life and soul are temporarily redeemed by the love of a princess, but eventually the devil is triumphant. In addition to the nationalistic story, Stravinsky retains the static quality and some of the melodic characteristics of his earlier works. At the same time, the work anticipates the imminent Neoclassical phase of Stravinsky's compositions, particularly in the sparse orchestration of just seven instruments, the clear tonal centers, the use of dance forms, and the generally detached emotions.

The *Marche royale* (*Royal March*) has a number of traditional features: it can be heard in an overall **A–B–A** form; there is a prevailing duple meter in a moderate tempo; and the trumpet, trombone, and drums—characteristic instruments of a march—are given prominent roles. But Stravinsky also plays with the most critical element of a march, the beat. Using polyrhythms and shifting meters, Stravinsky quietly creates an intricate rhythmic scheme that matches *Le sacre du printemps* in complexity. The detached humor and the B-flat tonality clearly suggest a Neoclassical conception.

28

Arnold Schoenberg

Pierrot lunaire, Op. 21, Nos. 18 and 21 (1912)

8CD: 7/ 24 – 27

4CD: 4/ 8 – 9

No. 18. *Der Mondfleck* (*The Moonfleck*)

Pic.
Kl. (B)
G.
Vcl.
mf quasi kadenzierend
f
pp
quasi kadenzierend
mf
sei_nes schwar - zen Rok - kes,
so spaziert Pier_
tr
sf

Pic.
Kl. (B)
G.
Vcl.
f
pp
sf
5
rot im lauen A_bend,
auf_ zu_suchen Glück und A - ben_teu_er.
5
sf
sf

Pic.
Kl. (B)
G.
Vcl.
cresc.
Plötzlich stört ihn was an sei_nem An_zug, er be_
25
9
sieht sich rings und fin_det rich_tig_ ei_nen wei_ßen Fleck
10
dim.

Pic.
Kl. (B)
G.
Vcl.
ppp
f
ff
pp
mfp
sf
p
des hel_len Mon_ _des auf dem Rük_ken sei_nes schwarzen Rockes. War_te!
denkt er: das ist so ein Gips _ fleck! Wischt und wischt, doch

Pic.
Kl. (B)
G.
Vcl.
15
(ärgerlich)
bringt ihn nicht her - un - ter!
(erregt)
Und so geht er
cresc.
gift - geschwollen wei - ter, reibt und reibt
bis an den frühen Morgen
(komisch bedeutsam)
ei - nen
hervor

TEXT AND TRANSLATION

Einen weissen Fleck des hellen Mondes	*With a fleck of white—from the bright moon—*
Auf dem Rücken seines schwarzen Rockes,	*on the back of his black jacket,*
So spaziert Pierrot im lauen Abend,	Pierrot strolls about in the mild evening
Aufzusuchen Glück und Abenteuer.	seeking his fortune and adventure.
Plötzlich stört ihn was an seinem Anzug,	Suddenly something strikes him as wrong,
Er besieht sich rings und findet richtig—	he checks his clothes and sure enough finds
Einen weissen Fleck des hellen Mondes	*a fleck of white—from the bright moon—*
Auf dem Rücken seines schwarzen Rockes.	*on the back of his black jacket.*
Warte! denkt er: das ist so ein Gipsfleck!	Damn! he thinks: that's a spot of plaster!
Wischt und wischt, doch—bringt ihn nicht herunter!	Wipes and wipes, but—he can't get it off.
Und so geht er, giftgeschwollen, weiter,	And so goes on his way, his pleasure poisoned,
Reibt und reibt bis an den frühen Morgen—	rubs and rubs till the early morning—
Einen weissen Fleck des hellen Mondes.	*a fleck of white—from the bright moon.*

No. 21. *O alter Duft aus Märchenzeit* (*O Scent of Fabled Yesteryear*)

27
poco rit.
Tempo
rit.
Tempo
Fl.
Kl. (A)
G.
Vcl.
nimmt Baß Klarinette in B
nimmt Bratsche
sehr innig
Wünschen macht mich froh nach Freu - den, die ich lang ver - ach - tet.
O
p espress.
Baß-Klarinette (B)
Bratsche.
p espress.
15
al - ter Duft aus Mär - chen - zeit, be - rau - schest wie - der mich.
All meinen
ppp
Ped.

nimmt Piccolo
Fl.
B-Kl (B)
Br.
Vcl.
Un-mut geb ich preis; aus meinem sonnumrahm-ten Fenster beschau ich frei die lie-be Welt und
Piccolo.
rit.
Tempo
molto rit.
Dämpfer aufsetzen
mit Dämpfer
träum hin-aus in sel-ge Weiten... O al-ter Duft aus Mär-chen-zeit!

TEXT AND TRANSLATION

O alter Duft aus Märchenzeit, *Berauschest wieder meine Sinne!* Ein närrisch Heer von Schelmerein Durchschwirrt die leichte Luft.	*O scent of fabled yesteryear,* *intoxicating my senses once again!* A foolish swarm of idle fancies pervades the gentle air.
Ein glückhaft Wünschen macht mich froh Nach Freuden, die ich lang verachtet: *O alter Duft aus Märchenzeit,* *Berauschest wieder mich!*	A happy desire makes me yearn for joys that I have long scorned: *O scent of fabled yesteryear,* *intoxicating me again.*
All meinen Unmut geb ich preis: Aus meinem sonnumrahmten Fenster Beschau ich frei die liebe Welt Und träum hinaus in selge Weiten . . . *O alter Duft aus Märchenzeit!*	All my ill humor is dispelled: from my sun-drenched window I look out freely on the lovely world and dream of beyond the horizon . . . *O scent of fabled yesteryear!*

Expressionism was a movement in literature, art, and music that sought to portray the dark side of the subconscious mind. The leading musical figure of this movement was Arnold Schoenberg (1874–1951), a Viennese composer who played a critical role in twentieth-century music as a composer, theorist, and teacher. The most important element of Schoenberg's Expressionistic style is his treatment of harmony, in which he pushes chromaticism, dissonance, and the lack of a tonal center (atonality) to new levels.

Schoenberg's early masterwork in Expressionism is the song cycle *Pierrot lunaire,* based on poems by the Belgian Symbolist poet Albert Giraud. Within these poems, the traditional clown figure of Pierrot is subject to nightmares and insanity, themes that are well suited for Expressionist settings. Each of the poems is a rondeau of thirteen lines, in which the first line recurs in lines 7 and 13, and the second line is repeated in line 8. The repetitive structure descends from the medieval rondeaux of Guillaume de Machaut.

A critical element of Expressionism is the exploration of new timbres. Schoenberg creates a unique sound by setting the cycle for the accompaniment of a chamber group of eight instruments played by five performers: piccolo/flute, B-flat clarinet/bass clarinet, violin/viola, cello, and piano. Each of the twenty-one songs has a unique combination of instruments supporting the voice. In addition, Schoenberg treats the voice in a nontraditional manner. Rather than using a full singing voice, the singer is asked to perform in a quasi-speaking style, which Schoenberg termed *Sprechstimme.*

The two songs in this anthology typify the variety of individual treatments found in the cycle as a whole. Song No. 18, *Der Mondfleck (The Moonfleck),* is accompanied by the piccolo, B-flat clarinet, violin, cello, and piano. Pierrot, disturbed by a white spot on his black jacket (a patch of moonlight), frantically tries to rub it off. Supporting this image are scurrying musical lines that include a three-voice fugue and canons in diminution and retrograde. In the final song of the set, No. 21 *O alter Duft aus Märchenzeit (O Scent of Fabled Yesteryear),* Schoenberg employs all eight musical instruments. The reflective mood of Pierrot is supported by a more serene musical setting. As Pierrot thinks of old times, the harmony incorporates more thirds and hints of traditional sounds.

29

Alban Berg

Wozzeck, Act III, Scene 4, Interlude, Scene 5 (1922)

8CD: 7/ 28 – 31

Wozz
p
da regt sich was.
whispered loudly
Still!
Cel
As
pp
(frog croaks)
(mp)
230
(spoken)
Al-les still und tot.
accel
Etwas
(shouting)
Mör-der!
Str m D
pppp
Holz
ff
Hfe
gliss
(quasi Des-Dur)
Trp m D
rascher
Mör - - - - der!!
235
again whispered
mf
Ha! da ruft's.
poco rit
gest Hr
Str
gliss (C-Dur)
Hfe
Ces
(quasi Ces-Dur glissando)
Pos m D

(poco rit) - - - a tempo
poco string - - - - - - poco rit - - molto
staggers a few more steps, searching, and comes upon the corpse
(spoken)
Wozz
Nein_ ich selbst.
Ma-rie! Ma-
p non legato e poco cresc - - - mf
Str
molto pp
fehlende Akkordtöne
Kl
Solo Br
Trp
etc
E H
Hr
Solo Vcl
Beck freihäng

Wieder langsamer, aber nicht schleppend
(quasi Hauptzeitmaß)
gato
240
[quasi
Wozz
rie! Was hast du für ei-ne ro - te Schnur um den Hals?
(Kl)
(Trp)
E H
2 Solo Gg
sempre pp
p espr
Hfe
sempre pp
Trp
Hr
Solo Br
Solo Vcl
port
etc

Walzertempo
poco string
(breaking into song)
Wozz
Hast Dir das ro - te Hals - band ver-dient, wie die Ohr - ring - lein,
poco cresc
245
sempre string
mit Dei-ner Sün - de!
(spoken)
Rasch (♩ = 100-120)
Was hän-gen Dir die
schwar - zen Haa - re so wild_?!_ Mör - der!_ Mör -
250

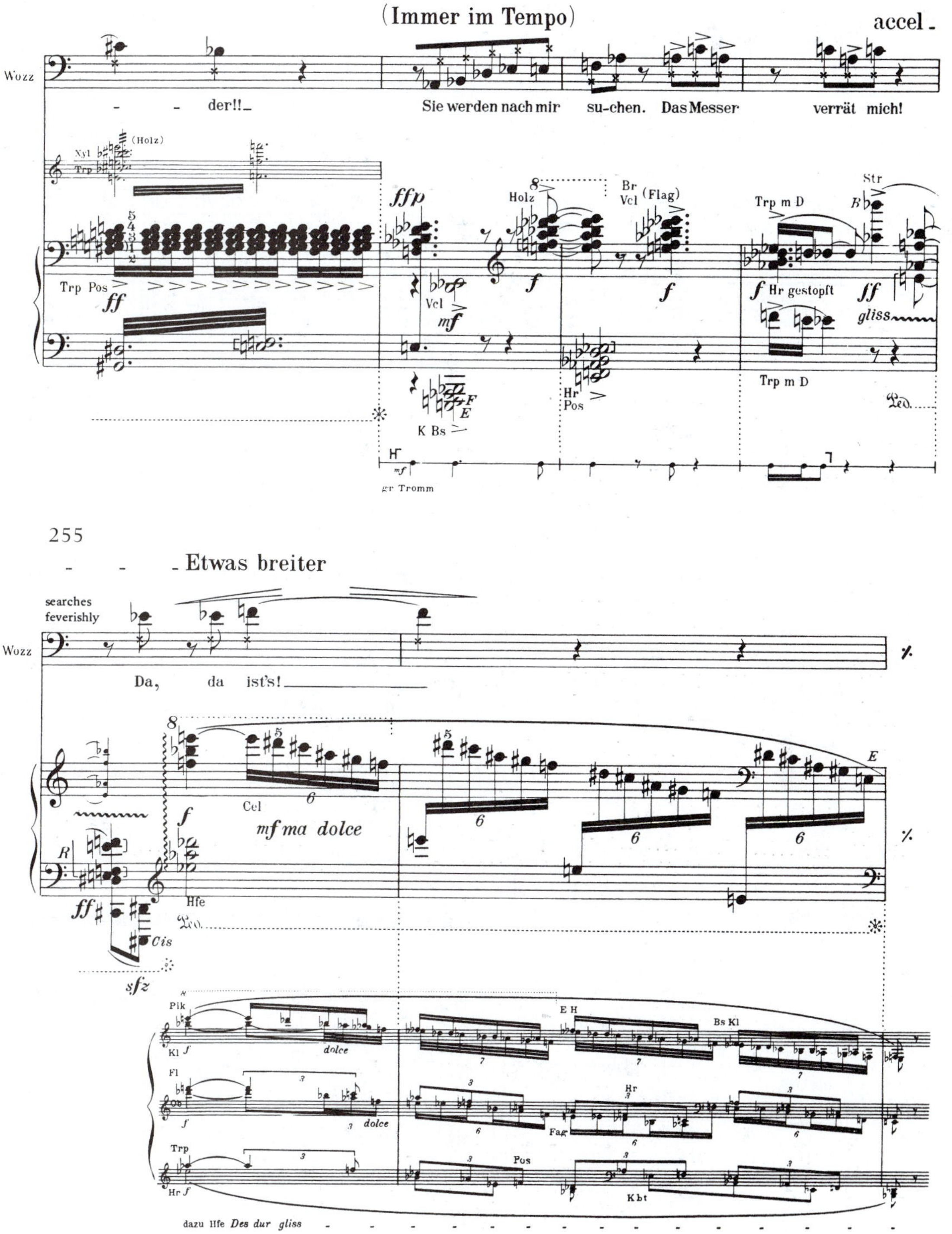

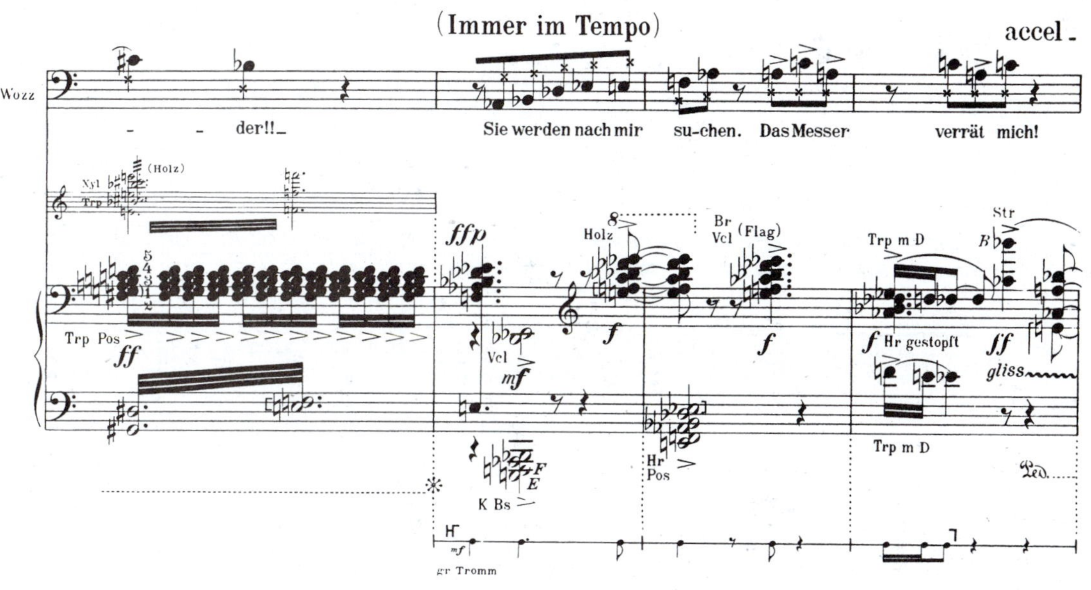

255

Etwas breiter

searches feverishly

Wozz

Da, da ist's!

8

Cel

mf ma dolce

6

E

R

ff

Cis

sfz

Hfe

Pik

Kl *f*

dolce

7

E H

Bs Kl

Fl

3

Hr

f

dolce

Fag

Trp

Pos

Hr *f*

Kbt

dazu Hfe *Des dur gliss*

Wie zu Anfang dieser Szene
(♩= ca 100)
ritard
quasi Hauptzeitmaß
(♩= 80)
am Teich
throws the knife in
Wozz
So! da hin-un-ter!
Es taucht ins
Holz Blech Holz
ff Str
dimin
p
Hfe
sfz
mf
poco a poco
Ped.
260
The moon rises blood-red from the clouds
dunk-le Was-ser wie ein Stein.
Holz Blech Holz
Pos Hr
E H Kl
Pos
E H
dimin
Pos
Fag
Hr
verlöschend
Blech Holz Blech etc.
diminuendo
ppp
senza cresc
Hfe
pp
(Ped.)
tr
kleines Tamtam
freihängendes Becken
looks up
265
pp
A-ber der Mond verrät mich
Der Mond ist blu-
6 Gg m D
Pos
alle 1. Gg ohne D
ppp
verlöschen
kl Tamtam
Becken
Hfe
verklingen lassen
gr Tamtam
(Ped.)
Ped.

Wozz
270
-tig. Will denn die ganze Welt_ es aus-plau-dern?!_ Das Messer,
(6 Solo Gg m D)
6 Br m D
6 Solo Gg (pizz) 2 Pik 2 Kl 2 Ob
6 Solo Br (pizz) je 2 Trp Hr Pos m D
alle Br o D

wades into
Wozz
es liegt zu weit vorn, sie findens beim Ba-den o-der wenn sie nach Muscheln tauchen.

Ganz frei ' a tempo
275
the pond
(with a somewhat singing voice)
(spoken)
Wozz
Ich find's nicht.
A-ber ich muß mich wa-schen.
Ich bin blu - tig.
Gg m D
ppp ged Blech allein.
pp
f Holz
Pkn
mf
pp
tief
Xyl
1.Gg m D richtig
2.Gg col leg gestr
(1.Gg)

moaning :
Wozz
Da ein Fleck und noch ei-ner.
Weh!
molto espr.
Gg
2 Hfe
poco f
ff
hoch
tief
sfz
Vcl
K Bs, Pos u Tub
Br
Kl
mf
Holz
f
Vcl

280
Wozz
Weh!
ich wa-sche mich mit
Blut —
das
hoch
Vcl
(Hr Hfe)
K Bs, Tub
K Bs, Pos
K Bs
mp
(Fag Hfe)
Kl
Bs Kl
Fag
K Fag
(he drowns . . .)
Was-ser ist Blut...
Blut...
(Beide Hände immer chromatisch)
Str
Es
2. K Bs
sempre Ped
Holz u Hfe
Vcl dazu
Br dazu
(Str allein am Steg o D)
1. K Bs
3. K Bs

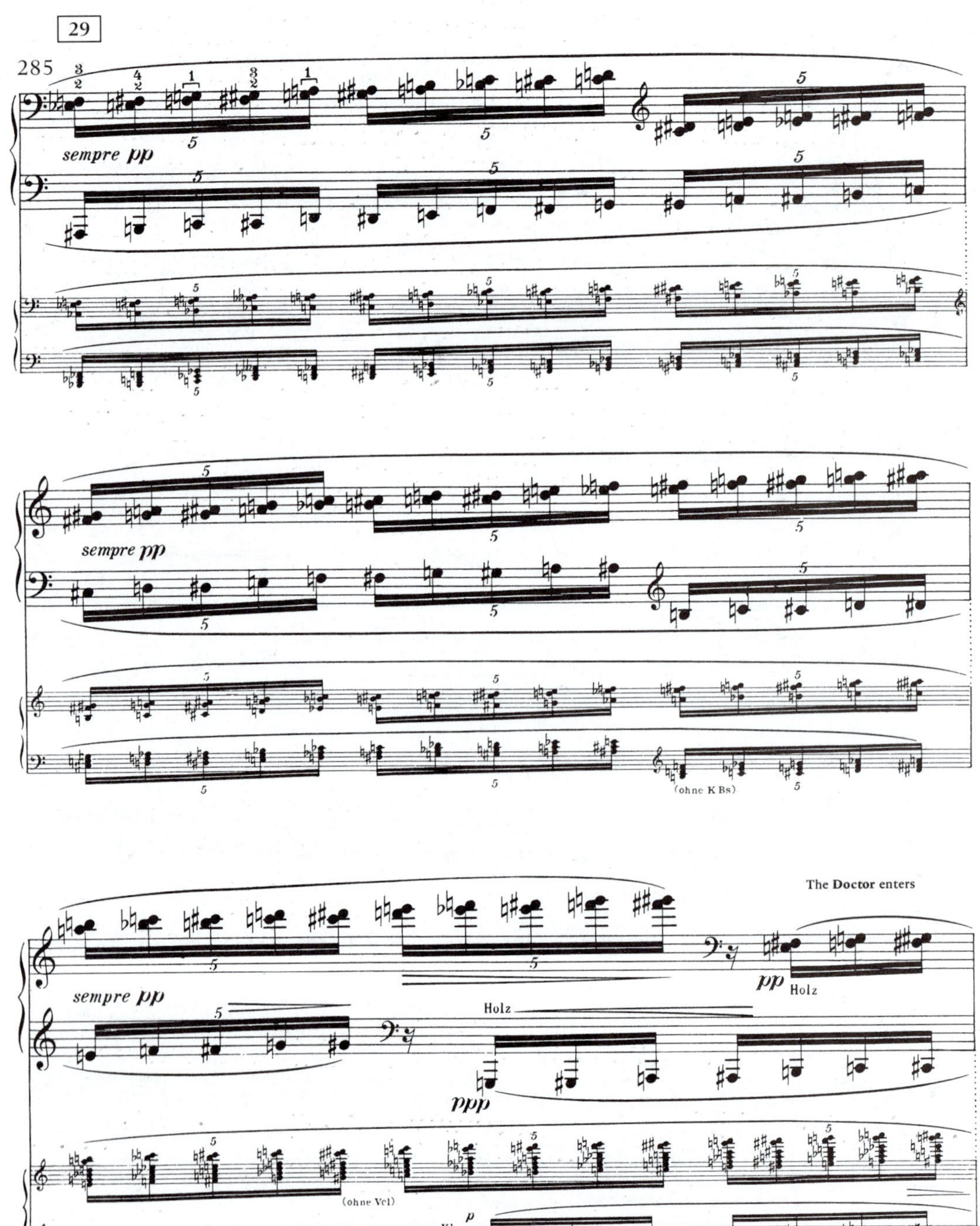
29
285
sempre pp
sempre pp
(ohne K Bs)
The Doctor enters
sempre pp
pp Holz
Holz
ppp
(ohne Vcl)
p
Kl
Fag
Bs Kl
2 Fag
K Fag

The **Captain** follows the Doctor (speaks)

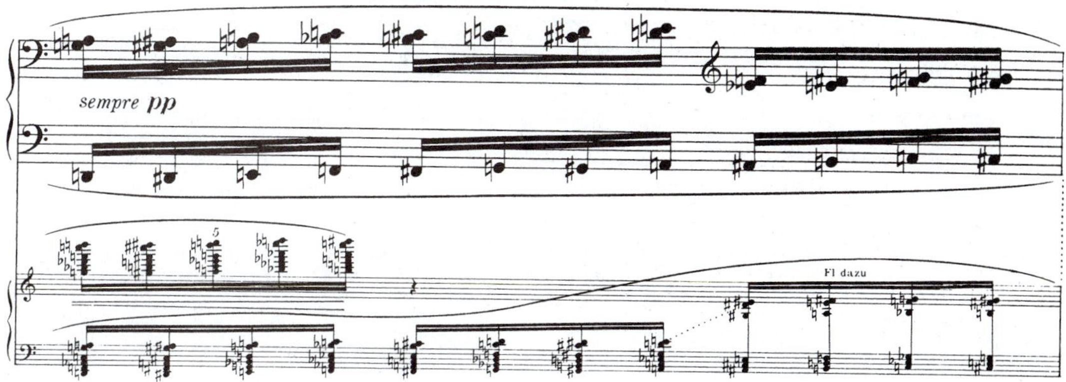

The **Doctor** (stands still): *p* Hören Sie? Dort!

Hauptmann: *p* Jesus! Das war ein Ton. (also stands still)

Doktor (pointing to the lake): Ja, dort!
Hauptmann: Es ist das Wasser
Fag
Hr
pp
Fag
Hr
pp
ohne K Bß
Hr, Fag
pp

im Teich. Das Wasser ruft. Es ist schon lange niemand ertrunken.
Gg
Br
Vel
ppp
pp (Str m D)
Str (ohne K Bß)
pp

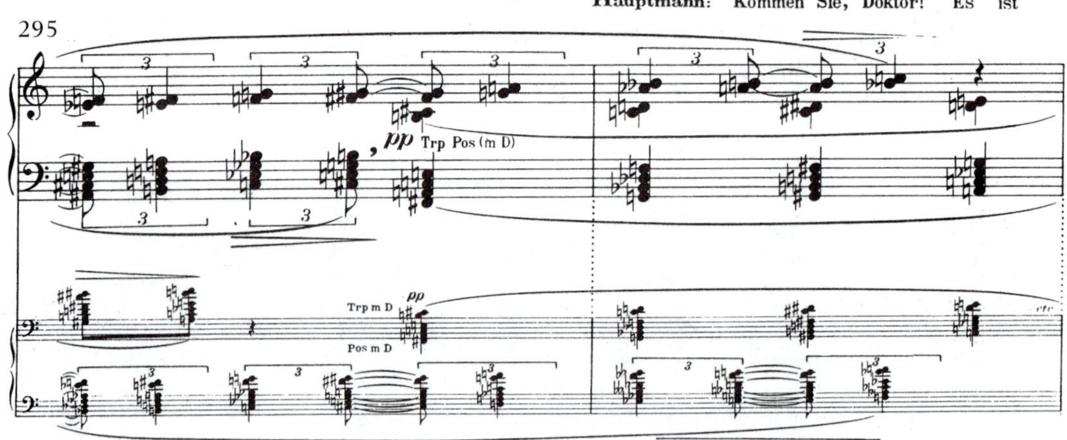
Hauptmann: Kommen Sie, Doktor! Es ist
295
pp Trp Pos (m D)
Trp m D
Pos m D
pp
etc.

300
nicht gut zu hören. (tries to drag off the Doctor)
Doktor (stands still and listens)
Str ppp
Fl Hr ppp
Kl Hr Bs Kl
6 Solo Str m D ppp
(pp) Das stöhnt — als stürbe ein Mensch.
6 Solo Str m D
pppp
Unkenrufe
Kl
p
Fl
p
Hr m D
Ped. (bis zum Schluß dieser Szene)
übergreifen
Ossia
305
Doktor: Da ertrinkt Jemand!
Hauptmann: Unheimlich! Der Mond rot, und die Nebel grau.
Hfe u. Cel
pp
pizz Vcl K Bs
The frog croaks continue to here

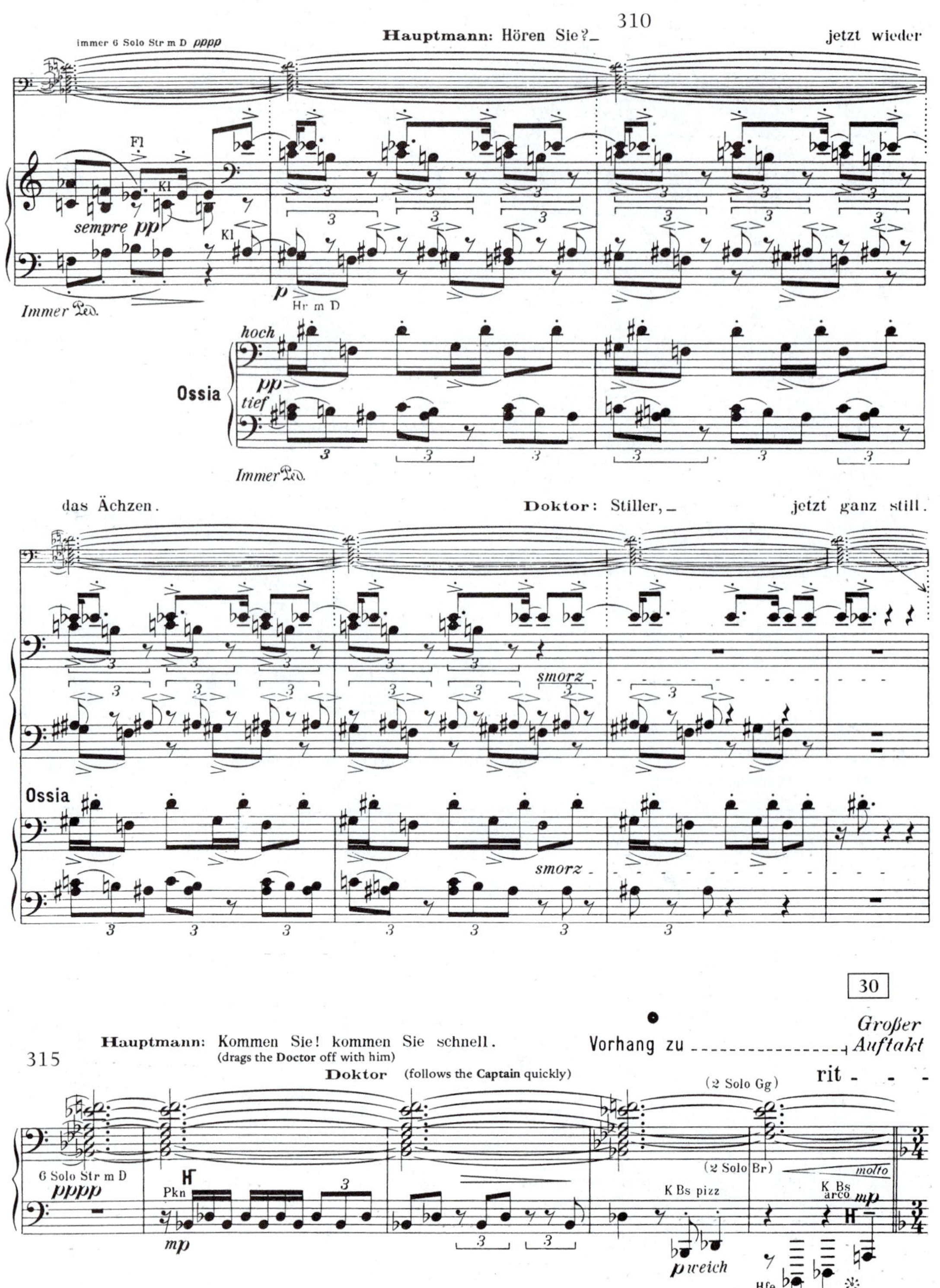
immer 6 Solo Str m D pppp
Hauptmann: Hören Sie?
310
jetzt wieder
Fl
Kl
sempre pp
Kl
Immer Ped.
p
Hr m D
hoch
pp
Ossia
tief
Immer Ped.
das Ächzen.
Doktor: Stiller,
jetzt ganz still.
smorz
Ossia
smorz
30
315
Hauptmann: Kommen Sie! kommen Sie schnell.
(drags the Doctor off with him)
Doktor (follows the Captain quickly)
Vorhang zu
Großer Auftakt
rit
(2 Solo Gg)
6 Solo Str m D
pppp
Pkn
mp
(2 Solo Br)
molto
K Bs pizz
p weich
K Bs arco
mp
Hfe
p (B Des)

320
Scene change
Adagio (♩= ♩= mindestens 46)
2.Gge
Br
p
(mp)
(K Bs)
Vcl dazu
2 Fag dazu
3
3
3. Fag u K Fag dazu
1.Ggn
Solo Gg
II. Spieler
pp
I. Spieler
325
Kl 2.Gg
3
Str allein
Fag dazu
1. Hälfte Ggn
alle Ggn
330
I
Ob dazu
3
Fl dazu
(Ob)
mf
3 Fag
zurücktreten
mp Hr
Pos
II
Orig 8va
Hr
K Bs

I
II
1. Gg
Hfe
(1) 5
(4)
6
Pos u 2. Gg
etc
Trp
Str
Pos
Hfe (Ganzton-Glissando)
335
nicht eilen
pp Holz u Trp
1. Gg u. Pos
molto
tief
sehr hoch
Pos
1. Gg dazu
ppp
Blech
2. Gg Trp
molto
Br
Pos
Vcl div
Kbt Tamtam
340
klagend
Ggn
poco f
(pp) Str allein
Br
(weg) espress
Hr (gest)
wie aus der Ferne, aber deutlich
Vcl
Fag
meno p

string
molto
I
II
menop
1.Gg u 4 Ob cresc
mp
Fag
mp
mf 3
cresc
3
Vel
Holz
pp
Vcl u. K-B
345
Bedeutend bewegter
(♩= 80-84)
ff furioso
Trp
Ob
(pizz)
(tief)
6
Pos
f
Str trem
f
Pk trem
(gr Trommschlag)
350
je 4
Kl. Fl
(pizz)
pizz
fp
cresc
Trp
Hr
f
f
Str
mf
f
3 Pos
m D
f
cresc

rall
Wieder etwas breiter (Andante)
Fl Kl
Str u Ob
espr
Trp
Pos Hfe
rauschend
weg!
cresc
Pke
Hfe
355
Wieder drängend
Kl
Hfe
hoch
Ob
molto
col leg
Pos
Hrn u Fag
kl Tromm
Br Vcl K Bs
tief
Wieder breiter
360
Trp
Gg Xyl
Ob
cresc
Br
alles übertönend
Hr Vcl
Pos
Br Vcl
weg
3 Pos
Hr Vcl
Hr
1 Pos
2 Pos
3 Pos
etc
Fag BB Kl
cresc
Holz
Str
Tub
gr Tromm

Breit
molto rit
365
Tempo I
12 Holzbl
Trp
(Tutti)
molto
Fl Kl Gg
(4 Pos)
Br
Hr
Schlagwerk
Hr Trp Br
Pos Hfe pizz 4 Pkn
Schon im neuen Tempo
(ohne Str)
dimin
weg
nicht hervortreten
(ohne Hr)
meno
(ohne Pkn)
ohne Pos Tb
espr
(quasi 4/4 Takt
31
Vorhang auf
370
molto
Str
Gg Fl Br
Cel
Ob Ggn
(Kl)
deutlich kadenzieren
molto
Hr Trp
Blech
Hfe
hoch
sehr hoch
Br u. Vcl
Pos Tub
Holz dazu
K Bß

5th (last) Scene In front of Marie's house (bright morning, sunshine)

Zweites Kind: Was is?
Erstes Kind: Weißt' es nit? Sie sind schon Alle 'naus.
(rall)
(♩. = 58)
Hfe
Es Kl
Trp m D
gr Tamtam
(Es Kl Trp)
Solo Gg m D
espr
Kl
Noch etwas langsamer
Wieder voriges Tempo
(♩. = 58)
380
Mariens Knabe (still riding)
Hopp,hopp!
Dritte Kind (to Marie's child): Du! Dein Mutter ist tot!
Rute
1.Gg (Flag)
Br (Flag)
Br
Vcl (Flag)
Vcl
Ob
Fl
(Br)
Hrn Hfe
Pkn gedämpft
'poco rit
a tempo, ma sempre rubato
Mariens Knabe
Hopp,hopp! Hopp,hopp!
Zweites Kind: Wo is sie denn?
Erstes Kind: Draus liegt sie, am Weg, neben dem Teich.
1.Gg
1 Trp m D
Es Kl
(poco espr.)
Str m D
Br Vcl
poco
4 Hr m D
kl Tromm gedämpft
etc

385
riding
Mariens Knabe
Hopp,hopp! Hopp,hopp! Hopp,hopp!
Drittes Kind: Kommt— anschaun!
Alle Kinder run off
Xyl
(poco rit)
(Es Kl)
Bs Kl
Solo Kl
ganz ohne Ausdruck
Solo Vcl
Str allein
Pke gedämpft
gr Tromm
dimin
p poco espress
Vorhang fällt
Mariens Knabe (alone) hesitates for a moment, then rides off after the other children
(ab) Leere Bühne
Etwas zögernd und molto rubato.
Allmählich wieder gleichmäßig fließend werden: Quasi Tempo I
[rit. acc. rit. acc. rit. acc. rit. acc. rit]
poco espress
Solo Br
Trp m D
Solo Gg m D
Hrm D
sempre pp, ma molto espr
pp sempre senza cresc e dim
Fl Cel
senza rit
390
(beide Hände hoch)
vierhändig
(tief)
Str m D ohne K Bß
molto p
(Hfe)
End of the opera

TEXT AND TRANSLATION

SCENE FOUR
INVENTION ON A CHORD OF SIX NOTES
Path in the wood by the pond. Moonlight, as before.
(Wozzeck stumbles hurriedly in, then stops, looking around for something.)

WOZZECK

Das Messer? Wo ist das Messer? Ich hab's dagelassen. Näher, noch näher. Mir graut's . . . da regt sich was. Still! Alles still und tot.	The knife? Where is the knife? I left it there. Around here somewhere. I'm terrified . . . something's moving. Silence. Everything silent and dead.

(Shouting)

Mörder! Mörder!	Murderer! Murderer!

(Whispering again)

Ha! Da ruft's. Nein, ich selbst.	Ah! Someone called. No, it was only me.

(Still looking, he staggers a few steps further and stumbles against the corpse.)

Marie! Marie! Was hast du für eine rote Schnur um den Hals? Hast dir das rote Halsband verdient, wie die Ohrringlein, mit deiner Sünde! Was hängen dir die schwarzen Haare so wild? Mörder! Mörder! Sie werden nach mir suchen. Das Messer verrät mich!	Marie! Marie! What's that red cord around your neck? Was the red necklace payment for your sins, like the earrings? Why's your dark hair so wild about you? Murderer! Murderer! They will come and look for me. The knife will betray me!

(Looks for it in a frenzy)

Da, da ist's!	Here! Here it is!

(At the pond)

So! Da hinunter!	There! Sink to the bottom!

(Throws the knife into the pond)

Es taucht ins dunkle Wasser wie ein Stein.	It plunges into the dark water like a stone.

(The moon appears, blood-red, from behind the clouds. Wozzeck looks up.)

Aber der Mond verrät mich, der Mond ist blutig. Will den die ganze Welt es ausplaudern? Das Messer, es liegt zu weit vorn, sie finden's beim Baden oder wenn sie nach Muscheln tauchen.	But the moon will betray me: the moon is blood-stained. Is the whole world going to incriminate me? The knife is too near the edge: they'll find it when they're swimming or diving for snails.

(Wades into the pond)

Ich find's nicht. Aber ich muss mich waschen.	I can't find it. But I must wash myself.
Ich bin blutig. Da ein Fleck—und noch einer.	There's blood on me. There's a spot here—and another.
Weh! Weh! Ich wasche mich mit Blut—	Oh, God! I am washing myself in blood—
das Wasser ist Blut . . . Blut . . .	the water is blood. . . blood . . .

(Drowns)
(The Doctor appears, followed by the Captain.)

CAPTAIN

Halt!	Wait!

DOCTOR *(Stops)*

Hören Sie? Dort!	Can you hear? There!

CAPTAIN

Jesus! Das war ein Ton!	Jesus! What a ghastly sound!

(Stops as well)

DOCTOR *(Pointing to the pond)*

Ja, dort!	Yes, there!

CAPTAIN

Es ist das Wasser im Teich. Das Wasser ruft.	It's the water in the pond. The water is calling.
Es ist schon lange Niemand ertrunken.	It's been a long time since anyone drowned.
Kommen Sie, Doktor!	Come away, Doctor.
Es ist nicht gut zu hören.	It's not good for us to be hearing it.

(Tries to drag the doctor away)

DOCTOR *(Resisting, and continuing to listen)*

Das stöhnt, als stürbe ein Mensch. Da ertrinkt Jemand!	There's a groan, as though someone were dying. Somebody's drowning!

CAPTAIN

Unheimlich! Der Mond rot, und die Nebel grau.	It's eerie! The moon is red, and the mist is grey.
Hören Sie? . . . Jetzt wieder das Ächzen.	Can you hear? . . . That moaning again.

DOCTOR

Stiller, . . . jetzt ganz still.	It's getting quieter . . . now it's stopped altogether.

CAPTAIN

Kommen Sie! Kommen Sie schnell! — Come! Come quickly!

(He rushes off, pulling the doctor along with him.)

SCENE CHANGE
INVENTION ON A KEY (D MINOR)

SCENE FIVE
INVENTION ON A QUAVER RHYTHM

In front of Marie's door. Morning. Bright sunshine.
(Children are noisily at play. Marie's child is riding a hobby-horse.)

CHILDREN

Ringel, Ringel, Rosenkranz, Ringelreih'n, Ringel, Ringel, Rosenkranz, Ring. . .	Ring-a-ring-a-roses, a pocket full of. . .

(Their song and game are interrupted by other children bursting in.)

ONE OF THE NEWCOMERS

Du, Käthe! Die Marie!	Hey, Katie! Have you heard about Marie?

SECOND CHILD

Was ist?	What's happened?

FIRST CHILD

Weisst' es nit? Sie sind schon Alle'naus.	Don't you know? They've all gone out there.

THIRD CHILD *(To Marie's little boy)*

Du! Dein'Mutter ist tot!	Hey! Your mother's dead!

MARIE'S SON *(Still riding)*

Hopp, hopp! Hopp, hopp! Hopp, hopp!	Hop, hop! Hop, hop! Hop, hop!

SECOND CHILD

Wo ist sie denn?	Where is she, then?

FIRST CHILD

Draus' liegt sie, am Weg, neben dem Teich.	She's lying out there, on the path near the pond.

THIRD CHILD

Kommt, anschaun!	Come and have a look!

(All the children run off.)

MARIE'S SON *(Continuing to ride)*

Hopp, hopp! Hopp, hopp! Hopp, hopp!	Hop, hop! Hop, hop! Hop, hop!

(He hesitates for a moment and then rides after the other children.)

TRANSLATED BY SARAH E. SOULSBY

Schoenberg's two most eminent students, Alban Berg (1885–1935) and Anton Webern, each created a distinctive style bound only by the commonality of Expressionism and serialism. Berg maintained ties to the lyricism and emotional intensity of late Romanticism, which he exploits fully in his masterpiece, the opera *Wozzeck.* Based on an early nineteenth-century play by Georg Büchner, the opera tells the disturbing tale of Wozzeck, a common soldier in the army who is abused both by his captain and by the army doctor. The only love in his life is Marie, and they have a young child born out of wedlock. Marie has an affair, and this pushes Wozzeck over the edge. Near a lake, he brutally murders her. Eventually Wozzeck drowns in the lake, which he perceives as a pool of blood. The frustrations of Wozzeck's hopeless life, as portrayed in Büchner's play, symbolize the political repressions of the post-Napoleonic years; based on real-life events, the opera explores Expressionistic themes of nightmares and insanity.

Berg organizes the opera into three acts, each with five scenes. Orchestral interludes serve as transitions between the scenes. In Act III, Scene 4, Wozzeck has returned to the scene of the murder. After observing Marie's dead body and admiring the "red necklace" around her neck, he looks for and finds the murder weapon. He throws the knife into the lake, but then panics that the knife did not go deep enough. In his effort to retrieve it he drowns. In a chilling touch, the captain and the doctor—symbols of authority in society—appear at the lake, hear the sounds of death, and leave quickly, rather than helping. The music, which had supported the scene with gentle chromaticism, surges forth during the interlude. Berg employs the full brute force of the orchestra, mixing dissonances and tonal elements, to express anguish over the events.

The final scene provides a simple yet unsettling close to the opera. The young child of Wozzeck and Marie is playing in the street along with other children. An older child runs in with news that Marie has been found, and the children all race out to see the dead body. Too young to understand, Marie's child rides on his hobbyhorse after the other children to the sounds of "Hop, hop." We are left to imagine his reaction to the gruesome scene that awaits him. Throughout the final scene, the innocence of the music, with its child-like compound meter, enhances the tragedy of the story.

30

Anton Webern

Symphony, Op. 21, Second movement (1928)

8CD: 7/ 32 – 34

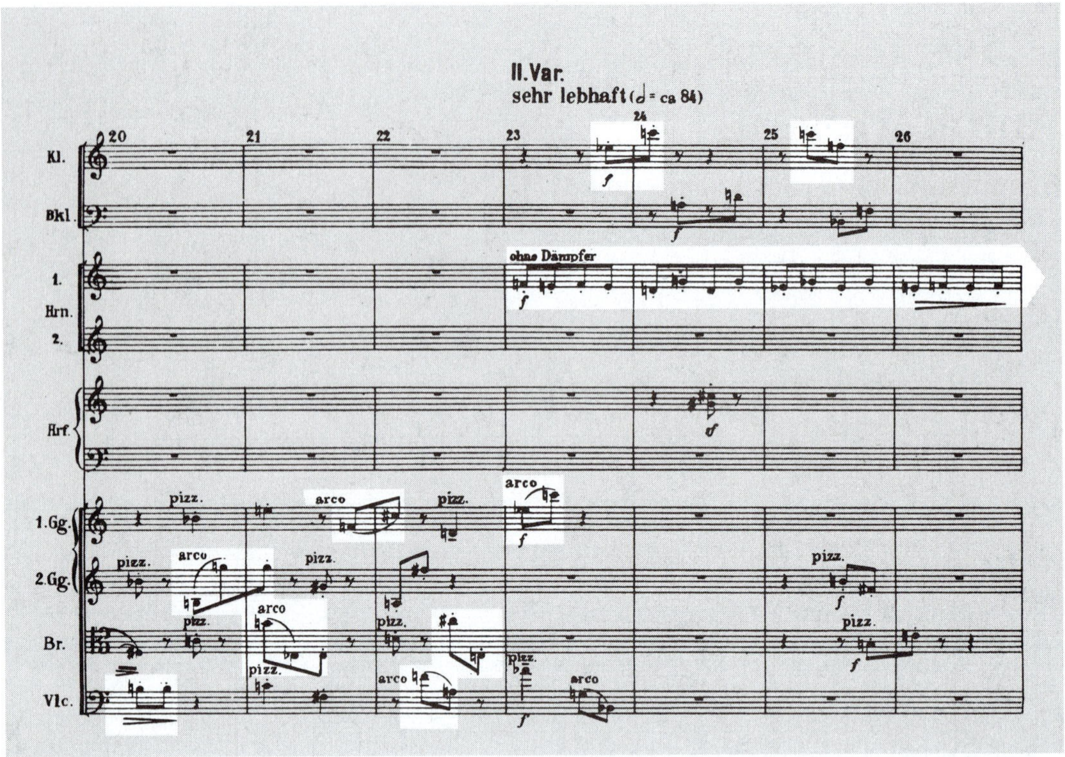

II. Var.
sehr lebhaft (𝅗𝅥 = ca 84)
Kl.
Bkl.
ohne Dämpfer
1.
Hrn.
2.
Hrf.
1. Gg.
2. Gg.
Br.
Vlc.
pizz.
arco

rit.
Kl.
Bkl.
1.
Hrn.
2.
Hrf.
1. Gg.
2. Gg.
Br.
Vlc.
pizz.

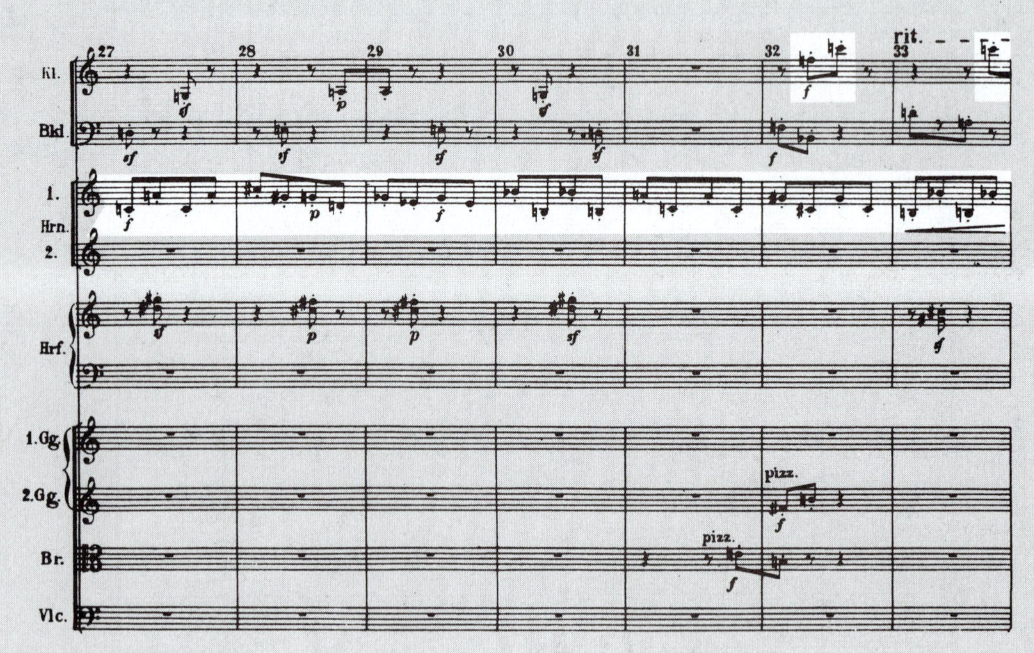

III. Var.
wieder mäßiger (𝅗𝅥 = ca 66)
Kl.
Bkl.
(o. Dpf.)
(m. Dpf.)
1. Hrn. 2.
Hrf.
pizz.
arco
1. Gg.
2. Gg.
Br.
Vlc.

rit.
tempo
Kl.
Bkl.
gedämpft
offen
Dämpfer auf
1. Hrn. 2.
Hrf.
pizz.
1. Gg.
2. Gg.
Br.
Vlc.

33
IV. Var.
molto rit.
äußerst ruhig (𝅗𝅥 = ca 40)
molto rit.
Kl.
Bkl.
1. Hrn. 2.
Hrf.
1. Gg.
2. Gg.
Br.
Vlc.
m.Dpf.
(m.Dpf.)
Solo arco
(Solo)
Solo
Solo arco
(Solo)
V. Var.
rit.
sehr lebhaft (𝅗𝅥 = ca 84)
Dämpfer ab
arco Alle (geteilt)
Alle (geteilt)
Alle (geteilt)
Alle (geteilt)

57
58
59
60
Kl.
Bkl.
1.
Hrn.
2.
Hrf.
1.Gg.
2.Gg.
Br.
Vlc.
pp
pp
p
pp
cresc.
pp
cresc.
cresc.
pp
cresc.
pp

61
62
63
64
Kl.
Bkl.
1.
Hrn.
2.
Hrf.
1.Gg.
2.Gg.
Br.
Vlc.
mf
p cresc.
mp cresc.
p cresc.
mp cresc.
p
cresc.
mp cresc.
p
cresc.
mp cresc.

VI. Var.
rit. - - - - - - - - marschmäßig (𝅗𝅥 = ca 66), nicht eilen
Kl.
Bkl.
1. Hrn. 2.
Hrf.
1. Gg.
2. Gg.
Br.
Vlc.
o. Dpf.
mf cresc.
gedämpft
offen
dim.
cresc.

74
75
76
77
Kl.
Bkl.
1.
Hrn.
2.
Hrf.
1.Gg.
2.Gg.
Br.
Vlc.
34
VII.Var.
etwas breiter
rit.
tempo
rit.
tempo rit.
78
79
80
81
82
83
(o.Dpf.)
(m.Dpf.)
pizz.
arco

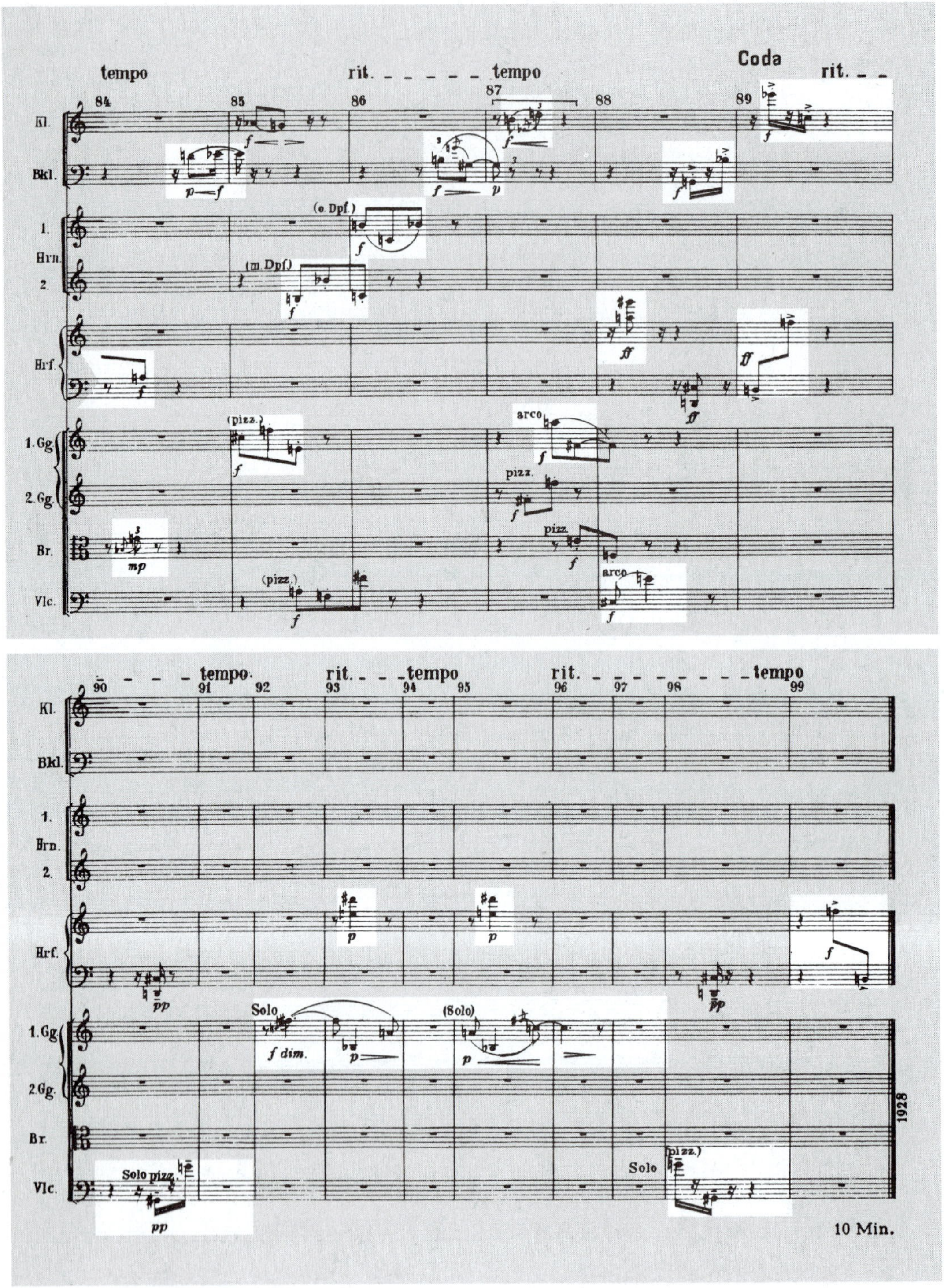

tempo rit. tempo Coda rit.

84 85 86 87 88 89

Kl.
Bkl.
1. Hrn. 2.
Hrf.
1. Gg.
2. Gg.
Br.
Vlc.

(e. Dpf.) (m. Dpf.) (pizz.) arco pizz. pizz. (pizz.) arco

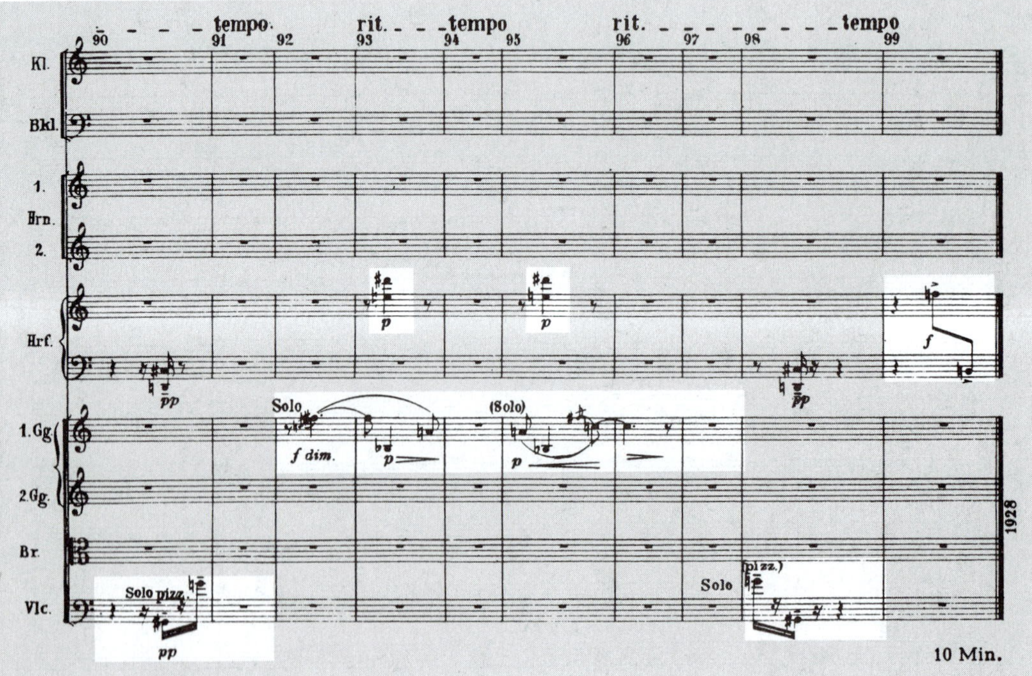

Anton Webern (1883–1945) explored the more radical side of Schoenberg's Expressionistic vision. Unlike Berg, Webern created a style based on a stricter adherence to atonality and a concise and nonexpressive musical language. Instead of creating traditional structures from thematic units, Webern expanded upon Schoenberg's device of *Klangfarbenmelodie* (tone-color melody) and fashioned a colorful sound fabric out of touches of timbre, as individual instruments play only a few notes in succession, often separated by rests and large intervals. The disjointed effect has been termed pointillism, after the distinctive use of color dots in the paintings of Georges Seurat.

Webern's manipulation of serial techniques, and particularly his application of serialism to musical elements other than pitch, had a pronounced influence on composers of the post–World War II generation. His celebrated Symphony, Opus 21, reflects some Neoclassical qualities, particularly in the two-movement format featuring a sonata-allegro form with a double canon followed by a theme-and-variation structure. Both movements are based on the same dodecaphonic tone row. The row is a palindrome, so that intervals of the retrograde are identical to those of the prime. At the center of the row is a tritone, which is also the interval that separates the first and last note of the series. These characteristics are reflected in the structure of the second movement as a whole. Most notable is the palindrome structure, which can be seen within each variation and in the structure of the movement as a whole. The theme of the second movement, which spans eleven measures, is based on the transposed inversion and retrograde inversion of the tone row from the first movement (A♮-F♯-G♮-G♯-E♮-F♮-B♮-B♭-D♮-C♯-C♮-E♭).

31

Béla Bartók

Concerto for Orchestra, Fourth movement, *Interrupted Intermezzo* (1943)

8CD: 7/ 35 – 41
4CD: 4/ 10 – 16

20
Fl. I
Cl. I in A
Bsn. I
Hn. I in F
Harp I
Vlns. I
Vlns. II
Vls.
Vcs.
D.Bs.
p, espr.
mp
* If the Flute has no low b, 1st Bassoon will play: and Flute tacet.

29
rallent. - - - a tempo
Fl. I
Ob. I
Hn. I in F
Harp I
Vlns. I
Vlns. II
Vls.
Vcs.
D.Bs.
arco
*real sound:

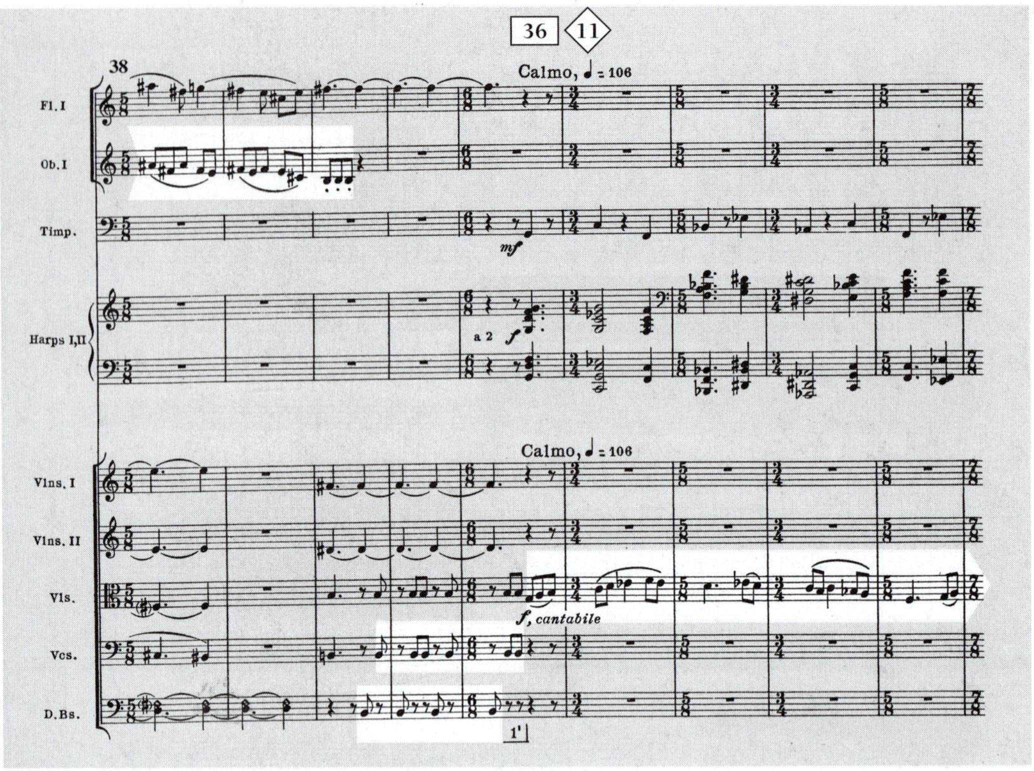

36
11
38
Calmo, ♩ = 106
Fl. I
Ob. I
Timp.
mf
Harps I,II
a 2
f
Calmo, ♩ = 106
Vlns. I
Vlns. II
Vls.
f, cantabile
Vcs.
D.Bs.
1'

47
C.A.
f
Timp.
Harps I,II
Vlns. I
f
Vls.
Vcs.
f
D.Bs.
f

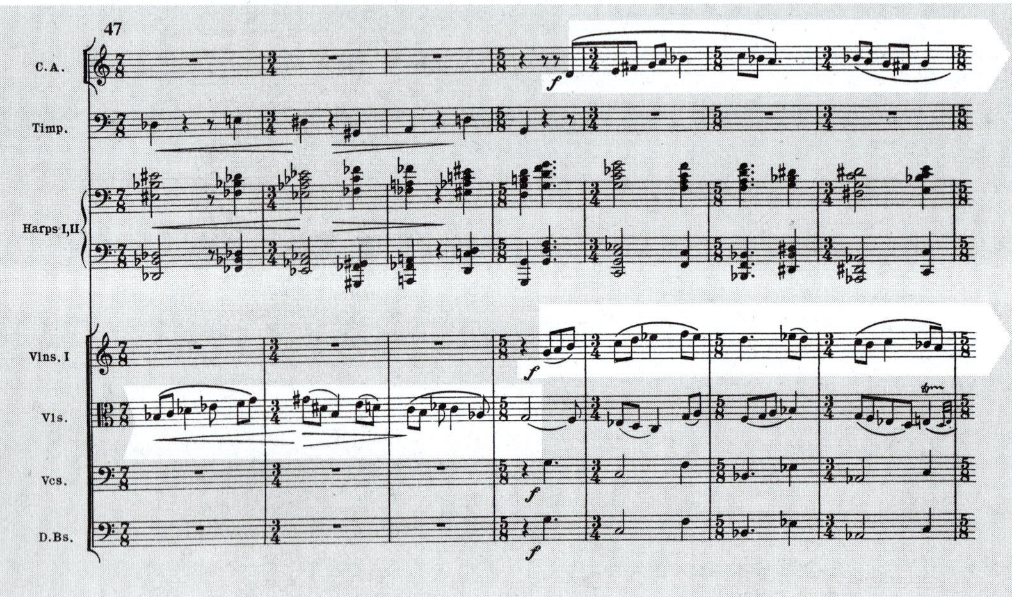

37 12

61

Tempo I. (♩= 114)

Fl. I
p

Ob. I
p

C.A.

Cl. I in A
p

Tempo I. (♩= 114)

Vlns. I
div.
p
unis. pizz.

Vlns. II
p

Vls.
non div.
p
p

Vcs.
pizz.
p
arco
p

D.Bs.
pizz.
p
arco
p

38
13
71
accelerando
Obs. I, II
Cl. I in B♭
Bsn. I
Hns. I, II in F
arco
Vlns. I
Vlns. II
Vls.
pizz.
Vcs.
D.Bs.
arco
1'
79
al Più mosso, 𝅗𝅥 = 94
Flts. I, II
Obs. I, II
Clts. in B♭
con sord.
Trpts. I, II in C
Trbs. I, II
Trb. III Tuba
sim.

87
I
Flts.
II, III
dim.
p
mf
I
Obs.
II, III
f
I
Clts. in B♭
II, III
Bsns. I, II
Hns. I, II in F
Trb. II
Trb. III Tuba
gliss.
D. Bs.
94
Tuba
Vlns. I
Vlns. II

39
14
101
I
Flts.
II, III
a 2
I
Obs.
II, III
I
Clts. in B♭
II, III
Bsns. I, II
Hns. I, II in F
(con sord.)
Trpts. I, II in C
I, II
Trbs.
III
Tuba
Trgl.
div.
unis.
gliss.
Vlns. I
div. II
Vlns. II
Vls.
D. Bs.
dim.
p, espr.

108
Flts.
I
II, III
Obs.
I
II, III
Clts. in B♭
I
II, III
Hns. I, II in F
senza sord.
con sord.
Trpts. in C
I, II
III
Trbs.
I, II
III
Tuba
with the thick end of a Side Drum stick
Cym.
Tam-Tam
[laissez vibrer]
Vlns. I
Vlns. II
Vls.
gliss.

40
15
115
Calmo, 𝅗𝅥 = 106
I Flts. II, III
dim.
I Obs. II, III
I Clts. in B♭ II, III
Hn. I in F
Trb. I
Harp I
div.
con sord.
pizz.
Vlns. I
Vlns. II
Vls.
Vcs.
D. Bs.
1'
122
Ob. I
non cresc.

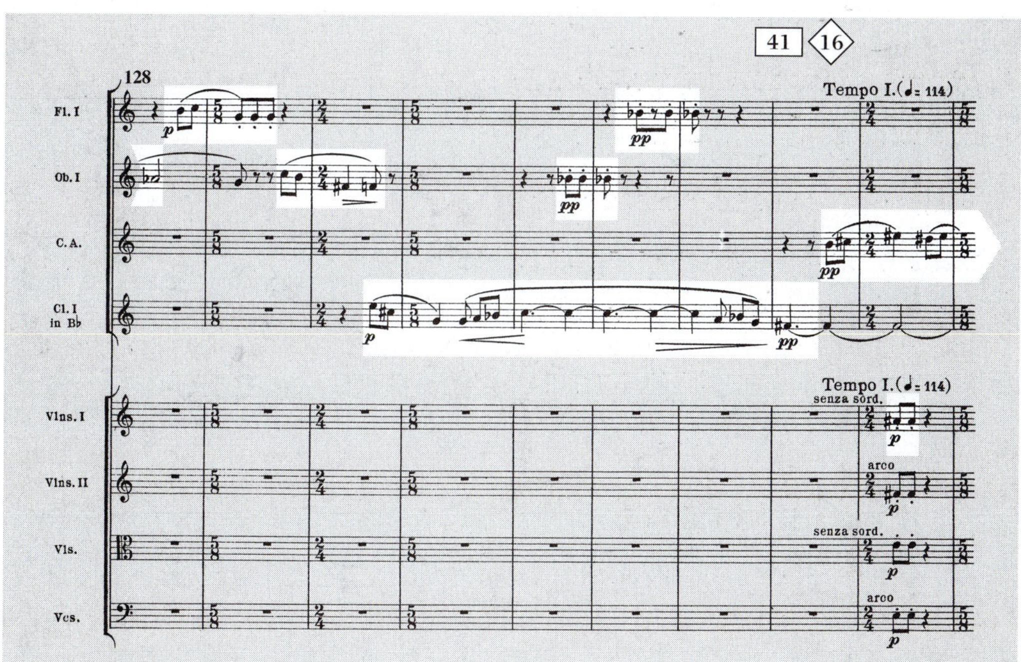
41
16
128
Tempo I. (♩= 114)
Fl. I
Ob. I
C. A.
Cl. I in B♭
Vlns. I
Vlns. II
Vls.
Vcs.
senza sord.
arco
senza sord.
arco

137
rallent. - - a tempo
rallent.
Fl. I
C. A.
Cl. I in B♭
I, III
Hns. in F
II
con sord.
con sord.
Vlns. I
Vlns. II
Vls.
Vcs.

quasi Cadenza
più volte
ad libitum
rubato
a tempo
pp
p
Fl. I
Ob. I
I, III
Hns. in F
II, IV
(senza sord.)
pp
colla parte
Vlns. I
Vlns. II
Vls.
Vcs.
144
(♩= 114)
Picc.
Obs.
Bsns.
pizz.
arco
D.Bs.

Béla Bartók (1881–1945) found a unique musical voice in the folk traditions of Eastern Europe. He studied the folk music of his native Hungary intently, writing numerous articles and collecting several anthologies of melodies. He then brought melodic, rhythmic, and harmonic aspects of these traditions into his own compositions. As a result, Bartók's music can be seen as a mixture of nationalist and neoclassical elements, along with his special gifts for color and dramatic flair.

Two years prior to his death, the terminally ill Bartók was commissioned by Serge Koussevitzky, the conductor of the Boston Symphony Orchestra, to write the *Concerto for Orchesta.* Bartók justified the title by explaining that he attempted "to treat the single orchestral instruments in a concertante or soloistic manner." In a very real sense, he composed a concerto for virtuoso orchestra.

The fourth movement, subtitled *Interrupted Intermezzo,* is set in a rondo pattern (**A-B-A′-C-B′-A′**). The **A** sections present a lively, folklike dance tune in the woodwinds. The shifting meters, reflecting the freedom of folk music, establish a playful mood. The beautiful lyrical melody in the **B** sections creates a striking contrast. Initially presented by the viola section with a harp accompaniment, the melody maintains the limited range and metrical variety of folk music. Section **C** centers on a theme from the Symphony No. 7 by Dmitri Shostakovich. Hardly a tribute to the Russian composer, the theme is mocked in a sarcastic, dissonant manner.

32

Sergei Prokofiev

Alexander Nevsky, Seventh movement (1939)

8CD: 7/ 42 – 45

11
на род - ной зем - ле не бы-вать вра - гу.
in our na - tive land foes shall ne - ver live.
ле не быть вра - гу,
land no foe shall live.
на род - ной зем - ле не бы - вать вра - гу.
in our na - tive land foes shall ne - ver live.
ле не быть вра - гу.
land no foe shall live.
maestoso
m.d.

16
Кто при - дёт бу - дёт на смерть бит.
Foes who come shall be put to death.
Кто при - дёт бу-дет на смерть бит.
Foes who come shall be put to death.
бу - дет
shall be

43
Allegro, ma non troppo ♩ = 84
21
Camp.
Xilof.
f Legni, Tr-be
Arpa, Archi
simile
26
ff
31 S.
f
Ве - се - ли - ся, пой,
Ce - le-brate and sing,
мать род-на - я Русь!
na - tive mo-ther Russ!
На - род-ной Ру - си
In our na-tive land
A.
f
Ве - се - ли - ся, пой,
Ce - le-brate and sing,
мать род - на - я Русь!
na - tive mo-ther Russ!
На - род-ной Ру - си
In our na-tive land

34
p subito
cresc.
не бы-вать вра-гу,
foes shall ne-ver live.
не ви-дать вра-гу
Foes shall ne-ver see
на-ших рус-ских сёл.
Rus-sian towns and fields.
p subito
cresc.
не бы-вать вра-гу,
foes shall ne-ver live.
не ви-дать вра-гу
Foesshall ne-ver see
на-ших рус-ских сёл.
Rus-sian towns and fields.
p
p subito
cresc.
37 S.
Кто при-дёт на Русь
They who march on Russ
бу-дет на смерть бит!
shall be put to death!
A.
Кто при-дёт на Русь
They who march on Russ
бу-дет на смерть бит!
shall be put to death!
T.
Не ви-дать вра-гу
Foes shall ne-ver see
B.
Не ви-дать вра-гу
Foes shall ne-ver see
V-ni
f espress.
m.d.

40
T.
на - ших рус-ских сёл,
Rus - sian towns and fields,
кто при - дет на
They who march on
Русь,
Russ
B.
m. s.
43
A.
На Ру - си род - ной, на Ру -
In our Rus - sia great, in our
T.
бу - дет на смерть бит.
shall be put to death.
На Ру - си род - ной, на Ру -
In our Rus - sia great, in our
B.
m. d.
46
A.
- си боль - шой не бы-вать вра - - гу!
na - tive Rus - sia no foe shall - live!
T.
- си боль - шой не бы-вать вра - - гу!
na - tive Rus - sia no foe shall - live!
B.
Meno mosso 𝅗𝅥 = 138
m. d.
f p

44
Legni
Tr-be
Corni
Fl.
Archi pizz.
Fl.
Ob.

Fl.
Cl.
Cl.
p
Fl.
Archi
Fag.
mf
C. ing.
Ob.
mp
p
Sax.

45
78
Alti
Bassi
mf
На Ру -
In our
Fl
Cl.
Fg.
Sax.
p
80
- си род - - ной, на Ру -
Rus - - sia great, in our
Fl.
(b)
Cl.
Fg.
Ob.
(b)
82
- си боль - - шой не бы -
na - tive Rus - - sia no
Fl.
3
3
Ob.

84
-вать
foe
вра
shall
гу.
live.
Fl.
Cl.
Cl.
86
Be
Ce
ce
le
p
Sax.
Ob.
88
-ли
-brate
ся,
and
пой,
sing,
mf
mf
Fl.
Fag.
Cl.
mf

90
мать род - на -
na - tive moth -
Cl.
92 S.
На Ру - си род -
In our Rus - sia
A
- я
er
Русь!
Russ!
T.
На Ру - си род -
In our Rus - sia
B.
- я
er
Русь!
Russ!
Ob.
Fl.
Fl., Archi
f espress.
Corni, Cl. b

95
-ной, на Ру - си боль - шой не бы - вать вра - - гу.
great, in our na - tive Rus - sia no foe shall live.
на Ру - си
in our
-ной, на Ру - си боль - шой не бы - вать вра - - гу.
great, in our na - tive Rus - sia no foe shall live.
на Ру - си
in our na-
8
8
100
Ве - се - ли - ся, пой, мать род-на - я Русь!
Ce - le - brate and sing, na-tive mo-ther Russ!
Ве - се - ли - ся, пой, мать род-на - я Русь!
Ce - le - brate and sing, na-tive mo-ther Russ!

105
Più largamente
S.
На ве - ли - кий празд - ник
To a fete in tri - umph
A.
T.
На ве - ли - кий празд - ник
To a fete in tri - umph
B.
Xil.
Camp.
Più largamente
Tr-be, Corni
Celli
Bassi
110
со - бра - ла - ся Русь. Ве - се - ли - ся,
all of Rus - sia came. Ce - le - brate, re -
со - бра - ла - ся Русь. Ве - се - ли - ся,
all of Rus - sia came. Ce - le - brate, re -
m.s.

115
Русь! joice,
Ве се - ce - le -
ли - ся, brate and
Русь, sing,
род - our
Русь! joice,
Ве - се - ce - le -
ли - ся, brate and
Русь, sing,
род - our
Camp.
Tr-ai
m.s. m.d.
pesante
120
poco allarg.
на - moth -
я er
мать! land!
на - moth -
я er
мать! land!
poco allarg
m.s.m.d.
m.s.

After over fifteen years of self-imposed exile, Sergei Prokofiev (1891–1953) returned to his homeland, the Soviet Union, eventually settling in Moscow in 1936. Among the most important works created during his Soviet years are several film scores made in collaboration with the nation's foremost film director, Sergei Eisenstein. The first of these resulted in the classic film *Alexander Nevsky* (1938), which tells the story of the thirteenth-century hero who defeated both the Swedish army and, two years later, the Germans. The later event, which culminates with Nevsky's brilliant victory on the frozen Lake Chudskoye, provides the subject for the film's plot.

Prokofiev extracted and refined some of the musical sections of the film to create a seven-movement cantata for mezzo-soprano, chorus, and orchestra. The last movement, subtitled *Alexander's Entry into Pskov,* is taken from the triumphant final portion of the film. Prokofiev creates a distinctive Russian character by tapping into the strong choral tradition of the country and by employing a folklike melody, reminiscent of Musorgsky. This final movement of the cantata not only exhibits a nationalistic character, but also projects in its fullness of sound the Soviet government's view of the powerful working class.

33

Olivier Messiaen

Quatuor pour la fin du temps (*Quartet for the End of Time*), Second movement, *Vocalise, pour l'Ange qui annonce la fin du Temps* (*Vocalise, for the Angel who announces the End of Time*) (1941)

8CD: 7/ 46 - 48

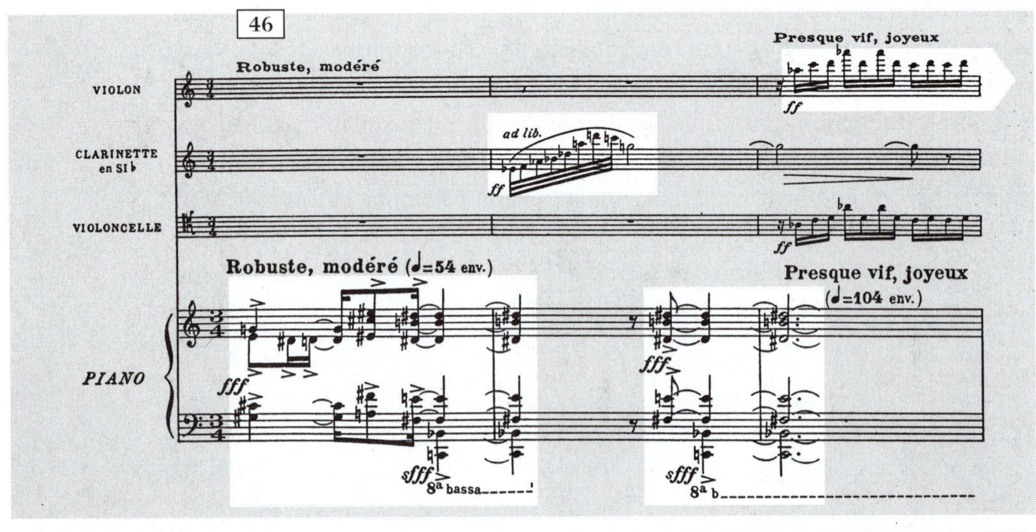

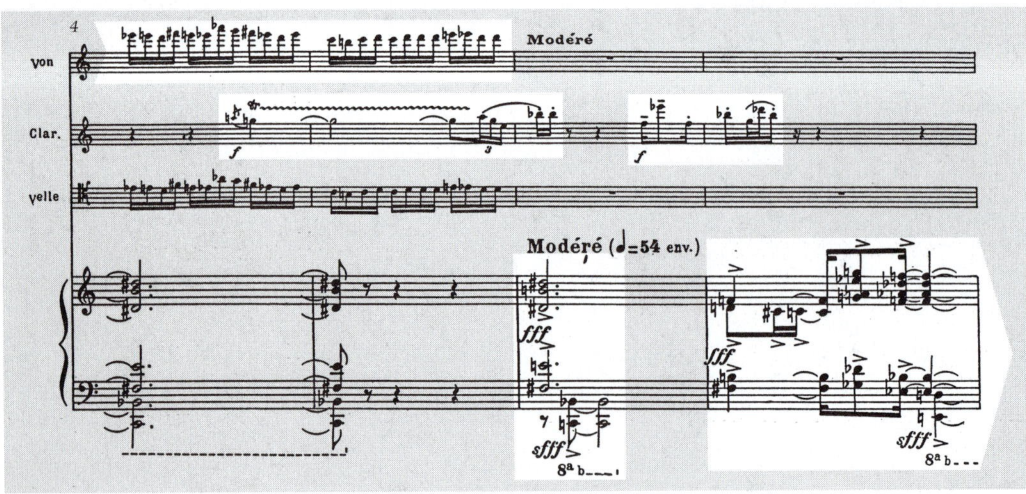

8
Presque vif
Modéré
Von
Clar.
Vcelle
ad lib.
Presque vif (♩=104 env.)
Modéré (♩=54 env.)
11
p cresc. molto
15
fff (fulgurant, pressez ce trait)

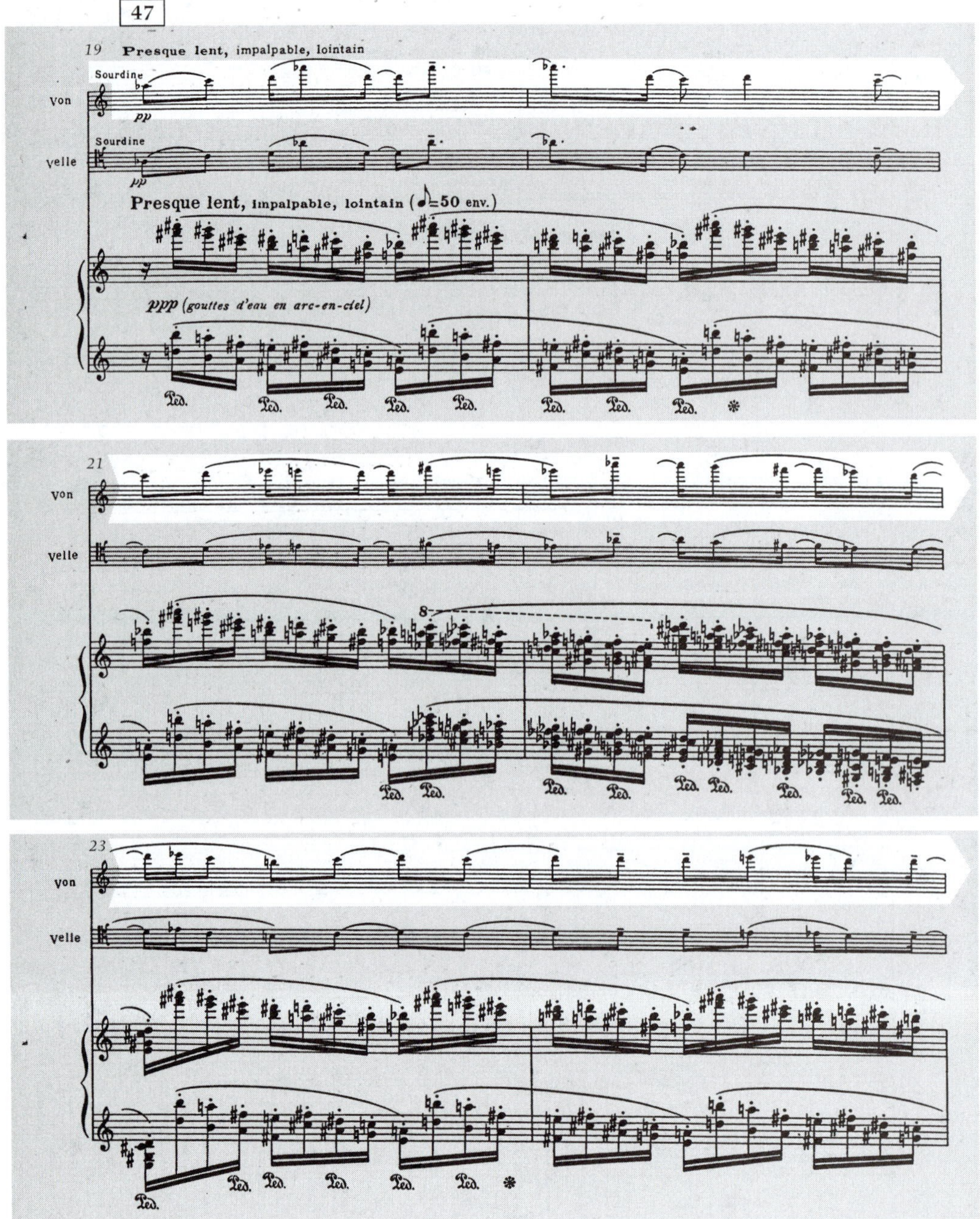
47
19
Presque lent, impalpable, lointain
Sourdine
Von
pp
Sourdine
Vcelle
pp
Presque lent, impalpable, lointain (♪=50 env.)
ppp (gouttes d'eau en arc-en-ciel)
21
Von
Vcelle
8
23
Von
Vcelle

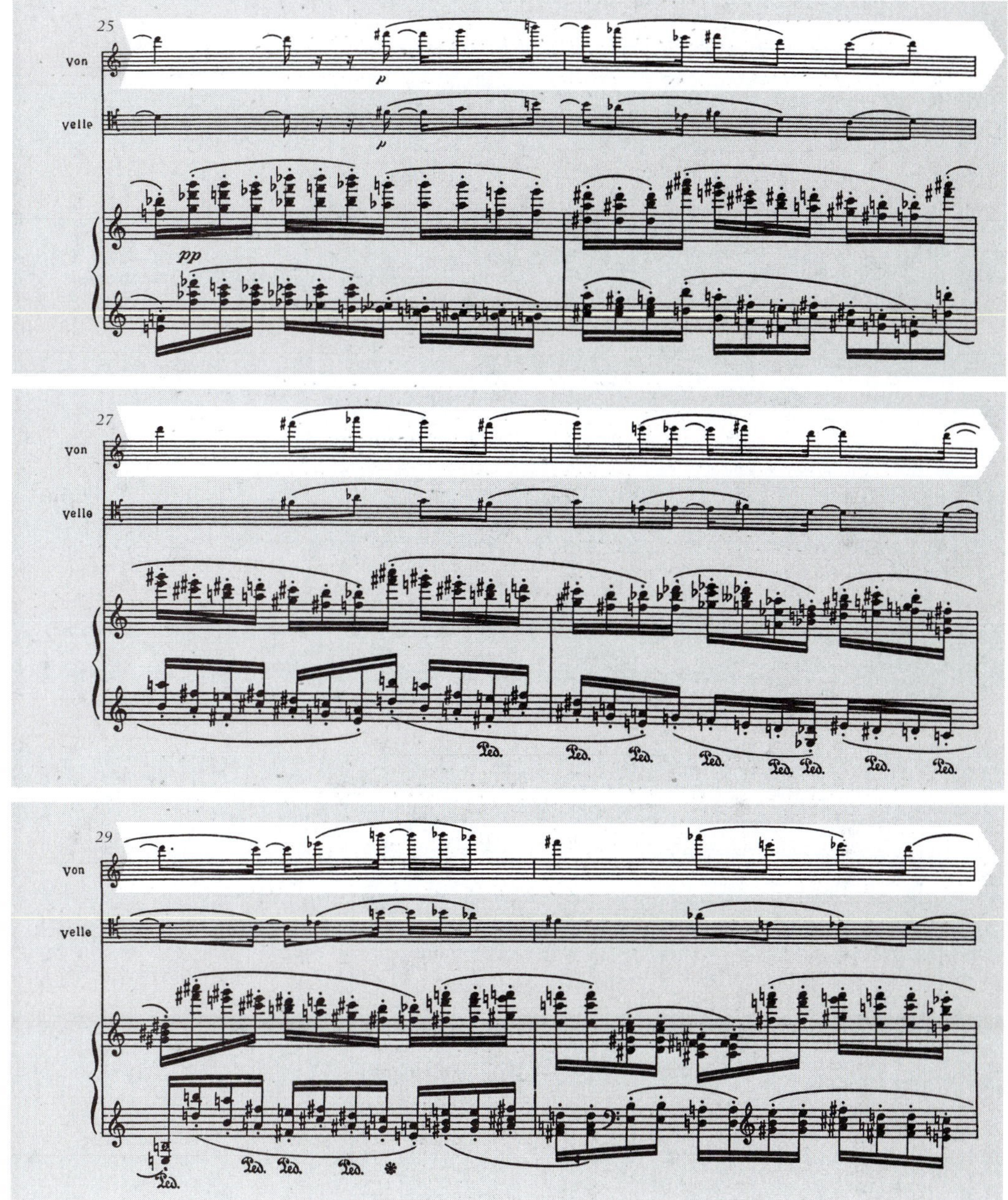
25
Von
p
velle
p
pp
27
Von
velle
Ped.
29
Von
velle
Ped.

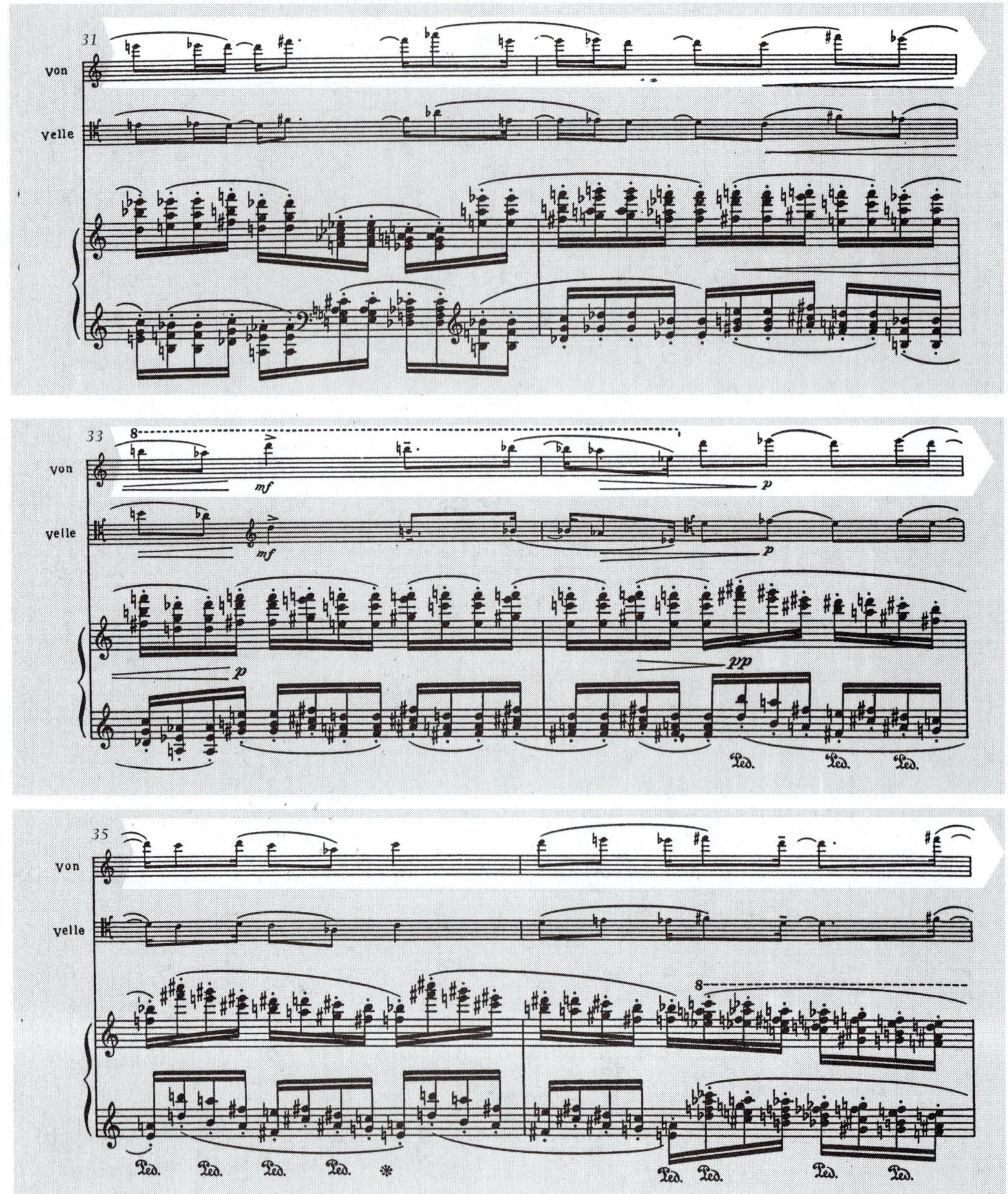
31
Von
Vcelle
33
Von
Vcelle
mf
p
pp
Ped.
35
Von
Vcelle
Ped.

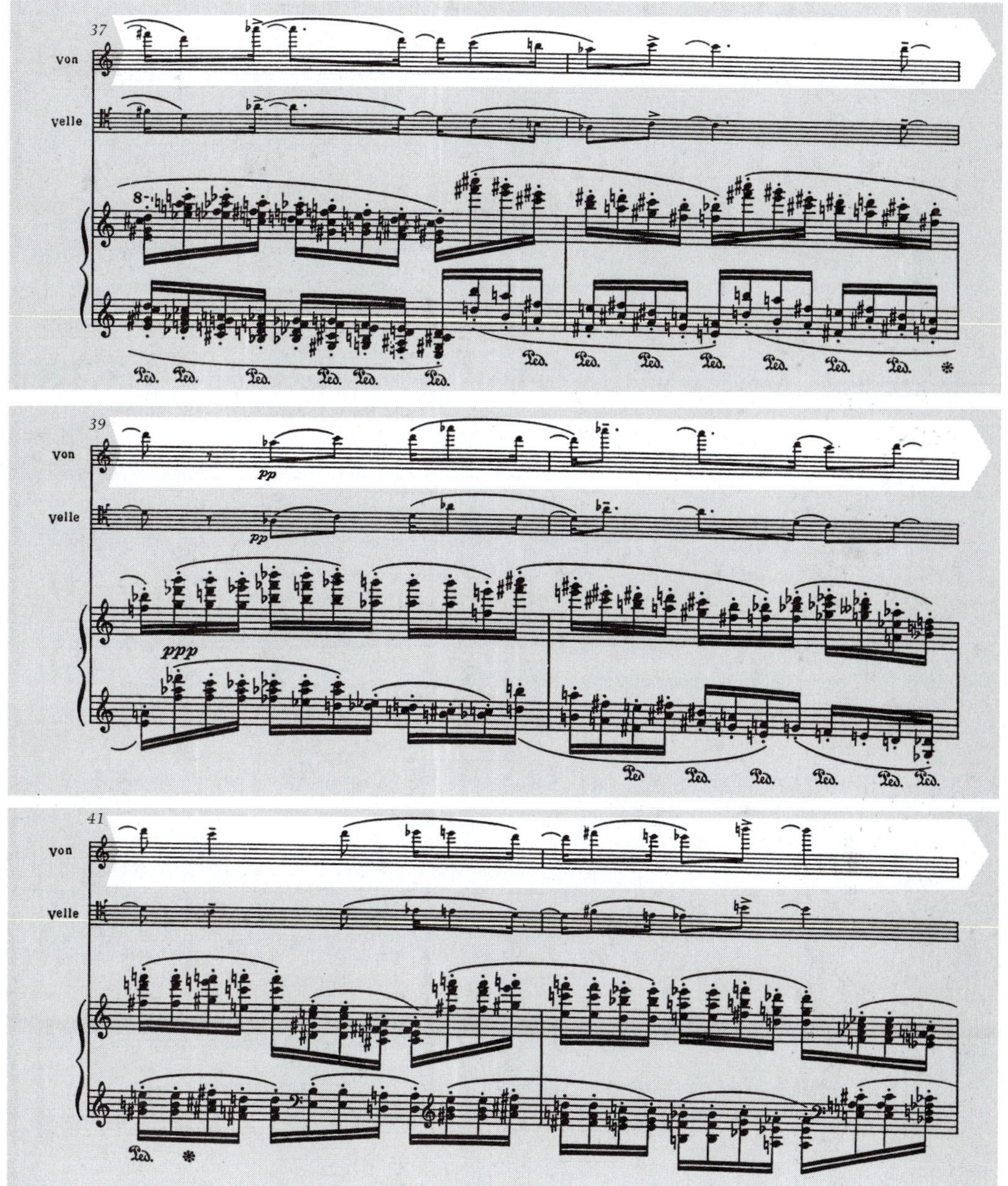
37
Von
Vcelle
8
39
pp
ppp
41

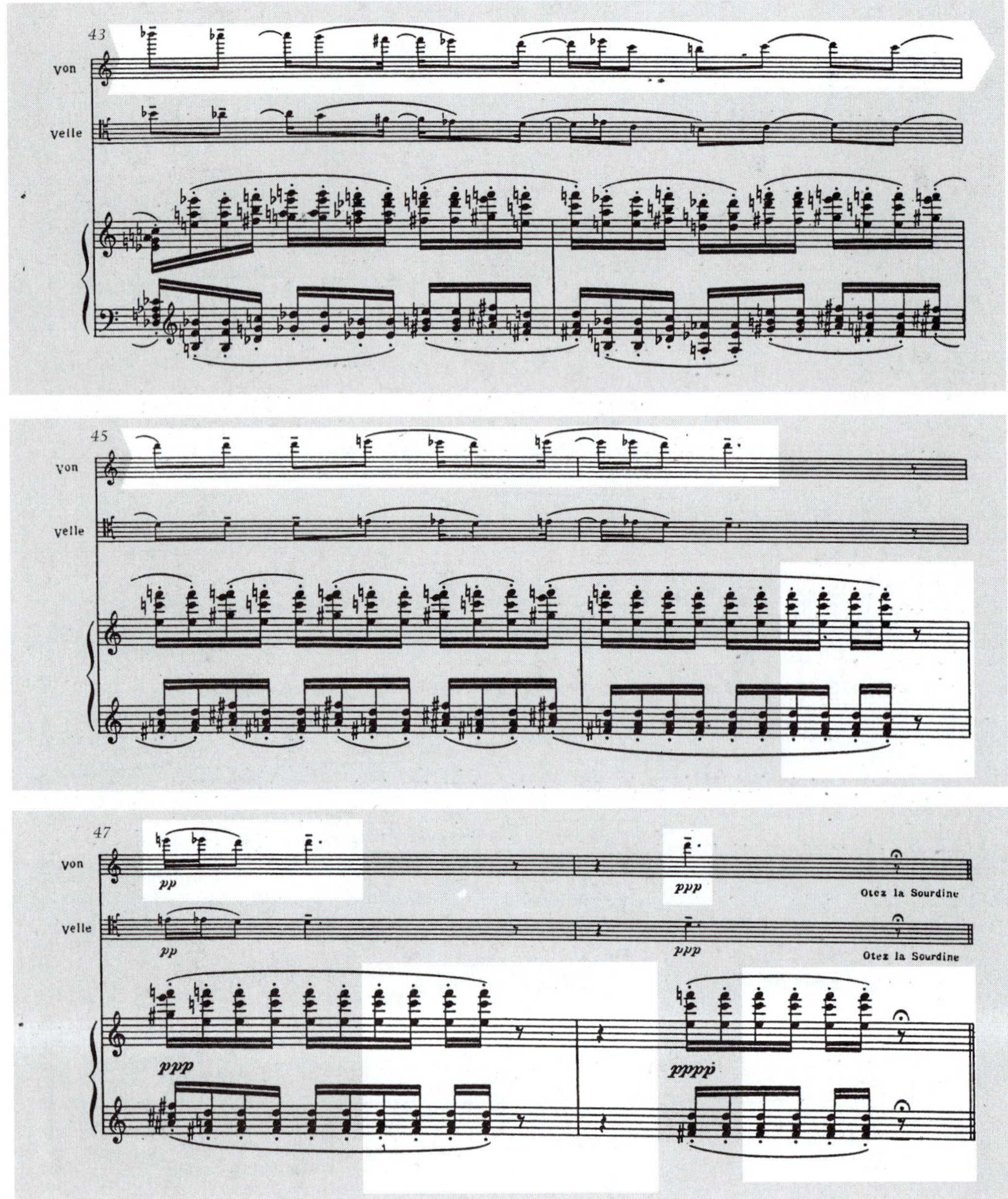
43
Von
Velle
45
Von
Velle
47
Von
pp
ppp
Otez la Sourdine
Velle
pp
ppp
Otez la Sourdine
ppp
pppp

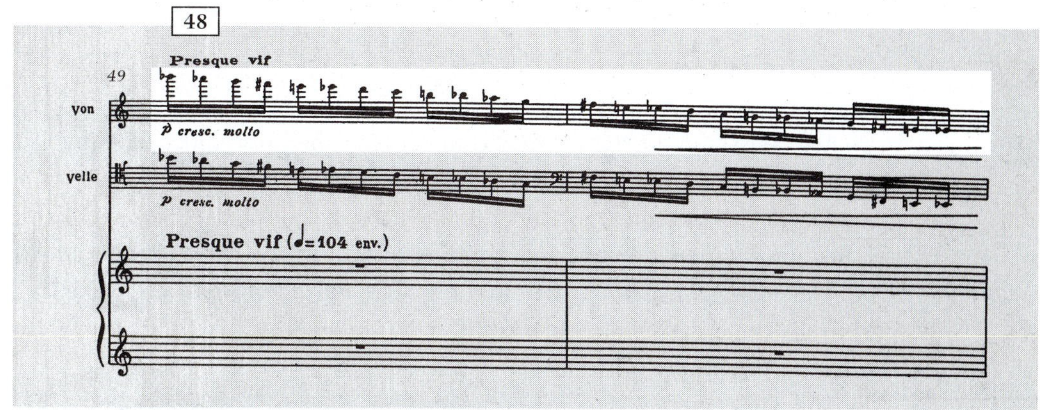
48
Presque vif
49
von
p cresc. molto
velle
p cresc. molto
Presque vif (♩=104 env.)

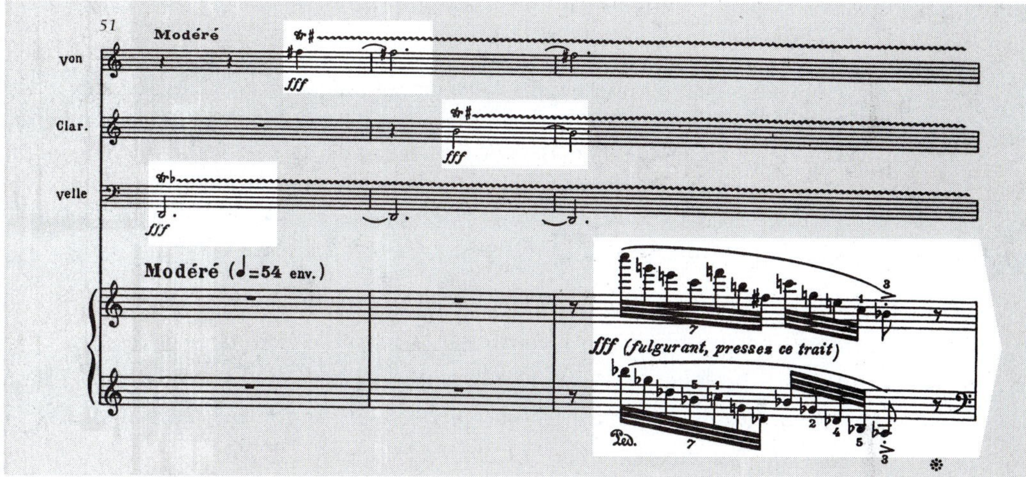
51
Modéré
von
fff
Clar.
fff
velle
fff
Modéré (♩=54 env.)
fff (fulgurant, pressez ce trait)
Ped.

54
Clar.
ff
fff
ff

Olivier Messiaen (1908–1992), one of Europe's foremost avant-garde composers, created his celebrated *Quatour pour la fin du temps (Quartet for the End of Time)* while imprisoned in a Nazi war camp. Interned with three other musicians—a clarinetist, violinist, and cellist—Messiaen wrote the quartet for this unusual combination, with an additional piano part for himself. The ensemble performed the work in front of five thousand fellow prisoners on January 15, 1941.

The work typifies Messiaen's religious mysticism. It is inspired by a passage in the Revelation of St. John, Chapter 10, which describes the seventh angel whose trumpet will announce the end of time.

> I saw an angel full of strength descending from the sky, clad with a cloud and having a rainbow over his head. His face was like the sun, his feet like columns of fire. He set his right foot on the sea, his left foot on the earth, and standing on the ocean and the earth, he raised his hand to the sky and swore by Him who lives in the centuries of centuries, saying: *There shall be no more Time,* but on the day of the seventh Angel's trumpet the mystery of God shall be accomplished.

The quartet has eight movements, which parallel the seven days of creation (God rested on the seventh day) and the eighth day of timeless eternity. In a preface to the score, Messiaen describes the second movement, entitled *Vocalise, pour l'Ange qui annonce la fin du Temps (Vocalise, for the Angel who announces the end of Time):*

> The first and third sections, very short, evoke the power of this mighty angel, a rainbow upon his head and clothed with a cloud, who sets one foot on the sea and one foot on the earth. In the middle section are the impalpable harmonies of heaven. On the piano, soft cascades of blue-orange chords envelop in their distant chimes the song of the violin and cello, which is almost like plainchant.

34

Charles Ives

The Things Our Fathers Loved (1917)

8CD: 7/ 49 - 50

11
faster and with more emphasis
in a gradually excited way
vil-lage cor-net band, play - ing in the square. The town's Red, White and Blue,
cresc.
14
ff
all Red, White and Blue Now! Hear the
più accel.
l.h.
ff
ff
16
songs! I know not what are the
l.h.
l.h.
l.h.
18
poco rall.
words But they sing in my
r.h.
l.h.
rit.

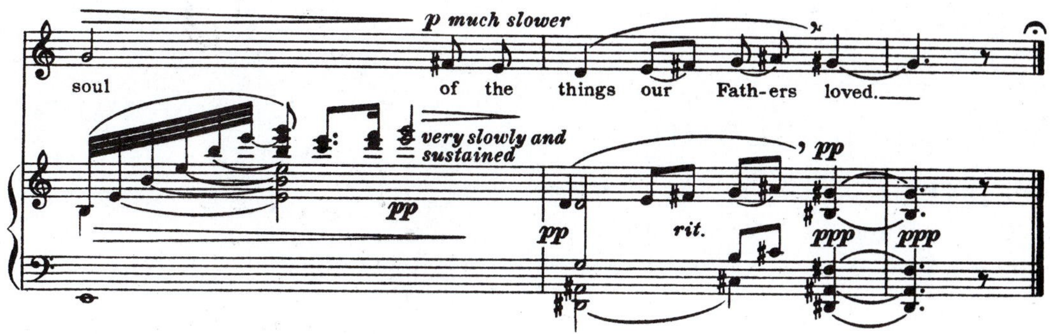

The New England composer Charles Ives (1874–1954) quietly created some of the most remarkable works in the history of American music. Staunchly nationalistic, Ives repeatedly drew inspiration from American events, transcendental ideas, and well-known popular, patriotic, and religious melodies. Today, he is recognized as a pioneer of the avant-garde, as many of his works anticipate future developments in American music.

Ives was a prolific composer of songs, writing over 150 works. *The Things Our Fathers Loved* (1917) typifies both his American spirit and innovative musical style. The text, written by Ives, is a nostalgic look at the American past through the melodies that linger in his memory. The vocal line is a pastiche of American tunes: *Dixie, My Old Kentucky Home, Nettleton, The Battle Cry of Freedom,* and *Sweet By-and-By.* Generally, the melodies are reshaped, but enough remains of the originals to be recognized. The piano accompaniment, which is separated from the vocal line both melodically and harmonically, creates a strong dissonant background.

35

William Grant Still

Afro-American Symphony,
Second movement (*Sorrow*) (1931)

8CD: 7/ 51 - 56

Editor's note: The layout of the instruments varies significantly with new score systems and over pages turns.

FLUTE 1
OBOE 1
con espressione
SOLO VLN.
1ST. VLNS.
2ND. VLNS.
VIOLAS
div.
'CELLI
div.
BASSES
CON ESPRESSIONE
16
FLUTE 1 2
FLUTE 3
OBOE 1
CLARINET 1 2
BASSOON 1
dolce
TRUMPET 1
Harmon Mute
HARP
SOLO
SOLO VLN.
VIOLAS
SOLI
'CELLI
doloroso
BASSES
16

poco riten.
a Tempo
FLUTE
OBOE
ENG. HORN
CLARINET 1
BASS CLAR.
BASSOON 1
TIMPANI
F – C – E
HARP
All of the Violins
1ST. VLNS.
2ND. VLNS.
VIOLAS
'CELLI
BASSES
SOLO
subito p
gliss.
53
rit. poco a poco
FLUTE 1
OBOE 1
ENG. HORN
CLARINET 1
BASS CLAR
BASSOON
HARP
1ST. VLNS
2ND. VLNS.
VIOLAS
'CELLI
BASSES
17

Editor's note: The English horn and bassoon parts are incomplete in this score.

rall.
a Tempo
ritard.
a Tempo
19
FLUTE 1 2 3
OBOE 1
SOLO
dolcroso
CLARINET 1
BASS CLAR.
SOLO
BASSOON 1 2
HORN 3
SOLO
closed
TROMBONE 1 2 3
Cup Mutes
dolce
TUBA
HARP
1ST. VLNS.
2ND. VLNS.
VIOLAS
'CELLI
BASSES.
ritard

FLUTE
OBOE
CLARINET
BASSOON
HORN
TRUMPET
TROMBONE
TUBA
HARP
1ST. VLNS.
2ND. VLNS.
VIOLAS
'CELLI
BASSES.
sonore
SOLO
Open
rit.
A.A.S.

55
20
a Tempo
poco a poco
FLUTE 1
SOLO
doloroso
BASSOON 1
SOLO
doloroso
simile
HARP
mp
poco a poco
1ST VLNS.
legatiss.
2ND VLNS.
legatiss.
VIOLAS
'CELLI
legatiss.
BASSES
poco a poco
20
a Tempo
56
ritard.
21
a Tempo
FLUTE 1
BASS CLAR.
BASSOON 1
1
TRUMPET
2
3
Cup Mutes
dolce
F - B♭ - E♭
TIMPANI
SOLO Muffled
VIB.
HARP
ritard.
a Tempo
1ST. VLNS.
Con sord.
2ND. VLNS.
con sord.
VIOLAS
con sord.
'CELLI
con sord.
quasi con sord.
BASSES
ritard.
a Tempo
21

William Grant Still (1895–1978) is one of the foremost African-American composers of the twentieth century. Associated with the Harlem Renaissance, Still mastered both classical and popular musical styles and often merged the two together. He achieved a number of firsts for an African-American: he was the first to conduct a major orchestra, the first to have an opera produced by a major American company, and the first to have a symphony performed by a major symphony orchestra. Conductor Howard Hanson premiered the *Afro-American Symphony* with the Rochester Philharmonic Orchestra in 1931.

The symphony reflects traditions from both classical and popular music. Like the classical symphony, it has four movements, each of which is in a modified sonata form. Attempting to avoid the restrictions of standard practices, Still referred to the sections of the sonata form as "divisions" rather than "exposition," "development," and "recapitulation." He also incorporated non-traditional key areas and took liberties with the structures. The opening division of the second movement resembles a standard exposition: first theme (rehearsal 15), second theme (rehearsal 17), and closing material. Divisions two and three (development and recapitulation), which begin at rehearsal numbers 18 and 20, focus on the first theme; the second theme is not recapitulated. Cyclic elements are also evident in this movement. The introduction and coda, scored for strings and timpani, make gentle references to material in the first movement, and the second theme is a variation of the opening theme of the symphony. In keeping with the twentieth-century symphonic style, the orchestration is colorful, and the harmony is enriched by extended chords.

The symphony is popular in spirit, as Still incorporates elements of blues, spirituals, jazz, and other African-American genres. The second movement suggests a spiritual; its first theme and countermelody, first heard in the oboe and flute, establish a plaintive mood that is maintained through the second theme. Still described the sounds at the end of the exposition as "the fervent prayers of a burdened people rising upward toward God," which is appropriately accompanied by a harp. Still suggested moods for each of the movements and later attached four poems by Paul Laurence Dunbar, whose works describe African-American life in dialect. For the second movement, called *Sorrow*, Still added this poem:

It's moughty tiahsome layin' 'roun'
Dis sorrer-laden earfly groun',
An' oftentimes I thinks, thinks I
'Twould be a sweet t'ing des to die
A' go 'long home.

36

Aaron Copland

Billy the Kid, Scene 1, *Street in a Frontier Town* (orchestral suite) (1939)

8CD: 7/ 57 - 61
4CD: 4/ 17 - 21

Instrumentation

Piccolo	Timpani	Bass drum
2 Flutes	Glockenspiel	Triangle
2 Oboes	Xylophone	
2 Clarinets	Tin whistle	Piano
2 Bassoons	Sleigh bells	
	Wood blocks	Violins I, II
4 French horns	Gourd	Violas
3 Trumpets	Snare drum	Cellos
3 Trombones	Slapstick	Double basses
Tuba	Cymbals	

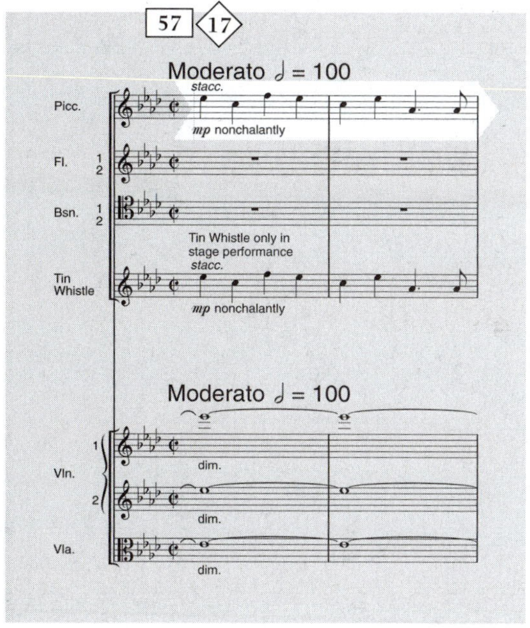

11
a tempo
rit.
Picc.
solo
stacc.
mp
Fl. 1
p
Clar. 1
p solo
solo
stacc.
mp
Bsn.
1
2
solo
p
Trgl.
(Trgl.)
sfp
p
Harp.
sfp
Piano
p
7
a tempo
rit.
Vl.
1
2
pizz.
sf
(pizz.)
p
pizz.
sf
(pizz.)
p
Vla.
pizz.
sf
Vlc.
C.b.
arco
p

19
Picc.
(solo)
mp
Ob. 1
solo
p
Clar.
(solo)
mp
p
Trpt. 1
con sordino
mp
(pizz)
Vl.
(pizz.)
Vla.
Vlc.

26
Picc.
d = 126
Fl. 1
mp
Ob. 1
mp
Clar. 1
Bsn. 1
mf
con sordino
mf
Hr.
Trpt. 1
mp
8
d = 126
Vl.
Vla.
arco
mf
Vlc.
mf

33
Picc.
Ob. 1
Bsn. 1
Hr. 1
Trpt. 1/2
con sordino
solo
mf
arco
Vl.
Vla.
Vlc.

40
Picc.
Fl. 1/2
Ob. 1/2
Clar. 1/2
Bsn. 1/2
Hr.
Piano
a2
1st solo
stacc.
solo
soli
p stacc.
9
Vl.
Vla.
Vlc.

46
Picc.
Fl.
1
2
Ob. 1/2
a2
f
Clar. 1/2
(a2)
Bsn. 1/2
Hr.
(senza sord.)
pp
(senza sord.)
pp
Trpt.
1
2
3
con sordino
pp
con sordino
pp
Trb.
1/2
3
Tb.
Timp.
Piano
Vl.
1
2
Vla.
Vlc.
Cb.

52
Picc.
Fl.
Ob.
a2
Clar.
a2
f
Bsn.
Hr.
senza sord.
stacc. mp
stacc.
mp
senza sord.
mp
Trpt.
Trb.
Tb.
Timp.
Piano
10
Vl.
stacc.
mp
Vla.
Vlc.
pizz.
Cb.

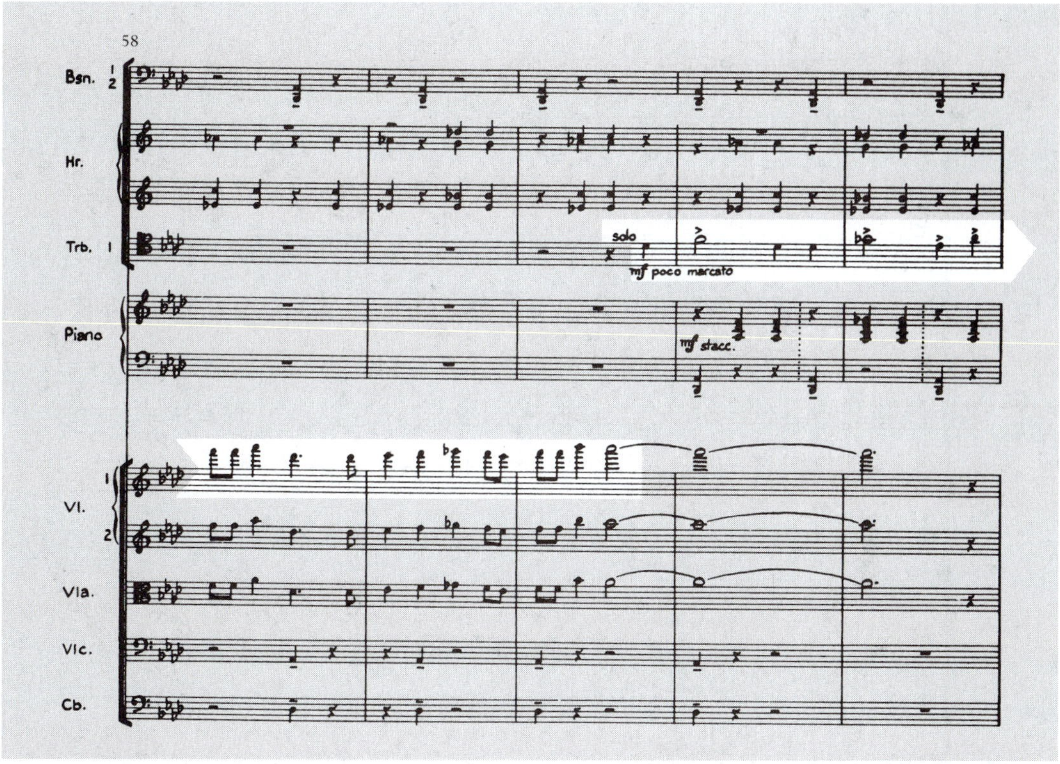

58
Bsn. 1 2
Hr.
Trb. 1
solo
mf poco marcato
Piano
mf stacc.
Vl. 1 2
Vla.
Vlc.
Cb.

63
Bsn. 1 2
Hr.
Trb. 1
Piano
Vl. 1 2
mp
Vla.
Vlc.
Cb.

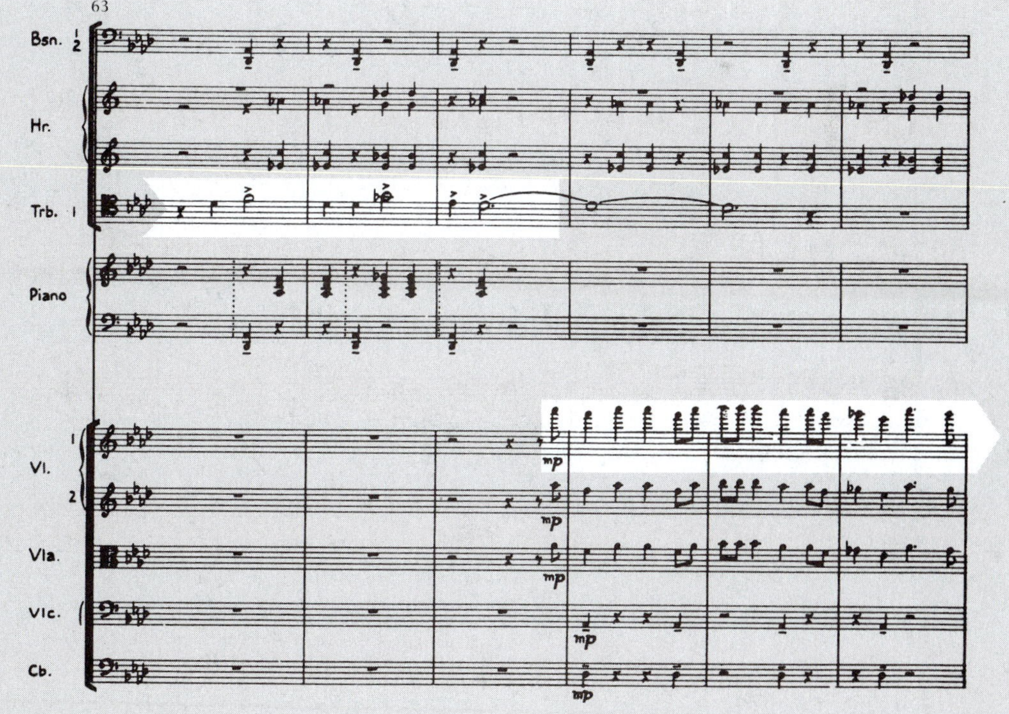

69
58
18
Picc.
Fl. 1 2
Ob. 1 2
Clar. 1 2
Bsn. 1 2
Hr.
(senza sord.)
solo
mf
1
Trpt.
2 3
con sordino
p
1
con sordino
Trb. 2
p
con sordino
3
p
con sordino
Tb.
p
Timp.
stacc
Piano
mf
11
1
Vl.
2
Vla.
Vlc.
Cb.

75
Picc.
Fl. 1 2
1° solo
Ob. 1 2
Clar. 1 2
1° solo
Bsn. 1 2
Hr.
Trpt. 1
2 3
Trb. 1
2
3
Tb.
Timp.
Perc.
Piano
Vl. 1
div.
2
pizz.
Vla.
pizz.
Vlc.
arco
Cb.
arco

81
Picc.
Fl. 1/2
Ob. 1/2
Clar. 1/2
Bsn. 1/2
Hr.
Trpt. 1
2/3
solo
Trb. 1
2
3
Tb.
Timp.
Perc.
Piano
12
Vl. 1
2
unis.
arco
Vla.
Vlc.
Cb.

87
Picc.
Fl. 1 2
Ob. 1 2
Clar. 1 2
Bsn. 1 2
Hr.
Trpt. 1 2 3
Trb. 1 2 3
Tb.
Timp.
Perc.
Piano
Vl. 1 2
Vla.
Vlc
Cb.
solo
pizz.
mp
mf
f

93
Fl. 1 2
Clar. 1 2
Bsn 1 2
Hr.
Trpt. 1
Trb. 1
Piano
Vl. 1 2
Vla.
Vlc.
Cb.
meno f
(senza sord.)
con sordino
solo
(pizz.)
13
99
p
pp
ppp
p dim. sempre
p dim

106
Picc.
Fl. 1 2
Ob. 1 2
Clar. 1 2
Bsn. 1 2
Hr.
Trpt. 1
2 3
Trb. 1 2
3
Tb.
Timp.
Cymb.
B. Drum.
Piano
Vl. 1
2
Vla
Vlc.
Cb.
ff marcato
a2
senza sordino
with hard stick
14
arco
div.

112
Picc.
Fl. 1 2
a2
Ob. 1 2
a2
Clar. 1 2
Bsn. 1 2
Hr.
Trpt. 1
2 3
Trb. 1 2
3
Tb.
Timp.
Cymb.
B. Drum
Piano
Vl. 1
2
Vla.
Vlc.
Cb.

59
19
♩ = 𝅗𝅥 precedente. (♩ = 138)
118
Picc.
Fl. 1 2
Ob. 1 2
a2
Clar. 1 2
Bsn. 1 2
f stacc.
Hr.
f stacc.
Trpt. 1 2 3
Trb. 1 2 3
senza sordino
Tb.
senza sordino
Timp.
Wood-bl.
mf
Sn. Drum
Cymb.
B. Drum
Piano
15
Vl 1 2
div.
Vla.
pizz.
Vlc.
Cb.

122
Picc.
Fl. 1 2
Ob. 1 2
Clar. 1 2
Bsn. 1 2
a2 stacc.
f
Hr.
1
Trpt.
2 3
solo f
solo f
1 2
Trb.
3
Tb.
Timp.
Woodbl.
Cymb.
B. Drum.
Piano
1
Vl.
2
Vla.
arco
Vlc.
f
Cb.

126
Picc.
Fl. 1 2
Ob. 1 2
Clar. 1 2
Bsn. 1 2
a2
Hr.
Trpt. 1 2 3
stacc.
Trb. 1 2 3
soli
legato, cantabile
Tb.
Timp.
Woodbl.
Cymb.
B. Drum
Piano
16
Vla. 1 2
unis.
pizz.
Vla
Vlc.
arco
Cb.
(pizz)

130
Picc.
Fl. 1 2
Ob. 1 2
Clar. 1 2
Bsn 1 2
a2
Hr.
1
Trpt.
2 3
1 2
Trb.
3
mf
Tb.
Timp.
Woodbl.
Piano
1
Vl.
2
Vla.
Vlc.
Cb.

134
Picc.
Fl. 1 2
Ob. 1 2
Clar. 1 2
Bsn. 1 2
a2
f
Hr.
Trpt. 1 2 3
Trb. 1 2 3
Tb.
Timp.
Woodbl.
Piano
Vl. 1 2
div.
arco
Vla.
Vlc.
(arco)
C.b.

138
Picc.
Fl. 1 2
a2
Ob. 1 2
a2
mf
Clar. 1 2
a2
Bsn. 1 2
a2
con sordino
mf
Hr.
solo
con sordino
Trpt. 1 2 3
mf
Trb. 1 2 3
Tb.
Timp.
Woodbl.
Piano
17
Vl. 1 2
Vla.
Vlc.
Cb.

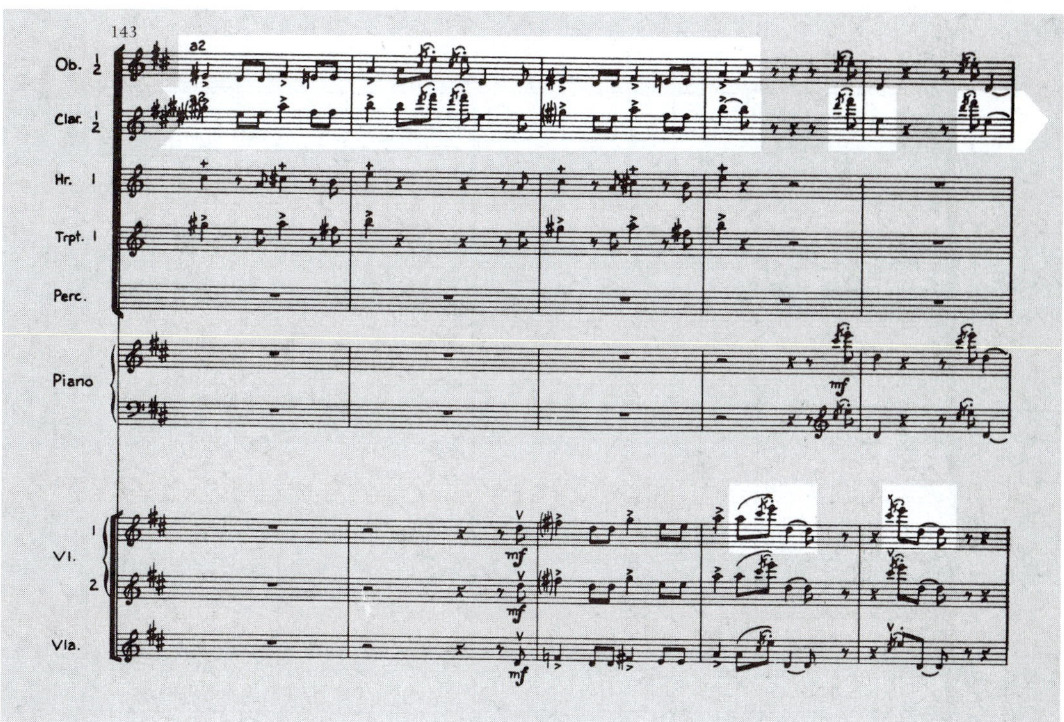
143
a2
Ob. 1 2
Clar. 1 2
Hr. 1
Trpt. 1
Perc.
Piano
mf
Vl.
Vla.
mf

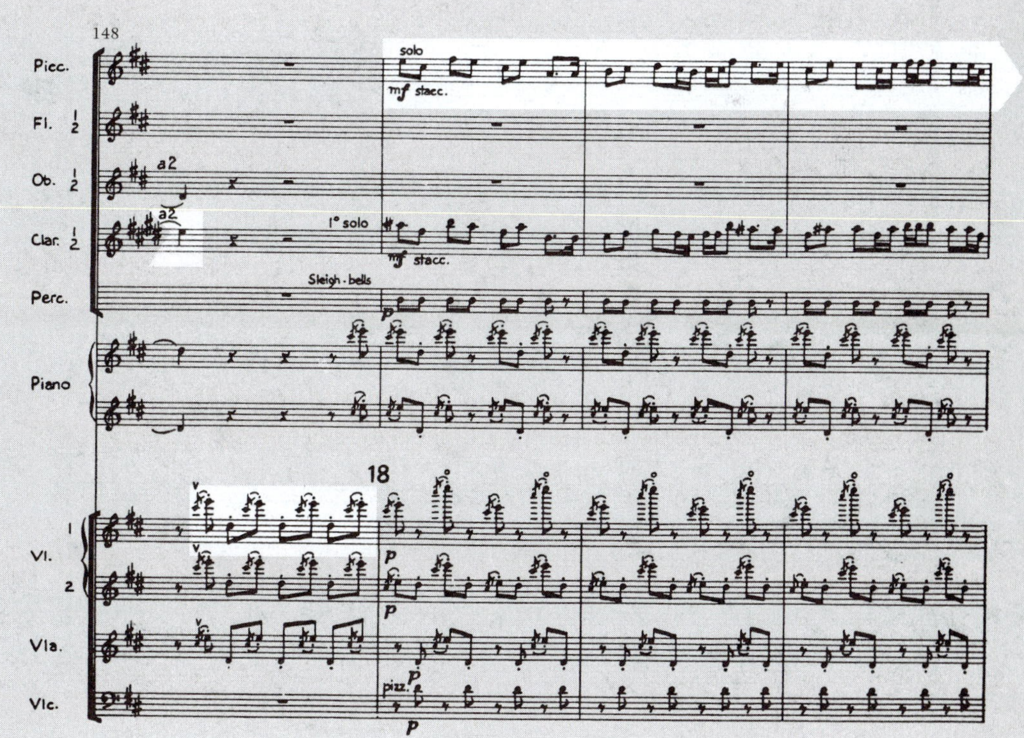
148
Picc.
solo
mf stacc.
Fl. 1 2
Ob. 1 2
a2
Clar. 1 2
1° solo
mf stacc.
Perc.
Sleigh-bells
p
Piano
18
Vl.
p
Vla.
Vlc.
pizz.
p

152
Picc.
Fl. 1 2
mf
a2
Ob. 1 2
mf
Clar. 1 2
mf
Bsn. 1 2
mf
Hr.
Trpt. 1 2 3
Trb. 1 2 3
Tb.
Timp.
Sleigh.b.
Woodbl.
Piano
Vl. 1 2
Vla.
Vlc.
Cb.

156
Picc.
Fl. 1 2
a2
Ob. 1 2
Clar. 1 2
Bsn. 1 2
Hr.
solo
cantabile
Trpt.
Trb.
Tb.
Timp.
Perc.
Piano
19
Vl.
Vla.
legato, cantabile
tenuto
Vlc.
arco
Cb.
div.

160
Picc.
Fl. 1 2
Ob. 1 2
Clar. 1 2
Bsn. 1 2
Hr. 1 2 3 4
Trpt. 1 2 3
Trb. 1 2 3
Tb.
Timp.
Perc.
Vl. 1 2
Vla.
Vlc.
Cb.

Mexican Dance and Finale

169
Picc.
Fl. 1 2
Ob. 1 2
Clar. 1 2
Bsn. 1 2
1°
Hr.
Trpt. 1
2 3
Trb. 1 2
3
Tb.
Timp.
Woodbl.
Gourd.
Piano
Vl. 1
2
Vla.
Vlc.
Cb.

175
Picc.
Fl. 1 2
Ob. 1 2
Clar. 1 2
Bsn. 1 2
1°
Hr.
Trpt. 1
2 3
Trb. 1 2
3
Tb
Timp.
Woodbl.
gourd.
Piano
21
Vl. 1
2
Vla.
Vlc.
Cb.

181
Picc.
Fl. 1 2
Ob. 1 2
Clar. 1 2
Bsn. 1 2
1°
Hr.
Trpt. 1 2 3
Trb. 1 2 3
Tb.
Timp.
Woodbl.
Gourd.
Piano
Vl. 1 2
Vla.
Vlc.
Cb.

187
Picc.
Fl.
Ob. 1 2
Clar. 1 2
Bsn. 1 2
Hr.
Trpt.
Trb.
Tb.
Timp.
Woodbl.
Gourd.
Piano
Vl.
Vla.
Vlc.
Cb.
solo
(10)
22
modo ordinario
pizz.

193
Picc.
Fl.
Ob.
Clar.
Bsn.
Hr.
Trpt.
Trb.
Tb.
Timp.
Woodbl.
Gourd.
Piano
23
Vl.
Vla
Vlc.
Cb.

199
Pict.
Fl. 1 2
Ob. 1 2
Clar. 1 2
Bsn. 1 2
1°
Hr.
1
Trpt.
2 3
1 2
Trb.
3
Tb.
Timp.
Woodbl.
Gourd.
Piano
1
Vl.
2
Vla
Vlc.
Cb.
col legno
col legno
col legno
(pizz)

205
Picc.
Fl. 1 2
Ob. 1 2
Clar. 1 2
Bsn. 1 2
1°
Hr.
1
Trpt.
2 3
1 2
Trb.
3
Tb.
Timp.
Woodbl.
Gourd.
Piano
1
Vl.
2
Vla.
Vlc
Cb.

211

61 21

Fl. 1 2

mp

Ob. 1 2

Clar. 1 2

mp

Hr.

mf

mp

mf

mp

Trpt. 1 2 3

24

Vl. 1 2

arco

legato

mf

modo ordinario

mf

Vla.

modo ordinario

mf

Vlc.

arco modo ordinario

mf

222
Ob. 1 2
Clar. 1 2
Bsn. 1 2
Hr.
25
Vl. 1 2
Vla.
(dim.)
Vlc.
solo mp
sul G....
p
mp

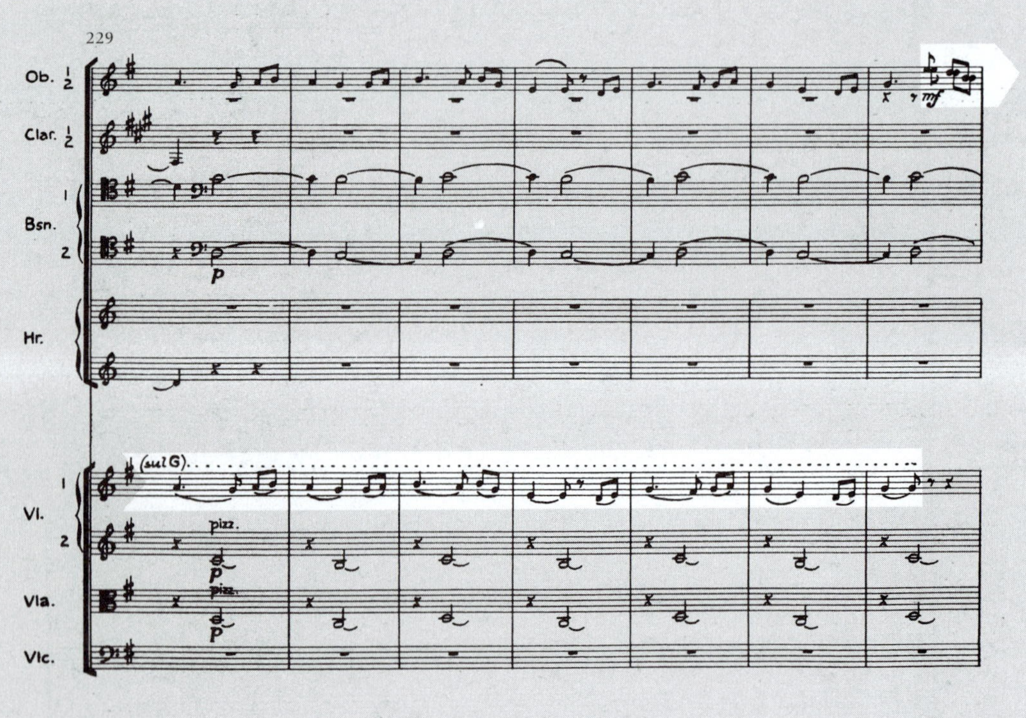
229
Ob. 1 2
Clar. 1 2
Bsn. 1 2
Hr.
Vl. 1 2
Vla.
Vlc.
(sul G)
pizz.
p
mf

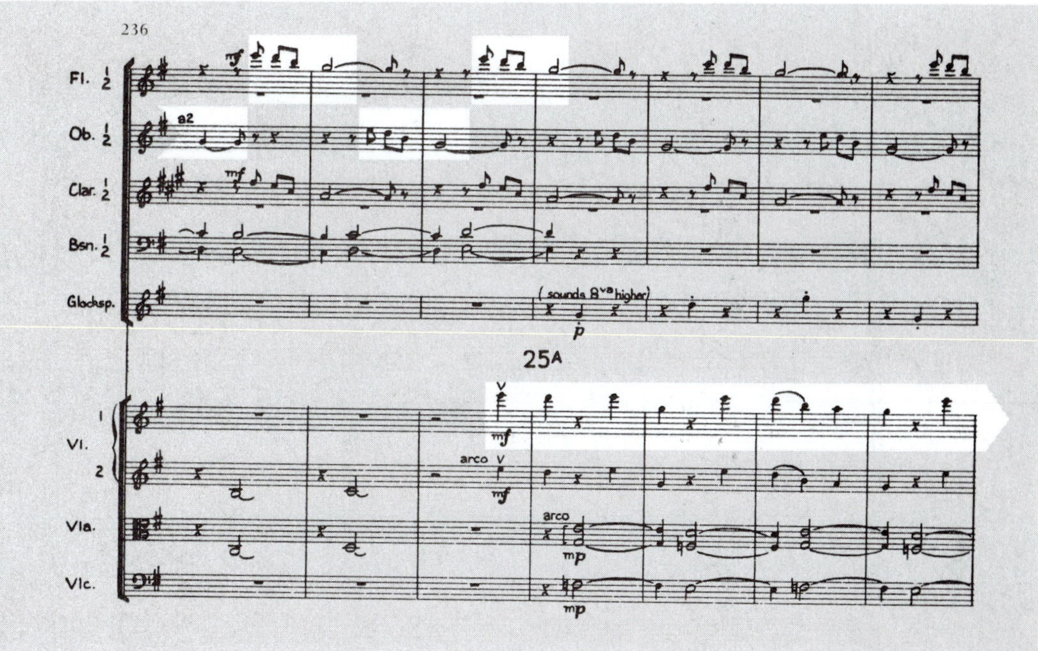
236
Fl. 1 2
Ob. 1 2
a2
Clar. 1 2
Bsn. 1 2
Glocksp.
(sounds 8va higher)
25A
Vl. 1 2
arco
Vla.
arco
Vlc.

243
Fl. 1 2
Ob. 1 2
a2
Clar. 1 2
senza sordino
Hr.
(con sordino)
senza sordino
(con sordino)
Glocksp.
Vl. 1 2
Vla.
Vlc.

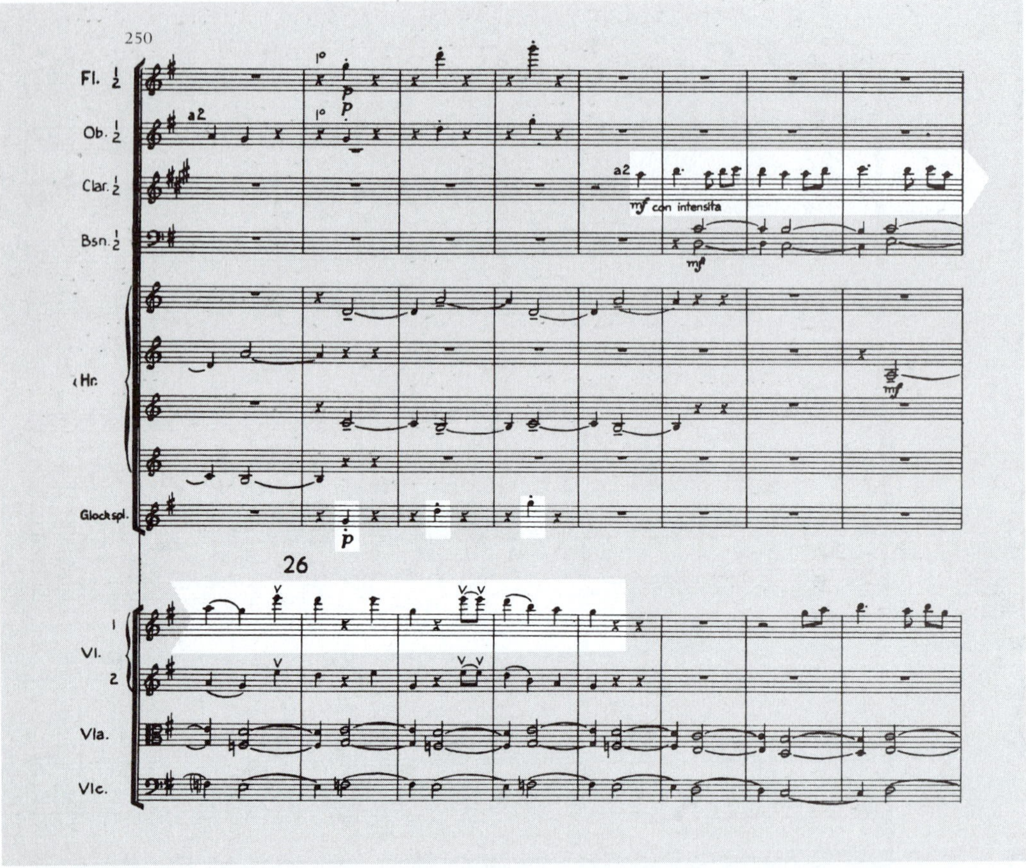

250

Fl. 1 2

Ob. 1 2

Clar. 1 2

Bsn. 1 2

Hr.

Glockspl.

Vl. 1 2

Vla.

Vlc.

a2 1° p 1° p

a2 mf con intensita

mf

mf

p

26

264
Picc
Fl. 1 2
(a2)
Ob. 1 2
a2
Clar. 1 2
(a2)
Bsn. 1 2
Hr.
senza sordino
solo
1
Trpt.
2 3
1 2
Trb.
3
Tb.
Timp.
Perc.
Piano
26A
1
Vl.
2
Vla.
Vlc.
Cb.
(arco)

270
Picc.
Fl. 1 2
Ob. 1 2
Clar. 1 2
Bsn. 1 2
Hr.
Trpt. 1 2 3
Trb. 1 2 3
Tb.
Timp.
Perc.
Piano
Vl. 1 2
Vla.
Vlc.
Cb.
stacc.
(a2)
marc.
a2
senza sord.
senza sordino

276
Picc.
Fl. 1 2
(a2)
Ob. 1 2
Clar. 1 2
Bsn. 1 2
Hr.
Trpt. 1 2 3
Trb. 1 2 3
Tb.
Timp.
Glockspl.
Xyloph.
Cymb. B. Drum
Piano
8va
27
Vl. 1 2
Vla.
Vlc.
Cb.

282
Picc.
Fl. 1 2
(a2)
Ob. 1 2
(a2)
Clar. 1 2
(a2)
Bsn. 1 2
(a2)
Hr.
Trpt. 1
2 3
fff
fff
Trb. 1 2
3
Tb.
Timp.
Glockspl.
Xylpph.
Cymb. B. Drum
ff
8va
Piano
Vl. 1
2
Vla.
Vlc.
Cb.

288
meno mosso
Picc.
Fl. 1/2
Ob. 1/2
Clar. 1/2
Bsn 1/2
Hr.
Trpt
Trb.
Tb.
Timp.
Glockspl.
Xyloph.
Slapstick
Cymb.
B. Drum.
Piano
27A
meno mosso
Vl.
Vla.
Vlc.
Cb.
div.
pizz.
arco

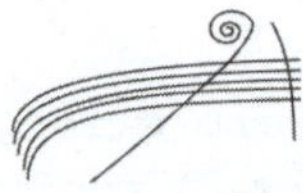

Aaron Copland (1900–1990) is generally recognized as America's foremost nationalist composer. This reputation largely rests on a series of ballets that he composed on American subjects, including the legend of Billy the Kid. Copland gives the following scenario for the opening scene of the ballet:

> The first scene is a street in a frontier town. Cowboys saunter into town, some on horseback, others on foot with their lassos; some Mexican women do a *jarabe,* which is interrupted by a fight between two drunks. Attracted by the gathering crowd, Billy is seen for the first time, a boy of twelve, with his mother. The brawl turns ugly, guns are drawn, and in some unaccountable way, Billy's mother is killed. Without an instant's hesitation, in cold fury, Billy draws a knife from a cowhand's sheath and stabs his mother's slayers. His short but famous career has begun.

The rest of the ballet treats Billy's later life, including a gun battle with his former friend Pat Garrett. At the end, a posse finally captures the tired and worn Billy.

Like Ives, Copland often quotes American tunes in his compositions. In this opening scene, he incorporates such traditional songs as *Goodbye, Old Paint; The Old Chisholm Trail; Git Along, Little Dogies; The Streets of Laredo;* and *Great Grand-Dad.* These songs of the Old West are woven into a general American sound that includes strong dance rhythms, syncopation, and a strong, effective orchestration. Copland sustains a lively, energetic mood with dissonances, polytonality, and polyrhythms. At the climax, the sound steadily builds in dissonance as *Goodbye, Old Paint* is obsessively repeated over a two-note ostinato.

37

Silvestre Revueltas

Homenaje a Federico García Lorca (*Homage to Federico García Lorca*), Third movement, *Son* (1937)

8CD: 7/ 62 - 69
4CD: 4/ 22 - 29

7
Picc.
Clar.
Trpt.I
Trpt.II
Trb.
Tuba
Pa.
Vln. I
Vln. II
Cbs.
marcatiss.
marc.
sf
mf
ff
sff
fff
pizz.
pizz. ff
15
63
23
f espress.
pp
piano sempre staccatissimo
arco

22
Picc.
Clar.
Trpt. I
ma con sordino
Trpt. II
Trb.
molto espress.
Tuba
Pa.
Vln. I
Vln. II
Cbs.

28
Picc.
Clar.
Trpt. I
Trpt. II
sord.
marc. ff
Trb.
sempre pp
Tuba
Pa.
Vln. I
Vln. II
Cbs.
arco

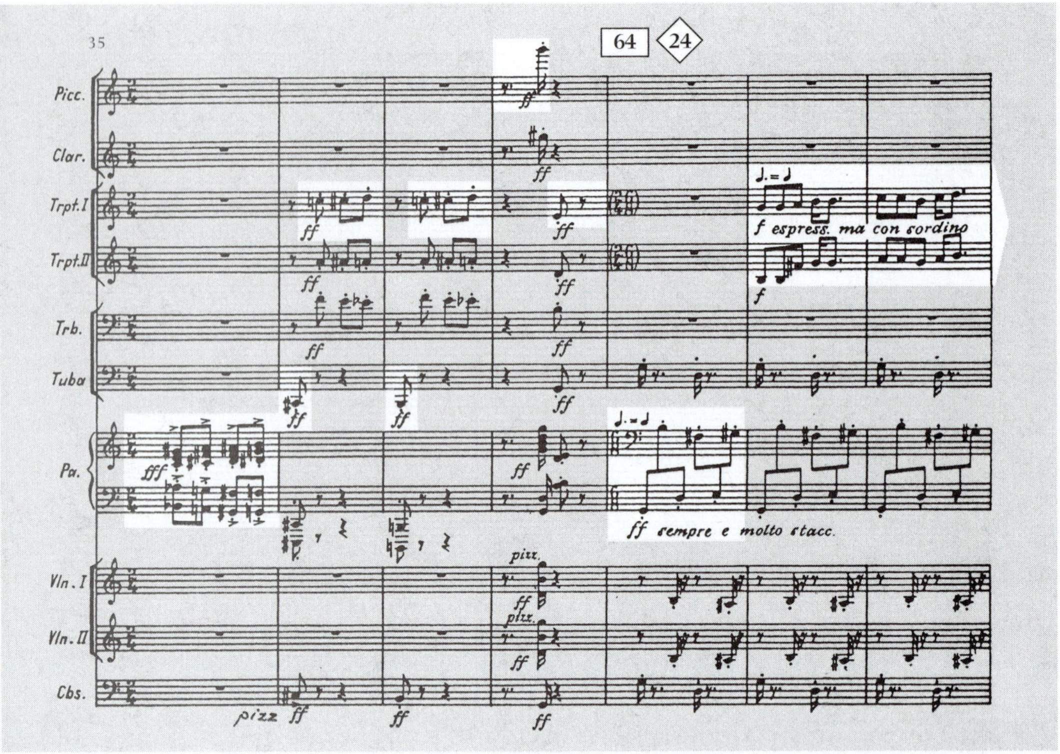

35
64
24
Picc.
Clar.
Trpt. I
Trpt. II
Trb.
Tuba
Pa.
Vln. I
Vln. II
Cbs.
fff
ff
f espress. ma con sordino
f
ff sempre e molto stacc.
pizz.
pizz

42
Picc.
Clar.
Trpt. I
Trpt. II
Trb.
Tuba
Pa.
Vln. I
Vln. II
Cbs.
mf
f
sf
sff
ff
sempre ff

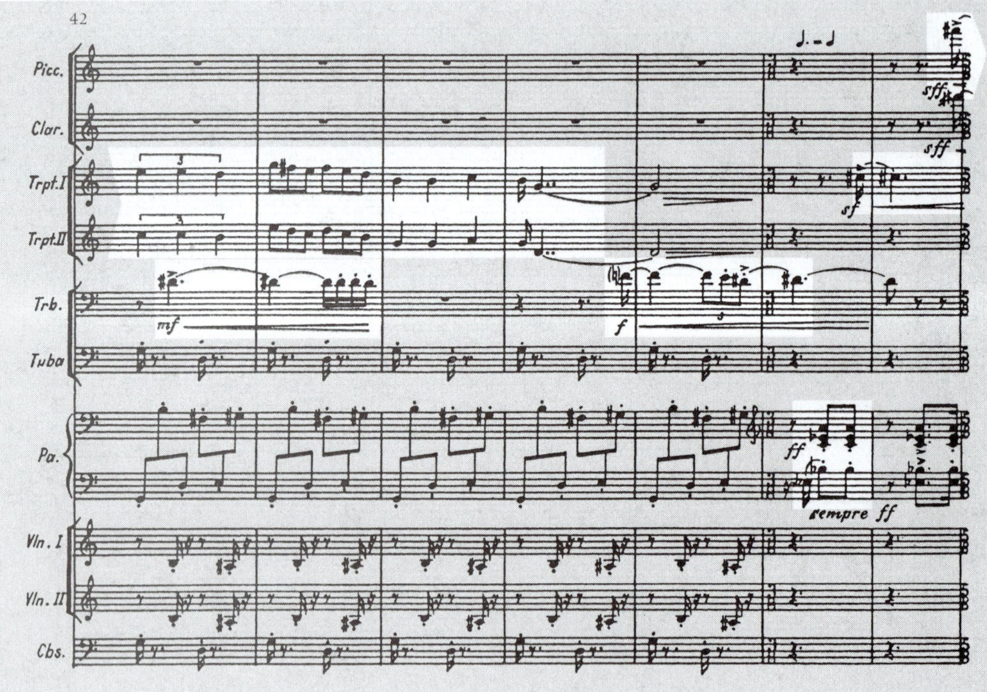

49
Picc.
Clar.
Trpt. I
Trpt. II
Trb.
Tuba
Pa.
Vln. I
Vln. II
Cbs.
ff
mf
f
arco
pizz

55
Picc.
Clar.
Trpt. I
Trpt. II
Trb.
Tuba
Pa.
Vln. I
Vln. II
Cbs.
f espress.
ff
arco

62
Picc.
Clar.
Trpt. I
Trpt. II
Trb.
Tuba
Pa.
Vln. I
Vln. II
Cbs.
sempre staccatissimo
pizz.
pizz. sff

68
Picc.
Clar.
Trpt. I
Trpt. II
Trb.
Tuba
Pa.
Vln. I
Vln. II
Cbs.
gliss.

73
Picc.
Clar.
Trpt. I
Trpt. II
Trb.
Tuba
Pa.
Vln. I
Vln. II
Cbs.
con sord.
gliss.

79
Picc.
Clar.
Trpt. I
Trpt. II
Trb.
Tuba
Pa.
Vln. I
Vln. II
Cbs.
con sord.
pizz.
arco

86
Picc.
Clar.
Trpt. I
Trpt. II
Trb.
Tuba
Pa.
Vln. I
Vln. II
Cbs.
f espress. molto
arco

92
65
25
Picc.
Clar.
Trpt. I
Trpt. II
Trb.
Tuba
Pa.
Vln. I
Vln. II
Cbs.
ff allegramente
allegramente
pizz. ff

98
Picc.
Clar.
(ad lib. 8va bassa)
Trpt. I
Trpt. II
Trb.
f sff
Tuba
f sff
Pa.
Vln. I
Vln. II
Cbs.
pizz. ff

104
Picc.
Clar.
Trpt. I
pp
Trpt. II
Trb.
f sff
mf
f subito
Tuba
f sff
f subito
Pa.
mf
stacc. e f subito
Vln. I
f
Vln. II
f
Cbs.
pizz. ff
pizz. f

110
Picc.
fff
sempre ff
Flatterzunge
Clar.
Trpt. I
Trpt. II
Trb.
Tuba
Pa.
Vln. I
Vln. II
Cbs.

116
Picc.
più fff
ff
Clar.
ff
Trpt. I
ff
Trpt. II
ff
Trb.
ff
Tuba
ff
Pa.
ff
pizz.
Vln. I
pizz.
Vln. II
pizz.
Cbs.
ff

122
Picc.
Clar.
Trpt. I
Trpt. II
Trb.
Tuba
Pa.
Vln. I
Vln. II
Cbs.
ff
con sord.
f
pizz. sempre f
66
26
128
pp con sord.
pp
ppp
p col legno ma
ppp

134
Picc.
Clar.
Trpt. I
Trpt. II
Trb.
Tuba
Pa.
Vln. I
Vln. II
Cbs.

67
27
140
Picc.
Clar.
Trpt. I
Trpt. II
Trb.
Tuba
Pa.
Vln. I
Vln. II
Cbs.
ff marcatiss.
m. d.
gliss. sobre blancas
gliss.
arco
arco
arco

145
Picc.
Clar.
Trpt. I
Trpt. II
Trb.
Tuba
Pa.
Vln. I
Vln. II
Cbs.
sobre blancas
pizz.

152
Picc.
Clar.
Trpt. I
Trpt. II
Trb.
Tuba
Pa.
Vln. I
Vln. II
Cbs.
mf ma molto marcato
mf ma molto stacc.
mf ma sempre marcato
arco
pizz. ff

68
28
158
Picc.
Clar.
Trpt. I
Trpt. II
Trb.
Tuba
Pa.
Vln. I
Vln. II
Cbs.
ff
ff
f
f
f espress.
f
f
arco f

164
Picc.
Clar.
Trpt. I
Trpt. II
Trb.
Tuba
Pa.
Vln. I
Vln. II
Cbs.
ff
ff
f marc.
f stacc.
f
f
marcatiss.
più f
ff
ff

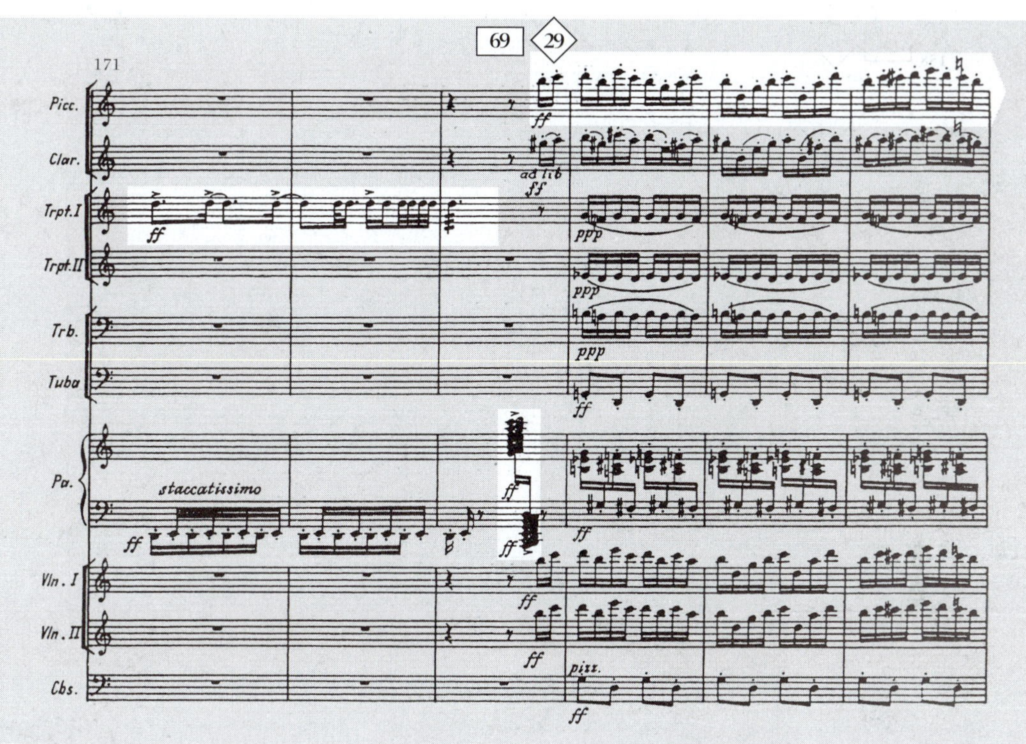
69
29
171
Picc.
Clar.
Trpt. I
Trpt. II
Trb.
Tuba
Pa.
Vln. I
Vln. II
Cbs.
ff
ad lib
ff
ppp
staccatissimo
pizz.

177
Picc.
Clar.
Trpt. I
Trpt. II
Trb.
Tuba
Pa.
Vln. I
Vln. II
Cbs.
sempre ppp
sempre ppp
sempre ppp

182
Picc.
Clar.
Trpt. I
ff
Trpt. II
ff
Trb.
ff
Tuba
ff sempre
Pa.
Vln. I
ff sempre
Vln. II
Cbs.

187
Picc.
f
sff
Clar.
f
sff
Trpt. I
f
staccatiss.
ff
Trpt. II
f
staccatiss.
ff
Trb.
8va
f
staccatiss.
ff
Tuba
8va
f
staccatiss
ff
secco
Pa.
ff
secco
ff
ff
Vln. I
sff
Vln. II
sff
Cbs.
arco
sff

Mexico produced a number of outstanding nationalist composers in the twentieth century. The varied musical traditions from the Amerindian, Hispanic, and Western cultures provided a rich palette for art music composers such as Carlos Chávez and Silvestre Revueltas (1899–1940). Achieving international acclaim, Revueltas created a distinctive style that combines folklike melodies and captivating dance rhythms with a dissonant and chromatic harmonic language.

The Spanish Civil War had a major impact on Revueltas, who was a staunch supporter of the Loyalist government that was destroyed by the Fascists. In 1936, the great Spanish poet Federico García Lorca was executed by a Fascist firing squad, and Revueltas responded with a three-movement orchestral work, *Homenaje a Federico García Lorca (Homage to Federico García Lorca)*. The third movement is entitled *Son*, which is a traditional Mexican dance that alternates between 3/4 and 6/8 meter. Following the somber second movement, entitled *Duelo (Sorrow)*, the finale appears as a joyful celebration of life.

Son presents three principal themes in a rondo-like pattern. The unusual orchestration is largely indebted to the sound of the Mexican mariachi band. Pairs of melodic instruments—two trumpets, two woodwinds (piccolo and E-flat clarinet), and two violin parts—dominate. String basses, a trombone, and a tuba provide the bass support, and the piano plays an essential harmonic function. Absent are middle-register instruments, such as the violas and cellos. Percussion instruments add distinctive colors to the ensemble. The lively dance rhythm of the *son* appears in the third theme, and throughout, Mexican folk sounds are underscored by strong dissonant harmonies.

38

Scott Joplin

Maple Leaf Rag (1899)

8CD: 7/ 70 – 74
4CD: 4/ 30 – 34

70 30

Editor's note: The Norton recording, from a Joplin piano roll, features embellishments added by the composer.

17
f stacc.
22
72
32
28
1.
2.
33
f
38
p
r. h.
l. h.
mf
73
33
43

49
TRIO.
54
74
34
60
1.
2.
65
70
76
1.
2.

The son of a former slave, Scott Joplin (1868–1917) was the first prominent African-American composer. Although he posthumously received a Pulitzer prize for his opera *Treemonisha,* Joplin is primarily remembered for his piano rags. A gifted improviser and pianist who worked in St. Louis, Chicago, and New York, Joplin was the principal figure in the craze for ragtime. Characterized by lively syncopated melodies set against a steady left-hand accompaniment, these works flourished during the 1890s.

The pinnacle of popularity for ragtime was reached in 1899, when Joplin's *Maple Leaf Rag* sold over one million copies. The dance itself is sectional, similar to the popular waltzes of Johann Strauss, Jr. and the marches of John Philip Sousa. The dance contains four principal melodic sections, called strains. Each strain is sixteen measures in length, and each is repeated. The opening strain makes a brief reappearance after the second strain, creating the following formal pattern: **A–A–B–B–A–C–C–D–D**.

39

George Gershwin

Piano Prelude No. 1 (published 1927)

8CD: 7/ 75 - 77

75

Allegro ben ritmato e deciso (M.M. ♩=100)

PIANO

f con licenzia

a tempo

ff

col 8

8

5

8

8

f

9

12

decresc.

Ped.

76
15
pp
cresc.
19
f
p
mf
22
decresc.
Ped.
p
26
cresc.
f
p
30
mf
mf
p

34
f
p
38
f
p
42
f
46
poco a poco cresc.
8
Ped.

77
ff
p
ff
f

American popular music, especially jazz, provided a source of inspiration for a number of European and American composers. Among these figures was the American jazz pianist George Gershwin (1898–1937), who created the most successful synthesis of the popular and classical worlds. A master of popular songs, many of which were written for Broadway or Hollywood musicals, Gershwin sought to integrate jazz elements into art music with his first major orchestral work, *Rhapsody in Blue* (1924). Among his other celebrated works fusing the two styles are the piano preludes, the Piano Concerto in F, the symphonic poem *An American in Paris,* and the folk opera *Porgy and Bess.* The Prelude No. 1, set in **A–B–A** form, features a syncopated accompaniment and a jazz-like melody with wide leaps, quick runs, and the characteristic "blues" lowering of the seventh degree in the opening phrase.

40

Billie Holiday

Billie's Blues (recorded 1936)

8CD: 7/ 78 – 84
4CD: 4/ 35 – 41

Introduction 78 35
(4 bars)—not transcribed

Chorus 1 79 36
ensemble (12 bars, standard blues changes)—not transcribed

Measures	4	2	2	2	2
Chord	I	IV	I	V	I

Chorus 2 80 37

Editor's note: This transcription shows pitch inflections, such as wide vibrato, slides, glisses, and scoops into notes, as well as slight rhythmic alterations, including delays and anticipations. Transcribed by Eric Fankhauser.

Chorus 3 81 38

Bb
F7
Bb7
delay
Eb7
ant.
My man woul-dn' gim-me no break - fast, Woul-dn' gim-me no din - ner,
Squawked a - bout my sup - per'n put me out - doors, Had the nerve to lay
a match - box on my clothes;
I did - n't
Clarinet
have so man - y but I had a long, long ways to go.

Chorus 4 82 39

Bb
F7
vib.
Eb7
Bb7
B°7

Chorus 83 40
B♭
F7
Trumpet (growl)
B♭
E♭7
F7
B♭
B♭7
E♭7
vib.
B♭
B♭
B°7
smear
Cmi7
vib.
delay
F7
B♭
Clar.
Chorus 6 84 41
B♭
F7
B♭
delay
Some men like me 'cause I'm hap - py, Some 'cause I'm snap - py,
B♭
B♭7
E♭7
Some call me hon - ey, oth - ers think I've got mon - ey, Some tell me,
B♭
F7
delay
"Ba - by you're built for speed," Now if you put that all to - geth - er, Makes me
B♭
Tpt.
E♭7
B♭
ev' - ry - thing a good man needs.

The blues is a category of African-American folk music that expresses misery and unhappiness. Emerging as a specific song type after 1900, the blues exerted a strong influence on jazz, both as a model of performance style and as a source of melodies. The simple repetitive structure of the blues made it ideal for improvisation. A blues melody typically consists of a twelve-measure tune (three four-measure phrases) that is repeated in a strophic fashion, often with improvised ornamentation. The standard harmonic progression for the tune is as follows:

Phrase one	Measures 1–4	I chord
Phrase two	Measures 5–6	IV chord
	Measures 7–8	I chord
Phrase three	Measures 9–10	V chord
	Measures 11–12	I chord

The blues was a performance vehicle for a number of black female singers, including the remarkable Billie Holiday (1915–1959). Developing an original sound characterized by a flexible vocal quality, subtle melodic nuances, and great expressiveness, Holiday became the premier jazz singer of her time. She performed and recorded with some of the major figures in jazz history. In addition, Holiday became one of the first black singers to break through racial barriers when she appeared with the white Artie Shaw orchestra.

This recording of *Billie's Blues* from 1936 features three principal soloists: voice (Billie Holiday), clarinet (Artie Shaw), and trumpet (Bunny Berigan). Supporting this group are a piano, guitar, string bass, and drums. The style of performance is typical of New Orleans jazz. Following a four-measure introduction, the soloists improvise on the given melody (known as the chorus) six times, three of which are instrumental. The clarinet and trumpet have distinct improvising styles, and Holiday embellishes the tune with scoops and dips on notes. The text for Holiday's first stanza is a typical three-line strophe, but the subsequent two verses are more extended.

Text

Lord, I love my man, tell the world I do,
I love my man, tell the world I do,
But when he mistreats me, makes me feel so blue.

My man wouldn't give me no breakfast,
Wouldn't give me no dinner,
Squawked about my supper and he put me outdoors,
Had the nerve to lay a matchbox on my clothes;
I didn't have so many but I had a long, long ways to go.

Some men like me 'cause I'm happy,
Some 'cause I'm snappy,
Some call me honey, others think I've got money,
Some tell me, "Baby you're built for speed,"
Now if you put that all together,
Makes me ev'rything a good man needs.

41

Billy Strayhorn/Duke Ellington

Take the A Train (recorded 1941)

8CD: 8/1-5

Transcribed by Brent Wallarab; edited by Gunther Schuller.

2
5
Alto 1
Alto 2
Tenor 1
unis.
mf
mp
Tenor 2
unis.
mf
mp
Baritone
unis.
mf
mp
St. mute
Tpt. 1
f
p
f
St. mute
Tpt. 2
f
p
f
St. mute
Tpt. 3
f
p
f
Trb. 1
mf
slow
p
mfp
mfp
mf
Trb. 2
mf
slow
p
mfp
mfp
mf
Trb. 3
mf
slow
p
mfp
mfp
mf
5
Piano
Guitar
C6
D7(♭5)
Bass
Drums

9
Alto 1
Alto 2
Tenor 1
Tenor 2
Baritone
Tpt. 1
Tpt. 2
Tpt. 3
Trb. 1
Trb. 2
Trb. 3
Piano
Guitar
Bass
Drums
G7
C6

13
Alto 1
Alto 2
Tenor 1
Tenor 2
Baritone
Tpt. 1
Tpt. 2
Tpt. 3
Trb. 1
Trb. 2
Trb. 3
Piano
Guitar
Bass
Drums
mf
mp
f
p
slow
mfp
C6
D7(♭5)

17
Alto 1
Alto 2
Tenor 1
Tenor 2
Baritone
Tpt. 1
Tpt. 2
Tpt. 3
Trb. 1
Trb. 2
Trb. 3
Piano
Guitar
Bass
Drums
G7
C6
C9

21
Alto 1
Alto 2
Tenor 1
Tenor 2
Baritone
mf
Tpt. 1
Tpt. 2
Tpt. 3
Trb. 1
Trb. 2
Trb. 3
Piano
Guitar
F 6
Bass
Drums

25
Alto 1
Alto 2
Tenor 1
mf
Tenor 2
mf
Baritone
mf
Tpt. 1
Tpt. 2
Tpt. 3
Trb. 1
Trb. 2
Trb. 3
25
Piano
D7
G7
Guitar
Bass
Drums

29
Alto 1
Alto 2
Tenor 1
p
mf
mp
Tenor 2
p
mf
mp
Baritone
p
mf
mp
Tpt. 1
f
p
f
p
Tpt. 2
f
p
f
p
Tpt. 3
f
p
f
p
Trb. 1
f
p
f
p
Trb. 2
f
p
f
p
Trb. 3
f
p
f
p
29
Piano
Guitar
C6/9
D9(♭5)
Bass
Drums

Solo as played by Ray Nance

37
lightly
mp
Alto 1
Alto 2
Tenor 1
Tenor 2
Baritone
Tpt. 1
Tpt. 2
Tpt. 3
Trb. 1
Trb. 2
Trb. 3
Piano
Guitar
C6
D9
Bass
Drums
mf

41
Alto 1
Alto 2
Tenor 1
Tenor 2
Baritone
Tpt. 1
Tpt. 2
Tpt. 3
Trb. 1
Trb. 2
Trb. 3
Piano
Guitar
Bass
Drums
mf
vib.
3
G7
D♭7
C6

45
Alto 1
Alto 2
Tenor 1
Tenor 2
Baritone
Tpt. 1
Tpt. 2
Tpt. 3
slight bend
bend
Trb. 1
Trb. 2
Trb. 3
Piano
Guitar
C 6
D 9
Bass
Drums
mp

49
Alto 1
mf
Alto 2
mf
Tenor 1
mf
Tenor 2
mf
Baritone
Tpt. 1
Tpt. 2
Tpt. 3
Trb. 1
Trb. 2
Trb. 3
49
Piano
G7
D♭7
C6
Guitar
Bass
Drums

53
Alto 1
Alto 2
Tenor 1
Tenor 2
Baritone
Tpt. 1
Tpt. 2
Tpt. 3
bend
vib.
3
Trb. 1
Trb. 2
Trb. 3
Piano
Guitar
F6
Bass
Drums

57
Alto 1
Alto 2
Tenor 1
Tenor 2
Baritone
Tpt. 1
Tpt. 2
Tpt. 3
bend
Trb. 1
Trb. 2
Trb. 3
57
Piano
mf
Guitar
D7
G7
Bass
Drums

61
Alto 1
Alto 2
Tenor 1
Tenor 2
Baritone
Tpt. 1
Tpt. 2
Tpt. 3
Trb. 1
Trb. 2
Trb. 3
Piano
Guitar
Bass
Drums
mp
vib.
C6
D9

65
Alto 1
Alto 2
Tenor 1
Tenor 2
Baritone
Tpt. 1
Tpt. 2
Tpt. 3
Trb. 1
Trb. 2
Trb. 3
65
Piano
Guitar
Bass
Drums
mf
mf
mf
mf
G7
D♭7
C6
f

69
Alto 1
Alto 2
Tenor 1
Tenor 2
Baritone
open
Tpt. 1
open
Tpt. 2
open
Tpt. 3
Trb. 1
Trb. 2
Trb. 3
69
Piano
Guitar
Bass
to sticks
choke
Drums
(mf)

*Solo as played by Ray Nance

77
Alto 1
Alto 2
Tenor 1
Tenor 2
Baritone
mp
mf
Tpt. 1
Tpt. 2
Tpt. 3
3
Trb. 1
Trb. 2
Trb. 3
77
Piano
Guitar
Fmi7
B♭7(♭9)
E♭6/9
Bass
Drums

81
Alto 1
Alto 2
Tenor 1
Tenor 2
Baritone
Tpt. 1
Tpt. 2
Tpt. 3
bend
squeeze
Trb. 1
Trb. 2
Trb. 3
81
Piano
Guitar
E♭6
F7(♭5)
Bass
Drums

85
Alto 1
Alto 2
Tenor 1
Tenor 2
Baritone
Tpt. 1
Tpt. 2
Tpt. 3
Trb. 1
Trb. 2
Trb. 3
Piano
Guitar
Bass
Drums
mp
mf
f
Fmi7
B♭7(♭9)
E♭6/9
E♭13

89
Alto 1
Alto 2
Tenor 1
Tenor 2
Baritone
Tpt. 1
Tpt. 2
Tpt. 3
shake
Trb. 1
Trb. 2
Trb. 3
Piano
Guitar
A♭6
Bass
Drums
mf
p

93
Alto 1
Alto 2
Tenor 1
Tenor 2
Baritone
Tpt. 1
Tpt. 2
Tpt. 3
1-2
3
1-2
Trb. 1
Trb. 2
Trb. 3
93
Piano
Guitar
F9
B♭9
Bass
Drums

97
Alto 1
Alto 2
Tenor 1
Tenor 2
Baritone
Tpt. 1
Tpt. 2
Tpt. 3
Trb. 1
Trb. 2
Trb. 3
97
Piano
E♭6
F7(♭5)
Guitar
Bass
Drums
mf
mp

101
5
Alto 1
Alto 2
Tenor 1
Tenor 2
Baritone
Tpt. 1
Tpt. 2
Tpt. 3
Trb. 1
Trb. 2
Trb. 3
Piano
Guitar
Bass
Drums
mf
mp
3
Fmi7
E13
E♭6
to brushes
dim.
mp
mf

105
Alto 1
Alto 2
Tenor 1
Tenor 2
Baritone
Tpt. 1
in hat
mp
Tpt. 2
in hat
mp
Tpt. 3
in hat
mp
Trb. 1
in hat
(or plunger)
mp
Trb. 2
in hat
(or plunger)
mp
Trb. 3
in hat
(or plunger)
mp
105
Piano
Guitar
E♭6
F7(♭5)
mp
Bass
mp
Drums
Brushes
mp
2

109
Alto 1
Alto 2
Tenor 1
Tenor 2
Baritone
mp
p
3
Tpt. 1
Tpt. 2
Tpt. 3
Trb. 1
Trb. 2
Trb. 3
109
Piano
Guitar
Fmi7
E13
E♭6
Bass
Drums

113
Alto 1
Alto 2
Tenor 1
Tenor 2
Baritone
Tpt. 1
Tpt. 2
Tpt. 3
Trb. 1
Trb. 2
Trb. 3
113
Piano
Eb6
F7(b5)
Guitar
Bass
Drums
2

117
Alto 1
Alto 2
Tenor 1
Tenor 2
Baritone
Tpt. 1
Tpt. 2
Tpt. 3
pp
Trb. 1
Trb. 2
Trb. 3
pp
117
Piano
Guitar
Fmi7
E13
E♭6
Bass
Drums

In the 1930s, the free improvisatory style of New Orleans jazz gave way to sophisticated arrangements for larger ensembles. Generally known as either the Big Band era or the Swing era, the period produced some outstanding musicians, one of the greatest of which was Duke Ellington (1899–1974). Born Edward Kennedy Ellington but known as "Duke," Ellington was a fine jazz pianist and a brilliant orchestrator. Ellington's band comprised of two trumpets, one cornet, three trombones, four or five saxophones (often doubling on clarinets), and a rhythm section consisting of two string basses, guitar, drums, vibraphone, and piano. In his distinctive orchestrations, Ellington treats each family of instruments as a unit, often having a soloist from one family accompanied by another group of instruments in close triadic harmonies.

Take the A Train was written and arranged by Billy Strayhorn (1915–1967), a frequent collaborator with Ellington. This recording, made on February 15, 1941, features Duke Ellington on the piano and Ray Nance on the trumpet. After Ellington's four-measure chromatic introduction, the saxophones present the principal theme, accompanied by the brass instruments. The thirty-two-measure chorus comprises four eight-measure phrases in the form **A–A–B–A.** In the remaining two choruses, Ray Nance improvises on the theme (both muted and unmuted), with bent notes, shakes (a wide vibrato produced by shaking the lip), and glissandi, while the saxophones either accompany or alternate with the soloist. An energetic four-measure interlude, interjecting a conflicting triple meter, separates the second and third choruses, and the coda contains two echoes of the final phrase of Chorus 3.

42

Dizzy Gillespie/Charlie Parker

A Night in Tunisia (recorded 1946)

8CD: 8/ 6 – 11
4CD: 4/ 42 – 47

Editor's note: The Norton Recording performance of the Introduction is as follows: 8-bar ostinato (bass and percussion); 4-bar saxophone ostinato.

6 42 Introduction (8 + 4 bar ostinato)

7 43 Chorus 1 (32 bars, **A-A-B-A**)

8 44 Interlude (12 bars)

9 45 Alto sax solo break; Chorus 2

10 46 Chorus 3 (32 bars, **A-A-B-A**)

11 47 Coda (8-bar ostinato)

New jazz styles, such as bebop, began to emerge in the late 1940s as a reaction to the controlled sounds of the Big Band era. Bebop, which features a small number of virtuoso soloists, returns to the original jazz emphasis on improvisation, but often with a frenetic character. Two bebop greats, Charlie "Bird" Parker (alto saxophone) and Miles Davies (trumpet), are featured in this 1946 recording of Dizzy Gillespie's popular *A Night in Tunisia*. Gillespie (1917–1993), also a trumpeter, was a founder of bebop and one of the greatest figures in jazz history. *A Night in Tunisia* is among a number of jazz classics that he composed.

The mood of the tune is established by a syncopated ostinato introduction. The thirty-two-measure chorus (**A-A-B-A**) is then presented by the trumpet (playing the **A** phrases) and saxophone (playing the **B** phrase). Following a brief saxophone interlude, the chord patterns of the chorus are repeated, featuring solos by the saxophone, guitar, and trumpet. Most notable are the extended improvisations, riffs (short melodic phrases), and Parker's famous break (a solo passage that interrupts the accompaniment). At the end of the work, the ostinato returns and gradually fades away.

43

Leonard Bernstein

West Side Story, Mambo and *Tonight* Ensemble (1957)

8CD: 8/12-20
4CD: 4/48-56

Instrumentation

Woodwinds

Most musical theater scores call for woodwind players (called reeds) to double on a variety of instruments. In *Mambo*, five reed books (numbered I-V) appear in different positions in the score, depending on the range of the instrument played (highest on the top line, lowest on the bottom).

Reed I: Alto saxophone
B-flat clarinet
Flute

Reed II: E-flat clarinet
B-flat clarinet

Reed III: B-flat clarinet
Tenor saxophone
Flute

Reed IV: Piccolo
Bass saxophone
B-flat clarinet
Flute

Reed V: Bassoon

Brasses

2 French horns
3 B-flat trumpets
2 Trombones

Percussion

Timpani
Bongos
Timbales
Conga
Pitched drums

Maracas
Cowbells
Guiro
Xylophone
Piano

Trap set:
Snare drum
Tenor drum
Brass drum
Cymbals

Strings

7 Violins
4 Cellos
Double bass

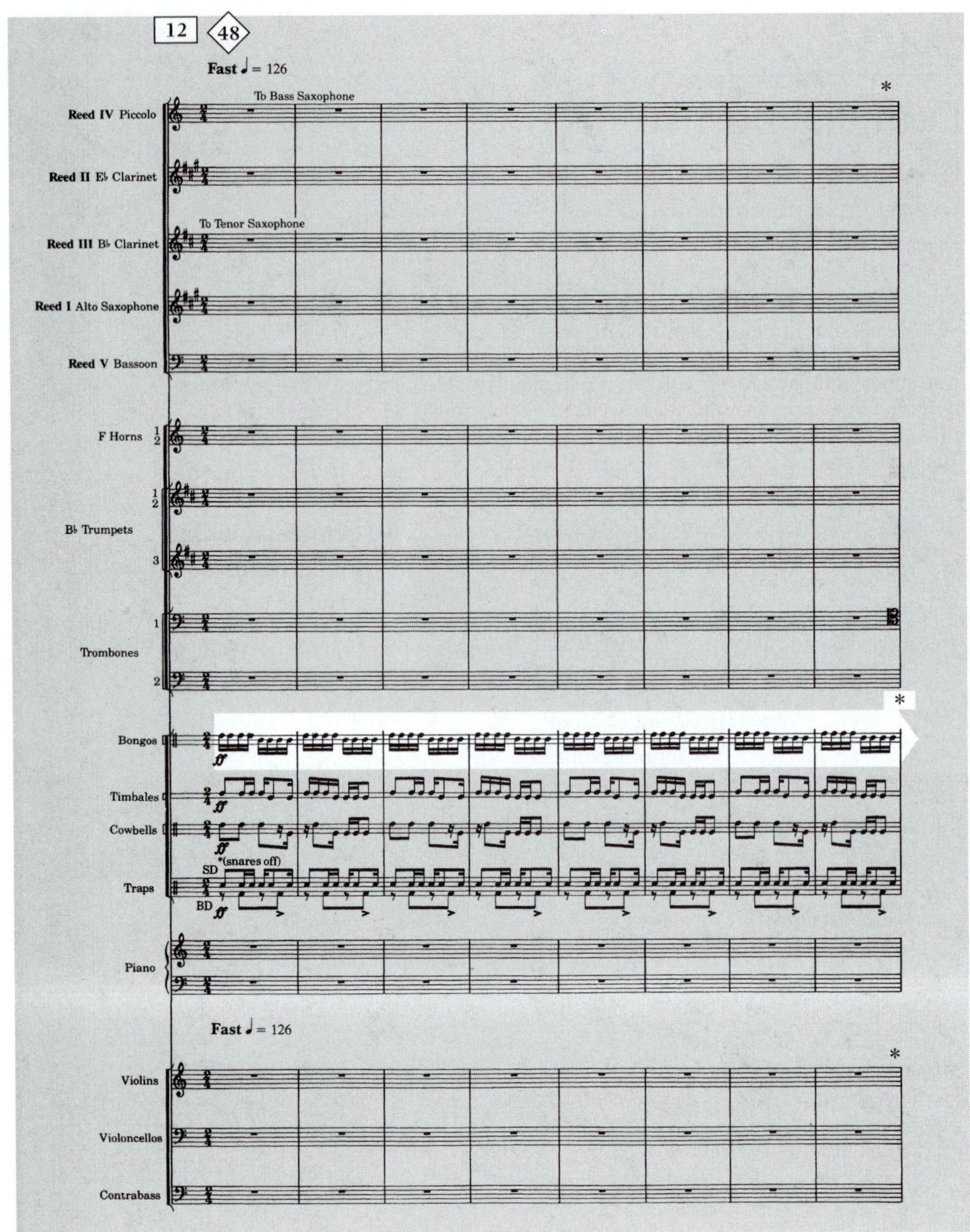

*Editor's note: *The Norton Recordings* performance, which is the original Broadway cast recording, cuts the following five pages and resumes at measure 43 (p. 798).

9
II E♭ Cl.
I Al. Sax.
III Ten. Sax.
IV Bs. Sax.
To Picc.
V Bsn.
a2
F Hns. 1 2
1 2
B♭ Tpts.
3
1
Tbns.
2
Timp.
Bongos
Timb.
Cowbells
Xylo.
SD
Traps
BD
Piano
JETS
Mam-bo!
Go!
SHARKS
Mam - bo!
Go!
Vlns.
Vcs.
Cb.

15
IV Picc.
II E♭ Cl.
I Al. Sax.
Ten. Sax.
V Bsn.
B♭ Tpts.
Tbns.
Bongos
Cowbells
Xylo.
Mambo ad lib.
SD (snares off)
BD
Traps
loco
Piano
Vlns.
Vcs.
pizz.
Cb.

22
II E♭ Cl.
I Al. Sax.
I Ten. Sax.
V Bsn.
f cresc.
F Hns. 1 2
ff cuivré
open
1
B♭ Tpts.
3
open
Tbns.
1
2
Bongos
Timb.
Cowbells
SD
Traps
BD
f cresc.
Piano
ff
Vlns.
1 2 3 4
5 6 7
Vcs.
arco
Cb.
f cresc.

29
II E♭ Cl.
I Al. Sax.
III Ten. Sax.
V Bsn.
f cresc.
F Hns. 1 2
ff cuivré
open
B♭ Tpts. 1 3
open
Tbns. 1 2
f cresc.
Bongos
f cresc.
Timb.
f cresc.
Cowbells
f cresc.
Traps
SD
BD
f cresc.
Piano
Vlns. 1 2 3 4
5 6 7
Vcs.
arco
Cb.
f cresc.

36
IV Picc.
II E♭ Cl.
I Al. Sax.
I Ten. Sax.
a2
F Hns. 1 2
B♭ Tpts. 1 3
Tbns. 1 2
1st only
Bongos
Timb.
Cowbells
SD
Traps
BD
Piano
Vlns. 1 2 3 4 5 6 7
Vcs.
Cb.

**Editor's note: The Norton Recordings* performance resumes here.

51
III Ob.
II E♭ Cl.
I B♭ Cl.
IV B♭ Cl.
V Bsn.
F Hns. 1 2
B♭ Tpts. 1 3
2
Tbns. 1
2
Bongos
Traps
SD
Piano
loco
f
Vlns. 1 2 3
4 5
6 7
Vcs. 1 2
3 4
Cb.
a2
pp
molto

59
IV Picc.
III Ob.
II E♭ Cl.
I B♭ Cl.
V B♭ Cl.
To Piccolo
V Bsn.
F Hns. 1 2
a2
1 3 ♭ Tpts. 2
Tbns. 1 2
Timp.
Bongos
Timb.
Cowbells
Xylo.
SD
Traps
BD
Piano
Mam-bo!
Vlns. 1 2 3 4 5 6 7
pizz.
1.2
3.4
5.6
unis.
Vcs.
Cb.

67
IV Picc.
III Ob.
II E♭ Cl.
I B♭ Cl.
V Bsn.
F Hns. 1 2
B♭ Tpts. 1 2 3
Tbns. 1 2
Bongos
Conga
Pitched Drs.
Cowbells
Xylo.
Traps
Piano
Vlns. 1 2 3 4 5 6 7
Vcs. 1 2 3 4
Cb.
cresc.
To Flute
a2
fall-off
gliss.
rim shots
SD
BD
TD
L.H. gliss.
at frog
arco
pizz.

74
IV Picc.
I Fl.
III Ob.
II E♭ Cl.
V Bsn.
F Hns. 1 2
a2
B♭ Tpts. 1 2 3
Tbns. 1 2
fall-off
Bongos
Conga
Pitched Drs.
Cowbells
Xylo.
gliss.
Traps
TD
BD
Piano
Vlns. 1 2 3 4 5 6 7
pizz.
Vcs.
unis.
Cb.
To B♭ Clarinet

81
IV Picc.
III Ob.
II E♭ Cl.
I B♭ Cl.
V Bsn.
F Hns. 1 2
a2
♭ Tpts. 1 2 3
Tbns. 1 2
Bongos
Conga
Pitched Drs.
Cowbells
Xylo.
Traps
Mambo ad lib.
TD
BD
SD
Tem. Blk.
rim shot
Piano
142
Vlns. 1 2 3 4 5 6 7
Vcs. 1 2 3 4
Cb.
cresc.

88
IV Picc.
III Ob.
II E♭ Cl.
I B♭ Cl.
V Bsn.
F Hns. 1 2
a2
B♭ Tpts. 1 2 3
p ma marc.
Tbns. 1 2
Bongos
Pitched Drs.
Cowbells
Xylo.
Traps
SD
Mambo ad lib.
TD
BD
(loco)
Piano
Vlns. 1 2 3 4 5 6 7
arco
Vcs. 1 2 3 4
Cb.
dim.

95
IV Picc.
III Ob.
II E♭ Cl.
I B♭ Cl.
V Bsn.
F Hns. 1 2
a2
poco f
Tpts. 1 2 3
marc.
Tbns. 1 2
Bongos
Pitched Drs.
Cowbells
Xylo.
Traps
TD
BD
Piano
loco
Vlns. 1 2 3 4 5 6 7
unis.
Vcs.
Cb.
cresc.
fff
ff
sfz

101
IV Picc.
III Ob.
II E♭ Cl.
I B♭ Cl.
V Bsn.
B♭ Tpts.
To D Trumpet
Solo
Tbn. 1
ad lib.
Conga
ad lib.
Cowbells
Guiro
Xylo.
Traps
BD
Piano
Vlns.
arco
Vcs.
arco
arco
Cb.

* maracas may be separate player.

114
13
49
IV Picc.
III Ob.
II E♭ Cl.
I B♭ Cl.
V Bsn.
F Hns. 1 2
D Tpt.
♭ Tpts. 1 3
Tbns. 1 2
Timp.
Bongos
Timb.
Pitched Drs.
Traps
Piano
Vlns.
Vcs.
Cb.
cresc.
To Tenor Saxophone
To Alto Saxophone
a2
(open)
ff
shake
sfz
f
SD
TD
BD

120
IV Picc.
II E♭ Cl.
I Al. Sax.
I Ten. Sax.
V Bsn.
F Hns. 1 2
a2
D Tpt.
shake
B♭ Tpts. 1 3
shake
shake
shake
Tbns. 1 2
Timp.
Bongos
Timb.
Pitched Drs.
Traps
TD
BD
Piano
Vlns.
Vcs.
Cb.

126
(Tony and Maria see each other)
IV Picc.
II E♭ Cl.
I Al. Sax.
I Ten. Sax.
V Bsn.
F Hns. 1 2
a2
D Tpt.
To B♭ Trumpet
B♭ Tpts. 1 3
2
open
Tbns. 1 2
gliss.
Timp.
with Maracas
ad lib.
Bongos
Timb.
Pitched Drs.
Traps
TD
BD
Susp. CYM
Piano
Vlns.
Vcs.
Cb.
pizz.

132
IV Picc.
II E♭ Cl.
I Al. Sax.
III Ten. Sax.
V Bsn.
F Hns. 1 2
a2
B♭ Tpts. 1 3
2
Tbns. 1 2
gliss.
a2
Timp.
Bongos
Timb.
Pitched Drs.
Traps
TD
BD
Piano
ALL
Go, Mam
Vlns.
Vcs.
Cb.

138
IV Picc.
II E♭ Cl.
I Al. Sax.
III Ten. Sax.
V Bsn
F Hns. 1/2
B♭ Tpts. 1 2 3
Tbns. 1/2
Timp.
Bongos
Timb.
Pitched Drs.
Traps
Piano
All
Vlns.
Vcs.
Cb.
a2
gliss.
valve gliss.
TD
BD
Susp. CYM
loco
- bo! Go, Mam - bo! Go, Mam - bo!

(The lights dim and the crowd disappears as Tony and Maria approach each other)
144
rall. molto
IV Picc.
To Flute
II E♭ Cl.
To B♭ Clarinet
I Al. Sax.
To Flute
III Ten. Sax.
To Flute
V Bsn.
a2
F Hns. 1 2
B♭ Tpts. 1 2 3
straight mute
straight mutes
Tbns. 1 2
Timp.
Bongos
Timb.
Pitched Drs.
Maracas
TD
Traps
BD
Piano
rall. molto
sul D
sul D
Vlns.
Vcs. 1 2 3 4
Cb.
ff
dim.
f dim.
mp
p
pp
ppp
SEGUE

Tonight

Ensemble

Maria, Tony, Anita, Riff, Bernardo*

*If the scene is staged with more than the designated five people, the members of the gangs may sing with their respective leaders.

14
(RIFF)
mf
The Puer - to Ri - cans grum - ble: "Fair
(BERN.)
mp sempre staccato
17
fight." But if they start a rum - ble, We'll rum - ble 'em
20
right.
mp
We're gon-na hand 'em a sur-prise To -
p

24
We're gon-na cut 'em down to size To -
night.
28
night.
mf
We said, "O. K., no rum-pus, No
mp sempre staccato
32
tricks". But just in case they jump us, We're read - y to

15
51
35
f
We're gon-na rock it to-night,
mix To - night!
We're gon-na rock it to-night,
cresc.
f marc.
mf
39
We're gon-na jazz it up and have us a ball!
We're gon-na jazz it up and have us a ball!
f subito
42
They're gon - na get it to - night; The more they turn it on, the
They're gon - na get it to - night; The more they turn it on, the
mf subito

44
hard-er they'll fall!
Well, they be-gan it!
hard-er they'll fall!
Well,
cresc.
47
And we're the ones to stop 'em once and for all,
they be-gan it! And we're the ones to stop 'em once and for all,
49
ANITA (sexily)
An-
To - night!
To - night!
cresc.
p subito
16
52

53
i - ta's gon - na get her kicks To - night.
56
We'll have our pri-vate lit-tle mix To - night.
60
He'll walk in hot and ti - red, So what? Don't
mp sempre staccato
64
mat - ter if he's ti - red, As long as he's hot

17
53
To - night!
TONY (warmly)
mf
To - night, to - night Won't be just an - y
mp
night, To - night there will be no morn - ing star.
più f
To - night, to - night, I'll see my love to -
cresc.

79
night And for us, stars will stop where they are.
83
18
54
f
To - day The min - utes seem like hours, The
3
f espr.
87
hours go so slow - ly, And still the sky is light.

91
mp
cresc.
Oh moon, grow bright, And make this end-less
cresc.
95
f
Come prima, in 4
day end-less night!
f
ff marcatissmo
99

102
RIFF (To Tony) mp
I'm count-ing on you to be there
sffz
dim.
p
105
To - night
When Dies-el wins it fair and square
109
To - night.
mf
That Puer-to Ri-can punk'll
mp
113
Go down And when he's hol-lered "Un-cle" We'll tear up the

19
55
117
MARIA (warmly)
mf
To - night, to - night Won't
TONY (abstractedly)
mp
All right.
(firmly)
town! So I can count on you, boy?
p
120
be just an - y night, To - night there will be
(a bit impatiently)
f
All right.
(spoken) (gently)
We're gon-na have us a ball. Womb to tomb!
simile

* The part of Anita may be augmented by voices in the wings from here to the end.

*The part of Maria may be augmented by voices in the wings from here to the end.

135
min - utes seem like hours, The hours go so
day, An-i-ta's gon-na have her day,
min - utes seem like hours, The hours go so
(lights on Riff)
fp
fp
sim.
They be - gan it,
sim.
gan it, they be - gan it
138
dim.
slow - ly, And still the sky is light.
Ber-nar-do's gon-na have his way To - night,
dim.
slow - ly, And still the sky is light.
They be - gan it.
f
And we're the ones To stop 'em once and for all!
dim.

141
pp
Oh moon, grow
to - night. To - night,
pp
Oh moon, grow
f
We'll stop 'em once and for all! The Jets are gon - na have their
dim. molto
pp
The Sharks are gon - na have their
pp
143
cresc. molto
bright, And make this end - less day end - less
cresc. molto
this ver - y night,
cresc. molto
bright, And make this end - less day end - less
cresc. molto
way, The Jets are gon - na have their day,
cresc. molto
way, The Sharks are gon - na have their day,
cresc. molto

146
night
To - night!
We're gon-na rock it to-night!
night
To - night!
We're gon-na rock it to-night,
To - night!
We're gon-na rock it to-night,
To - night!
149

Leonard Bernstein (1918–1990), one of America's foremost musicians of the twentieth century, achieved critical success as a concert pianist, conductor, and composer. His masterwork is the Broadway musical *West Side Story,* which adapts Shakespeare's *Romeo and Juliet* to a modern New York setting. The musical centers on two rival gangs, the established Jets and the Puerto Rican Sharks, which are equivalent to the rival families in the Shakespeare tragedy. Bernstein emphasizes the ethnic differences between the gangs by incorporating elements of both American jazz and Latin American popular music. With these diverse styles, Bernstein creates a highly unified work that has immense popular appeal yet retains its ties to Western classical music.

The mambo is played at the neighborhood dance, which is equivalent to the masked ball in the Shakespeare drama. Bernstein uses this energetic Afro-Cuban dance, with its fast tempo and accented syncopation, to reflect the presence of the Sharks. Bongos, cowbells, shouts from the dancers, loud dissonances, and jazzy riffs contribute to the frenzied character of the dance. At the end, the music quickly fades as Tony and Maria see each other for the first time.

The *Tonight* Ensemble mixes popular elements within an operatic setting. The ensemble is in three sections. During the opening section, the two gangs sing an energetic melody over a menacing marching bass line. After alternating the material, the two gangs sing simultaneously. Anita joins in with a new verse, which closes this section. The second section is a reprise of Tony and Maria's balcony love song, *Tonight.* Set against a beguine rhythm (another Latin American popular dance), the melody is sung in its full **A-A'-B-A'** format. Upon the repetition of the tune by Maria, the final section emerges, and the two musical ideas are combined together. At the climax, both Tony and Maria sing of their love, while Anita and both gangs sing of hatred. The common element linking the two is the word "tonight."

44

John Cage

Sonatas and Interludes, Sonata V (1946)

8CD: 8/ 29 - 30
4CD: 4/ 65 - 66

Table of Preparations

TONE	MATERIAL	STRINGS LEFT TO RIGHT	DISTANCE FROM DAMPER (INCHES)	MATERIAL	STRINGS LEFT TO RIGHT	DISTANCE FROM DAMPER (INCHES)	MATERIAL	STRINGS LEFT TO RIGHT	DISTANCE FROM DAMPER (INCHES)
A				SCREW	2-3	1 1/4*			
G				MED. BOLT	2-3	1 3/8*			
F				SCREW	2-3	1 5/8*			
E				SCREW	2-3	1 13/16*			
E♭				SCREW	2-3	1 3/4*			
D				SM. BOLT	2-3	2*			
C♯				SCREW	2-3	1 9/16*			
C				FURNITURE BOLT	2-3	2 3/16*			
B				SCREW	2-3	2 1/2*			
B♭				SCREW	2-3	1 7/8*			
A				MED. BOLT	2-3	2 7/8*			
A♭				SCREW	2-3	2 1/4*			
G				SCREW	2-3	3 3/4*			
F♯				SCREW	2-3	2 15/16*			
F	SCREW	1-2	3/4*	FURN. BOLT + 2 NUTS	2-3	2 1/8*	SCREW + 2 NUTS	2-3	3 1/4*
E				SCREW	2-3	1 13/16*			
E♭				FURNITURE BOLT	2-3	1 7/8			
C♯				SCREW	2-3	1 15/16			
C				SCREW	2-3	1 1/16			
B	(DAMPER TO BRIDGE = 4 7/16; ADJUST ACCORDINGLY)			MED. BOLT	2-3	3 3/4			
A				SCREW	2-3	4 7/16			
G♯	RUBBER	1-2-3	4 1/2	FURNITURE BOLT	2-3	1 1/4			
F♯				SCREW	2-3	1 3/4			
F				SCREW	2-3	2 5/16			
E	RUBBER	1-2-3	5 3/4						
E♭	RUBBER	1-2-3	6 1/2	FURN. BOLT + NUT	2-3	6 7/8			
D				FURNITURE BOLT	2-3	2 9/16			
D♭	RUBBER	1-2-3	3 5/8						
C				BOLT	2-3	7 1/8			
B				BOLT	2-3	2			
B♭	SCREW	1-2	10	SCREW	2-3	1	RUBBER	1-2-3	8 1/4
G♯	(PLASTIC (SEE G))	1-2-3	2 5/16				RUBBER	1-2-3	4 1/2
G	PLASTIC (OVER 1 - UNDER 2-3)	1-2-3	2 7/8				RUBBER	1-2-3	10 1/8
D♯	(PLASTIC (SEE D))	1-2-3	4 1/4				RUBBER	1-2-3	5 7/16
D	PLASTIC (OVER 1 - UNDER 2-3)	1-2-3	4 1/8				RUBBER	1-2-3	9 3/4
D♭	BOLT	1-2	15 1/2	BOLT	2-3	14/16	RUBBER	1-2-3	14 1/8
C	BOLT	1-2	14 1/2	BOLT	2-3	7/8	RUBBER	1-2-3	6 1/2
B	BOLT	1-2	14 3/4	BOLT	2-3	9/16	RUBBER	1-2-3	14
B♭	RUBBER	1-2-3	9 1/2	MED. BOLT	2-3	10 1/8			
A	SCREW	1-2	5 7/8	LG. BOLT	2-3	5 7/8	SCREW + NUTS	1-2	1
A♭	BOLT	1-2	7 1/8	MED. BOLT	2-3	2 1/4	RUBBER	1-2-3	4 1/8
G	LONG BOLT	1-2	8 3/4	LG BOLT	2-3	3 1/4			
D				BOLT	2-3	14/16			
D (8va. bas)	SCREW + RUBBER	1-2	4 7/16						
D (16va. bas)	ERASER (OVER D UNDER C♯ + E♭) AM. PENCIL CO. #346	1	6 3/4						

*MEASURE FROM BRIDGE.

[Mutes of various materials are placed between the strings of the keys used, thus effecting transformations of the piano sounds with respect to all of their characteristics.]

V
29
65
30
66
mf

California-born John Cage (1912–1992) established himself as a major American avant-garde composer during the 1930s. Greatly influenced by Eastern philosophies and musical styles, Cage is best remembered as an advocate of indeterminacy and for his expansion of the boundaries of musical sound to include more of what had generally been considered as noise. In 1938, he invented the "prepared" piano, which is created by inserting various objects, such as nails, screws, wood, and leather, between the strings of a grand piano. Depending on the nature of the material and its placement, a great variety of sounds can be created, ranging from altered pitches to nonpitched effects.

Sonatas and Interludes is a set of works for prepared piano dating from 1946–48. These sixteen sonatas are grouped in sets of four. Between each group, Cage inserts an interlude. In the preface, Cage gives specific instructions on how to prepare the piano, indicating that forty-five of the eighty-eight strings are to be prepared with various materials at prescribed distances from the damper. Sonata V, set in a binary form, has a limited pitch content, primarily centering on the five pitches between B and E-flat. Because of the prepared alterations, many of these notes produce a nonpitched, percussive sound. The unusual timbre and hypnotic quality of the movement as a whole are reminiscent of the character of a Javanese gamelan ensemble; Cage's interest in Asian music is also apparent in his attempt to portray, in this set of piano works, the eight permanent emotions of [East] Indian aesthetics: the erotic, the heroic, the odious, anger, mirth, fear, sorrow, and the wondrous.

45

Pierre Boulez

Notations IV (1945, rev. 1978)

8CD: 8/ 31 – 33

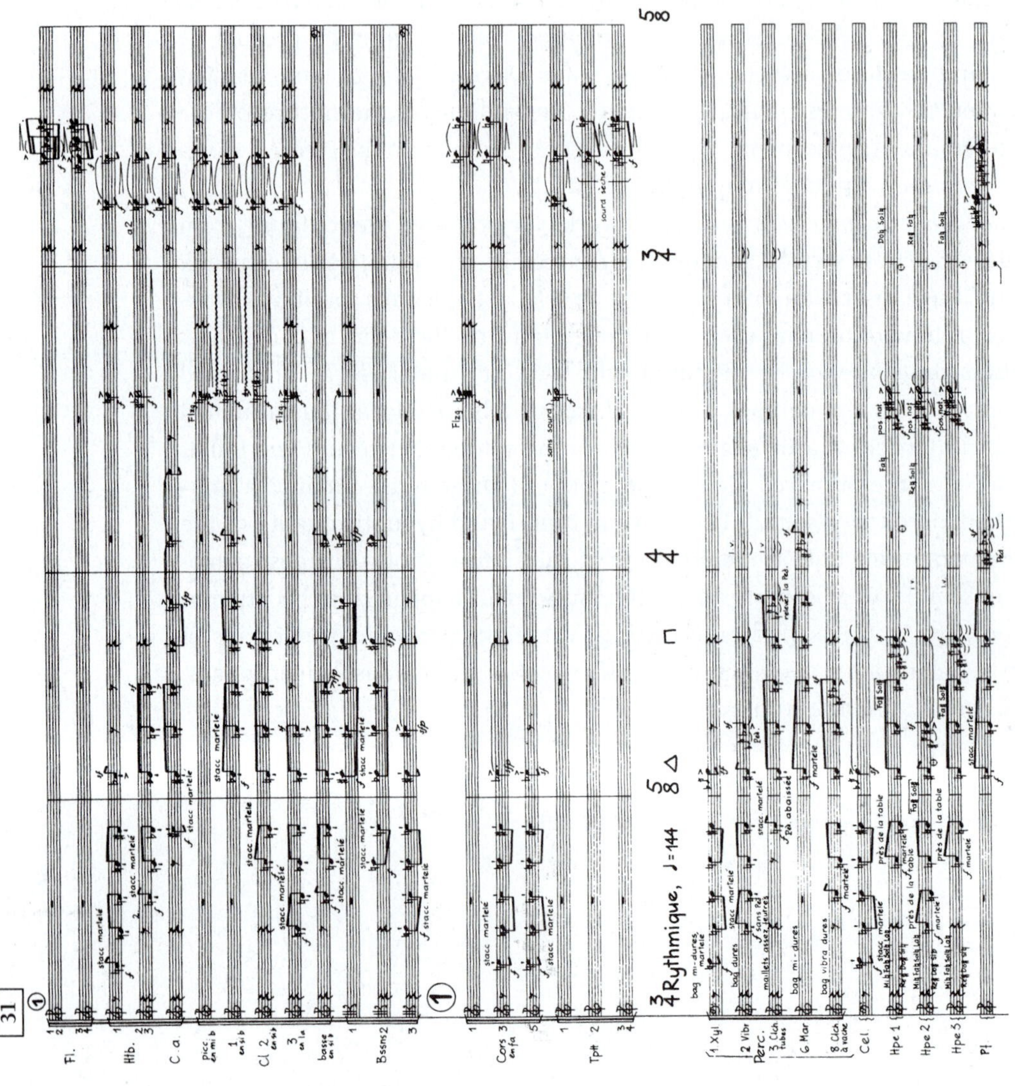

Editor's note: Due to the very large format of this score, *The Norton Scores* presents only the first page of the orchestral version of *Notations IV*, set across pages 834–35; however, the original piano version is included, with track markings to aid in following the recording.

Rythmique, ♩=144
Viol. I
Viol. II
Altos
Vc.
stacc. martelé
sul pont
pos nat
pizz
div

Pierre Boulez (b. 1925) was one of the leading figures of the avant-garde movement following World War II. A student of Messiaen, the young French composer explored complex serial and rhythmic techniques that produced dense yet colorful compositions. One of the products of his early infatuation with serialism is a set of twelve short piano works entitled *Notations* (1945), which was published as Opus 1.

Notations IV from this set, marked *Rhythmique*, draws all of its pitch material from two related hexachords that together encompass all twelve tones of the chromatic scale. The left hand plays one hexachord in an ostinato fashion. The first five pitches (A–E–F–G–F sharp) are notated as sixteenth notes, and the final A♭ is sustained for various lengths. Although the movement contains twelve measures, the bar lines do not delineate regular metrical units; instead, they indicate the beginning of each ostinato.

The right hand responds to the ostinatos with a variety of rhythmic gestures. In the first measure, the right hand enters after the entire ostinato has been played, but in each succeeding measure, the entrance of the right hand comes earlier until both hands play simultaneously at measure seven. The primary hexachord of the right hand (D–C–C♯–B–B♭–E♭) is a transposed retrograde version of the left-hand hexachord. The first measure presents the initial two notes of the hexachord, and one note is added in each measure until E♭ arrives in measure five. This progression builds density and dissonance, intensifying in measures ten through twelve. In these final measures, the right hand introduces a third hexachord, which reorders the pitches of its original hexachord.

After achieving international recognition as an orchestra conductor, Boulez expanded and arranged the first four movements of *Notations* for a large symphony orchestra in 1978. In *Notations IV*, Boulez divides the strings into nine stands of first violins, eight stands of second violins, seven stands of violas, and six stands of cellos (each stand accommodates two players). In addition, he employs five percussionists playing different pitched instruments, three harpists, two keyboardists, and numerous wind and brass players. With these varied sources, Boulez explores a variety of colorful effects and employs dense contrapuntal textures. Because of the extended orchestration, the complete score for this work is too large for the page dimensions of this anthology. Only one page is reproduced; the piano version can be used as skeleton guide to the work as a whole.

In the orchestral score, bar lines indicate metric units, and rehearsal numbers mark the beginning of each of the twelve ostinatos. In the opening measures, the ostinato is presented canonically with six entrances, each separated by an eighth note. The final note of the last entrance is sustained and emphasized through dissonances. This basic pattern recurs for each statement of the ostinato, following the general treatment found in the piano version. The final chord of each ostinato is systematically lengthened and then shortened across in the movement, creating the effect of a palindrome. With a system that Boulez calls "frequency multiplication," chords are built by multiplying the first intervals of the pitch sequence, thereby intensifying the overall dissonance.

46

George Crumb

Ancient Voices of Children, First movement, *El niño busca su voz* (*The Little Boy Is Looking for His Voice*) (1970)

8CD: 8/ 34 – 36

4CD: 4/ 67 – 69

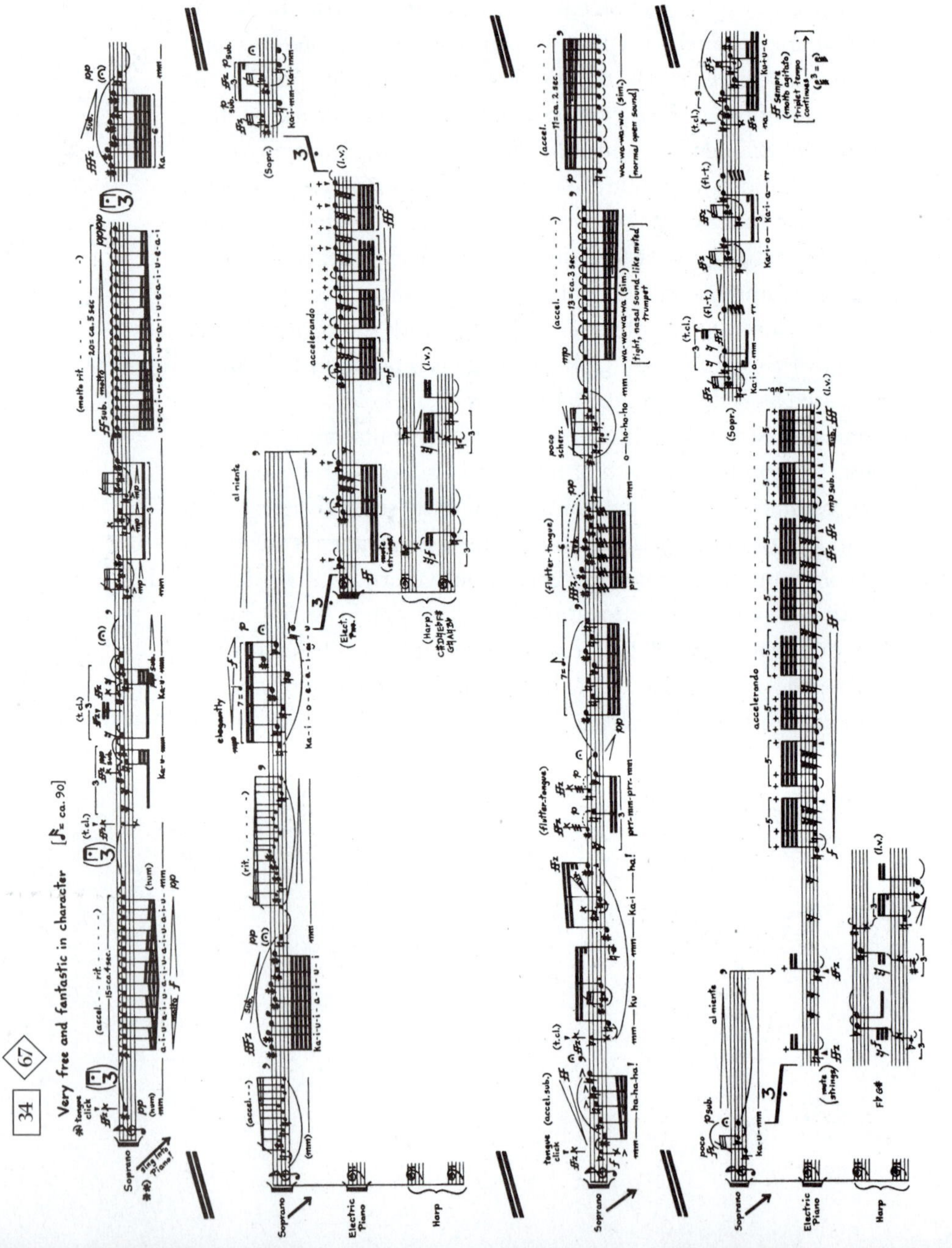

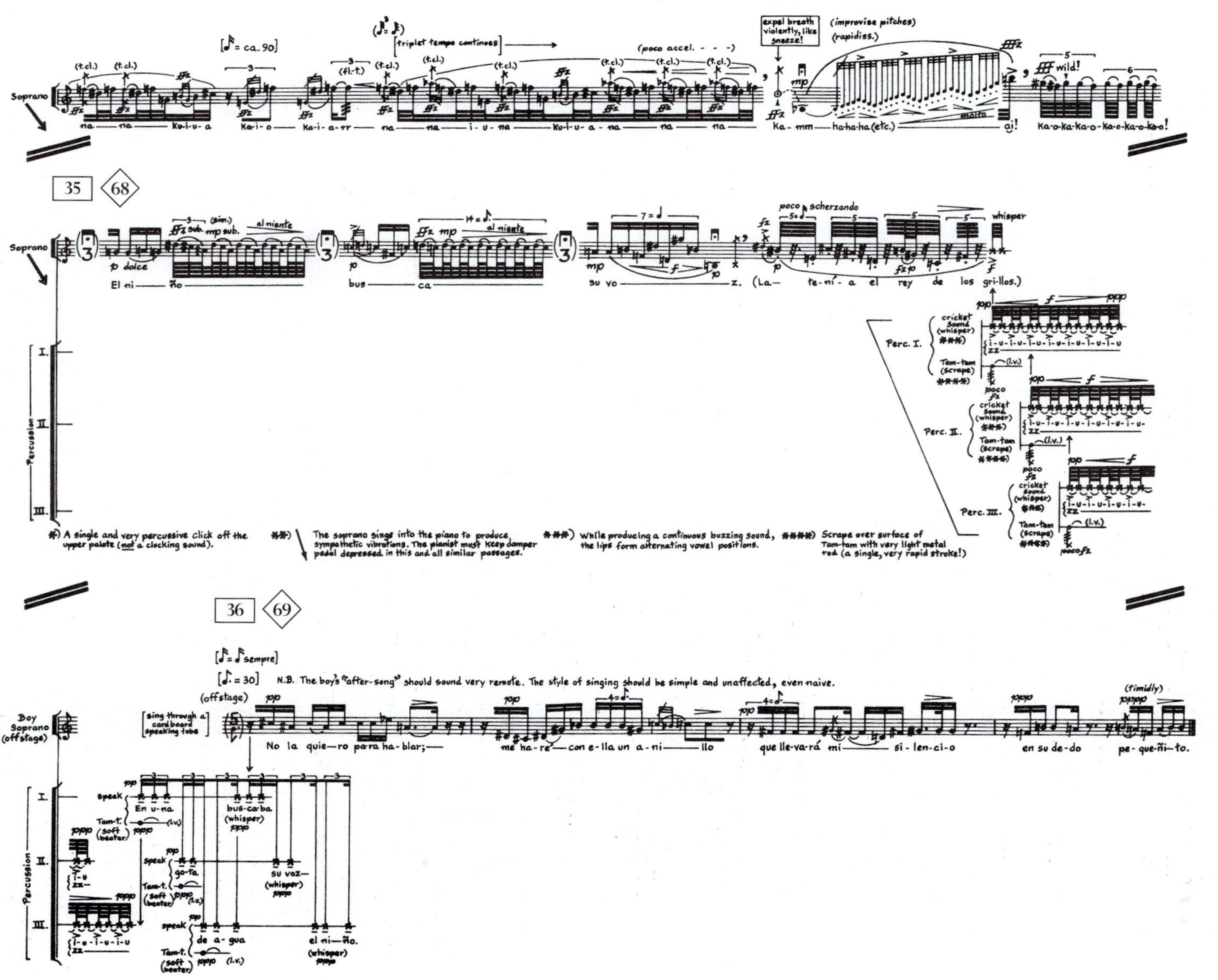
Soprano
(improvise pitches)
(rapidiss.)
expel breath violently, like sneeze!
triplet tempo continues
(poco accel. - - -)
na — na — Ku-i-u-a Ka-i-o — Ka-i-a-rr — na — na — i-u-na — Ku-i-u-a-na — na — na — Ka-mm — ha-ha-ha (etc.) — aj!
wild!
Ka-o-ka-ka-o-ka-o-ka-o-ka-o!
35 68
Soprano
p dolce
al niente
poco scherzando
whisper
El ni— ño bus— ca su vo— z. (La— te-ni-a el rey de los gri-llos.)
Percussion
Perc. I. cricket sound (whisper) Tam-tam (scrape)
Perc. II. cricket sound (whisper) Tam-tam (scrape)
Perc. III. cricket sound (whisper) Tam-tam (scrape)
A single and very percussive click off the upper palate (not a clucking sound).
The soprano sings into the piano to produce sympathetic vibrations. The pianist must keep damper pedal depressed in this and all similar passages.
While producing a continuous buzzing sound, the lips form alternating vowel positions.
Scrape over surface of Tam-tam with very light metal rod (a single, very rapid stroke!)
36 69
sempre
N.B. The boy's "after-song" should sound very remote. The style of singing should be simple and unaffected, even naive.
Boy Soprano (offstage)
(offstage)
sing through a cardboard speaking tube
(timidly)
No la quie—ro para ha-blar;— me ha-re—con e-lla un a-ni—llo que lle-va-rá mi — si-len-ci-o en su de-do pe-que-ñi—to.
speak En u-na
bus-ca-ba (whisper)
speak go-ta
su voz— (whisper)
speak de a-gua
el ni—ño. (whisper)
Tam-t. (soft beater)

TEXT AND TRANSLATION

El niño busca su voz. (La tenía el rey de los grillos.) En una gota de agua buscaba su voz el niño.	The little boy is looking for his voice. (The king of the crickets had it.) In a drop of water the little boy looked for his voice.
No la quiero para hablar; me haré con ella un anillo que llevará mi silencio en su dedo pequeñito.	I don't want it to speak with; I will make a ring of it so that he may wear my silence on his little finger.
FEDERICO GARCÍA LORCA	*Translated by W. S. Merwin*

George Crumb (b. 1929) is one of America's foremost contemporary composers. A professor at the University of Pennsylvania, Crumb has created a number of works that are justifiably acclaimed for their unique musical colors and strong emotional content. *Ancient Voices of Children* is a song cycle based on fragments of poems by the great Spanish literary figure Federico García Lorca. These poetic excerpts are grafted into a five-song structure that also includes two instrumental dance interludes.

The cycle is set for an ensemble that features soprano, boy soprano, oboe, electric piano, harp, mandolin, and numerous percussion instruments. Unique timbres are created from these instruments, as well as from the addition of other unusual instruments such as a musical saw, a toy piano, and various non-Western percussion instruments. The soprano opens the cycle with a vocalise sung into the piano with the pedals down, thereby creating an aura of sound from sympathetic vibrations. The boy soprano sings from off-stage until the end of the cycle. Other unusual effects include the mistuning by a quarter-step of one of each pair of mandolin strings, the use of a paper-threaded harp, and the "bending" of the piano pitch by applying a chisel to the strings.

The first song of the cycle, *El niño busca su voz (The Little Boy Is Looking for His Voice)*, features a virtuosic vocal line that was originally intended for mezzo-soprano Jan DeGaetani. In addition to the elaborate vocalise, the singer is required to click her tongue, use flutter tonguing, and make other unique sounds. The accompanying ensemble consists of electric piano, harp, and percussionist, who, like the voice, whisper and make additional vocal noises. At the end, the boy soprano enters from off-stage, singing through a cardboard speaking tube. The mixture of sounds from different cultures and time periods is described by Crumb:

> In composing *Ancient Voices of Children* I was conscious of an urge to fuse various unrelated stylistic elements. I was intrigued with the idea of juxtaposing the seemingly incongruous: a suggestion of Flamenco with a Baroque quotation (*Bist du bei mir,* from the Notebook of Anna Magdalena Bach), or a reminiscence of Mahler with a breath of the Orient. It later occurred to me that both Bach and Mahler drew upon many disparate sources in their own music without sacrificing "stylistic purity."

47

György Ligeti

Désordre (*Disorder*), from *Etudes pour Piano*, Book I (1985)

8CD: 8/ 37 – 39

Composer's directions: Use the pedal very discreetly throughout the entire piece.
Editor's note: Measure numbers pertain to left hand.

29
36
1 2 3
43
38
52

62
8bassa
crescendo poco a poco
71
8bassa
8va
più crescendo
81
8bassa
39
8va
fff crescendo molto
Poco
simile
p
mf
f
fff sub.
91
fff
8bassa
Ped.

Composer's directions:
*Dynamic balance: the right hand should play somewhat louder than the left, so that the accented chords in both hands sound equally loud (until the end of the piece).
Gradually add more pedal (but always sparingly).
*Gradual *crescendo* (until the end): the accents gradually become *ff*, then *fff* (with the right hand constantly louder), the eighth notes gradually *mp*, then *mf*.

8va
128
135
141

György Ligeti (1923–2006) left his Hungarian homeland in 1956 and immediately began to add his own distinctive voice to the European avant-garde movement. He achieved quasi-celebrity status when three of his compositions—*Atmosphères*, the Requiem, and *Lux aeterna*—were used in Stanley Kubrick's classic film *2001: A Space Odyssey* (1968). In these works, Ligeti explored the use of fixed pitches to create large clusters of tones.

At the end of the 1970s, Ligeti's style began to change as he turned toward a complex polyrhythmic technique and moved away from the static quality of his earlier compositions. Among his later works are fifteen piano études, published in three books: Book I has six works (1985), Book II has eight works (1988), and Book III contains only one work—"White on White" (1995). In the tradition of fellow Hungarian Franz Liszt, each étude is given a subtitle. The first étude, *Désordre* (*Disorder*), presents a complex web of rhythmic patterns that, at a vigorous tempo, creates an effect well suited to its title. Two distinct rhythmic processes can be observed: additive metric patterns (5 + 3 or 3 + 5)—an influence of African rhythm—and the simultaneous playing of triple and duple patterns. With the quick tempo, the complexities of the rhythmic patterns are not heard, but rather the focus is on the overall effect that grows in intensity and diminishes only at the end.

48

Bright Sheng

China Dreams: Prelude (1995)

8CD: 8/ 40 – 45
4CD: 4/ 70 – 75

* Grace note on the beat.

12
Picc.
Fl. 1 2
Ob. 1 2
(a2)
E.H.
pp sub.
E♭ Cl.
mp
p
B♭ Cl. 1
p
mp
p
Bs. Cl.
Bn. 1 2
pp
(pp)
Cbn.
Hn. in F
Tpt. in C 2
con sord.
mp
Tpt. in B♭ 3
con sord.
mp
con sord.
mp
Tbn.
Tuba
(Chimes)
p
Perc.
(Glock.)
pp
Pno.
(p)
mf
f
Harp
ff
Vn.
unis.
pizz.
p
pizz.
mp
f
Va.
(p)
f
div.
Vc.
unis., pizz.
p
Cb.
(p)
mp
p

17
Picc.
Fl. 1 2
Ob. 1 2
(a2)
E.H.
E♭ Cl.
to B♭ Cl. 2
B♭ Cl. 1
Bs. Cl.
Bn. 1 2
Cbn.
Tpt. in C 1 2
con sord.
legato
Tpt. in B♭ 3
Tbn. 1 2
Tuba 3
Perc. 1 2
(Chimes)
Pno.
Harp
G♭
D♭ C♭
F♭
Vn. I II
div.
Va. (div. a4) 1 2 3 4
arco
Vc.
Cb.

rit.
B♭ Cl.
Bs. Cl.
Bn.
Cbn.
solo
Tpt. in C
Tpt. in B♭
Tbn.
Pno.
rit.
Vn.
Va. (div. a4)
unis.
Vc.
Cb.
41
71
Meno mosso ♩ = 63
B♭ Cl. 1
to B♭ Cl. 3
Bs. Cl.
(w/nails)
gliss.
Harp
E♮ F♭ G♭ A♮
D♮ C♭ B♭
G♭ – G♮
C♭ – C♮
F♭ – F♮
Meno mosso ♩ = 63
Vn. I
solo
pizz., gliss.
solo
Vn. II
gli altri
poco tasto, non vibrato
arco
ppp sempre
unis., sul tasto, non vibrato
Va.
ppp sempre
poco tasto
sul tasto, non vibrato
arco
Vc.
ppp sempre
poco
poco tasto
* Glissando occurs at the end of the first note value.

42
72
accel.
♩ = 76 (più mosso)
32
Picc.
Fl. 1 2
Ob. 1 2
E.H.
B♭ Cl. 1 2 3
B♭ Clarinet
Bn. 1 2
a2
molto
Hn. in F 1 3 2 4
1. open
Tpt. in C 1 2
(con sord.)
Tbn. 2 3
con sord.
Perc. 1 2
(Chimes)
Pno.
Harp
simile
F♮ – F♯
B♮
F♮
C♮
solo
Vn. I
gli altri
non vib.
vib.
pizz., gliss.
ppp sempre
Vn. II
(pizz.)
ord.
sola
Va.
le altre
soli
Vc.
1 solo
2 soli (pizz.)
non div.
pizz.
Cb.
* Bass clef notation for horns sounds a fifth lower.

♩ = 72
Picc.
Fl.
Ob.
E.H.
B♭ Cl.
Bn.
Hn. in F
Tpt. in C
Tbn.
Perc.
(Chimes)
Pno.
Harp
Vn.
Va.
Vc.
Cb.
(tutti, unis.)
(tutte, unis.)
tutti, non div.
molto
1. solo open
gliss.
E♮ F♯ G♯ A♮
D♮ C♯ B♮
* Glissando occurs at the end of the first note value.

44

accel. to ♩ = 76 *(più mosso)*

Picc.

Fl. 1 2

B♭ Cl. 1 3

Hn. in F 1 2

Tbn. 3

gliss.

Perc. 2

Glock.

Pno.

mp

Harp

mf

accel. to ♩ = 76 *(più mosso)*

Vn. I II

Va.

Vc.

pizz.

p

pp

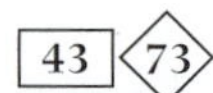

♩ = 72

48

Picc. 1 2 (1.) f a2 ff

Fl. 1 f ff ff

Fl. 2 f to Picc. 2

Ob. 1 2 a2 ff

E.H. ff

E♭ Cl. E♭ Clarinet ff

B♭ Cl. 1 ff

B♭ Cl. 3 f ff

Bn. 1 2 a2 ff

Hn. in F 1 3 (1.) mp mf f a2 ffp mp

Hn. in F 2 4 (2.) mp mf f a2 ffp mp

Tbn. 2 senza sord. mp f ffp mp

Tbn. 3 senza sord. p mf ffp mp

Perc. 1

Perc. 2 (Glock.)

Pno. (mp) mf f ff ff p f 8ba

Harp fff E♭ F♯ G♭ A♭ D♭ C♭ B♮ ff

♩ = 72

Vn. I arco pp mp f ff p f

Vn. II arco p f ff p f

Va. p arco p f ff p f

Vc. p mf arco ff p f

Cb. (pizz.) p mf div. f ff fff

52
Picc. 1 2
Fl. 1
Ob. 1 2
E.H.
E♭ Cl.
B♭ Cl. 1 3
Bn. 1 2
Hn. in F 1 3 2 4
Tpt. in C 1 2
senza sord.
Tbn. 2 3
Pno.
Harp
Vn. I II
Va.
Vc.
Cb.

55
Picc.
Fl.
Ob.
E.H.
E♭ Cl.
B♭ Cl.
Bn.
Hn. in F
Tpt. in C
1. to Tpt. in D
Tbn.
Pno.
Harp
Vn.
Va.
Vc.
Cb.

58
Picc.
Fl.
Ob.
E.H.
E♭ Cl.
B♭ Cl.
Bn.
Hn. in F
Tpt. in C
Tpt. in B♭
Tbn.
Tuba
Timp.
Pno.
Harp
Vn.
Va.
Vc.
Cb.
to B♭ Cl.
to Cl. in A
to Bs. Cl.
senza sord.
a2 soli
soli
gliss.
solo
double wood mallet
E♭ F♮ G♯ A♭
D♭ C♮ B♯

44
74
♩ = 69
62
Picc.
Fl.
Ob.
E.H.
A Cl.
B♭ Cl.
Bs. Cl.
Bn.
Cbn.
Hn. in F
Tpt. in D
Tpt. in C
Tpt. in B♭
Tbn.
Tuba
Timp.
Perc.
Pno.
Vn.
Va.
Vc.
Cb.
a2
(a2)
A Clarinet
B♭ Clarinet
Bass Clarinet
Trumpet in D
Chimes
Bass Drum (wood sticks)
Large Suspended Cymbal
free bowing

Picc.
Fl.
Ob.
E.H.
A Cl.
B♭ Cl.
Bs. Cl.
Bn.
Hn. in F
Tpt. in D
Tpt. in C
Tpt. in B♭
Tbn.
Timp.
(Chimes)
(B.D.)
Perc.
(Cym.)
Vn.
Va.
Vc.
Cb.

45
75
rit.
♩ = 60
Picc.
Fl.
Ob.
E.H.
A Cl.
B♭ Cl.
Bs. Cl.
Bn.
Hn. in F
Tpt. in D
Tpt. in C
Tpt. in B♭
Tbn.
Tuba
Timp.
Perc.
Vn.
Va.
Vc.
Cb.
solo, wood mallets
(Chimes)
(B.D.)
(Cym.)
Glock.
free bowing
pizz.
arco
solo

rit.
Picc. 1
Fl. 1
Ob. 1 2
E.H.
to B♭ Cl.
A Cl. 1
to E♭ Cl.
B♭ Cl. 2
to B♭ Cl. 3
Bs. Cl.
Bn. 1 2
Hn. in F 1 3
2 4
to Picc. Tpt. in B♭
Tpt. in D 1
Tpt. in C 2
Tpt. in B♭ 3
Tbn. 1 2
Tuba 3
Timp.
Perc. 1 2 3
Harp
A♮
A♭
D♮
rit.
1 solo pizz.
Vn. I II
sola
Va.
le altre
solo
Vc.
gli altri
Cb.
pizz.
fff
ppp
pppp
attacca

Inspired by the mixture of eastern European folk and Western classical music in the compositions of Bartók, Bright Sheng (b. 1955) has explored a similar blend of Asian and Western music in his own works. Born in Shanghai, Sheng was forced to work in the Qinghai province near Tibet during the Cultural Revolution. When the universities reopened, he was one of the first students accepted at the Shanghai Conservatory. With a strong background in the traditions of Chinese folk and Western classical music, Sheng came to New York in 1982 and continued his studies at Queens College and Columbia University. He has applied his distinctive style to a variety of genres, including vocal, chamber, and symphonic works, and has received numerous awards and commissions.

China Dreams is a four-movement symphonic suite. Each movement was composed separately; the first, entitled *Prelude*, was commissioned and premiered by the Houston Symphony. The Western elements of the work include its structural similarity to a symphony, the setting for a standard western orchestra, and passages of dense modernism. These features are balanced by Chinese sounds, such as the imitation of Chinese instruments and performing techniques, pentatonic melodies, quick ornamentation, and the free treatment of rhythm and meter.

The free-flowing *Prelude* can be heard in three sections. The first two alternate gentle tunes with a contrasting melody characterized by quick ornamental turns. The movement begins with a pentatonic tune in the oboe and English horn, accompanied by the horn, violas, and plucked lower strings. The contrasting melody interrupts the serenity of this tune in two successively louder entrances (mm. 11 and 18). At the close of the first section, the opening melody returns in the bass clarinet. The second section, beginning in measure 26, resembles the slow movement of Bartók's *Music for Strings, Percussion, and Celesta* in its combination of a quiet melody in the violas, contrapuntal entrances, and quick percussive notes in the upper strings. As the dynamics crescendo, the intrusive theme returns (m. 35), initiating another loud and dissonant passage.

The third section features another lyric tune, which begins in the violins (m. 43), moves to the bass clarinet (m. 45) and returns forcibly in the strings (m. 50). At this point, Sheng divides the orchestra into three layers: the strings play the sustained melody passionately, the woodwinds perform fast figures with thirty-second notes, and the brasses crescendo to an intense climax marked by harsh dissonances, dynamics up to ***ffff***, and timpani and trombone glissandos (m. 64). In this dream of China, the conclusion of the first movement may be a recollection of the nightmare-like terror of the Cultural Revolution.

49

Tod Machover

Hyperstring Trilogy: Begin Again Again . . ., excerpts (1991, rev. 2004)

8CD: 8/ 46 – 51
4CD: 4/ 76 – 81

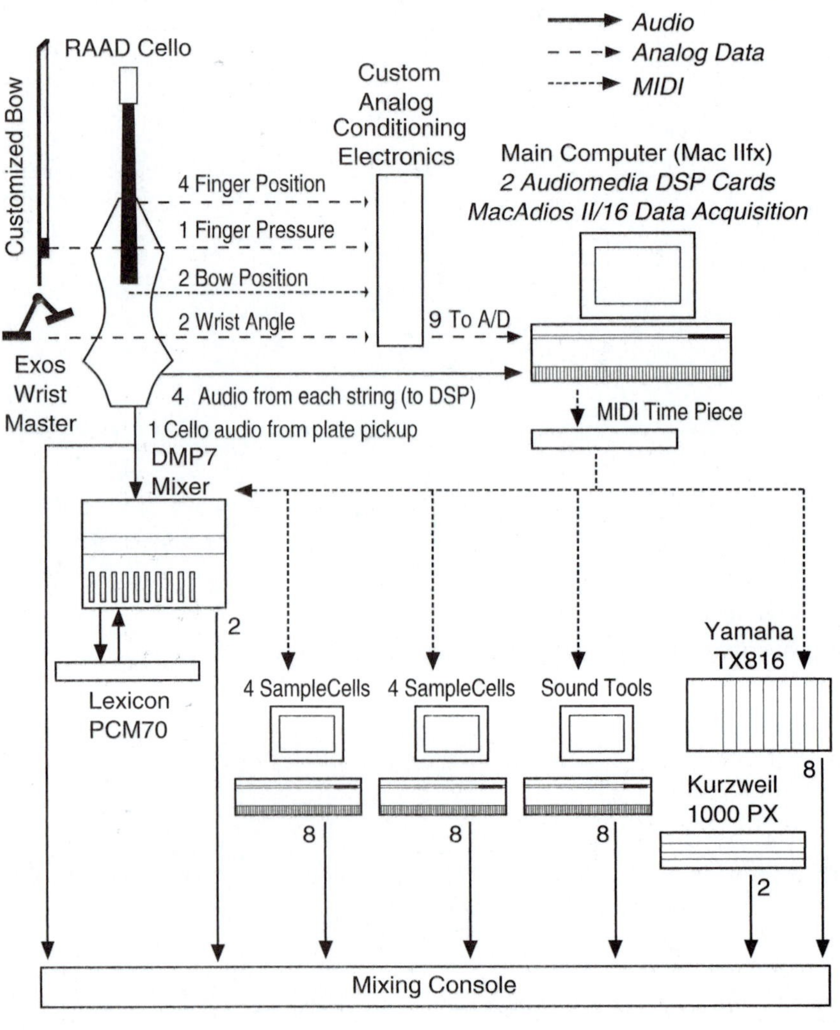

The Hypercello System

The Hypercello was designed by Tod Machover and his group at the MIT Media Lab to allow the performer to shape, modify, and control a whole range of extensions and enhancements to natural cello sound, all through intuitive interpretation of the music performed. To do this, it was necessary to capture, analyze, and interpret the most significant aspects of cello performance, and to turn this information into new sounds and textures.

The figure on the left shows the Hypercello system and the major data paths. The system is comprised of three main parts: the Hypercello and Hyperbow with associated sensors, the sound generation and sound processing devices, and the main computer running the Hyperinstrument software. Information from the cellist is interpreted and transduced three times before becoming recognizable audio: from physical motion to analog sensing data, from the digitized sensing data to MIDI, and from MIDI to audio. The final transformation from electronic audio to acoustic sound is made using a multichannel mixing console and conventional stereo loudspeakers in a concert hall sound system.

In the first stage of the process, the following parameters are measured: right hand wrist angle in two dimensions (flexion and deviation), finger pressure on the bow, bow position in two dimensions, left hand finger position on strings, loudness of each of the four strings, and the pitch of each string.

In the second stage of transformation, intelligent software modules—different for each section of the composition—analyze data collected from the parameters above, associate this data with musical descriptions, and then send instructions to sound production and processing devices. A wide range of mapping techniques was used for this piece, from adding special timbral or textural effects called up by changes in bowing or articulation (as in the piece's opening section), to sustaining chosen melody notes to create counterpoint and harmony (as in Very Emphatic), to silencing the cello's own sound and using performance parameters to control and "shepherd" huge timbral clouds and clusters (as heard at the very end of the excerpt included here).

For the last stage of the Hypercello process, a large array of sample playback devices, synthesizers, and effects processors translates the MIDI instructions into audio that is merged and coordinated with the live cello playing. The following equipment is used to create this "hypersound": Digidesign SampleCell sample playback units (eight in all), a Yamaha TX-816 sound generator bank, a Yamaha DMP-7 automated mixer and processor, a Lexicon PCM-70 sound processor, and a Kurzweil PX-1000 synthesizer.

The goal is for the entire Hypercello system to truly feel like a new kind of integrated "instrument" rather than like a dialogue with a machine.

—Tod Machover

46
76
Intro
♩ = 50
ord.→sul pont.
sul tasto
→ord.
→sul pont.
ppp pp ppp
mp
p
f
p
Arrows indicate notes/events with special Hyperelectronics. Use extra pressure with Hyperbow to prolong note and/or create special timbral shadow. Bow position and amount of bow used modify evolution of timbre.
rit.
a tempo
ord.
Bounce
1 0 1 0 1
mf p
mp
f
p
sul pont. ord.
sul pont.
dolce
ord.
sul pont.
mp
fp
mf
p
ord.
fp fp
mf
f
mp

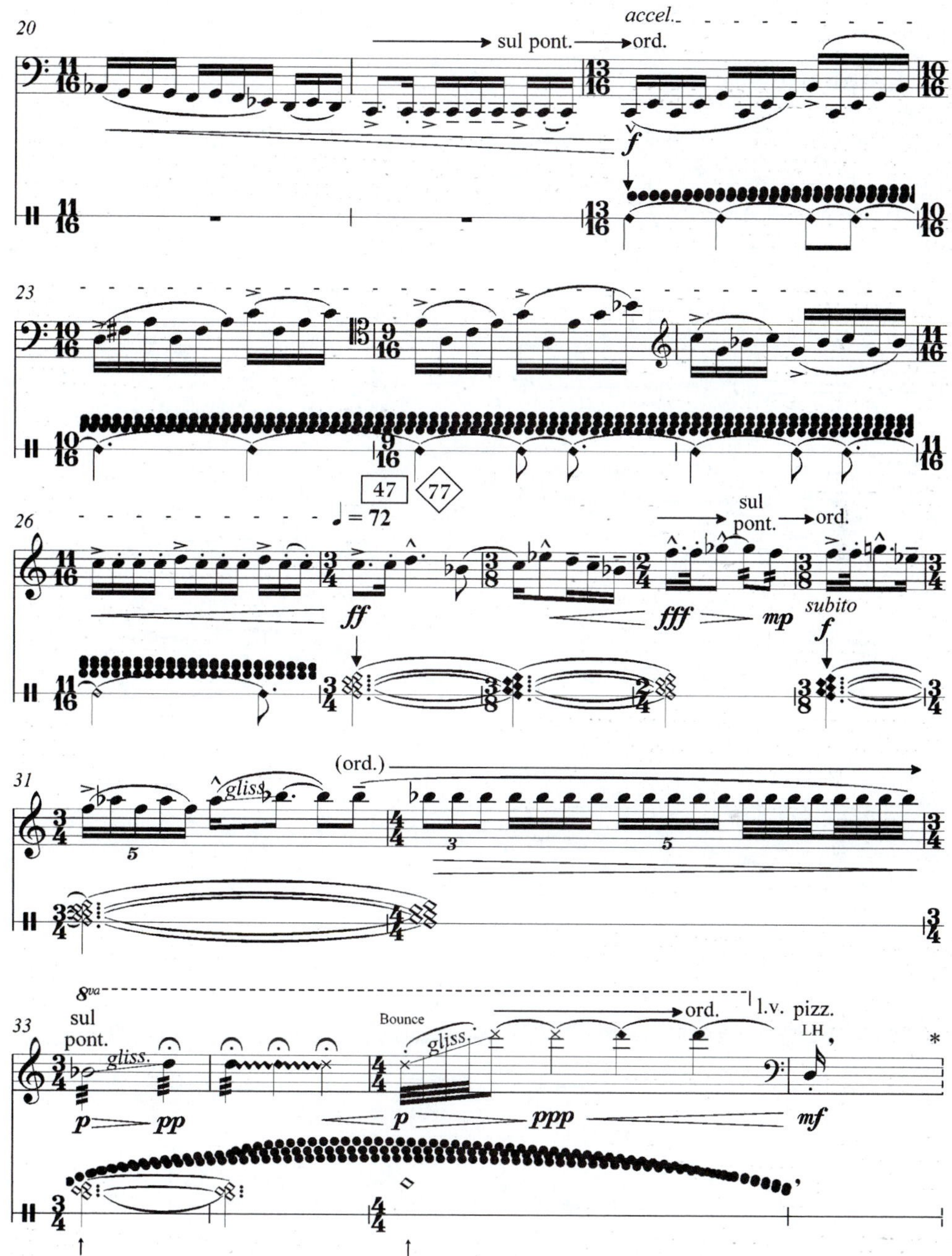

**Editor's note:* At this point in the music, the score and recording skip to measure 261.

48
78
Very Emphatic
261
♩ = 160
mf sf mp f mf f mf f
Bow position and pressure cause extra timbral emphasis, i.e. harsh pressure = timbral crash; closer-to-frog = denser clusters.
266
mp f mp mf f sf
Warm and Singing
272
accel.
♩ = 240
ff f sff f ff mf
Amount of bow and of bow change creates varied "shadow textures", i.e. more of each generates broader accompaniment flurries.
277
f mp f
282
ff mp mf
287
f
292
mf f mf

297
f
mp
fp
f
302
mp
mf
mp
mf
p
sf
307
fp
sf
p
sf
p
sf
p
mp
312
sf
mp
f
mf
317
f
mp
322
mf
p
f
326
mp
sf
mp
sf
mf
sf
f

331
mf
sf
sub.
p
f
sub.
p
f
sf
sf
336
sub.
p
f
sub.
p
341
mf
sf
p
345
sempre
mf
348
352

356
f
mf
f
361
mf
49
79
365
con bravura
f
ff
sff
mf
ff
Bow movement controls accompaniment texture.
371
mf
sf
mp
mf
mp
Fast, long bow strokes cause note played to be sustained and folded into "timbral harmony."
Playing near frog favors note sustain; playing near tip "clears" sustained notes.
377
sf
mp
f
mp
mf
382
sf
mp
mf
p
mf

388
mp
5
3
f
sff
mf
3
5
393
3
sf
mf
ff
mf
3
398
f
3
mp
5
3
mf
403
3
ff
407
3
mf
3
3
3
3
sff
mf
411
3
3

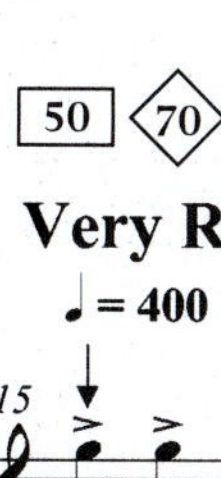

Very Rapid and Precise

♩ = 400

All aspects of playing influence Hyperelectronics, which also follow pitches and adjust harmony accordingly. Harsh accents at frog - including quick bow movement - to generate bass crashes at arrows. More bow-per-unit-time increases timbral complexity of accompaniment. Tempo adjusted to 8th-note rate of live playing.

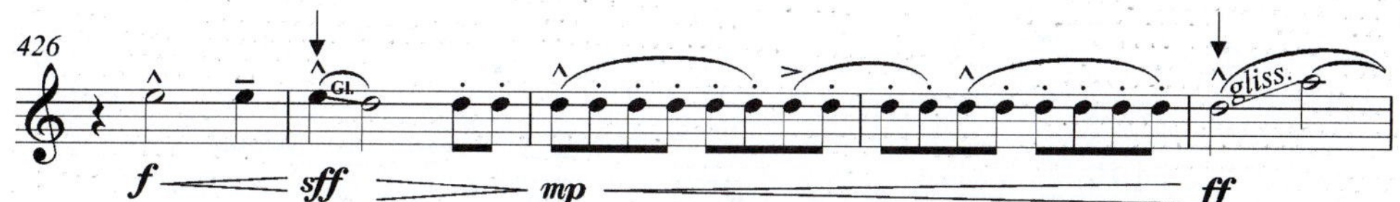

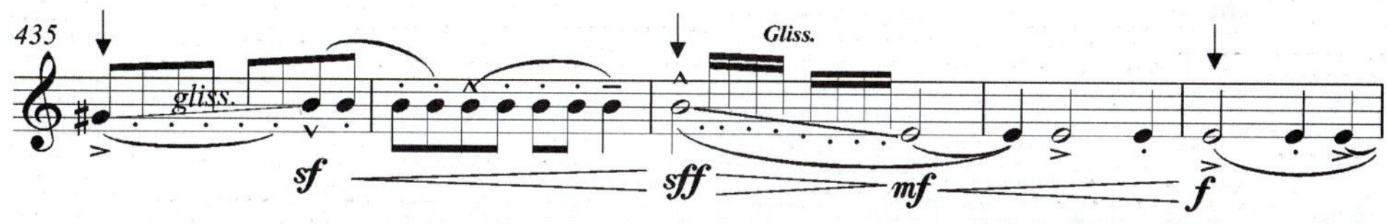

445
gliss.
sf
p
449
Gl.
Gl.
mf
ff
gliss.
mp
455
Gl.
sf
sf
sf
sf
460
ff
mf
465
gliss..
gliss.
f
469
sf
sf
sf
sf
sf
gliss.

473
Gliss.
sf
sff
478
mp
f
sf
sf
sf
483
gliss.
sff
f
mf
488
p
f
493
gliss.
gliss.
gliss.
ff
sff
mf
497
gliss.
gliss.
gliss.
f
sff
f
sff

501
51
71
almost hysterical!
mf
505
pizz.
LH
arco
ff
sf
f
In addition to previous hypercontrols, each timbral modification and bowing style change (including pizzicato) influences accompaniment differently. Experiment, but in general more frenetic and varied playing - in technique and sound - produces similar results in shadowed materials.
510
gliss.
sff
515
p
519
Bounce
523
sfff
Timbre Dream
526
fff

Quickly fade out live, amplified cello sound; Hypercello controls shape complex timbral masses in this section. Pitch played on Hypercello is central frequency for "swarming" timbres; the longer a note is played, the more the electronic timbre clusters around that note. Every cello articulation and timbre (i.e. tremolo, pizzicato, sul ponticello, harmonics) is mirrored and augmented in electronics.

The combination of musicians and computers in live performance has fascinated musicians for decades. One of the most successful composers in this interactive genre is Tod Machover (b. 1953). A native New Yorker, Machover has an eclectic training that includes cello performance, computer studies, lessons with Elliot Carter and Roger Sessions, and interests in Ives, Cage, and rock music. He spent five years in Paris serving as Director of Musical Research at Pierre Boulez's IRCAM, the French government center for contemporary music, and he is currently Professor of Music and Media at the MIT Media Lab. His compositions, including the opera *VALIS* (1986), have explored a variety of approaches to performance with electronic music. One element of this work is the use of hyperinstruments—standard acoustical instruments that are enhanced through electronic means.

Yo-Yo Ma premiered *Begin Again Again . . .* for solo hypercello in 1991 at the Tanglewood Festival. The work requires an electronic cello and a computer with several unique programs. Sensors are attached to the performer's hands and wrists that can measure the angle, placement, and speed of the bow as well as the movement of the left hand. The musician directly controls certain electronic responses, but these devices also allow the computer to generate sounds somewhat spontaneously.

Conceived as the first of three works based on Dante's *Divine Comedy*, *Begin Again Again . . .* represents the *Inferno*. The musical line centers on middle D; it tries to ascend higher but is constantly pulled lower. The title refers to the repetitive variation structure of the twenty-five minute work, in which the same melodic ideas are continuously recycled. Machover divides the composition into two movements: the first is dramatic, and the second is lyrical. Each movement begins with a theme that is followed by four variations. This anthology contains the introduction and variations three and four from the first movement.

Begin Again Again . . . was inspired in part by the Sarabande of Bach's unaccompanied Cello Suite No. 2. The introduction is set in the same key center as the model, and thematic references to Bach are clearly audible in the first few measures. Thereafter, certain melodic contours of Bach are imitated, the sarabande rhythm (second beat accent) appears occasionally, and Baroque devices such as arpeggiated chords and ornaments are mimicked (tremolos function as trills). References to Bach notwithstanding, the overall sound is fresh and invigorated with modern bowing techniques, virtuosic flourishes, reverberating pitches from the computer, and an extreme range of dynamics. A chromatic descent can be heard in the lower register, beginning with the first D and steadily moving downward to an arrival on the open C, the lowest note of the cello (m. 21). From here, the melodic line makes a frenetic rise of over four octaves, and the Introduction closes with a colorful cascade of wavering sounds hovering at the cello's highest pitch in the movement.

The subsequent variations focus on different aspects of the theme and grow in intensity. Variation three, entitled Very Emphatic, begins with the rise and fall of a half-step as heard at the beginning of the introduction, but now starting on the low C. Various motives from the Introduction recur as the range gradually expands upward, but the lower register predominates. The half-step figure on C returns at measure 109, and the melodic line marked *con bravura* begins a lengthy ascent. This moment parallels the conclusion of the introduction, but the ascent is slower and shorter.

The fourth variation is marked Very Rapid and Precise, and a strong regular pulse propels this section with a rock-like intensity. Unlike the previous variation, the upper register of the cello is explored with repeated notes, accents, hard pizzicatos, and slides between notes. Machover adds the performance direction "Almost Hysterical!" (m. 91) as the movement drives towards a climax. At the end, the return of the low C is reinforced by a left-hand pizzicato. From the instrument's lowest pitch, Machover asks the cellist to ascend rapidly and play "a violent noise-like sound as high on fingerboard as possible." Reverberations from the computer are sustained, and a fantastic collage of sounds lingers at the end.

50

Arvo Pärt

Cantate Domino canticum novum (O sing to the Lord a new song) (1977; revised 1996)

8CD: 8/52–55
4CD: 4/82–85

R. Bourdon 8'
Flûte 4'
Octave 2'

G.O. Bourdon Doux 8'
Flûte 4'

S
e - jus: an - nun - ti - a - te de di - e in di - em sa - lu - ta - re e - jus.
A
e - jus: an - nun - ti - a - te de di - e in di - em sa - lu - ta - re e - jus.
T
B

3
S
An - nun - ti - a - te in - ter gen - tes glo - ri - am e - jus, in o - mni - bus
A
An - nun - ti - a - te in - ter gen - tes glo - ri - am e - jus, in o - mni - bus
T
An - nun - ti - a - te in - ter gen - tes glo - ri - am e - jus, in o - mni - bus
B
An - nun - ti - a - te in - ter gen - tes glo - ri - am e - jus, in o - mni - bus
R.
R.

4
53
83
S
po - pu - lis mi - ra - bi - li - a e - jus.
A
po - pu - lis mi - ra - bi - li - a e - jus.
T
po - pu - lis mi - ra - bi - li - a e - jus. Quo - ni - am ma - gnus Do - mi - nus, et
B
po - pu - lis mi - ra - bi - li - a e - jus.
G.O.

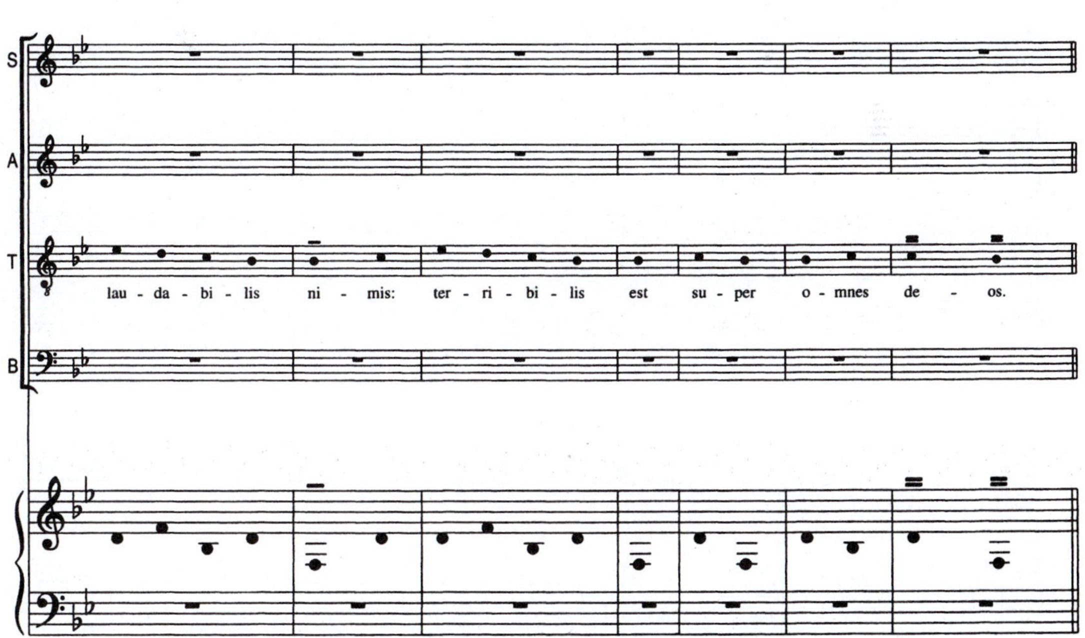
S
A
T
lau - da - bi - lis ni - mis: ter - ri - bi - lis est su - per o - mnes de - os.
B

5
S
A
T
Quo - ni - am o - mnes di - i gen - ti - um dae - mo - ni - a: Do - mi - nus au - tem coe - los
B
Quo - ni - am o - mnes di - i gen - ti - um dae - mo - ni - a: Do - mi - nus au - tem coe - los
R.
G.O.

6
S
Con - fes - si - o et pul - chri - tu - do in con - spe - ctu e - jus:
A
Con - fes - si - o et pul - chri - tu - do in con - spe - ctu e - jus:
T
fe - cit. Con - fes - si - o et pul - chri - tu - do in con - spe - ctu e - jus:
B
fe - cit. Con - fes - si - o et pul - chri - tu - do in con - spe - ctu e - jus:
G.O.
G.O.

S
A
T
B
san - cti - mo - ni - a et ma - gni - fi - cen - ti - a in san - cti - fi - ca - ti - o - ne e - jus.
san - cti - mo - ni - a et ma - gni - fi - cen - ti - a in san - cti - fi - ca - ti - o - ne e - jus.
san - cti - mo - ni - a et ma - gni - fi - cen - ti - a in san - cti - fi - ca - ti - o - ne e - jus.
san - cti - mo - ni - a et ma - gni - fi - cen - ti - a in san - cti - fi - ca - ti - o - ne e - jus.

7
54
84
S
A
T
B
Af - fer - te Do - mi - no pa - tri - ae gen - ti - um, af - fer - te Do - mi - no glo - ri - am
R.

S
A
T
B
et ho - no - rem: af - fer - te Do - mi - no glo - ri - am no - mi - ni e - jus.

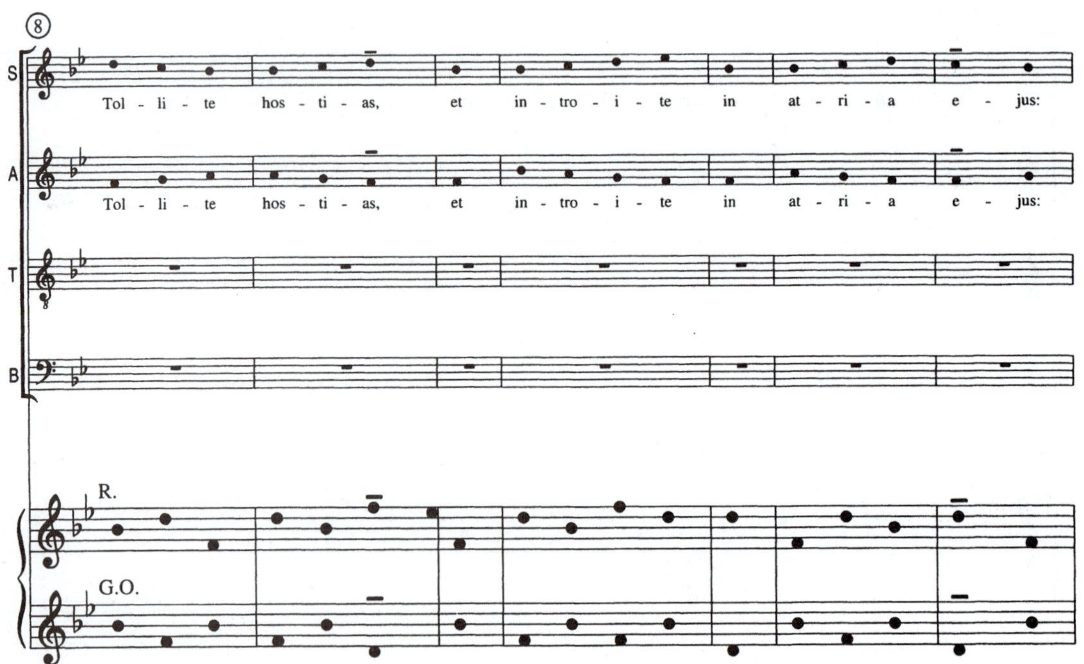
8
S
A
T
B
Tol - li - te hos - ti - as, et in - tro - i - te in at - ri - a e - jus:
Tol - li - te hos - ti - as, et in - tro - i - te in at - ri - a e - jus:
R.
G.O.

S
ad - o - ra - te Do - mi - num in at - ri - a san - cto e - jus.
A
ad - o - ra - te Do - mi - num in at - ri - a san - cto e - jus.
T
B
9
S
Com - mo - ve - a - tur a fa - ci - e e - jus u - ni - ver - sa ter - ra:
A
Com - mo - ve - a - tur a fa - ci - e e - jus u - ni - ver - sa ter - ra:
T
Com - mo - ve - a - tur a fa - ci - e e - jus u - ni - ver - sa ter - ra:
B
Com - mo - ve - a - tur a fa - ci - e e - jus u - ni - ver - sa ter - ra:
R.
R.

S
A
T
B
di - ci - te in gen - ti - bus qui - a Do - mi - nus re - gna - vit.
di - ci - te in gen - ti - bus qui - a Do - mi - nus re - gna - vit.
di - ci - te in gen - ti - bus qui - a Do - mi - nus re - gna - vit.
di - ci - te in gen - ti - bus qui - a Do - mi - nus re - gna - vit.

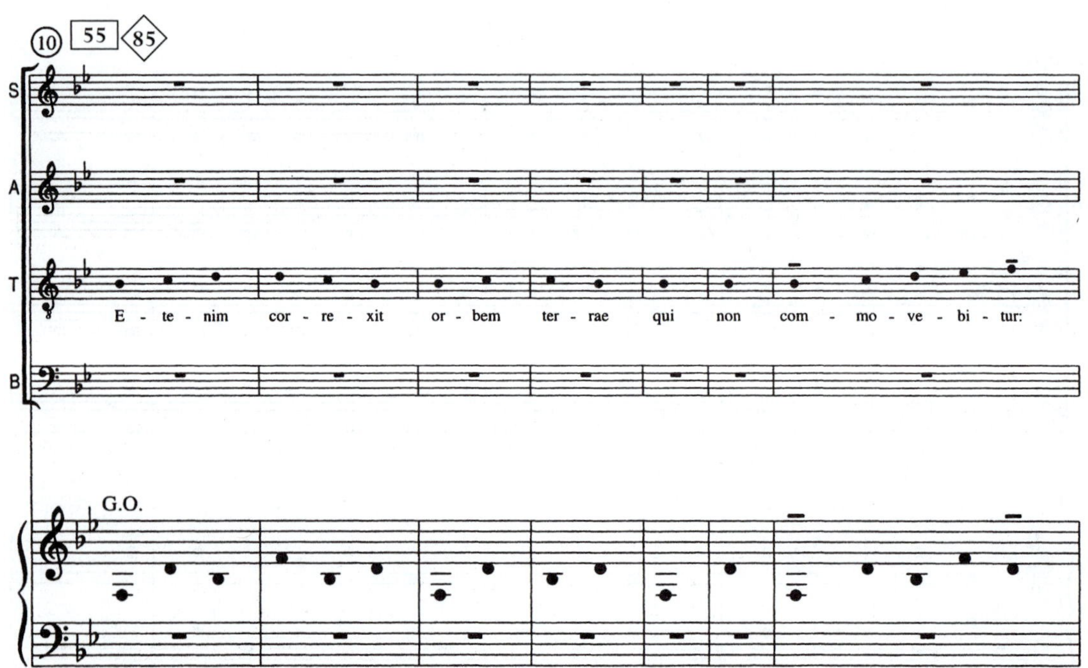
10
55
85
S
A
T
B
E - te - nim cor - re - xit or - bem ter - rae qui non com - mo - ve - bi - tur:
G.O.

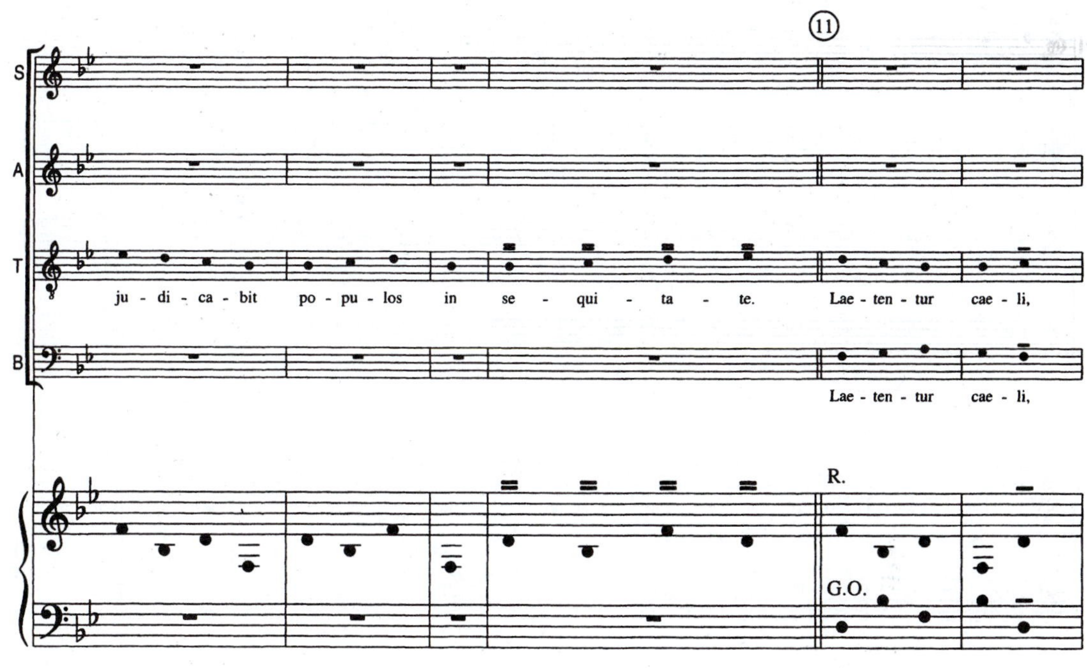
11
S
A
T
B
ju - di - ca - bit po - pu - los in se - qui - ta - te. Lae - ten - tur cae - li,
Lae - ten - tur cae - li,
R.
G.O.

S
A
T
B
et ex - sul - tet ter - ra: com - mo - ve - a - tur ma - re, et ple - ni - tu - do
et ex - sul - tet ter - ra: com - mo - ve - a - tur ma - re, et ple - ni - tu - do

S
A
T
e - jus: gau - de - bunt cam - pi, et o - mni - a quae in e - is sunt.
B
e - jus: gau - de - bunt cam - pi, et o - mni - a quae in e - is sunt.

12
S
Tunc ex - sul - ta - bunt o - mni - a li - gna sil - va - rum a fa - ci - e Do - mi - ni,
A
Tunc ex - sul - ta - bunt o - mni - a li - gna sil - va - rum a fa - ci - e Do - mi - ni,
T
Tunc ex - sul - ta - bunt o - mni - a li - gna sil - va - rum a fa - ci - e Do - mi - ni,
B
Tunc ex - sul - ta - bunt o - mni - a li - gna sil - va - rum a fa - ci - e Do - mi - ni,
G.O.
G.O.

13
S
qui - a ve - nit: quo - ni - am ve - nit ju - di - ca - re fer - ram. Ju - di - ca - bit
A
qui - a ve - nit: quo - ni - am ve - nit ju - di - ca - re fer - ram. Ju - di - ca - bit
T
qui - a ve - nit: quo - ni - am ve - nit ju - di - ca - re fer - ram. Ju - di - ca - bit
B
qui - a ve - nit: quo - ni - am ve - nit ju - di - ca - re fer - ram. Ju - di - ca - bit
G.O.
G.O. + Bourdon 16'

S
or - bem ter - rae in ae - qui - ta - te, et po - pu - los in ve - ri - ta - te su - a.
A
or - bem ter - rae in ae - qui - ta - te, et po - pu - los in ve - ri - ta - te su - a.
T
or - bem ter - rae in ae - qui - ta - te, et po - pu - los in ve - ri - ta - te su - a.
B
or - bem ter - rae in ae - qui - ta - te, et po - pu - los in ve - ri - ta - te su - a.

TEXT AND TRANSLATION

Cantate Domino canticum novum: Cantate Domino omnis terra. Cantate Domino, et benedicite nomini ejus: Annuntiate de die in diem salutare ejus. Annuntiate inter gentes gloriam ejus, In omnibus populis mirabilia ejus.	O sing to the Lord a new song: Sing to the Lord, all the earth. Sing to the Lord, bless his name; Tell of his salvation from day to day. Declare his glory among the nations. His marvelous works among all the peoples.
Quoniam magnus Dominus, et laudabilis nimis: Terribilis est super omnes deos. Quoniam omnes dii gentium daemonia: Dominus autem coelos fecit. Confessio et pulchritudo in conspectu ejus: Sanctimonia et magnifcentia in sanctificatione ejus.	For great is the Lord, and greatly to be praised. He is to be feared above all gods. For all the gods of the people are idols; But the Lord made the heavens. Honor and majesty are before him; Strength and beauty are his salvation.
Afferte Domino patriae gentium, Afferte Domino gloriam et honorem: Afferte Domino gloriam nomini ejus. Tollite hostias, et introite in atria ejus: Adorate Dominum in atria sancto ejus. Commoveatur a facie ejus universa terra: Dicite in gentibus quia Dominus regnavit.	Ascribe to the Lord, O families of the peoples. Ascribe to the Lord glory and strength; Ascribe to the Lord the glory due his name. Bring an offering, and come into his courts. Worship the Lord in holy array. Tremble before him, all the earth; Say among the nations, "The Lord reigns.
Etenim corexit orbem terrae qui non commovebitur: Judicabit populus in aequitate. Laetentur caeli, et exsultet terra:	Yea, the world is established, it shall never be moved. He will judge the peoples with equity." Let the heavens be glad, and let the earth rejoice:
Commoveatur mare, et plenitudo eius: Gaudebunt campi, et omnia quae in eis sunt.	Let the sea roar, and all that fills it; Let the field exult, and everything in it.
Tunc exsultabunt omnia ligna silvarium A facie Domini, quia venit: Quoniam venit iudicare terram. Judicabit orbem terrae in aequitate, Et populos in veritate sua.	Then shall all the trees of the wood sing for joy Before the Lord, for he comes; For he comes to judge the earth. He will judge the world with righteousness, And the peoples with his truth.

Arvo Pärt (b. 1935) was born in Estonia, one of the republics of the former Soviet Union. Despite limited opportunities and lack of access to international music, Pärt rose to prominence as one of the region's leading composers. His early works combine serial techniques and a strong Neoclassical fascination with the traditions of Western music, particularly the music of Bach. After an extended break in composition, during which he studied medieval and Renaissance music, he developed a new sound that he calls tintinnabulation (after the Latin word for the ringing of bells). Because of his strong religious convictions, Pärt left the Soviet Union and settled in West Berlin, where he composed numerous sacred works.

Cantate Domino canticum novum (O sing to the Lord a new song) reflects both Pärt's interest in medieval traditions and his distinctive tintinnabular style. Based on Psalm 95 (96 in the Protestant Bible), this work is set for SATB choir and organ. Reflecting the freedom of Gregorian chant, Pärt uses a free notation: measure lines do not mark off regular metric units, but rather separate individual words. Moreover, the rhythm is indicated by a notation system similar to that of Gregorian chant. Pärt uses black note heads only, without stem lines. Each note is of equal value (approximating an eighth note), but the addition of a single dash above a note doubles its value (quarter note), and two dashes triple the value (a dotted quarter note).

The work can be divided into four sections. Each section has three phrases: a monophonic opening phrase, a two-voice phrase moving primarily in contrary motion, and a four-voice phrase, in which the added voices double the homorhythmic contrary motion of the established voices. The overall effect of the work is similar to both Gregorian chant and early organum. The fullness of sound achieved by the expansion to a four-voice texture can be seen as word painting, as it reinforces images such as "declare his glory among the nations" and "all the trees of the woods sing for joy." The tintinnabular sound is created by the repetition of the pitch center (B-flat) and the triadic organ accompaniment. Pärt indicates specific organ registrations in the score.

51

John Adams

Tromba lontana (Distant Trumpet) (1986)

8CD: 8/ 56 – 60

4CD: 4/ 86 – 90

56 86

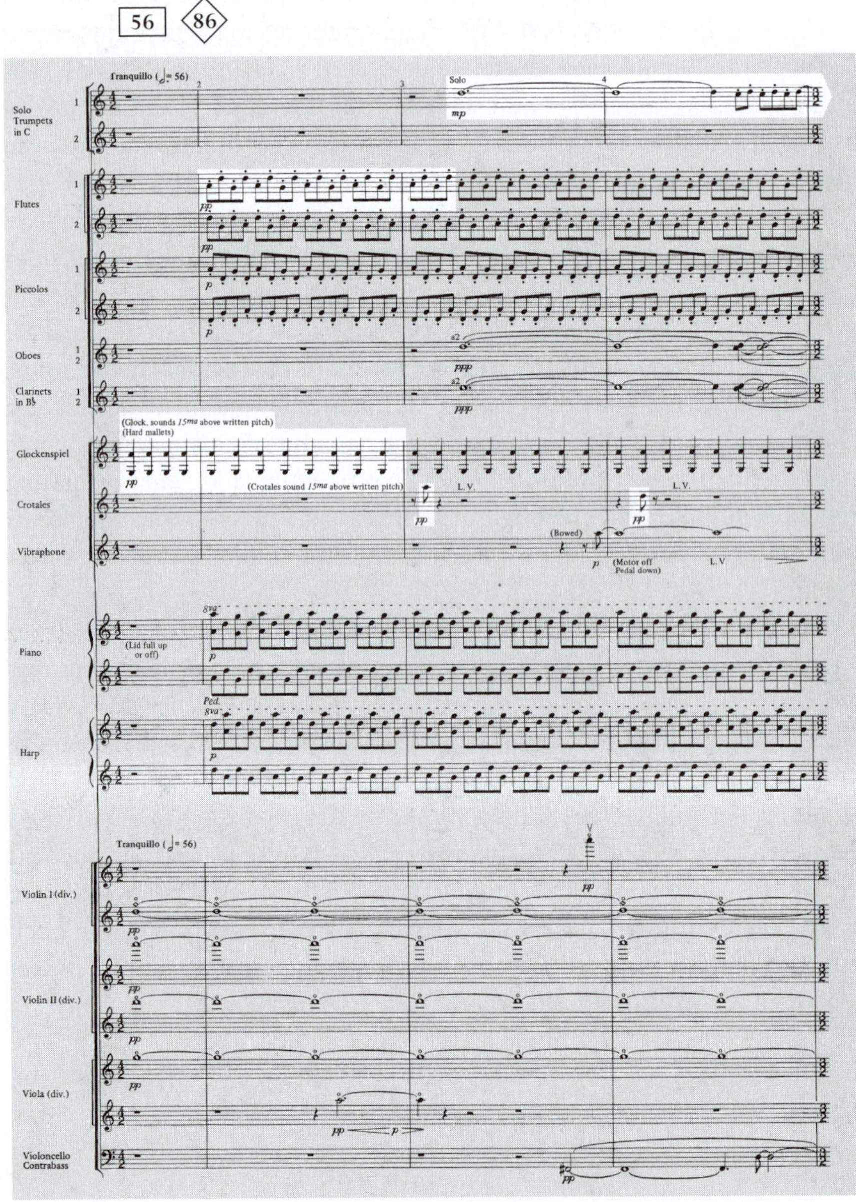

Solo Tpts. in C
Fls.
sim.
Piccs.
Obs.
Cls. in B♭
sempre ppp
Glock.
Crot.
Vibr.
L.V.
Piano
(8va)
Harp
Vln. I
sempre pp
Vln. II
Vla.
Vcl. Cbs.
sempre legato e pp

9
10
11
12
Solo Tpts. in C
Fls.
Piccs.
Obs.
Cls. in B♭
Glock.
Crot.
Vibr.
(Bowed)
L. V.
Piano
(8va)
Harp
(8va)
Vln. I
Vln. II
sempre pp
Vla.
Vcl. Cbs.

13
14
15
16
Solo Tpts. in C
mp
Fls.
Piccs.
Obs. 1 2
Cls. 1 in B♭ 2
Glock.
Crot.
pp
Vibr.
L. V.
p
Piano
(8va)
Harp
Vln. I
gliss.
Vln. II
pp (off the string)
Vla.
pizz.
arco
Vcl. Cbs.

57
87
17
18
19
20
Solo Tpts. in C
1
2
mf
pp
Solo
mp
Fls.
Piccs.
Obs.
sempre ppp
Cls. in B♭
Glock.
sempre pp
Crot.
pp
Vibr.
p
L. V.
(8va)
Piano
Harp
Mutes on
Vln. I
p
pp
mp
Vln. II
Vla.
mf
Vcl. Cbs.

21
22
23
24
Solo Tpts. in C
Fls.
Piccs.
poco f
Obs.
Cls. in B♭
Hns. in F
Glock.
Crot.
Vibr.
(mallets)
Piano
(8va)
Harp
Vln. I
Vln. II
Mutes on
sim.
gliss.
Vla. unis.
Vcl. Cbs.

25
26
27
28
29
Solo Tpts. in C
mp
Fls.
sim.
Piccs.
Obs.
Cls. in B♭
Hns. in F
p
Glock.
Crot.
pp
Vibr.
Piano
(8va)
(Ped. sempre)
Harp
Vln. I
mf
gliss.
Vln. II
sim.
pp
Vla.
Vcl. Cbs.

58
88
30
31
32
33
Solo Tpts. in C
Fls.
Piccs.
Obs.
Cls. in B♭
Hns. in F
Glock.
Crot.
Vibr.
Piano
Harp
Vln. I
Vln. II
Vla.
Vcl. Cbs.
sempre staccato
poco f
mf
p
pp
(Ped.)
(8va)
gliss.
sim.
(pp)

34
35
36
Solo Tpts. in C
Fls.
Piccs.
Obs.
Cls. in B♭
Hns. in F
Glock.
Crot.
Vibr.
Piano
Harp
Vln. I
Vln. II
Vla.
Vcl. Cbs.
sim.
poco f
a2
mf
p
(8va)
mp
Mutes on

37
38
39
Solo Tpts. in C
Fls.
Piccs.
sim.
Obs.
Cls. in B♭
Hns. in F
mp
mf
Glock.
sempre pp
Crot.
p
To Suspended Cym.
Vibr.
(8va)
Piano
Harp
Vln. I unis.
Vln. II
Vla.
Vcl. Cbs.

40
41
42
Solo Tpts. in C
poco f
p
Fls.
Piccs.
mp
Obs.
Cls. in B♭
Hns. in F
mf
Glock.
sempre pp
Susp. Cym.
(soft mallets)
tr
pp
Vibr.
Piano
(8va)
Harp
Vln. I
Vln. II
Vla.
Vcl. Cbs.

43
44
45
Solo Tpts. in C
Fls.
Piccs.
Obs.
Cls. in B♭
Hns. in F
Glock
Susp. Cym.
Vibr.
Piano
Harp
Vln. I
Vln. II
Vla.
Vcl. Cbs.
poco f
mf
pp
(8va)
(Ped.)

46
47
48
Solo Tpts. in C
1
2
poco f
Fls.
Piccs.
Obs.
ppp
Cls. in B♭
Hns. in F
mf
poco f
p
Glock.
Susp. Cym.
tr
f
Vibr.
3
(8va)
Piano
Harp
Vln. I
Vln. II
Vla.
Vcl. Cbs.

49
50
51
Solo Tpts. in C
Fls.
Piccs.
Obs.
Cls. in B♭
Hns. in F
Glock.
Susp. Cym.
Vibr.
Piano
Harp
Vln. I
Vln. II
Vla.
Vcl. Cbs.
poco f
mf
p
f
(Ped.)
(8va)

52
53
54
Solo Tpts. in C
1
2
poco f
p
Fls.
Piccs.
sim.
(mp)
Obs. 1 2
Cls. in B♭ 1 2
Hns. in F
Glock.
sempre pp
Susp. Cym.
f
Vibr.
3
sempre p
(8va)
Piano
Harp
Vln. I
Vln. II
Vla.
Vcl. Cbs.

59
89
Solo Tpts. in C
Fls.
Piccs.
Obs.
Cls. in B♭
Glock.
Susp. Cym.
Vibr.
Piano
Harp
Vln. I
Vln. II
sempre staccato
sempre staccato
Vla.
Vcl. Cbs.

58
59
60
Solo Tpts. in C
Fls.
Piccs.
Obs.
Cls. in B♭
Glock.
Susp. Cym.
Vibr.
(mallets)
Ped.
Piano
(8va)
Harp
Vln. I
Vln. II
Vla.
Vcl. Cbs.
sim.

60
90
Solo Tpts. in C
Fls.
Piccs.
Obs.
Cls. in B♭
Glock.
Susp. Cym.
Vibr.
Ped.
(Ped. sempre)
L.V.
Piano
Harp
Vln. I
Vln. II
Vla.
Vcl. Cbs.

64
65
66
Solo Tpts. in C
Fls.
Piccs.
Obs.
Cls. in B♭
Glock.
Crot.
Vibr.
Piano
Harp
Vln. I
Vln. II
Vla.
Vcl. Cbs.
mf
mp
p
(8va)

67
68
69
Solo Tpts. in C
Fls.
Piccs.
Obs.
Cls. in B♭
Glock.
Crot.
Vibr.
Piano
Harp
Vln. I
Vln. II
Vla.
Vcl. Cbs.
mf
mp
pp
(Ped.)
(8va)
loco

70
71
72
Solo Tpts. in C
Fls.
Piccs.
sim.
Obs.
niente
Cls. in B♭
Glock.
Crot.
Vibr.
mp
(Ped.)
Piano
Harp
Vln. I
Vln. II
p
Vla.
Vcl. Cbs.

73
74
75
Solo Tpts. in C
mp
niente
Fls.
p
Piccs.
pp
Obs.
Cls. in B♭
Glock.
Crot.
Vibr.
Piano
Harp
Vln. I
(p)
Vln. II
Vla.
Vcl. Cbs.
pp

In 1971, Harvard graduate John Adams (b. 1947) ventured away from the East coast and settled in San Francisco, where he began teaching at the San Francisco Conservatory of Music. Within a decade he rose to national prominence, and he received international acclaim for his opera *Nixon in China* (1987). A product of the postmodern climate, Adams's diverse influences include Schoenberg's Expressionism and rock music. He is a leading proponent of minimalist music, but his works are also steeped in the emotional freedom of New Romanticism. Adams won a Pulitzer Prize in 2002 for *On the Transmigration of Souls*, a work commissioned by the New York Philharmonic in memory of the September 11 attacks on the World Trade Center.

Tromba lontana (*Distant Trumpet*) is a fanfare premiered by the Houston Symphony Orchestra in 1986 for the Texas Sesquicentennial celebrations. The title refers to the two solo trumpets that are placed on opposite sides of the stage. The accompanying orchestra includes four French horns, woodwinds, strings, harp, and percussion. The musical fabric is divided into three parts: a rhythmic pulse of quarters, eights, or sixteenths; long sustained pitches; and trumpet solos. The opening shimmers with a Far Eastern aura created by the bell-like instruments, string harmonics, and repetitious figures. Reflecting Adams's approach to minimalism, the mood changes slowly and intensifies through added pitches, expanding ranges, faster figurations, stronger and more frequent dissonances, and a general rise in dynamics. Initially, the trumpets answer each other antiphonally, but as the mood darkens they play together, often creating overlapping dissonances. Eventually the tension subsides, and the work comes to a quiet and somber close, a mood that is atypical of fanfares.

52

Libby Larsen

Sonnets from the Portuguese, Nos. 5 and 6 (1993)

8CD: 8 / 61 – 62
4CD: 4 / 91 – 92

a tempo
5
1
Fl.
Ob.
Cl.
Bsn
Hrn
Harp
Perc.
Sop
world of ours!
I will not gain say love called
Vln
Vla
Vnc
Cb
pizz.

19
freely
a tempo
Fl.
Ob.
Cl.
Bsn
Hrn
Harp
Perc.
Sop
love
for-sooth
I have
heard
love
Vln
Vla
Vnc
Cb
mf
p
f

14
2
Fl.
p
Ob.
1
Cl.
2
lightly
Bsn
pp
cresc.
Hrn 1 2
p
Harp
Perc.
2
mf
Sop
talked in my ear - ly youth, and since, not so long back but that the
2
1
Vln
2
Vla
Vnc
arco lightly
Cb
pp
cresc.

17
ritard
Fl.
Ob.
Cl.
Bsn
Hrn
Harp
Perc.
Sop
Vln
Vla
Vnc
Cb
3
a tempo ♩ = 144
flow'rs then gath - ered smell still.

22
Fl.
Ob.
Cl.
Bsn
Hrn
Harp
Perc.
Sop
Vln
Vla
Vnc
Cb
Mus - sel - men and Gai - ors throw hand-ker-chiefs at a smile and

26
Fl.
Ob.
Cl.
Bsn
Hrn
Harp
Perc.
Sop
Vln
Vla
Vnc
Cb
4
have no ruth for an - y weep-ing.

p (whitely)
poco a poco crescendo
Sop
Pol - y - pheme's white tooth slips on the nut if
poco a poco crescendo
non vib.
pp
cresc.
Vln
1
2
non vib.
pp
cresc.
non vib.
Vla
pp
cresc.
Vnc
pp

ff
Sop
af - ter - fre - quent show's the shell is o - ver smooth
Vln
1
2
ff
ff
Vla
ff
sul pont.
Vnc
ppp
ff

38
Fl.
Ob.
1
Cl.
2
Bsn
Hrn 1 2
Harp
Perc.
Sop
and not so much will turn the thing called love to hate
1
Vln
2
Vla
Vnc
Cb

44
freely
a tempo
freely
Fl.
Ob.
Cl.
Bsn
Hrn
Harp
Perc.
Sop
or else to o-bliv-ion. But thou art not such a
con sord.
Vln
Vla
Vnc
Cb

48
⑥
Fl.
Ob.
1
Cl.
2
Bsn
Hrn 1 2
Harp
Perc.
Sop
lov-er my be-lov - ed, Thou canst wait through sor-row and
Vln 1
Vln 2
Vla
Vnc
Cb
senza sord., non vib.
p

51
poco rit.
7 a tempo
Fl.
mp
dolce
ppp
Ob.
1
Cl.
2
f
Bsn
Hrn 1 2
p
Harp
Perc.
poco rit.
7 a tempo mp
Sop
sick-ness to bring souls to touch and think it
poco rit.
7 a tempo
+ vib.
1
Vln
2
ppp
mf
Vla
Vnc
pizz.
Cb
p

56
Fl.
Ob.
Cl.
Bsn
Hrn
Harp
Perc.
Sop
Vln
Vla
Vnc
Cb
mp
p
f
ff
pizz.
soon when oth-ers cry too late, too late! too late!

No. 6, "How do I love thee?"

6
freely, recitative ①
a tempo
Fl.
Ob.
Cl.
Bsn
Hrn
Harp
Perc.
Sop
Vln
Vla
Vnc
Cb
mp
mf gently
love thee?
Let me count the ways.
I love thee from the depth and

10
poco a poco accelerando
poco a poco crescendo
Fl.
Ob.
Cl. 1 2
Bsn
Hrn 1 2
Harp
Perc.
Sop
breath and height my soul can reach, My soul can reach, My
Vln 1 2
Vla
Vnc
Cb
cresc.

13
Fl.
Ob.
warmly
mf decresc.
1
Cl.
2
Bsn
mf
f
Hrn 1 2
Harp
f
Perc.
Sop
f
mp
soul can reach when feel - ing out of sight for the ends of Being and i - deal
1
Vln
2
f decresc.
pp
Vla
Vnc
arco
Cb

17
ritard
2 a tempo
Fl.
Ob.
1
Cl.
2
Bsn
Hrn 1 2
Harp
Perc.
Sop
1
Vln
2
Vla
Vnc
Cb
mf
p
p legato
a2
orchestra bells
mp gently
mf warmly
Grace.
I love thee to the lev'l of ev-'ry day's Most quiet need,
pizz.

20
③ Piu Mosso
Fl.
Ob.
1
Cl.
2
Bsn
mf
p
Hrn 1 2
Harp
Perc.
③ Piu Mosso
mf
Sop
by Sun _ and can-dle-light.
I love thee free-ly as men strive for Right;
③ Piu Mosso
1
Vln
2
Vla
Vnc
f
2
arco
Cb
p

poco a poco accelerando to ④
24
Fl.
p gently
sub. ***p***
Ob.
p
pp
Cl. 1 2
p
Bsn
mf
Hrn 1 2
Harp
Perc.
poco a poco accelerando to ④
Sop
mp
mf
I love thee pure - ly, as they turn from Praise. I love thee with a pass-ion put to
poco a poco accelerando to ④
Vln 1 2
mf
Vla
mf
sub. ***p***
sub. ***p***
Vnc
mf
pizz.
Cb
p

27
Fl.
Ob.
Cl.
Bsn
Hrn
Harp
Perc.
Sop
Vln
Vla
Vnc
Cb
mf cresc.
mf
p
mp cresc.
1.
mf warmly
a2
sub. p cresc.
mf cresc.
with anticipation
mp cresc.
f
use In my old griefs, and with my child-hood's faith. Ah
pp
arco

30
4 ritard
♪= 60
Fl.
Ob.
Cl. 1
Cl. 2
Bsn
Hrn 1 2
Harp
Perc.
Sop
Vln 1
Vln 2
Vla
Vnc
Cb
f
p
pp legato
mp
pp
mf
pizz.
I love thee with a love I seemed to

35
accelerando
Fl.
Ob.
Cl.
Bsn
Hrn
Harp
Perc.
Sop
lose With my lost saints, I love thee with the breath, smiles, tears, of
Vln
Vla
Vnc
Cb
p warmly, cresc.

38
ritard
⑥ ♪= 92
Fl.
mp warmly
Ob.
mp warmly
very legato
warmly
mf
Cl. 1 2
mp warmly
mp warmly
mp warmly
Bsn
f
Hrn 1 2
a2
mf
pp
very legato
warmly
1.
mf
p
pp
Harp
ff
p gently
Perc.
ritard
⑥ ♪= 92
Sop
all my life!
ritard
⑥ ♪= 92
Vln 1 2
f
p
mf
f
Vla
f
p
mf
f
Vnc
f
p
mf
f
arco
Cb
mp warmly
mf

43
warmly
ritard
Fl.
Ob.
Cl.
Bsn
Hrn
Harp
Perc.
Sop
Vln
Vla
Vnc
Cb
niente
sub. p
and, if God choose, I shall but love thee bet - ter af - ter

7 ♪= 92
47
Fl.
mf warmly
2
p
ritard
p gently
Ob.
p gently
1
Cl.
2
p gently
p gently
Bsn
p gently
Hrn 1 2
1.
mf warmly
2
p
a2
p
Harp
p gently
Perc.
tam-tam
pp
chime
p lontano
7 ♪= 92
ritard
Sop
death.
7 ♪= 92
ritard
1
Vln
2
p warmly
p warmly
Vla
2
mf warmly
p
Vnc
p warmly
Cb
pizz.
mf
arco
p warmly

Libby Larsen (b. 1950) is one of America's leading composers of the late twentieth and early twenty-first centuries. Forgoing the security of a university position, Larsen has built a career on commissions, composer-in-residence positions, work in music education, and performance of contemporary music. In these endeavors, she has maintained a strong link to the general public, and her works are frequently performed by professional musical organizations around the country.

Women artists and historical figures have been a constant source of inspiration for Larsen. The song cycle *Sonnets from the Portuguese* derives its text from Elizabeth Barrett Browning's collection of poems bearing the same title. Written secretly during Elizabeth's courtship with the prominent Victorian poet Robert Browning, these love poems were published after their marriage in 1850. Robert suggested the title of the collection in order to give the impression that the poems were translations rather than intimate expressions of their love. The poems are modeled after the sonnets of Petrarch: each has fourteen lines with the rhyme scheme abba abba cdcdcd.

Larsen set six of the forty-four poems in this collection, and the last two are included in this anthology. Accompanying the voice is a chamber ensemble consisting of a flute, an oboe, two clarinets, a bassoon, two horns, a string quintet, a harp, and percussion. These instruments represent the primary colors of a symphony orchestra (excepting trumpets and low brass). In setting the texts, Larsen worked closely with singer Arleen Auger, who premiered the songs. Auguer's 1994 recording won a Grammy.

Larsen's sensitivity to the English language and to the meaning of the text is certainly evident in "O, yes!" (Song No. 5), based on Sonnet 40. The poem shifts through three moods. It begins with an exuberant affirmation of love, but then turns darker with references to "Musselmans and Giaours" (Muslims and infidels) and to the mythical Polyphemus, figures that are supposedly unfeeling. In setting the middle section, Larsen employs harsh harmonies and irregular accents. A dramatic silence highlights the reference to "hate" and "oblivion," but the growing intensity of the poem is halted when the speaker thinks of her lover, and the opening mood is restored with an unaccompanied soprano melisma. The outer portions of the song are both playful and lyric. Although the structure is through-composed, the third portion is connected to the first with the return of an earlier melodic phrase just after rehearsal 5 and the closing imitative interplay of a two-note motive that mirrors the opening of the song.

The final song of the cycle (Song No. 6) is based on Elizabeth Barrett Browning's celebrated Sonnet 43, "How do I love thee?" As in "O, yes!," Larsen's setting is through-composed, although there is a reprise of the instrumental introduction just prior to the final statement of the text. The mood is sustained throughout the song by a prevailing duple compound meter, warm orchestration, and poignant harmony resulting from frequent seventh chords. To its opening question the poem presents eight responses, which can be seen in pairs. Larsen reinforces this structure by using similar material for the beginnings of the love declarations. With the first, the voice rises a major ninth to a soaring climax, reflecting the text "my soul can reach." The next phrase nearly matches the range with a simple octave leap for the reference to the "sun." This motive reappears three times at the end of the song, just after the poet has vowed to love even "after death." The final two notes of this cadential motive are identical to the pitches sung for the initial question, on the words "love thee."

53

Abing (Hua Yanjun)

Er quan ying yue (*The Moon Reflected on the Second Springs*) (recorded 1950)

8CD: 8/63–65
4CD: 4/93–95

63 93 Statement (Variation) 1

64 94 Statement (Variation) 2

65 95 Statement (Variation) 3

Statement (Variation) 4 (not on Norton recording)

Editor's note: The music above is a notated version of the first statement of the melody as heard on the Norton recording; the following three statements represent elaborations or variations on the same melody.

According to the official Chinese biography, Abing (1883–1950) was born Hua Yanjun. Orphaned, he was adopted by a Daoist monk who taught him music. Abing was later expelled from the Daoist temple after performing sacred music in a secular setting. He wandered through China, singing and playing the erhu as a street musician, and, in his mid-thirties, he lost his sight. Near the end of his life, Abing recorded several works, of which *The Moon Reflected on the Second Springs* is the most famous.

The principal instrument of the work is an erhu, a two-stringed fiddle, generally tuned a fifth apart. The sound box, which rests on the lap, is covered with snakeskin and projects a strong, sometimes nasal sound. Lacking a fingerboard, the instrument creates a sound that moves in a continuum of pitch. The sound has a strong, vocal-like quality. In the recording, the erhu is accompanied by a yangqin, a hammered dulcimer. The melody has four phrases derived from a pentatonic scale. The entire melody is presented four times; each is varied with diverse ornamentation. The climax occurs in the third statement, when the erhu is played in the upper register. Our recording stops with this statement.

54

Traditional Cajun Music

Jongle à moi (Think of Me)

8CD: 8/66–69
4CD: 4/96–99

Transcription by Roger Hickman

Editor's note: The recorded performance includes trills, slides, scoops, double stops, and drones not notated in this transcription.

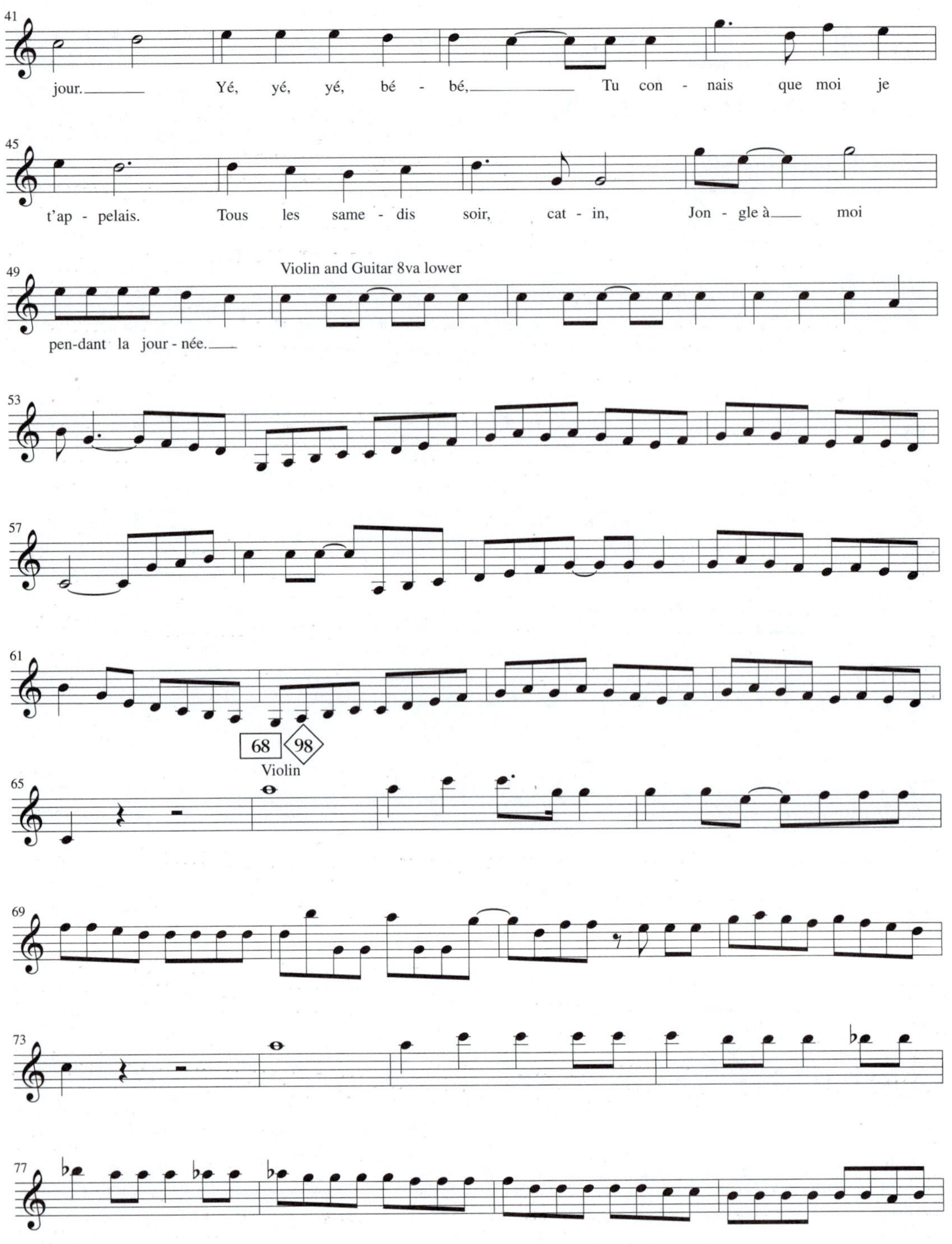
41
jour.
Yé, yé, yé, bé - bé,
Tu con - nais que moi je
45
t'ap - pelais.
Tous les same - dis soir, cat - in,
Jon - gle à moi
49
Violin and Guitar 8va lower
pen-dant la jour - née.
53
57
61
68
98
Violin
65
69
73
77

81
85
89
93
97
101
105
109
113
69
99
Voice
O O O, yé yail - le, Quoi faire t'es comme
117
ça? Jon - gle à moi, cat - in, bé - bé, Oué, une foir par

121
jour.
Yé, yé, yé, bé - bé,
Tu con - nais moi je
125
t'ai - mais.
Jon - gle à moi, jo - line, bé - bé,
Tous les soirs et
129
Violin
toutes les jour - nées.
133
137
141
145
Guitar
149
153
Guitar
158

TEXT AND TRANSLATION

O mais, o, yé yaille, Quoi faire t'es comme ça? Jongle à moi, catin, bébé, O, une fois par jour. Yé, yé, yé, bébé, Tu connais que moi je t'appelais Tous les samedis soir, catin, Jongle à moi pendant la journée.	Oh, but oh, yé yaille, Why are you like that? Think of me, darling baby, At least once a day. Yé, yé, yé, baby, You know that I called for you Every Saturday night, darling, Think of me during the day
O mais, o, yé yaille, Quoi faire t'es comme ça? Jongle à moi, catin, bébé, Oué, une fois par jour. Yé, yé, yé, bébé, Tu connais moi je t'aimais Jongle à moi, joline, bébé, Tous le soirs et toutes les journées.	Oh, but oh, yé yaille, Why are you like that? Think of me, darling baby, At least once a day. Yé, yé, yé, baby, You know that I love you Think of me, darling baby, Every night and every day.

In the middle of the eighteenth century, Acadian residents descended from French colonists were expelled from their home in Canada by the British and dispersed to various locations in the United States. In southwestern Louisiana, the so-called Cajuns intermingled with the Creoles, people of mixed French, Spanish, and African or Afro-Caribbean descent. Both Cajun music and Creole music, called *zydeco*, have maintained distinct characteristics, but each has also exerted strong influences on the other.

BeauSoleil, led by Michael Doucet, is one of the leading groups in the popular revival of Cajun music. The ensemble features traditional Cajun instruments—a fiddle, guitar, washboard, and drums, and the accordion, the principal instrument of zydeco. *Jongle à moi (Think of Me)* is a traditional Cajun fiddle tune, consisting of a pair of eight-measure phrases, sometimes alternating with an eight-measure phrase that acts as a bridge. The tune is sung twice in this performance.

The fiddle predominates in the instrumental sections, although the accordion and guitar occasionally vie for the lead. Typical Cajun fiddle techniques can be heard, including drones (playing a repeated pitch on one string while playing the melody on another), double stops (playing two notes at the same time), slides, and trills. The texture is sometimes heterophonic, with several instruments elaborating on the tune at the same time.

Appendix A

Reading a Musical Score

Clefs

The music for some instruments is written in clefs other than the familiar treble and bass. In the following example, middle C is shown in the four clefs used in orchestral scores:

The *alto clef* is primarily used in viola parts. The *tenor clef* is employed for cello, bassoon, and trombone parts when these instruments play in a high register.

Transposing Instruments

The music for some instruments is customarily written at a pitch different from its actual sound. The following list, with examples, shows the main transposing instruments and the degree of transposition. (In some modern works—such as the Stravinsky *Le sacre du printemps* included in volume two of this anthology—all instruments are written at their sounding pitch.)

Instrument	Transposition	Written note	Actual sound
Piccolo Celesta	sounds an octave higher than written	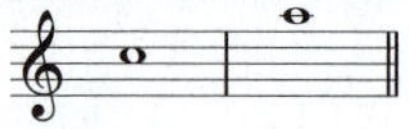	
Trumpet in F	sounds a fourth higher than written		
Trumpet in E	sounds a major third higher than written		
Clarinet in E♭ Trumpet in E♭	sounds a minor third higher than written		
Trumpet in D Clarinet in D	sounds a major second higher than written	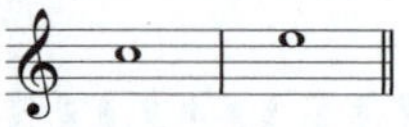	
Clarinet in B♭ Trumpet in B♭ Cornet in B♭ French horn in B♭, alto	sounds a major second lower than written	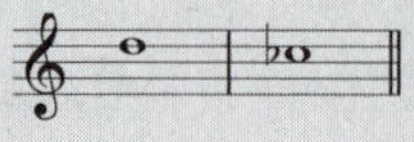	
Clarinet in A Trumpet in A Cornet in A	sounds a minor third lower than written		
French horn in G Alto flute	sounds a fourth lower than written	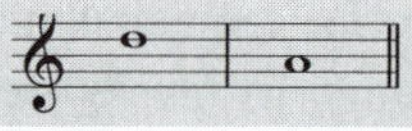	
English horn French horn in F	sounds a fifth lower than written	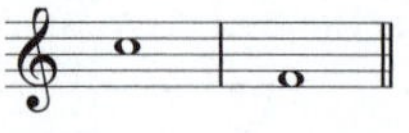	
French horn in E	sounds a minor sixth lower than written		
French horn in E♭ Alto saxophone	sounds a major sixth lower than written	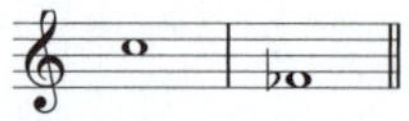	
French horn in D	sounds a minor seventh lower than written		
Contrabassoon French horn in C Double bass	sounds an octave lower than written	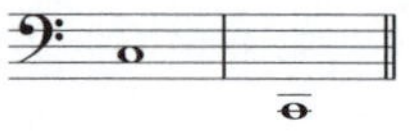	
Bass clarinet in B♭ Tenor saxophone (written in treble clef)	sounds a major ninth lower than written	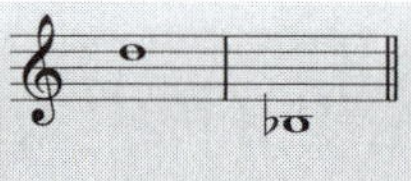	
Tenor saxophone (written in bass clef)	sounds a major second lower than written	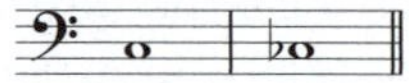	
Bass clarinet in A (written in treble clef)	sounds a minor tenth lower than written		
Bass clarinet in A (written in bass clef)	sounds a minor third lower than written	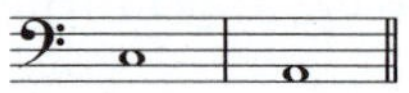	
Baritone saxophone in B♭ (written in treble clef)	sounds an octave and a major sixth lower than written	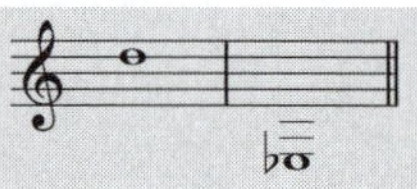	
Bass saxophone in B	sounds two octaves and a major second lower than written		

Appendix B

Instrument Names and Abbreviations

The following tables set forth the English, Italian, German, and French names used for the various musical instruments in these scores, and their respective abbreviations (when used). Latin voice designations and a table of the foreign-language names for scale degrees and modes are also provided.

Woodwinds

English	Italian	German	French
Piccolo (Picc.)	Flauto piccolo (Fl. Picc.)	Kleine Flöte (Kl. Fl.)	Petitite flûte
Flute (Fl.)	Flauto (Fl.); Flauto grande (Fl. gr.)	Grosse Flöte (Gr. Fl.)	Flûte (Fl.)
Alto flute	Flauto contralto (fl. c-alto)	Altflöte	Flûte en sol
Oboe (Ob.)	Oboe (Ob.)	Hoboe (Hb.); Oboe (Ob.)	Hautbois (Hb.)
English horn (E. H.)	Corno inglese (C. or Cor. ingl., C.i.)	Englisches Horn (E. H.)	Cor anglais (C. A.)
E♭ clarinet	Clarinetto piccolo (clar. picc.)		
Clarinet (C., Cl., Clt., Clar.)	Clarinetto (Cl., Clar.)	Klarinette (Kl.)	Clarinette (Cl.)
Bass clarinet (B. Cl.)	Clarinetto basso (Cl. b., Cl. basso, Clar. basso)	Bass Klarinette (Bkl.)	Clarinette basse (Cl. bs.)
Bassoon (Bsn., Bssn.)	Fagotto (Fag., Fg.)	Fagott (Fag., Fg.)	Basson (Bssn.)

English	Italian	German	French
Contrabassoon (C. Bsn.)	Contrafagotto (Cfg., C. Fag., Cont. F.)	Kontrafagott (Kfg.)	Contrebasson (C. bssn.)
Alto saxophone Tenor saxophone Baritone saxophone	Sassofone	Saxophon	Saxophone
Surrusophone	Sarrusofano	Sarrusophon	Sarrusophone

Brass

English	Italian	German	French
French horn (Hr., Hn.)	Corno (Cor., C.) [*pl.* Corni.]	Horn (Hr.) [*pl.* Hörner (Hrn.)]	Cor; Cor à pistons
Trumpet (Tpt., Trpt., Trp., Tr.)	Tromba (Tr.) [*pl.* Tbe.]	Trompete (Tr., Trp.)	Trompette (Tr.)
Trumpet in D	Tromba piccola (Tr. picc.)		
Cornet	Cornetta [*pl.* Cornetti., Ctri]	Kornett	Cornet à pistons (C. à p., Pist.)
Trombone (Tr., Tbe., Trb., Trm., Trbe.)	Trombone (Tromb) [*pl.* Tromboni (Tbni., Trni.)]	Posaune (Ps., Pos.)	Trombone (Tr.)
Bass trombone Tuba (Tb.)	Tuba (Tb., Tba.)	Tuba (Tb.) [*also* Basstuba (Btb.)]	Tuba (Tb.)
Ophicleide (Oph.)	Oficleide	Ophikleide	Ophicléide

Percussion

English	Italian	German	French
Percussion (Perc.), Battery	Percussione	Schlagzeug (Schlag.)	Batterie (Batt.)
Kettledrums (K. D.)	Timpani (Timp., Tp.)	Pauken (Pk.)	Timbales (Timb.)
Snare drum (S. D.,sn.)	Tamburo piccolo (Tamb. picc.) Tamburo militare (Tamb. milit.)	Kleine Trommel (Kl. Tr.)	Caisse claire (C. cl.): Tambour militaire (Tamb. milit.)
Tenor drum (T. D.)	Cassa rullante	Rührtrommel	Caisse roulante
Bass drum (B. drum, B. D.)	Gran cassa (Gr. Cassa, Gr. C., G. C.) Gran tamburo (Gr. Tamb.)	Grosse Trommel (Gr. Tr.)	Grosse caisse (Gr. c.)
Cymbals (Cym., Cymb.) Tam-Tam (Tam.-T.)	Piatti (P., Ptti., Piat.) Cinelli	Becken (Beck.)	Cymbales (Cym.)

English	Italian	German	French
Tambourine (Tamb.)	Tamburino (Tamb.)	Schellentrommel; Tamburin	Tambour de Basque (T. de B., Tamb. de Basque)
Triangle (Trgl., Tri.)	Triangolo (Trgl.)	Triangel	Triangle (Triang.)
Glockenspiel (Glock.)	Campanelli (Cmp.)	Glockenspiel	Carillon
Bells; Chimes tubular bells, orchestral bells	Campane (Cmp., Camp.)	Glocken	Cloches
Antique cymbals	Crotali; Piatti antichi	Antike Zimbeln	Crotales; Cymbales antiques
Sleigh bells (S.bells)	Sonagli (Son.)	Schellen	Grelots
Xylophone (Xyl.)	Xilofono	Xylophon	Xylophone
Marimba			
Vibraphone	Vibrafone	Vibraphon	Vibraphone
Cowbells		Herdenglocken	
Crash cymbal			Grande cymbale chinoise
Siren	Sirena	Sirene	Sirène
Lion's roar			Tambour à corde
Slapstick			Fouet
Wood blocks			Blocs chinois
Castanet (Cast.)	Castagnette	Kastagnette	Castagnette
Bongos			
Bell tree			
Tom tom			
Conga			
Guiro			
Maracas (Marac.)			

Strings

English	Italian	German	French
Violin (V., Vl., Vln., Vi., Vn.)	Violino (V., Vl., Vln., Viol.)	Violine (V., Vl., Vln.); Geige (Gg.)	Violon (V., Vl., Vln.)
Viola (Va., Vl.) [*pl.* Vas.]	Viola (Va., Vla.) [*pl.* Viole (Vle.)]	Bratsche (Br.)	Alto (A.)
Violoncello; Cello (Vcl., Vc.)	Violoncello (Vc., Vlc., Vcllo.)	Violoncell (Vc., Vlc.)	Violoncelle (Vc.)
Double bass (D. Bs.)	Contrabasso (Cb., C. B.) [*pl.* Contrabassi or Bassi (C. Bassi, Bi.)]	Kontrabass (Kb.)	Contrebasse (C. B.)

Other Instruments

English	Italian	German	French
Harp (Hp., Hrp.)	Arpa (A., Arp.)	Harfe (Hrf.)	Harpe (Hp.)
Piano (Pa.)	Pianoforte (P.-f., Pft.)	Klavier	Piano
Celesta (Cel.)	Celesta	Celesta	Céleste
Harpsichord	Cembalo	Cembalo	Clavecin
Harmonium (Harmon.)	Armonium	Harmonium	Orgne sulon
Organ (Org.)	Organo	Orgel	Orgue
Synthesizer			
Guitar	Chitarra	Gitarre (Git.)	Guitare
Mandolin (Mand.)			
Sampler			
Uilleann pipes			
Accordion	Fisarmonica	Ziehharmonika	Accordéon
Concertina		Konzertina	
Erhu			
Yangqin			

Voice Designations

English	German	French	Italian
Soprano (S)	Sopran	Soprano	Soprano
Alto (A), contralto	Alt	Contralte	Contralto
Tenor (T)	Tenor	Tenor	Tenor
Bass (B)	Bass	Basse	Basso
Voice	Singstimme	Voix	Voie, canto
Voice in Sprechstimme	Rezitation		
Chorus	Chor	Chœrur	Coro

Names of Scale Degrees and Modes

English	Italian	German	French
C C-sharp	do do diesis	C Cis	ut ut dièse
D-flat D D-sharp	re bemolle re re diesis	Des D Dis	ré bémol ré ré dièse
E-flat E E-sharp	mi bemolle mi mi diesis	Es E Eis	mi bémol mi mi dièse

English	Italian	German	French
F-flat F F-sharp	fa bemolle fa fa diesis	Fes F Fis	fa bémol fa fa dièse
G-flat G G-sharp	sol bemolle sol sol diesis	Ges G Gis	sol bémol sol sol dièse
A-flat A A-sharp	la bemolle la la diesis	As A Ais	la bémol la la dièse
B-flat B B-sharp	si bemolle si si diesis	B H His	si bémol si si dièse
C-flat	do bemolle	Ces	ut bémol

Modes

English	Italian	German	French
major	maggiore	dur	majeur
minor	minore	moll	mineur

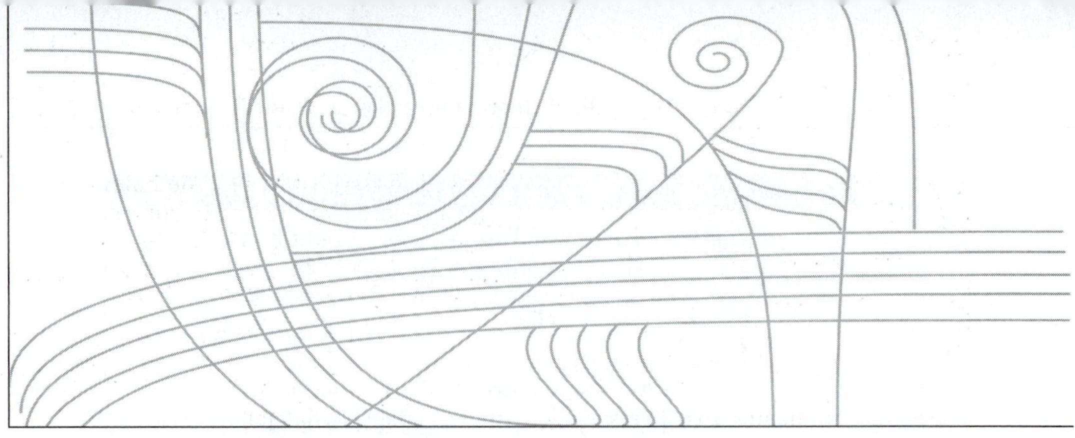

Appendix C

Glossary of Musical Terms Used in the Scores

The following glossary is not intended to be a complete dictionary of musical terms, nor is knowledge of all these terms necessary to follow the scores in this book. However, as listeners gain experience in following scores, they will find it useful and interesting to understand the composer's directions with regard to tempo, dynamics, and methods of performance.

In most cases, compound terms have been broken down and defined separately, as they often recur in varying combinations. A few common foreign-language words are included in addition to the musical terms. Note that names and abbreviations for instruments and for scale degrees will be found in Appendix B.

8va If written above a passage, an indication to play the passage an octave higher; if written below a passage, an indication to play the passage an octave lower.

16va If written above a passage, an indication to play the passage two octaves higher; if written below a passage, an indication to play the passage two octaves lower.

+ Closed (hi-hat cymbals).

o Open (hi-hat cymbals).

𝄋 Sign (segno).

a The phrases *a 2, a 3* (etc.) indicate the number of parts to be played by 2, 3 (etc.) players; when a simple number (1, 2, etc.) is placed over a part, it indicates that only the first (second, etc.) player in that group should play.

ab Off.

abaisée Lower, push down (the pedal).

aber But.

accelerando (accel.) Growing faster.

accentato, accentué Accented.

accompagnando Accompanying.

accompagnemento Accompaniment.

accordato, accordez Tune the instrument as specified.

adagio Slow, leisurely.
affettuoso With emotion.
affrettare (affrett.) Hastening a little.
agitando, agitato Agitated, excited.
al fine "The end"; an indication to return to the start of a piece and to repeat it only to the point marked "fine."
alla breve Indicates two beats to a measure, at a rather quick tempo.
allargando (allarg.) Growing broader.
alle, alles All, every, each.
allegramente Allegro, happily.
allegretto A moderately fast tempo (between allegro and andante).
allegrezza Gaiety.
allegro A rapid tempo (between allegretto and presto).
allein Alone, solo.
allmählich Gradually (*allmählich wieder gleich mässig fliessend werden,* gradually becoming even-flowing again).
alta, alto, altus (A.) The deeper of the two main divisions of women's (or boys') voices.
am Steg On the bridge (of a string instrument).
ancora Again.
andante A moderately slow tempo (between adagio and allegretto).
andantino A moderately slow tempo.
Anfang Beginning, initial.
anima Spirit, animation.
animando With increasing animation.
animant, animato, animé, animez Animated.
aperto Indicates open notes on the horn, open strings, and undamped piano notes.
a piacere The execution of the passage is left to the performer's discretion.
appassionato Impassioned.
appena Scarcely, hardly.
apprensivo Apprehensive.
archet Bow.
archi, arco Played with the bow.
arditamente (ardito) Boldly.
arpeggiando, arpeggiato (arpegg.) Played in harp style, i.e., the notes of the chord played in quick succession rather than simultaneously.
arrêt Break (as in *arrêt long,* long break).
articulato Articulated, separated.
assai Very.
assez Fairly, rather.
attacca Begin what follows without pausing.
a tempo At the original tempo.
auf dem On the (as in *auf dem G,* on the G string).
Ausdruck Expression.
ausdrucksvoll With expression.
äusserst Extreme, utmost.
avec With.

bacchetta, bacchetti (bacch.) Drumsticks (*bachetti di spugna,* sponge-headed drumsticks).
baguettes Drumsticks (*baguettes de bois, wooden drumsticks; baguettes d'éponge,* sponge-headed drumsticks; *baguettes dures,* hard mallets; *baguettes midures,* medium-hard mallets or drumsticks.
bass, bassi, basso, bassus (B.) The lowest male voice.
battere, battuta, battuto (batt.) To beat.
beaucoup A lot.
Becken Cymbals.
bedeutend bewegter With significantly more movement.
behaglich heiter Pleasingly serene or cheerful.
beider Hände With both hands.
ben Very.
bend A slight alteration, or lowering, of the pitch.
bewegt Agitated.
bewegter More agitated.
bisbigliando, bispiglando (bis.) Whispering.
bis zum Schluss dieser Szene To the end of this scene.
blancos White keys (*glissando sobre blancos, glissando* on the white keys of the piano).
blasen Blow.

Blech Brass instruments.
blues African-American form of secular folk music, related to jazz, that is based on a simple, repetitive, poetic-musical structure.
bogen (bog.) Played with the bow.
bois Woodwind.
bouché Muted.
bourdon Organ stop of capped flue pipes producing a dark sound.
break A jazz term for a fast, solo passage, usually without accompaniment.
breit Broadly.
breiter More broadly.
bridge On a bowed string instrument, a wedge-shaped device that holds the strings in place and transmits the vibrations to the body of the instrument. On a piano, a rail that holds the strings and transmits vibrations to the soundboard.
brilliante Brilliant.
brio Spirit, vivacity.
brushes Fan-shaped wires that are bound together and used to play the snare drum and cymbals, especially in jazz.
burden Refrain.

cadenza (cad., cadenz.) An extended passage for solo instrument in free, improvisatory style.
calando (cal.) Diminishing in volume and speed.
calma, calmo Calm, calmly.
cantabile (cant.) In a singing style.
cantando In a singing manner.
cantata Vocal genre for solo singers and instrumentalists based on a lyric or dramatic poetic narrative. It generally consists of several movements, including recitatives, arias, and sometimes ensemble numbers.
canto Voice (as in *col canto,* a direction for the accompaniment to follow the solo part in tempo and expression).
cantus An older designation for the highest part in a vocal work.
capriccio Capriciously, whimsically.
cedendo Yielding.
cédez Slow down.
changez Change (usually an instruction to retune a string or an instrument).
chanson French song.
Chinese ride A type of cymbals used particularly in jazz and popular music.
chiuso closed, stopped. See *gestopft.*
choke A sudden stopping of vibration, as on the cymbals.
chorus In jazz, a single statement of the melodic-harmonic pattern (e.g., 12-bar blues).
chromatisch Chromatic.
circa (ca.) About, approximately.
coda The last part of a piece.
col, colla, colle, coll' With the.
colore Colored.
come prima, come sopra As at first, as previously.
commodo Comfortable, easy.
con With.
corda String; for example, *seconda (2a) corda* is the second string (the A string on the violin).
corto Short, brief.
court Short.
crescendo (cres.) An increase in volume.
cuivré Played with a harsh, blaring tone.
cupa, cupo Gloomy, somber.
cup mute In brass instruments, a mute with a lip that forms a cup over the bell.

da capo (D.C.) Repeat from the beginning.
dal segno (D.S.) Repeat from the sign.
damper A felt-covered device on a piano that prevents a string from vibrating except when the key is depressed.
Dämpfer (dpf.) Mutes.
dazu In addition to that, for that purpose.
de, des, die Of, from.
début Beginning.
deciso Determined, resolute.
declamando In a declamatory style.
decrescendo (decresc., decr.) A decreasing of volume.
dehors Prominent, standing out.

delay Playing behind the beat, common in blues and jazz.
delicato Delicate, delicately.
dem To the.
détaché With a broad, vigorous bow stroke, each note bowed singly.
deutlich Distinctly.
d'exécution Performance.
diminuendo, diminuer (dim., dimin.) A decreasing of volume.
distinto Distinct, clear.
divisés, divisi (div.) Divided; indicates that the instrumental group should be divided into two parts to play the passage in question.
dolce Sweetly and softly.
dolcemente Sweetly.
dolcissimo (dolciss.) Very sweetly.
dolente Sad.
dolore, doloroso With sorrow.
Doppelgriff Double stop.
doppio Double (as in *doppio movimento*, twice as fast).
doux Sweetly.
drammatico Dramatic.
drängend Pressing on.
dreifach Triple.
dreitaktig Three beats to a measure.
dur Major, as in G dur (G major).
durée Duration.

e, et And.
eilen To hurry.
ein One, a.
elegante Elegant, graceful.
Empfindung Feeling.
energico Energetically.
enharmonic Pitches that are the same but are spelled differently (e.g., C-sharp and D-flat).
espansione Expansion, broadening.
espressione With expression.
espressivo (espr., espress.) Expressively.
étouffez Muted, dampened.
etude Study piece that focuses on a particular technical problem. Though not originally conceived as a concert piece, some etudes are frequently performed in the concert hall.
etwas Somewhat, rather.
expressif Expressively.

facile Simple.
falsetto Male voice singing above normal range, with light sound.
fantasie Free instrumental piece of fairly large dimensions, in an improvisational style.
feroce Fierce, ferocious.
feutré Felted; in mallet percussion, softer mallets.
fin, fine End, close.
Flatterzunge (Flatterz., Flzg.), fluttertongue A special tonguing technique for wind instruments, producing a rapid, trill-like sound.
flebile Feeble, plaintive, mournful.
fliessend Flowing.
forte (f) Loud.
fortepiano (fp) Loud, then soft immediately.
fortissimo (ff) Very loud (*fff* indicates a still louder dynamic).
forza Force.
forzando (fz) Forcing, strongly accented.
forzandissimo (ffz) Very strongly accented.
fou Frantic.
frappez To strike.
frei Freely.
freihäng., freihängendes Hanging freely. An indication to the percussionist to let the cymbals vibrate freely.
frisch Fresh, lively.
fuoco Fire.
furioso Furiously.
furore Fury, rage.

ganz Entirely, altogether.
Ganzton Whole tone.
gedämpft (ged.) Muted.
geheimnisvoll Mysteriously.
geschlagen Pulsating.
gestopft (gest.) Stopping the notes of a horn; that is, the hand is placed in the bell of the horn to produce a muffled sound. Also *chiuso*.
geteilt (get.) Divided; indicates that

the instrumental group should be divided into two parts to play the passage in question.

getragen Sustained.

gewöhnlich As usual.

giocoso Humorous.

giusto Moderately.

gli altri The other players; those not playing a solo.

glissando (gliss.) Rapid scales produced by running the fingers over all the strings.

gradamente Gradually.

grande Large, great.

grande orgue (G.O.) The main division of an organ (great organ, English; *Hauptwerk*, German).

grandezza Grandeur.

grandioso Grandiose.

grave Slow, solemn; deep, low.

grazioso Gracefully.

Griffbrett Fingerboard.

grosser Auftakt Big upbeat.

grotesque Absurd, fantastic, monstrous.

growl A rough, "dirty" tone produced by brass and woodwinds instruments; used in jazz.

gut Good, well.

Hälfte Half.

harmonics Individual, pure sounds that are part of a musical tone; on string instruments, crystalline tones in the very high register, produced by lightly touching a vibrating string at a certain point.

Harmon mute In brass instruments, a brand name of wa-wa mute; common in jazz.

hat A brass mute in the shape of a derby hat, held by the brim; used in jazz.

Hauptzeitmass Original tempo.

hauteur réelle In the octave notated, designation for transposing French horns.

head The tune and chord progression, in jazz.

hervortreten Prominent.

hi-hat Pair of cymbals suspended horizontally on a stand and operated with a foot pedal; part of a drum set used in jazz.

hoch High, nobly.

Holz Woodwinds.

Holzschlägel Wooden drumstick.

hyperinstruments Acoustical instruments that are enhanced electronically to expand the possibilities of expressivity and virtuosity; developed by Tod Machover at MIT.

im gleichen Rhythmus In the same rhythm.

immer Always.

impalpable Imperceptively.

in Oktaven In octaves.

insensibilmente Slightly, imperceptibly.

intensa Intensely.

interlude A connecting musical passage between movements or large sections of a work.

istesso tempo Duration of beat remains unaltered despite meter change.

jeté On a string instrument, the bow is thrown so that it bounces on the string with a series of rapid notes.

jeu Playful.

jusqu'à Until.

kadenzieren To cadence.

klagend Lamenting.

kleine Little.

klingen To sound.

komisch bedeutsam Very humorously.

kurz Short.

laissez To allow; *laisser vibrer*, to let vibrate.

langsam Slow.

langsamer Slower.

languendo, langueur Languor.

l'archet See archet.

largamente Broadly.

larghetto Slightly faster than largo.

largo A very slow tempo.

lasci, lassen To abandon.

lebhaft Lively.

lebhafter Livelier.

legatissimo A more forceful indication of *legato*.
legato Performed without any perceptible interruption between notes.
légèrement, leggieramente Lightly.
leggierissimo Very light.
leggiero (legg.) Light and graceful.
legno The wood of the bow (*col legno gestrich*, played with the wood).
leitmotif "Leading motive," or basic recurring theme, representing a person, object, or idea, commonly used in Wagner's operas and in some film music scores.
lent Slow.
lentamente Slowly.
lento A slow tempo (between andante and largo).
l.h. Abbreviation for "left hand."
libetum Liberty (*ad libitum*, at liberty, at the pleasure of the performer).
licenzia License with tempo (*con licenzia*, with license or liberty).
Lied, Lieder German for "song"; generally associated with the solo art song of the nineteenth century, usually accompanied by piano.
liricamente Lyrically.
loco Indicates a return to the written pitch, following a passage played an octave higher or lower than written.
loin Distant, faraway.
Luftpause Pause for breath.
lunga Long, sustained.
lusingando Caressing.

ma, mais But.
maestoso Majestic.
mailloche Timpani mallet.
mambo Dance of Afro-Cuban origin with a highly syncopated quadruple-meter rhythmic pattern.
mano derecha Right hand (m.d.), in piano music.
mano izquierda Left hand (m.i.), in piano music.
marcatissimo (marcatiss.) With very marked emphasis.
marcato (marc.) Marked, with emphasis.
marcia March.
marschmässig, nicht eilen Moderate-paced march, not rushed.
martelé, martellato Hammered; in piano playing, a hammer-like touch; in bowed string instruments, forcefully releasing each stroke.
marziale Military, martial, march-like.
mässig Moderately.
mässiger More moderately.
melodia Melody.
même Same.
meno Less.
mettez With (as in *mettez les sourdines*, with the mutes).
mezza, mezzo Half, medium.
mezzo forte (mf) Moderately loud.
mezzo piano (mp) Moderately soft.
mezzo voce With half voice, restrained.
mindestens At least.
misterioso Mysterious.
misura (misurato) Measured.
mit With.
moderatissimo A more forceful indication of *moderato*.
moderato, modéré At a moderate tempo.
moins Less.
molto Very, much.
mordenti Biting, pungent.
morendo Dying away.
mormorato Murmured.
mosso Rapid.
moto Motion.
mouvement (mouv., mouvt.) Tempo (as in *au mouvement*, a tempo).
movimento Movement, pace.
muta, mutano Change the tuning of the instrument as specified.

nach After.
naturalezza A natural, unaffected manner.
nel modo russico In the Russian style.
neuen New.
nicht Not.

niente Nothing.
nimmt To take; to seize.
noch Still.
node A point at which vibrations do not occur.
non Not.
notturno, nocturne "Night piece"; introspective work common in the nineteenth century; often for piano.
nuovo New.

obere, oberer (ob.) Upper, leading.
oder langsamer Or slower.
offen Open.
ohne Without.
ondeggiante Undulating movement of the bow, which produces a tremolo effect.
open On a French horn, removing the hand or mute; unmuted.
ordinairement Ordinarily, normally.
ordinario (ord., ordin.) In the usual way (generally canceling an instruction to play using some special technique).
ossia An alternative (usually easier) version of a passage.
ôtez vite les sourdines Remove the mutes quickly.
ottava Octave (as in *8va,* octave higher than written; *8 basso, 8 bassa,* octave lower than written; *16 va,* two octaves higher than written).
ottoni Brass.
ouvert Open.

parte Part *(colla parte, colle parti,* the accompaniment is to follow the soloist[s] in tempo).
part song A secular, a cappella choral work.
passionato Passionately.
passione Passion, emotion.
Paukenschlägel Timpani stick.
pavillons en l'air An indication to the player of a wind instrument to raise the bell of the instrument upward.
pedal, pedale (ped., P.) (1) In piano music, indicates that the damper pedal should be depressed; an asterisk indicates the point of release (brackets below the music are also used to indicate pedaling); (2) on an organ, the pedals are a keyboard played with the feet.
per During.
perdant fading (as in *en se perdant,* dying away).
perdendosi Gradually dying away.
pesante Heavily.
peu Little, a little.
piacevole Agreeable, pleasant.
pianissimo (pp) Very soft (*ppp* indicates a still softer dynamic).
piano (p) Soft.
piena Full.
più More.
pizzicato (pizz.) The string plucked with the finger.
plötzlich Suddenly, immediately.
plunger A plunger-shaped trombone mute that is held in the left hand and moved in front of and away from the bell; used in jazz.
plus More.
pochissimo (pochiss.) Very little, a very little.
poco Little, a little.
poco a poco Little by little.
Polonaise A dance form in a moderate tempo; originated in Poland.
ponticello (pont.) The bridge (of a string instrument).
portamento Continuous smooth and rapid sliding between two pitches.
portando Carrying.
position naturel (pos. nat.) In the normal position (usually canceling an instruction to play using some special technique).
possibile Possible.
precedente Previous, preceding.
precipitato Rushed, hurried.
prelude Instrumental opening that precedes a larger work or serves as an introduction; usually in a free form.
premier mouvement (1er mouvt.) At the original tempo.
prenez Take up.

prepared piano Piano whose sound is altered by the insertion of various materials (metal, rubber, leather, or paper) between the strings; invented by John Cage.
préparez Prepare.
près de la table On harp, play near the soundboard with the nails.
presque Almost, nearly.
presser To speed up.
prestissimo A more forceful indication of *presto*.
presto A very quick tempo (faster than allegro).
prima, primo First, principal.
principale First, principal, solo.
punto Point.

quarta Fourth.
quasi Almost, as if.
quinto Fifth.

rag Late-nineteenth-century African-American dance genre for piano characterized by highly syncopated melodies; contributed to early jazz styles.
ralentissez Slow down.
rallentando (rall., rallent.) Growing slower.
rapidamente Quickly.
rapide Rapid, fast.
rapidissimo (rapidiss.) Very quickly.
rasch Quickly.
rascher More quickly.
rauschend Rustling, roaring.
Recit A manual on the French organ for solo stops.
recitative, recitativo (recit.) A vocal style designed to imitate and emphasize the natural inflections of speech.
rein Perfect interval.
relever To raise, to lift up.
reprenez Take again, put on again.
Requiem Roman Catholic Mass for the Dead.
resonante Resonating.
respiro Pause for breath.
retenu Held back.
revenir au tempo Return to the original tempo.
r.h. Abbreviation for "right hand."
rianimando Reanimating.
richtig Correct (*richtige Lage*, correct pitch).
rien Nothing.
rigore di tempo Strictness of tempo.
rigueur Rigor, strictness.
rinforzando (rf, rfz, rinf.) A sudden accent on a single note or chord.
risoluto In a resolute or determined manner.
ritardando (rit., ritard.) Gradually slackening in speed.
ritenuto (riten.) Immediate reduction of speed.
ritmato, ritmico Rhythmic.
ritornando, ritornello (ritor.) Refrain.
robuste Robustly.
rubato A certain elasticity and flexibility of tempo, consisting of slight accelerandos and ritardandos according to the requirements of the musical expression.
ruhig Quietly.

saltando Leaping.
sans Without.
scat A jazz vocal style that sets syllables without meaning (vocables) to an improvised vocal line.
Schalltrichter Horn.
scherzando (scherz.) Playful.
schlagen To strike in a usual manner.
Schlagwerk Striking mechanism.
schleppen, schleppend Dragging.
Schluss Cadence, conclusion.
schnell Fast.
schneller Faster.
schon Already.
Schwammschägeln Sponge-headed drumstick.
scorrevole Flowing, gliding.
sec, secco (sèche) Dry, simple.
secunda Second.
segno Sign; used to mark the beginning or ending of a repeated section (*dal segno, D.S.*, from the sign; *sino al segno*, until the sign).
sehr Very.
semplice Simple.
semplicità Simplicity.

sempre Always, continually.
senza Without.
serre Short, pronounced (*tres serre*, very short or pronounced).
sesquialtera In Spanish and Latin American music, an unequal meter based on the alternation of duple and triple time within groups of six beats.
sforzando (sf., sfz.) With sudden emphasis.
sforzandissimo (sff, sffz) With very loud, sudden attack.
shake An effect on a brass instrument resembling an exaggerated vibrato, produced by shaking the instrument against the lips while playing; used in jazz.
simile (sim.) In a similar manner.
sin Without.
Singstimme Singing voice.
sino al Up to the . . . (usually followed by a new tempo marking, or by a dotted line indicating a terminal point).
si piace Especially pleasing.
smear An exaggerated bending of a semitone or tone down and then up again; often played with a harsh tone; used by brass instruments in jazz.
smorzando (smorz.) Dying away.
sobre On.
sofort Immediately.
soli, solo (s.) Executed by one performer.
son Traditional Mexican dance song that alternates between compound duple and triple meters (sesquialtera).
son naturel Natural sound; on a brass instrument, played without valves.
sonoro Sonorous, resonant.
sopra Above; in piano music, used to indicate that one hand must pass above the other.
soprano (S.) The voice classification with the highest range.
sordini, sordino (sord.) Mute.
sostenendo, sostenuto (sost.) Sustained.
sotto voce In an undertone, subdued, under the breath.
sourdine (sourd.) Mute.
soutenu Sustained.
spiel, spielen Play (an instrument).
Spieler Player, performer.
spirito Spirit, soul.
spiritoso In a spirited manner.
Sprechstimme Early-twentieth-century vocal style in which the melody is spoken at approximate pitches rather than sung on exact pitches; developed by Arnold Schoenberg.
spugna Sponge.
squeeze Squeezing the embouchure to raise the pitch; used in jazz.
staccatissimo Extremely detached or staccato.
staccato (stacc.) Detached, separated, abruptly, disconnected.
stentando, stentare, stentato (stent.) Delaying, retarding.
stesso The same.
Stimme Voice.
stimmen To tune.
stopped On a French horn, closing the opening of the bell with the hand or a mute.
straight mute (st. mute) A conical or pear-shaped brass mute in which the wider end is closed.
strascinare To drag.
straziante Agonizing, heart-rending.
Streichinstrumente (Streichinstr.) Bowed string instruments.
strepitoso Noisy, loud.
stretto In a non-fugal composition, indicates a concluding section at an increased speed; *also tight, strict, exact, as in rubato stretto.*
stringendo (string.) Quickening.
subito (sub.) Suddenly, immediately.
suite Multimovement work made up of a series of contrasting dance movements, generally all in the same key.
suivez Follow (as in *suivez le solo*, follow the solo line).
sul On the (as in *sul* G, on the G string).

superius In older music, the uppermost part.
sur On.

tacet The instrument or vocal part so marked is silent.
tanto A lot, much.
tasto Fingerboard (as in *sul tasto*, bow over the fingerboard).
tasto solo In a continuo part, this indicates that only the string instrument plays; the chord-playing instrument is silent.
tema Theme.
tempo primo (tempo I) At the original tempo.
teneramente, tenero Tenderly, gently.
tenor, tenore (T.) The highest male voice.
tenuto (ten., tenu.) Held, sustained.
tertia Third.
through-composed Song structure without large internal repetitions, where each stanza is set to different music.
tief Deep, low.
timbre Tone color.
timpanista Timpanist.
touche Key; note; fingerboard (as in *sur la touche*, on the fingerboard).
toujours Always, continually.
tranquillo Quietly, calmly.
tre corde (t.c.) Release the soft (or *una corda*) pedal of the piano.
tremolo (trem.) On string instruments, a quick reiteration of the same tone, produced by a rapid up-and-down movement of the bow; also a rapid alternation between two different notes.
trepak A Russian dance in fast duple meter, featuring the kicking of the legs from a squatted position.
très Very.
trill (tr.) The rapid alternation of a given note with the diatonic second above it. In a drum part, it indicates rapid alternating strokes with two drumsticks.
trio In a dance movement or a march, a contrasting middle section.
tromba Trumpet (as in *quasi tromba*, trumpet-like).
Trommschlag (Tromm.) Drumbeat.
troppo Too much.
tutta la forza Very emphatically.
tutti Literally, "all"; usually means all the instruments in a given category as distinct from a solo part.

übergreifen To overlap.
übertonend Drowning out.
umstimmen To change the tuning.
un One, a.
una corda (u.c.) With the "soft" pedal of the piano depressed.
und And.
unison (unis.) The same notes or melody played by several instruments at the same pitch. Often used to emphasize that a phrase is not to be divided among several players.
unmerklich Imperceptible.

velocissimo Very swiftly.
verklingen lassen To let die away.
vibrare, vibrer To sound, vibrate.
vibrato (vibr.) To fluctuate the pitch on a single note.
vierfach Quadruple.
vierhändig Four-hand piano music.
vif Lively.
vigoroso Vigorous, strong.
violento Violent.
viva, vivente, vivo Lively.
vivace Quick, lively.
vivacissimo A more forceful indication of vivace.
voce Voice (as in *colla voce*, a direction for the accompaniment to follow the solo part in tempo and expression).
volles Orch. Entire orchestra.
vorbereiten Prepare, get ready.
Vorhang auf Curtain up.
Vorhang zu Curtain down.
vorher Beforehand, previously.
voriges Preceding.

Waltzertempo In the tempo of a waltz.
weg Away, beyond.
weich Mellow, smooth, soft.

wie aus der Fern As if from afar.
wieder Again.
wie zu Anfang dieser Szene As at the beginning of this scene.

zart Tenderly, delicately.
Zeit Time; duration.
zögernd Slower.
zu The phrases *zu 2, zu 3* (etc.) indicate the number of parts to be played by 2, 3 (etc.) players.
zum In addition.
zurückhaltend Slackening in speed.
zurücktreten To withdraw.
zweihändig With two hands.

Appendix D

Concordance Table for Recordings and Listening Guides

The following table provides cross-references to the Listening Guides (LG) in *The Enjoyment of Music*, Tenth Edition, by Kristine Forney and Joseph Machlis (New York: W. W. Norton, 2007). The table also gives the track numbers for each work on both recording sets (see "A Note on the Recordings," p. xvii).

LG #	Shorter LG #	Score Number, Composer, Title	Score Page	8-CD Set	4-CD Set
43	25	1. Schubert: *Erlkönig*	1	5 (1–8)	2 57–64)
42		2. Schubert: Lied, *Die Forelle* (*The Trout*)	9	5 (9–11)	—
	—	3. Schubert: Quintet in A major for Piano and Strings (*Trout*), Fourth movement	15	5 (12–18)	—
44	26	4. R. Schumann: *Dichterliebe*, No. 1: "Im wunderschönen Monat Mai"	32	5 (19–20)	2 65–66)
46	—	5. Chopin: Prelude in E minor, Op. 28, No 4	35	5 (21–22)	—
45	27	6. Chopin: Polonaise in A major, Op. 40, No. 1 (*Military*)	37	5 (23–27)	2 67–71)
47	—	7. Liszt: *La campanella* (*The Little Bell*)	45	5 (28–37)	—
48	28	8. C. Schumann: *Notturno*, from *Soirées musicales*, Op. 6	55	5 (38–41)	3 (1–4)
49	29	9. Gottschalk: *Le banjo*	62	5 (42–48)	3 (5–11)
50	30	10. Berlioz: *Symphonie fantastique*		5 (49–54)	3 12–17)
		Fourth movement	76	5 (55–61)	—
		Fifth movement	97		
51	31	11. Smetana: *Vltava* (*The Moldau*)	152	5 (62–69)	3 (18–25)
52	32	12. Brahms: Symphony No. 3 in F major, Op. 90, Third movement	217	5 (70–72)	3 (26–28)
53	—	13. Dvořák: Symphony No. 9 in E minor, *From the New World*, First movement	235	6 (1–9)	—

LG #	Shorter LG #	Score Number, Composer, Title	Score Page	8-CD Set	4-CD Set
54	—	14. Felix Mendelssohn: Violin Concerto in E minor, Op. 64, First movement	288	6 (10–18)	—
55	—	15. Beach: Violin Sonata in A minor, Second movement	338	5 (73–75)	—
56	33	16. Brahms: *Ein deutsches Requiem*, Fourth movement	346	6 (19–23)	3 (29–33)
57	34	17. Fanny Mendelssohn Hensel: *Unter des Laubdachs Hut*	358	6 (24–27)	3 (34–37)
58	35	18. Verdi: *Rigoletto*, Act III, excerpts	363	6 (28–33)	3 (38–43)
59		19. Wagner: *Die Walküre*, Act III			
	36	*The Ride of the Valkyries* (opening)	388	6 (34–39)	3 (44–49)
		Finale, closing section	404	6 (40–44)	—
60	—	20. Bizet: *Carmen*, Act I, Scenes 4 and 5	411	6 (45–51)	—
61	37	21. Puccini: *Madama Butterfly*, "Un bel dì"	434	6 (52–53)	3 (50–51)
63	38	22. Tchaikovsky: *The Nutcracker*, Three Dances	440	6 (54–62)	3 (52–54)
64	—	23. Mahler: *Das Lied von der Erde* (*The Song of the Earth*), Third movement	488	6 (63–66)	—
65	39	24. Debussy: *Prélude à "L'après-midi d'un faune" (Prelude to "The Afternoon of a Faun")*	500	7 (1–5)	3 (55–59)
66	—	25. Ravel: *Don Quichotte à Dulcinée*, Two Songs	533	7 (6–11)	—
67		26. Stravinsky: *Le sacre du printemps*, Part I			
	40	Introduction (closing)	549	7 (12)	4 (1)
		Danses des adolescentes	550	7 (13–16)	4 (2–5)
		Jeu du rapt	569	7 (17–18)	4 (6–7)
68	—	27. Stravinsky: *L'histoire du soldat: March royale*	582	7(19–23)	—
69	41	28. Schoenberg: *Pierrot lunaire*			
		No. 18 *Der Mondfleck*	592	7 (24–25)	4 (8–9)
		No. 21 *O alter Duft aus Märchenzeit*	598	7 (26–27)	
70	—	29. Berg: *Wozzeck*, Act III, Scene 4, Interlude, and Scene 5	603	7 (28–31)	—
71	—	30. Webern: Symphony, Op. 21, Second movement	629	7 (32–34)	—
72	42	31. Bartók: *Concerto for Orchestra*, Fourth movement	638	7 (35–41)	4 (10–16)
95	—	32. Prokofiev: *Alexander Nevsky*, Seventh movement	650	7 (42–45)	—
86	—	33. Messiaen: *Quatuor pour la fin du temps, Vocalise*	664	7 (46–48)	—
73	—	34. Ives: *The Things Our Fathers Loved*	673	7 (49–50)	—
74	—	35. Still: *Afro-American Symphony*, Second movement	676	7 (51–56)	—
75	43	36. Copland: *Billy the Kid*, Scene I, *Street in a Frontier Town*	685	7 (57–61)	4 (17–21)
76	44	37. Revueltas: *Homenaje a Federico García Lorca*, Third movement, *Son*	727	7 (62–69)	4 (22–29)
78	46	38. Joplin: *Maple Leaf Rag*	744	7 (70–74)	4 (30–34)
82	—	39. Gershwin: Piano Prelude No. 1	748	7 (75–77)	—

(*Continued*)

LG #	Shorter LG #	Score Number, Composer, Title	Score Page	8-CD Set	4-CD Set
79	47	40. Holiday: *Billie's Blues*	753	7 (78–84)	4 (35–41)
80	—	41. Strayhorn/Ellington: *Take the A Train*	758	8 (1–5)	—
81	48	42. Gillespie/Parker: *A Night in Tunisia*	789	8 (6–11)	4 (42–47)
83	49	43. Bernstein: *West Side Story* *Mambo* *Tonight* Ensemble	 791 814	 8 (12–13) 8 (14–20)	 4 (48–49) 4 (50–56)
89	52	44. Cage: *Sonatas and Interludes*, Sonata V	831	8 (29–30)	4 (65–66)
87	—	45. Boulez: *Notations IV*	834	8 (31–33)	—
88	51	46. Crumb: *Ancient Voices of Children*, first movement	838	8 (34–36)	4 (67–69)
91	—	47. Ligeti: *Désordre*, from *Etudes pour Piano*, Book I	842	8 (37–39)	—
93	54	48. Sheng: *China Deams: Prelude*	848	8 (40–45)	4 (70–75)
97	57	49. Machover: *Hyperstring Trilogy: Begin Again Again . . .*, excerpts	866	8 (46–51)	4 (76–81)
98	58	50. Pärt: *Cantate Domino canticum novum*	881	8 (52–55)	4 (82–85)
99	59	51. Adams: *Tromba lontana*	894	8 (56–60)	4 (86–90)
100	60	52. Larsen: *Sonnets from the Portuguese*, Nos. 5 and 6	917	8 (61–62)	4 (91–92)
94	55	53. Abing: *Er quan ying yue* (*The Moon Reflected on the Second Springs*)	945	8 (63–65)	4 (93–95)
84	50	54. BeauSoleil: *Think of Me* (*Jongle à moi*)	947	8 (66–69)	4 (96–99)

Credits

p. 9 Schubert: *Die Forelle* (*The Trout*) from *Lieder I, Sopran oder Tenor*. Used by permission of C. F. Peters Corporation. **p. 15 Schubert:** Piano Quintet in A major (*Trout*), fourth movement. Edited by Anke Butzer and Jurgen Neubacher. ©1988 Ernst Eulenburg & Co GmbH. Used by permission of European American Music Distributors LLC, sole U.S. and Canadian agent for Ernst Eulenburg Ltd. **p. 32 Robert Schumann:** *Dichterliebe* (*A Poet's Love*), No. 1: "Im wunderschönen Monat Mai." From DICHTERLIEBE, A NORTON CRITICAL SCORE by Robert Schumann, edited by Arthur Koman. Copyright © 1971 by W. W. Norton & Company, Inc. Used by permission of W. W. Norton & Company, Inc. **p. 37 Chopin:** Polonaise, Op. 40, No. 1 from *Frédérick Chopin: Nocturnes and Polonaises*, New York, NY: Dover Publications, Inc. **p. 55 Clara Schumann:** *Notturno*, from *Soirees musicales*, Op. 6 for Piano. Used by permission of Carl Fischer, LLC, on behalf of Hildegard Publishing Company (Theodore Presser Company). **p. 62 Gottschalk:** *Le Banjo* from *Gottschalk: A Compendium of Piano Music*, ed. Eugene List, N5360. Used by permission of Carl Fischer, LLC. **p. 76 Berlioz:** *Symphonie fantastique*, Fourth and Fifth movements. From HECTOR BERLIOZ: FANTASTIC SYMPHONY, A NORTON CRITICAL SCORE by Hector Berlioz, edited by Edward T. Cone. Copyright © 1971 by W. W. Norton & Company, Inc. Used by permission of W. W. Norton & Company, Inc. **p. 217 Brahms:** Symphony No. 3 in F major, Third movement. Used by kind permission of European American Music Distributors LLC, sole U.S. and Canadian agent for Ernst Eulenburg & Co GmbH. **p. 235 Dvořák:** Symphony No. 9 in E minor, First movement. Edited by Klaus Doge. © 1986 Ernst Eulenburg & Co GmbH. All Rights Reserved. Used by permission of European American Music Distributors LLC, sole U.S. and Canadian agent for Ernst Eulenburg & Co GmbH. **p. 288 Felix Mendelssohn:** Violin Concerto in E minor, Op. 64, First movement. Used by kind permission of European American Music Distributors LLC, sole U.S. and

Canadian agent for Ernst Eulenburg Ltd. **p. 346 Brahms:** *Ein deutsches Requiem*, Fourth movement. Edition Peters No. 3672. Used by permission of C.F. Peters Corporation. **p. 358 Fanny Mendelssohn Hensel:** *Unter des Laubdachs Hut* from CHB 5234 Wb. 2062. © 1989 by Breitkopf & Haertel, Wiesbaden. Used by permission. **p. 363 Verdi:** "La donna è mobile" and "Un dí, se ben rammentomi" from *Rigoletto*, Act III. Copyright © 1957 (Renewed) by G. Schirmer, Inc. (ASCAP). International Copyright Secured. All Rights Reserved. Reprinted by Permission. **p. 388 Wagner:** *Die Walküre*, Act III, Opening, *The Ride of the Valkyries*, and Finale, closing section. English translation by Frederick Jameson. Copyright © 1936 (Renewed) by G. Schirmer, Inc. (ASCAP). International Copyright Secured. All Rights Reserved. Reprinted by Permission. **p. 411 Bizet:** Carmen, Act I, scenes 4–5. English translation by Ruth and Thomas Martin. Copyright © 1958 (Renewed) by G. Schirmer, Inc. (ASCAP). International Copyright Secured. All Rights Reserved. Reprinted by Permission. **p. 434 Puccini:** "Un bel dí," from *Madame Butterfly*, no. 2428. English translation by John Gutman. Copyright © 1963 (Renewed) by G. Schirmer, Inc. (ASCAP). International Copyright Secured. All Rights Reserved. Reprinted by Permission. **p. 440 Tchaikovsky:** *The Nutcracker*, Three Dances. Used by kind permission of European American Music Distributors LLC, sole U.S. and Canadian agent for Ernst Eulenburg & Co GmbH. **p. 488 Mahler:** *Das Lied von der Erde*, Third movement. Copyright 1912 by Universal Edition A.G., Wien. Copyright renewed, assigned 1952 to Universal Edition (London) Ltd, London. © This edition, revised by the Internationale Gustav-Mahler-Gesellschaft, copyright 1962 by Universal Edition A.G., Wien, and Universal Edition (London) Ltd., London. © renewed. All Rights Reserved. Used by permission of European American Music Distributors LLC, U.S. and Canadian agent for Universal Edition A.G., Wien and Universal Edition (London) Ltd., London. **p. 533 Ravel:** *Chanson romanesque* and *Chanson à boire* from *Don Quichotte à Dulcinee*. Music: Maurice Ravel. Lyrics: Paul Morand. © 1934 Joint ownership Redfield and Nordice. Exclusive representation Editions Durand, Paris, France. Reproduced by permission of Editions Durand. **p. 549 Stravinsky:** *Le sacre du printemps*, Part I: Introduction (end), *Danses des adolescentes*, and *Jeu du rapt* from *Rite of Spring*, Orchestral score, Hawkes Pocket Scores. © Copyright 1912, 1921 by Hawkes & Son (London) Ltd. Copyright Renewed. Reprinted by permission of Boosey & Hawkes, Inc. **p. 582 Stravinsky:** *L'histoire du soldat*: *Marche royale*. Music by Igor Stravinsky. Copyright © 1987, 1992 by Chester Music Ltd. International Copyright Secured. All Rights Reserved. Reprinted by Permission of G. Schirmer, Inc. (ASCAP). **p. 592 Schoenberg:** *Pierrot lunaire*, Op. 21, Nos. 18 & 21. Used by permission of Belmont Music Publishers, Pacific Palisades, CA 90272. **p. 603 Berg:** *Wozzeck*, Op. 7: Act III, Scene 4. Full score Copyright 1926 by Universal Edition A.G., Vienna. Full score Copyright renewed. English translation Copyright 1952 by Alfred A.

Kalmus, London. English translation Copyright renewed. All Rights Reserved. Used by permission of European American Music Distributors LLC, U.S. and Canadian agent for Universal Edition A.G., Vienna. **p. 629 Webern:** Symphony, Op. 21, Second movement. Copyright 1929 by Universal Edition. Copyright renewed. All Rights Reserved. Used by permission of European American Music Distributors LLC, sole U.S. and Canadian agent for Universal Edition. **p. 638 Bartók:** *Concerto for Orchestra*, Fourth movement: *Interrupted Intermezzo*. © Copyright 1946 by Hawkes & Son (London) Ltd. Copyright Renewed. Reprinted by permission of Boosey & Hawkes, Inc. **p. 650 Prokofiev:** *Alexander Nevsky*, Op. 78 Seventh movement. Copyright © 1941 (Renewed) by G. Schirmer, Inc.(ASCAP). International Copyright Secured. All Rights Reserved. Reprinted by Permission. **p. 664 Messiaen:** *Quatuor pour la fin du temps*, Second movement: *Vocalise pour l'ange qui annonce la fin du temps*. © 1941 by Editions Durand. Used by permission. **p. 673 Ives:** *The Things Our Fathers Loved* from *Fourteen Songs*. Copyright © 1955 by Peer International Corporation. Copyright Renewed. This arrangement Copyright © 2006 by Peer International Corporation. International Copyright Secured. All Rights Reserved. Reprinted by Permission of Hal Leonard Corp. **p. 676 Still:** *Afro-America Symphony*, Second movement. Copyright © 1935 by J Fischer and Bro. Copyright © Renewed 1962 and transferred to Novello & Company Limited 1970. All Rights Reserved. International Copyright Secured. Reprinted by Permission. **p. 685 Copland:** *Billy the Kid*, Scene 1, *Street in a Frontier Town*. © Copyright 1941 by The Aaron Copland Fund for Music, Inc. Copyright Renewed. Boosey & Hawkes, Inc., Sole Publisher &Licensee. Reprinted by permission. **p. 727 Revueltas**: *Homenaje a Federico García Lorca*, Third movement, *Son*. © Southern Music Publication Co./Peermusic Classical. **p. 753 Holiday:** *Billie's Blues*. Copyright © 1956, 1962 by Edward B. Marks Music Company. Copyright Renewed. This arrangement copyright © 2006 by Edward B. Marks Music Company. International Copyright Secured. All Rights Reserved. Used by Permission of Hal Leonard Corp. **p. 744 Joplin:** *Maple Leaf Rag*. From *Scott Joplin: Complete Piano Rags*, New York, NY: Dover Publications, Inc. **p. 748 Gershwin:** Piano Prelude No. 1. © 1927 (Renewed) WB MUSIC CORP. in the U.S.A. Rights throughout the World excluding the U.S.A. and British Reversionary Territories controlled by NEW WORLD MUSIC COMPANY (LTD.) and Administered by WB MUSIC CORP. Rights throughout the British Reversionary Territories controlled by CHAPPELL & CO. All Rights Reserved. Used by Permission. **p. 758 Strayhorn:** *Take the A Train*. Copyright © 1941; Renewed 1969 Dimensional Music Of 1091 (ASCAP) and Billy Strayhorn Songs, Inc. (ASCAP) for the U.S.A. This arrangement Copyright © 2006 Dimensional Music Of 1901 (ASCAP) and Billy Strayhorn Songs, Inc. (ASCAP) for the U.S.A. Rights for Dimensional Music Of 1901 and Billy Strayhorn Songs, Inc. Administered by Cherry Lane Music Publishing Company, Inc. Internal Copyright Secured. All Rights Reserved.

Reprinted by permission of Hal Leonard Corp. **p. 789 Gillespie/Parker:** *A Night in Tunisia*. By John "Dizzy" Gillespie and Frank Paparelli. Copyright © 1944 UNIVERSAL MUSIC CORP. Copyright Renewed. This arrangement Copyright © 2006 UNIVERSALMUSIC CORP. All Rights Reserved. Used by Permission of Hal Leonard Corporation. **p. 791 Bernstein:** *West Side Story*: *Mambo* and *Tonight* ensemble. © Copyright 1956, 1957, 1958, 1959 by Amberson Holdings LLC and Stephen Sondheim. Copyright Renewed. Leonard Bernstein Music Publishing Company LLC, Publisher. Boosey & Hawkes, Inc., Sole Agent. Reprinted by permission. **p. 831 Cage:** Sonata V from *Sonatas and Interludes*. Copyright ©1960 by Henmar Press Inc. Reprinted by permission of C. F. Peters Corporation. **p. 834 Boulez:** *Notations IV*. © 1985 by Universal Edition A.G., Vienna. All Rights Reserved. Used by permission of European American Music Distributors LLC, U.S. and Canadian agent for Universal Edition A.G., Vienna. **p. 839 Crumb:** *Ancient Voices of Children*, First movement. Copyright © 1970 by C. F. Peters, 373 Park Avenue South, New York, NY 10016. Reprinted with permission of the publishers who published the score of the complete work under Peters Edition No. 66303. **p. 843 Ligeti:** *Désordre* from *Etudes pour Piano*, Book I. © Schott Musik International, 1986. All Rights Reserved. Used by permission of European American Music Distributors LLC, sole U.S. and Canadian agent for Schott Musik International. **p. 849 Sheng:** *China Dreams*, Prelude. Copyright © 1995 by G. Schirmer, Inc. (ASCAP). International Copyright Secured. All Rights Reserved. Reprinted by Permission. **p. 866 Machover:** *Begin Again Again . . .* from *Hyperstring Trilogy*. Reprinted by permission of BMG Music Publishing. **p. 881 Pärt:** *Cantate Domino canticum novum*, Psalm 95. © 1980, 1997 by Universal Edition A.G., Vienna. All Rights Reserved. Used by kind permission of European American Music Distributors LLC, sole U.S. and Canadian agent for Universal Edition A.G.,Vienna. **p. 894 Adams:** *Tromba lontana* from Two Fanfares for Orchestra. © Copyright 1986 by Hendon Music, Inc., a Boosey & Hawkes company. Reprinted by permission of Boosey and Hawkes, Inc. **p. 917 Larsen:** *Sonnets from the Portuguese*, Nos. 5 and 6. Music by Libby Larsen. Words by Elizabeth Barrett Browning. © 1998 Oxford University Press, Inc. Used by permission. All rights reserved.

Index of Forms and Genres

A roman numeral following a title indicates a movement within the work.

Notes

Notes

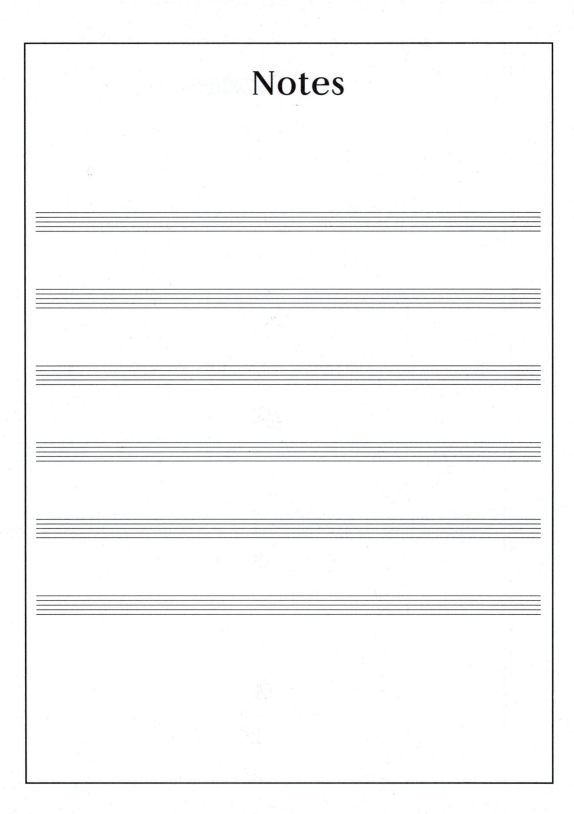

Notes

Notes

Notes

Notes